NEW PATHS TO DEMOCRATIC DEVELOPMENT IN LATIN AMERICA

The Rise of NGO-Municipal Collaboration

◆ ◆ ◆

edited by
CHARLES A. REILLY

LYNNE
RIENNER
PUBLISHERS

BOULDER
LONDON

Published in the United States of America in 1995 by
Lynne Rienner Publishers, Inc.
1800 30th Street, Boulder, Colorado 80301

and in the United Kingdom by
Lynne Rienner Publishers, Inc.
3 Henrietta Street, Covent Garden, London WC2E 8LU

Library of Congress Cataloging-in-Publication Data
New paths to democratic development in Latin America: the rise of NGO-
    municipal collaboration / edited by Charles A. Reilly.
        p. cm.
    Includes bibliographical references and index.
    ISBN 1-55587-557-2 (alk. paper)
    1. Urban policy—Latin America. 2. Non-governmental
organizations—Latin America. 3. Community development—Latin
America. 4. Municipal government—Latin America. 5. Municipal
services—Latin America. I. Reilly, Charles A.
HT127.5.N49 1995
338.98—dc20   94-31381
                                                             CIP

British Cataloguing in Publication Data
A Cataloguing in Publication record for this book
is available from the British Library.

Printed and bound in the United States of America

5 4 3 2 1

To my mother and father

CONTENTS

PREFACE

Democracy and development remain elusive in Latin America. Even as earlier generations looked upon the state as the driving force for change, many enthusiasts now opt for the "magic of markets." Others, however, have discovered that civil society harbors a promising mix of nongovernmental development organizations (NGOs), community associations, and social movements that policymakers—both public and private, national and international—would enlist to grapple with problems stemming from debt, economic adjustment, austerity measures, and poverty. The boundaries between states, markets, and civil society are fluid, continually modified by princes and princesses, by merchants and entrepreneurs, and recently, for the first time in much of the region's history, by ordinary citizens. Machiavelli, Adam Smith, de Tocqueville, and Rousseau could each lend an interpretive hand, but citizens active in organized civil society will have to fashion the form and substance of twenty-first-century Latin American citizenship.

During authoritarian periods, these organizations of civil society have defined themselves by their opposition to the state. But as governments move toward formal democracy, so too must NGOs redefine themselves and find new ways to relate to both states and markets. Thus, negotiation replaces opposition as groups born out of protest learn to propose specific policies and programs. Organizations accomplished at servicing local clientele now seek to expand their activities, to "scale up," just as government programs, obliged to accommodate international rules of finance, must scale back services despite growing numbers of "new" and "old" poor. The principal arena for redefining social policy is the cities, where 72 percent of Latin America's total population of 432 million now reside. But despite their position on the front lines, municipal governments are fiscally ill-equipped to address the problems of their residents. Under such circumstances, municipalities may welcome (or at least tolerate) NGOs and grassroots social movements that help implement and even shape social policy and services.

Joining the growing body of literature examining NGOs and social movements in Latin America, this volume reaches beyond the study of the organizations themselves to explore the complex ties they form with local and state governments to deliver services to constituents. The authors analyze collaborative ventures among municipal governments, social movements, and NGOs in the region that offer citizens a measure of hope for meeting housing, health, education, and environmental needs through experimentation, contracting, extension, and self-provisioning.

Based on field research carried out during 1990–1991, these studies in Argentina, Brazil, Chile, Colombia, Mexico, and Peru chronicle important developments as democracy takes hold despite the challenges (and setbacks) of fiscal shortfalls, social tensions, political competition, and economic hardship. This research on municipal-NGO joint ventures aims to advance both democracy and development by concentrating on the local "capillaries" of society, where demands, supports, and information are exchanged to keep the political organism healthy. As an American politician once remarked, "All politics is local." Ultimately, democratization and development, like effective poverty reduction and social problem solving, are local as well. Following de Tocqueville's lead, *New Paths to Democratic Development in Latin America* examines how, prodded by NGOs and social movements, policymakers in contemporary Latin American cities are redefining the "art of association" and "equality of conditions."

—*Charles A. Reilly*

ACKNOWLEDGMENTS

Many people have contributed to this volume, which sums up several years of field work, conferences, and debates chronicling new dimensions and levels of Latin American democratization. Gabriel Camara of Mexico shares intellectual responsibility for initiating the enterprise and bore the onus of organizing two very successful conferences in Tepoztlan, Mexico, to move the agenda forward, while encouraging the Inter-American Foundation to teach what it has learned. Sergio Martínez and Tere Gomez provided warm Mexican hospitality. Marcela Jiménez of Santiago, Chile, organized another comparative workshop that led to the publication of *Municipios y Organizaciones Privadas,* the first product of this enterprise. I am grateful to each of the authors who contributed chapters to this collection, as well as to Armando Bartra, Fernando Calderón, Hamilton Farias, and Marcela Jiménez, who prepared studies that informed our discussions, and to many more people who participated in the several workshops.

Various colleagues at the Inter-American Foundation read and commented upon various chapters, as did a number of outside readers including Guillermo O'Donnell and Jordi Borja. Their comments improved the collection in many ways—although, with the coauthors, I take responsibility for the final product, which does not necessarily reflect the views of the sponsoring institutions. My wife, Marta Torres Reilly, applied Latin American empathy, experience, and common sense to reading, typing, and critiquing much of the manuscript.

Laura Mullahy and Anne Martin contributed far more than just research assistance to the project. Laura coauthored a chapter and, with Elisavinda Echeverri-Gent, prepared the extensive bibliography. Anne Martin oversaw multiple versions of the manuscript in Portuguese, Spanish, and English through successive iterations. Leyda Appel saw to translations to and from the three languages with consummate skill and speed.

Lynda Edwards edited the manuscript, concerned for readers who live beyond the cramped language confines of social and political sciences. Every page was improved by her careful eye and exacting pencil. The production side of the manuscript fell to Maria Barry and Marnie Morrione, who once again proved themselves top-caliber publishing professionals.

I am grateful to the Inter-American Foundation for giving me time and space to carry out this project. As it becomes more flexible, corrigible, and attentive to the working relationships of NGOs and social movements within swiftly changing contexts, the foundation can enhance its contribution to the empowerment of poor people in Latin America. If the past four decades of development efforts have focused on the state, this volume bears witness to the conviction that citizens must forge new kinds of partnerships between the "local" state and civil society and between citizens of global society if either development or democracy is to flourish in this hemisphere.

—C.A.R.

Acronyms

General

CLACSO	Latin American Council of Social Sciences
GSO	Grassroots Support Organization
IAF	Inter-American Foundation
MO	Membership Organization
NGO	Nongovernmental Organization
PVO	Private Voluntary Organization

Argentina

CEADEL	Center for the Support of Local Development
CREATS	Rosario Community Studies and Technical Assistance Center
CRICSO	Social Science Research Center of Rosario
MCHP	Community Movement for Popular Habitat
PSP	Popular Socialist Party
UCR	Radical Civic Union

Brazil

FREI	Rural Foundation for Education and Integration
INAMPS	National Institute of Medical Assistance and Social Welfare
PHC	Pastoral Health Commission
Pólis	Institute of Research, Training, and Advisory Services in Social Policy

Chile

ACI	Agency for International Cooperation
ACR	Catholic Rural Action
AHC	Academy of Christian Humanism

CEPLAN	Center for Planning Studies
CIASPO	Center for Research and Action in Popular Health
CIEPLAN	Economic Research Corporation for Latin America
CODEIR	Corporation of Respiratory Patients
CONAR	National Committee to Aid Refugees
COPACHI	Committee for Cooperation for Peace
FLACSO	Latin American Faculty of Social Sciences
FOSIS	Fund for Social Solidarity and Investment
IER	Institute for Rural Education
INFOCAP	Institute for Popular Education and Training
INPROA	Institute for Agricultural Promotion
PET	Labor Economics Program
SOINDE	Interdisciplinary Society for Development

Colombia

CINEP	Center of Research and Popular Education
CUT	Central Workers' Union
IDEMA	Institute of Agricultural Marketing

Mexico

ANADEGES	Analysis, Decentralization, and Management
CDyPE	Ecological Defense and Preservation Committee
CDP	Committee for Popular Defense of Durango
CNC	National Peasant Confederation
COCEI	Coalition of Workers, Peasants, and Students of the Isthmus
CNOP	National Confederation of Popular Organizations
CONAMUP	National Coordinating Body of the Urban Popular Movement
FNDP	National Democratic Popular Front
INI	National Indigenous Institute
PAN	National Action Party
PMS	Mexican Socialist Party
PNR	National Revolutionary Party
PRD	Party of the Democratic Revolution
PRI	Institutional Revolutionary Party
PRM	Mexican Revolutionary Party
PRONASOL	National Solidarity Program
PRT	Revolutionary Workers Party
SEDAC	Adult Education Services Civil Association

Peru

ANC	National Association of Centers
APRA	American Popular Revolutionary Alliance
CEP	Center for Studies and Publications
DESCO	Center for the Study and Promotion of Development
IEP	Institute of Peruvian Studies
ILD	Institute for Liberty and Democracy
PUM	Unified Mariátegui Party
SINAMOS	National System to Support Social Mobilization
UDP	Popular Democratic Unity

1

Public Policy and Citizenship

CHARLES A. REILLY

As debt, structural adjustment, and austerity blanketed Latin America during the 1980s and more and more people moved to the cities, basic services for housing, health, and education declined in both quantity and quality. Whether through retreat of the state or advance by the market, poverty grew and social programs evaporated in many countries. In the short term, economic adjustment and poverty alleviation have proven to be conflicting goals. We have seen food riots explode in Argentine, Brazilian, and Venezuelan cities; random violence can break out anywhere. Beset by regressive economic measures and disastrous social policy, many Latin Americans no longer wait passively for change. During the coming decade, fiscal, political, and ideological shifts will constrain governments, international donors, and the nongovernmental organizations (NGOs) and movements of civil society to redefine their identities and strategies. When they do so, these policymakers will have to factor citizen "policytakers" into their equations.

There is good news to offset the unequal economic distribution and uneven growth in most Latin American countries, a contrasting movement toward democracy and the (re)discovery of civil society. Civil society, an aggregation of voluntary associations, organizations, movements, and networks engaged in collective action, is defined by Hegel as "beyond the family but short of the state" (from Hegel's *Philosophy of Right*). Complementing state and market with civil society, Alan Wolfe observes that "civil society points toward families, neighborhoods, voluntary organizations, unions, and spontaneous grassroots movements" (1991: 1).

The boundaries between state, market, and civil society are fluid, frequently modified by princes and princesses, by merchants and entrepreneurs, and now, for the first time in much of the region's history, by ordinary citizens. The writings of Machiavelli, Adam Smith, de Tocqueville, and Rousseau could lend an interpretive hand, but citizens acting through

1

organized civil society will have to furnish form and substance for twenty-first-century Latin American citizenship.

Besides the catchall concept of civil society, two relatively unattended institutions have lately entered Latin American political discourse and debate: nongovernmental organizations and municipal governments. As Columbus "discovered" America, so many in the development community have recently discovered nongovernmental development organizations, or NGOs, within civil society. These legally constituted, nonprofit associations deliver services, mobilize interests, encourage self-reliance, and act as advocates for improving citizens' life conditions and opportunities. In the United States, they are usually called private voluntary organizations (PVOs). Grassroots support organizations (GSOs) are a subset of this broad NGO spectrum, "a civic developmental entity that provides services (and/or) allied support to local groups of disadvantaged rural or urban households and individuals" (Carroll 1992: 9). Membership organizations (MOs), another subset of NGOs, represent and are accountable to their members, articulate their demands, and provide services to individual citizens and groups ranging from grassroots neighborhood organizations in Rio de Janeiro to national federations of indigenous peoples in Colombia. Finally, civil society is spiced by a wide variety of social movements that ebb and flow around specific issues, interests, and populations. Throughout this volume, authors use the term "NGO" as a shorthand for all these expressions of civil society.

Many NGOs and social movements afford their members opportunities to express their views and to participate in decisions, while their leadership learns something of responsiveness and accountability. This experience of "secondary" citizenship in the associations of civil society multiplies opportunities for negotiation, competition, contained conflict, and the search for consensus. As real-world academies for democracy, NGOs permit people to taste the full menu of rights and responsibilities, including, but not restricted to, voting, which characterizes "primary" citizenship.

Established NGOs are changing their operations, their leadership, even their sources of financial support, while new NGOs spring up virtually overnight. Some, pushed by state financial austerity or pulled by escalating human needs, have moved from confrontation to cooperation, engaging in joint ventures with local governments to provide goods and services to the urban poor. This by itself is significant. But another unanticipated outcome of economic crisis, structural adjustment, and austerity may be the revival of city and local government. Could Latin America, like Italy, come to rely on a "sottogoverno" for stability despite restive changes at the top?

Municipal governments will increasingly become the setting where people who experienced secondary citizenship through membership in NGOs may graduate into a fuller realization of citizenship. While Latin America historically operated on centralized models inherited from the colonial times, these coexisted with formal, though ineffective, municipal government structures.

In this book, researchers from Latin America and the United States analyze nongovernmental development organizations and social movements interacting with national, regional, and local governments in programs of housing and health care, waste disposal and urban environmental protection, and education. The contributors explore the hypothesis that, during the 1990s, significant joint ventures in service delivery between local governments and NGOs will evolve in Latin America.

As authoritarian regimes fade and economies founder, NGO-municipal collaborative ventures, contracts, and cost sharing will grow more significant—for both development and democracy. *New Paths to Democratic Development in Latin America* aims to alert government policymakers and the development-assistance community to these emerging actors and relationships. It also aspires to open new lines of reflection on the political economy of development and democracy through lessons culled from case studies in six Latin American countries. These include cases of local administration by agencies of central or provincial governments, which often complement but sometimes compete with local governments.

Labor unions, which have played significant roles historically in corporatist urban Latin America, are not the focus here, although a shift to territorial or factory-level organization may be significant. Neither are political parties included, except obliquely, as in the Mexico case study, where a party emerging from NGOs and social movements sought to inject new forms of political representation into the party and electoral systems. The party/movement phenomenon has appeared also in Argentina and Brazil but has not crystallized sufficiently to be analyzed in detail.

The case studies illustrate how grassroots collective action may stimulate at least a measure of change at the "mezzo" or intermediate level. From the perspective of policymakers and macrolevel donors engaged in policy dialogue and conditionality, the book raises the issue not of *whether* services should be provided, but of *who* should provide them and (to a lesser degree) how they can be financed. Whether NGOs and social movements are adversaries, collaborators, or surrogates for the local state; whether privatization is yet another instrument for excluding the poor majority; whether the survival strategies of the urban poor must be built on self-provisioning; whether joint NGO-municipal ventures are feasible and viable; and whether Latin American development in the postadjustment period will include growth in national economies as well as in the scope of citizenship benefits for the majority—these are the underlying questions. Although expanding and prolonging the productive potential of each society is fundamental, it is not the focus here. Our emphasis is on expanding citizenship, human capital, and organizational capacity, all of which make increased and sustained production, as well as consumption, possible.

The case studies featured in this book illustrate NGO-government relationships in different activities. The Argentine case, for example, examines collaboration between NGOs and the municipal government in the city of Rosario, focusing on habitat issues, community organization, and popular housing. In Chile, the role of NGOs in health care is examined, underlining new contractual mechanisms linking these organizations to the state. The Brazilian cases include social movements organized to improve primary health care in the periphery of São Paulo, proposals for financing urban mass transit, and community efforts in various cities to manage waste through garbage collection, separation, and recycling. The Mexican case examines what Tarrow (1989) calls a "social movement organization" galvanized around environmental issues in the city of Durango. The Peruvian and Colombian chapters trace the evolution of the NGO movement in these very different Andean political settings as both countries grapple with government decentralization and widespread violence.

The cases are drawn from both primary and secondary cities: NGOs in major cities often serve as research and development think tanks, as well as experimental sites for service delivery; NGOs in secondary cities and smaller municipalities are often important sources of technical expertise for public-sector development programs.

The Inquiry

This volume presents the views of seventeen authors who have been studying and comparing relations between nongovernmental development organizations and local governments in six democratizing Latin American countries: Argentina, Brazil, Chile, Colombia, Mexico, and Peru. Initiated in 1989 by the Inter-American Foundation, this research program identified illustrative cases of collaboration between popular organizations and the public and private sectors to provide needed services in Latin American cities. The studies explore the hypothesis that, during the 1990s, significant new joint ventures will evolve based on NGO-municipal linkages. Better understanding of such collaboration (and the conflict it may entail) should contribute to improved strategies for grassroots development and urban service delivery.

Underlying the research was the premise that, without local involvement, there can be neither development nor democracy. Indeed, the growing stream of literature on gaining and consolidating democracy (and the ebb and flow of literature on development) underline the uncertainty and reversibility of both. Thus, the researchers undertook a study of the *kinds* of democracy emerging in Latin American cities through collaboration and conflict, negotiation and bargaining, pacts and impasses, services and self-help. Their case studies explore the ways democracy, development, and (in some cases) decentralization intersect locally, either through conflict or through collaboration.

The authors are affiliated with nongovernmental development organizations, research institutions, development agencies, and government agencies linked to the NGO universe. Each is involved in the formulation and implementation of public (and private) social policy. Their chapters include assessments of the evolution of NGOs, social movements, and NGO-governmental relationships in each country as well as case studies of conflict or of collaborative ventures in specific urban sectoral areas (health, housing, and environment).

Poverty and Citizenship

The ranks of the poor in Latin American are growing, as they are in the United States. However, unlike the United States, their numbers are staggering: in 1989, there were 183 million poor people in Latin America, representing 44 percent of the entire population (Economic Commission for Latin America and the Caribbean 1990). Of those, over half were urban poor, whose proportion had increased from 37 to 55 percent between 1970 and 1986 (see Table 1.1).

Poverty may be viewed from various perspectives. We can, for example, look at it from the viewpoint of the economist:

Table 1.1   Estimates of Poverty Incidence and Distribution in Latin America, 1970–1989

	Households			Total Population			
	1980	1986	1989[a]	1970	1980	1986	1989[a]
Population (millions)	69	87	94	283	331	396	416
Poor (millions)	24	32	35	113	136	170	183
Poverty Incidence (%)[b]							
National	35	37	37	40	41	43	44
Urban	25	30	31	26	30	36	36
Rural	54	53	54	62	60	60	61
Poverty Distribution (%)[c]							
National	100	100	100	100	100	100	100
Urban	49	58	59	37	46	55	57
Rural	51	42	41	63	54	45	43

Sources: Mesa Lago 1992, Altimir 1982, Economic Commission for Latin America and the Caribbean (ECLAC) 1990.

Notes: a. Projection.

b. Percentages of national, urban, and rural populations under the absolute poverty line.

c. Percentages of urban and rural poor in total national poor population.

> Poverty has been defined as the inability to maintain a minimum standard of living or to purchase the minimum basket of goods and services required for the satisfaction of basic needs; the poor, then, are those who fall under such a minimum level or "poverty line" (Mesa Lago 1992: 6).

Or, we can see the poor as people enmeshed in a host of relationships beyond the solely economic. Viewed in this light, the definition of poverty would encompass not only a lack of access to adequate income but also a lack of access to information, to networks of social support, to adequate time and sufficient space, and to participation in the decisions that shape their lives: that is, the tools for accumulating social power (Friedmann 1988). Finally, we can consider the poor as protagonists as well as receivers, or targets, of policy; that is, the poor are both policymakers *and* policytakers.

Local Governments

The public sector is being redefined in Latin America as democratization inches forward and privatization gains support. Although centralist traditions run deep, antedating the conquest and reinforced by subsequent revolutions by the left and by military regimes of the right, state corporatism (a system of interest representation) is on the wane. "The State" is being dissected. Corporatist labor organizations have declined as well. Reluctantly, long-insulated industrial and commercial associations are yielding to pressures for trade liberalization. In many countries, traditional political parties are in disrepair or are realigning themselves. Clientelism, the bonding between individuals of unequal power and social status through the exchange of economic and/or political resources (resembling U.S. "machine" or "pork barrel" politics) is also waning. State and provincial governments, long the arena of isolated clientelistic politics, struggle to contain incursions of the center by technocrats. Municipal governments, too, enter the realm of competitive or semicompetitive politics—their attributions and functions expanded by constitutions and statutes, their capacity to provide services to citizens frustrated by nearly empty treasuries.

State, provincial, and local governments—all lacking resources—are now being asked by central government to shoulder more of the burden for social and economic development. Most Latin American constitutions celebrate municipal autonomy, but they contribute little to its vitalization. In most countries, municipalities subsist on meager and dwindling transfers rather than on an independent tax base. Some countries are electing local officials for the first time, many of them riding to victory on reform platforms that stir high expectations. When they crash into fiscal reality consisting of stubborn bureaucracies and empty coffers, disenchantment is the first outcome.

Some municipalities opt to downsize, contracting services through nongovernmental organizations and unloading social services onto the non-profit and for-profit private sector. Other municipal authorities, recognizing that informality in the economy contributes to endemic fiscal crisis, have begun to levy new taxes and to "formalize" even microentrepreneurs. The leaders of resource-poor, major and mid-sized cities of Latin America are discovering as well that demands and supports are often mediated, not by traditional parties, but by nongovernmental development organizations rooted in churches, neighborhoods, and associations of people engaged in service delivery and productive activities. While the sector of the economy is being celebrated as the latest development fad, the informal sector of the polity based on informal associations also deserves emphasis.

NGOs in Civil Society

In recent years, nongovernmental development organizations have moved into portions of the informal space vacated by government. These groups include relatively well-organized grassroots support organizations (GSOs) that provide goods and services to groups of the organized poor; member-ship organizations (MOs) like cooperatives and neighborhood associations; and the more ephemeral, sometimes single-issue, and frequently vociferous social movements of the poor at local, regional, or national levels. While organic metaphors in politics can be problematic, we may think of NGOs and grassroots communities, popular associations, and social movements— the latter particularly significant in Mexico and Brazil—as the "capillaries" of civil society. Tiny, interactive, the beginning and end of a circuit—they are the point at which finance, information, demands, and supports (like wastes, oxygen, and nutrients for the body) are exchanged to keep democ-racy healthy. Clearly, there is abundant social energy available outside the state.

Enthusiasm for NGOs in civil society must be tempered with the carbon of capacity and the calibration of scale. Advocates of privatization and antagonists of government rhapsodize about the potential of NGOs, and, indeed, many of these organizations played pivotal roles in opposing authoritarian regimes and opening paths to democratic transitions. It is also true that nongovernmental development organizations can be effective lab-oratories for testing and delivering services to some of the poor, as several of the chapters in this book demonstrate quite clearly. Microexperiments are not enough, however, given the scale of poverty and inequitable distrib-ution in Latin America. As Mario Padrón, a Peruvian spokesman for NGOs, remarked shortly before his death, "Don't ask us to carry more than our capacity, and then blame the failure of the next development decade on us—we can't carry the load" (interview with the author, 25 February 1987, Washington, D.C.).

Even if NGOs could shoulder such burdens, many of their leaders resist implementing decisions made elsewhere. To become surrogate bearers of state services is not the goal of these men and women, especially when they have no say in policy formulation or program design. One position, at the extreme end of the scale, would dismiss all NGO service delivery, self-help, and localism as a neoliberal subterfuge (and imply that de Tocqueville should have known better). Others would accept Keynes's dictum that "The important thing for government is not to do things which individuals are doing already, and to do them a little better or a little worse, but to do those things which at present are not done at all" (World Bank/Johns Hopkins 1991: 128). That is still a large order.

Just as there are inefficient, opportunistic, and bankrupt states or markets, there are inefficient, opportunistic, and bankrupt NGOs. Social movements are frequently ephemeral. The levers of power within Latin American societies are not managed by NGOs or social movements, although these groups often deal with the unintended consequences of decisions made elsewhere. Political scientists worry about governability as the increase in anomic violence and threats to personal and collective security throughout Latin America suggest a breakdown in civility, a deterioration that NGOs alone cannot remedy. Let us reread de Tocqueville.

Human Rights, Basic Needs:
The Stuff of Citizenship

Among the laws that rule human societies there is one which seems to be more precise and clear than all the others. If men are to remain civilized or to become so, the art of associating together must grow and improve in the same ratio in which the equality of conditions is increased.
—de Tocqueville, *Democracy in America*

The art of association and equality of conditions should progress in the same ratio, argued de Tocqueville in his reflections on North America. While artful association takes hold at all levels of Latin American society, equality of conditions remains an aspiration. If the goal is democratic development based on citizenship and qualitative relationships like accountability and participation, what are the concrete manifestations of the obligations and benefits implicit in citizenship? What is the blend of rights and responsibilities? The range of human needs confronting citizens and local governments includes health and housing, food and nutrition, personal and public safety, education, leisure and recreation, transportation, communication, and psychic states such as self-esteem. In each national and local setting, expectations vary on what is a matter of rights, what is charity, and what is likely to be obtained only through self-help or self-provision of services. In Brazil, for example, it was the withdrawal of previously available health care that provoked a movement of social protest (see Cohn, Chapter 5 in this book). In Durango, Mexico, squatters occupied land, laid out streets, and built dwellings; then, with the help of university students, they pressured progressively for land titles, water, electricity, and other urban services.

To what degree can citizens count on government (and which layer of government?) for such needs as personal security, consumer protection, income maintenance, health services, education, housing, economic safety nets, garbage collection, water, sanitation, and electricity? On the other side of the coin, what are the same citizens' behavioral obligations? What financial payments, taxes, and in-kind or voluntary contributions must they make? What other types of support are citizens expected to furnish? How many of their basic needs (some of which we consider rights) should citizens meet on their own, unassisted?

The interplay between political, economic, and social democracy is too complex to be fully explored here. Similarly complex are the issues of elite interests and power and of the appropriate role of external actors in mediating the process and checking the abuses of local elites. Who formulates priorities for allocating resources and adjudicating among competing interests? Local governments are frequently captives of entrenched elite interests, and national-level reformers argue that "bypass" surgery is required to permit democratic impetus from below. The case studies in this volume, especially the ones from Mexico, offer strong justification for this position.

The authors discuss different development services and how democratic practices emerging from citizen activity and awareness vary within NGOs, social and movements, municipal governments. These democratic practices may vary considerably from eighteenth- and nineteenth-century European, or twentieth-century North American notions of citizens' rights and responsibilities. Social movements addressing particular issues (land invasions, health care, water, and sanitation) or emanating from different formulations of collective identities (gender and ethnicity) bring new substance to the rights and responsibilities of citizenship. Citizens invent citizenship.

We will not attempt to define this new substance issue here except to insist that it is ultimately linked to its local origin. To sectoral categories of analysis, we must add spatial ones. Territory does matter; people live and work somewhere, and man and woman are ultimately the measure of citizenship. Much depends on reforms from the top; for example, the evolution of social security, state-provided health services, mandated sexual equality in employment, union recognition, worker representation in management, safety nets, protection of children's rights, and similar rights and benefits. But today, conservatives praise "mediating structures," Foucault's followers push the "microphysics" of power, and corporate managers test "flexible specialization"; all insist that empowerment and ideas for problem solving are best generated from below.

The relationship of citizens and services is under scrutiny everywhere. There is a congenital defect in state delivery of social services beyond conservative assaults and bureaucratic bungling, especially where societies are differentiated into myriad levels, layers, and classes. Poverty is not a simple condition. It manifests itself among the rural poor, single parents, street children, recent migrants, undocumented persons, dismissed public employees, and unemployed factory workers, to name but a few. Central governments seldom enjoy the resources, flexibility, or imagination needed to fashion programs that can reach such diversified, highly specific human needs. Can decentralized governmental units or joint ventures with organizations of civil society deliver goods and services better than central administrations deliver them? Mounting evidence suggests that sometimes they can.

By way of introduction to a set of policy recommendations, let us examine one such joint venture, an example of multilevel, multiactor policymaking and policytaking. The following description of a tripartite involvement—NGO, local government, and community—in education illustrates how policy issues bridge distinct governmental levels and both public and private sectors. It will concretize issues and frame the policy recommendations to follow.

Luiz Freire Center—Recife, Brazil

The rapid growth of urban populations coupled with declining social expenditures has overwhelmed state and municipal school systems throughout much of Latin America. Services decline, parents seek other options, and alternative school systems appear. In Recife, Brazil, nearly 124,000 of the children between the ages of seven and fourteen who do not attend public school receive basic education through a network of community organizations serviced by the Luiz Freire Center. Like most grassroots support organizations, this NGO provides more than one service. In addition to basic education for children (and illiterate adults), the center offers legal assistance, communications services, and health care. The center is one of many nonformal NGO education programs that respond more effectively to the needs of the urban poor than do the understaffed, underbuilt state and municipal formal schools.

Like many such programs in democratizing settings, the program receives contributions from government ministries of justice, education, and culture as well as from a variety of private international donor agencies. The newly drafted Brazilian Constitution and the State Constitution of Pernambuco (which the center helped draft) endorse the use of public funds for "community and philanthropic schools that demonstrate their social function and nonprofit purpose" (Brad Smith 1987: 31–32).

The center carries out an active outreach program, providing technical assistance and training to state and NGO organizations throughout Brazil, that extends even to the state educational secretariats in Maranhão and Santa Catarina. The recent request of the governor of the state of Pernambuco to have the center participate in an evaluation of state programs would have been unheard of in more authoritarian times. During the past year, the center sponsored civic assemblies where political parties aired their platforms on educational policy. Besides its interaction with government entities, the center serves as the nucleus of a social movement that sustains individual educational programs and that lobbies for more effective public policy in education. With the collaboration of the federal University of Pernambuco, the center has developed a program leading to a graduate degree in pedagogy with a specialization in popular education.

What are the implications for policy? The center's leading activist role characterizes democratization in many similar resource-scarce settings of Latin America today. Public-private collaboration is recognized as a necessity by a new and pragmatic generation of activists. Moreover, cooperation between specialized, technical GSOs (such as the center) and more diffuse social movements pursuing popular health, education, and legal rights characterizes a new stage in the evolution of urban coalitions. Some observers think these new social actors will eventually displace the NGO, if not the state, and the NGO will wither away. At the very least, new social actors and changing intergovernmental relations suggest that we should pay greater attention to the emerging "mezzo" level of policy. In Latin America's policy drama, NGOs and social movements have moved to center stage.

Strength and Weakness in State and Civil Society: Subnational Units

Discussion of strong and weak states usually focuses on regimes and on nationally articulated elites and institutions. It can be useful, however, to start from below. Manuel Castells wrote that "the municipality is the decentralized level of the state, the most penetrated by civil society, the most accessible to the governed, and the most directly connected to the daily life of the masses" (1981: 300). Many would argue that NGOs and social movements prepare people within civil society for an encounter with the state at local, regional, and national levels and in so doing contribute to their democratization. Collective relationships as well as individual relationships link state and civil society territorially; services may be provided and taxes paid on that basis and demands and supports mediated there as well.

Along with territoriality, other issues need to be addressed that range from public administration proposals for deconcentration to suggestions (usually by incumbent politicians) that decentralization somehow correlates with democratization. The world is not so neat, however, and local organizations to ensure even minimal exercise of democracy, must frequently circumvent national-level oligarchs or local-level power brokers (*caciques* and *coroneis*) by turning to sympathetic technocrats within the federal government. Often, democracy carries limiting adjectives (e.g., "tutelary" and "delegative" democracy) because of clientelistic and authoritarian legacies. The residues of populism, clientelism, and even corporatism appear at the local level (although the most salient corporatist structures are embedded primarily in the central state). Castells further observed that "central state-municipal relations are the clearest indicator of the general relations between the State and Civil Society" (1981: 300). I prefer that the linkage be examined, not just through intergovernmental relations, but at each government level and in its relationships to individuals and associations of civil society.

Figure 1.1 illustrates the convergence of state and civil society as a setting for social policy in each country. On the horizontal axis, civil society is ranked according to my assessment of and feel for the number and

Figure 1.1   Configuring Social Policy

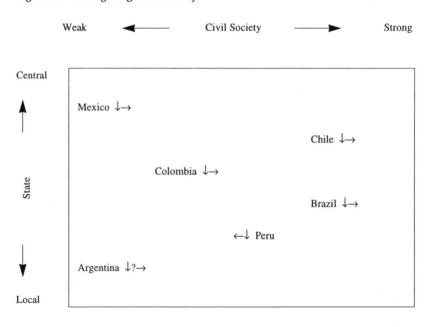

salience of NGOs and organized social movements active in urban social programs and, at least indirectly, influencing policy. (A recently published *Guide to Directories of NGOs* by the Inter-American Foundation refers to over 11,000 Latin American NGOs.) Civil society is the setting for demands and supports by organizations of and for the poor as well as by the individuals who may receive services and pay taxes. I have ventured to locate each of the book's six countries within this space, with an arrow indicating my assessment of directionality toward or away from a stronger civil society in the 1990s.

The vertical axis identifies the level of governmental involvement in decisionmaking vis-à-vis social policy. Here, the emphasis is on the locus of relevant (social) program and policymaking decisions, whether made by the central or local governmental and administrative apparatus. I assume a trend toward greater devolution of decisionmaking to local units, but that must be established in each case. This illustration does not deal with fiscal capacity, intergovernmental transfers, efficiency, or efficacy of government services—important variables but beyond the scope of this graphic.

Country Comparisons

Despite each country's radically different starting point, direction, and pace of evolution, most authors in this book expect the frequency of collaborative ventures between NGOs and local governments to accelerate during the 1990s, although their salience will vary. Such variations stem primarily from differences in the NGO community and in the juridical and fiscal health of municipalities.

Argentina and Mexico resemble each other because of their small, recently spawned NGO sectors within historically weak civil societies. Contrasting evidence from Buenos Aires and Rosario make it difficult to gauge movement toward or away from democratic participation in Argentina. In Brazil and Chile, on the other hand, large NGO sectors emerged under heavy-handed dictatorships. NGOs in both countries shared church origins, relied heavily on foreign support, and offered highly diverse programmatic activities. A key difference between the latter two countries is that in the years of democratization, since 1992, Chilean NGO leaders have moved rapidly into the public sector while Brazilian NGOs have remained firmly planted outside government precincts. Another difference is that most mayors in Chile remained appointees of the Pinochet regime until the municipal elections held on 28 June 1992 while Brazilian mayors have been elected throughout both authoritarian and democratizing periods.

Peruvian NGOs offer a beleaguered center amidst fear and violence, and some observers hope for improved NGO-government links through regional decentralization. If Hernando de Soto's informal sector is celebrated by the center-right (and in Washington), the self-provisioning experience of Villa El Salvador merits equal time by the center-left (and throughout Latin America). The performance of NGOs in health care during the 1991 cholera crisis sent an upbeat message from an otherwise depressing Peruvian situation. In contrast, Colombia rides high on the crest of civic enthusiasm, municipal political reform, and decentralization, all of which augur well for further democratization.

Let us examine more closely some of the insights from each country as discussed in this book.

Argentina: Negotiated Interaction

Marcello Cavarozzi and Vincente Palermo analyze relationships between the state and popular neighborhood organizations (*sociedades de fomento*), emphasizing the comparatively late development of civil society associations in a comparatively weak state. Based on field work conducted in 1987 and 1988, the authors trace the evolution of neighborhood organizations in the very poor southern and western portions of Buenos Aires and their relationships with the state and with municipal governments. The authors suggest that if inflation, a shrinking public sector, and a deteriorating economy lowered living standards of both existing and "new" poor in the late 1980s, inflated political discourse, fiscal impotency, and clientelistic leadership diminished the scope and salience of participation through popular organizations. The result was indifference, rather than dissent, and the apparent decline of neighborhood associations in Buenos Aires.

Roberto Martínez Nogueira's study of three NGOs in housing and community development (working in close collaboration with the mayor of Rosario) sketches a more optimistic picture of Argentine NGOs and social movements. In Rosario, Argentina, Martínez Nogueira examined several NGOs as they interacted with two successive municipal administrations and popular organizations in established neighborhoods and squatters' settlements, or *villas*. Rosario was notorious for an outburst of looting and rioting in 1989, and again in 1990, as a response to austerity, inflation, and the deteriorating situation of the urban poor. (Similar outbursts occurred in Brazilian cities during the same period and, most recently, in Caracas, Venezuela.) Such rioting strengthened the arguments of those who insisted that subsidies for urban food, transport, job creation, and the like could not be cavalierly suspended. In response, the World Bank initiated a series of social emergency programs in some Latin American countries to cushion the worst effects of the initial phases of economic structural adjustment. These emergency funds occasioned the Bank to begin dealing directly with subnational political actors and NGOs—perhaps initiating new patterns for a multilayered presence of the development bank in the region.

In Rosario, a hierarchy of needs emerged from the local organizations. Food and nutrition, work, land, housing, health, collective infrastructure, recreation, and cultural activities were the principal rank-ordered needs that motivated action. The first four needs were the most urgent during the worst periods of social emergency, the latter after the emergency had ameliorated and, throughout these years, in the more established, less poor communities. Community priorities were also dictated by vulnerability; children and the elderly received attention, food, nutrition, and health care before others during the worst times. Martínez Nogueira observes that it was women who played the primary mobilizational role; their community centers coalesced around needs for child day care and help for the elderly.

At first inclined to seek long-term, sustainable development roles, the Rosario NGOs learned to design short-term, welfare-type programs to legitimate their presence during the worst years of social crisis, inflation, and unemployment. In the transition from welfare to organizational capacity building and development, philosophy sometimes yielded to circumstance. Other local organizations matured, learning how to negotiate, first with the NGOs, then with the municipal authorities. Important as well was the process of learning what could be realistically expected from municipal officials and what would require self-provisioning. Finally, Martínez Nogueira observed that political activism varied considerably between older, established neighborhoods and the villas. The former, weighted down by spokespersons and organizational remnants of clientelistic parties, tended to be competitive and fragmented. The villas, lacking ties to political parties, were poorer but more collaborative.

According to Martínez Nogueira, as negotiated interaction occurs between NGOs and clients and between NGOs and the municipality, it is characterized by a progression from welfare to development emphasis. Jorge Caballeros, mayor of Rosario, told me that "the city's economy and fiscal capacity must be rebuilt. We cannot respond to the needs of the poor without working closely with NGOs" (Interview, Rosario, 10 November 1991).

Brazil's "Supercitizens": NGO-Movement Linkages

The chapter by Rubem Cesar Fernandes and Leandro Piquet Carneiro of the Institute for Religious Studies (ISER) features a survey of over one hundred Brazilian NGO leaders conducted in August 1991 during a meeting establishing the National Association of Brazilian NGOs. The NGOs are a self-identified subset of civil associations that multiplied dramatically in the 1970s and 1980s in Brazil. They offer consulting services, popular education, applied research and information services, leadership training, video production, and technical assistance to grassroots groups and popular movements. Fernandes and Piquet define the principal NGO function as advisory, or "value-based contractual relationships," linked to the transmission of know-how, involving mutual trust, and partial affinity of purpose.

The Fernandes and Piquet survey finds that the majority of Brazilian NGO leaders were inspired by either church or leftist political philosophies. Many had suffered directly from repression (two lost their political rights, eleven were tried in military tribunals, six lost their jobs, seventeen were jailed, seven were tortured, six were exiled, and six more went into voluntary exile). A significant number of NGOs, however, are led by a new generation of activists unmarked by experience under authoritarianism. While opposition to the government might be expected among these organizations, 43 percent of the NGOs participating in the survey had received funding from federal, state, or municipal government sources. A surprising 66 percent of the respondents said that they believed NGOs should be subject to some government regulation, but they were ambivalent about its extent since both proponents and opponents fear excessive government control.

Like NGOs in Chile, Brazilian NGOs are closely linked to international donors. As Fernandes and Piquet note:

> NGOs cannot exist without international relations. Independent of the state, contrary to the market, far from fragile domestic philanthropy, NGOs find support in a system of international cooperation . . . the NGO circuit is one of the most internationalized in Brazilian society.

Brazilian NGOs come in large and small sizes. Twelve of the NGOs surveyed have annual budgets in excess of U.S.$500,000; eight exceed $1 million. These large units are well-institutionalized and self-consciously "professionalized," offering a wide range of services and entering easily into partnerships with international donors and local government entities. They are evolving some characteristics of the market, notes Fernandes, as they explore whether to charge fees for consulting and technical assistance and to sell services or products to finance their programs. These nonprofit NGOs "are small businesses that operate in counterpoint to the market," resisting the central paradox of mercantile exchange, "the more markets universalize, the more they exclude." While many of them began as charitable entities, the authors note that even "good shepherds need marketing experts."

The 102 organizations included in the survey are a cross section of a single network self-identified as NGOs. Other networks include women's movements, Afro-Brazilian organizations, environmentalists, domestic employees, and the homeless. Civic and political issues are at the core of NGO discourse. NGOs remind Fernandes and Piquet of Citizen Rousseau, who carries the "general will around in his heart." They are not representatives, but they have delegated themselves to speak for the poor; they may be small, but they cultivate a totalizing vision. In bumper-sticker language, "NGOs are supercitizens."

Amélia Cohn's Brazilian case study examines health-care demands, citizenship, and social movements in São Paulo. Cohn's study drives home the strong reaction of social movements when previously available services are withdrawn. She also demonstrates the effect of high-tech (and high-cost) medicine, which can lead to popular rejection of more efficient, primary health-care models. As in U.S. cities, Brazil's hospital emergency rooms have become the sole source of medical care for the urban poor.

One product of democratization in Brazil, as elsewhere, has been the large number of municipal governments managed by a new generation of politicians closely identified with popular movements but not particularly well-versed in city management. However, high popular expectations and small coffers test even experienced managers. One of our chapters examines the Institute of Research, Training, and Advisory Services in Social Policy (Pólis), a São Paulo NGO set up explicitly to provide technical assistance to municipalities seeking greater popular participation. Pólis offers an interesting perspective on the changing boundaries between public and private sectors, as NGOs become trainers and information clearinghouses for government officials. In this case study, Silvio Caccia Bava of Pólis and Laura Mullahy chronicle innovative efforts of Brazilian citizens' groups and municipal governments to improve urban transportation and to collect, separate, and recycle garbage, examples of urban environmental problem solving well within reach of community associations collaborating with the public sector. Applied researchers in NGOs like Pólis play valuable roles, facilitating research and development, policy advocacy, and technology transfer.

Chile's Concertación

Brian Loveman's overview of local-level democratization in Chile traces the evolution of NGOs, emphasizes the role of international donors in the process, and calls attention to the many former NGO leaders who moved into the *concertación* government. Governance brings new perspectives, including efforts by the new Chilean government to channel such aid efforts into its own policy (and political) priorities.

The administrative and regulatory framework ruling Chilean NGOs today leaves space for municipal-NGO collaboration, and, unlike Mexico, it seems to be effective. For example, municipal responsibilities currently include urban planning and administration, water and sanitation, housing, transportation, and public utilities. Municipal discretionary authority can include social welfare, health, education, environmental protection, adult education and employment development, recreation, road maintenance, and emergency relief. Most of these services are also provided by NGOs to limited numbers of clients, and mechanisms for collaboration are available. Chilean municipalities are technically empowered to charge fees, grant concessions, contract public and private entities, manage property, and distribute subsidies and grants to nonprofit organizations (Loveman 1991).

Although the administrative and regulatory framework seems propitious, the political sphere is more complicated. Mayors in most cities remained Pinochet appointees through June 1992 and enjoyed clear dominance over the municipal council. Furthermore, municipal-reform legislation proposed by the concertación has been delayed several times by Congress.

On another level, the creation of a Fund for Solidarity and Social Investment and the Agency for International Cooperation demonstrate a more proactive stance by the concertación government vis-à-vis NGOs. While less encompassing or directive than the National Solidarity Program in Mexico, the actions of these state entities designed to articulate with NGOs will likely be a source of both tension and negotiation. As Loveman notes, there is irony in the fact that most NGO leaders during past decades originally favored state-centric solutions to the problems of development.

Cooperation, rather than conflict, characterizes the Chilean health-care study by Judith Salinas and Giorgio Solimano; NGOs now collaborate with the Ministry of Health and municipal governments in primary health-care delivery. Salinas and Solimano trace the history of public health services in Chile and the role of nearly three hundred health-related NGOs. Employing more than two thousand health and social science professionals in the health care field, these NGOs work in primary health care, mental health (including a subspecialty devoted to victims of repression, torture, and human rights violations), health promotion and education, and health policy research. The authors studied six of these health-related NGOs, three of them with strong ties to public-sector health services. Some of the programs are quite large; for example, the Hogar de Cristo, a church-related hospital and clinic network, cared for 7,328 patients in 1990.

Chilean public health services have been decentralized since Pinochet's administrative reforms, which included "the municipalization of primary health care." The authors list three categories of Chilean health NGOs: welfare, solidarity, and research-oriented. Research-oriented NGOs have played a significant role in formulating and implementing health policy. Health NGOs have progressed from refuge institutions during the dictatorship to technical-political protagonists in the formulation of public policy. The diversity of mechanisms linking public and private sectors in health care range from coordinating agreements to formal contracts. The relative ease whereby NGOs bid for and win contracts with government agencies relates, at least in part, to the considerable migration of Chilean NGO leadership to government jobs in the past two years.

Colombia: A Wave of Civic Enthusiasm

Pedro Santana Rodríguez's chapter chronicles Colombia's recent efforts at decentralization and municipal-NGO collaboration. The Colombia NGO "Foro" and a consortium of NGOs currently leading a national-level civics campaign have energized a wave of civic change in that country. It is remi-

niscent of the heady days of concertación in Chile in 1989–1990, or the
1987–1988 period, when Brazilians drafted their new constitution.
Colombians seem bound to make democracy work, counting heavily on
municipal governments and on NGOs with their networks.

Santana Rodríguez describes recent efforts in Colombia to restore
democratic practice through administrative and political decentralization.
Local elections have been introduced, fiscal decentralization has permitted
municipalities to generate local revenues and to receive transfers from the
federal government, and a number of participatory mechanisms such as
local administrative councils have been set up in the neighborhoods in thirty Colombian cities. NGO-municipal collaboration has become routine in
local planning, primary health care, housing, food and marketing, garbage
collection and recycling, microenterprise promotion, day care, and urban
transport.

While the transition to democracy is not simple, its consolidation is
even more complex. It brings confrontation, conflict, and demands for
equity and efficiency. As Santana notes:

> Traditionalist tendencies linger in Colombia as expressed in clientelist
> practices, irrationality, lack of planning, and delayed municipal reforms.
> Planning becomes a means of participation and negotiation when a partic-
> ipatory methodology is adopted; traditionalist tendencies can be combated
> when power rests at the local level. . . . The municipality has become an
> arena in which traditional and antidemocratic interests confront those
> seeking to create democratic and participatory localities.

Colombia is riding a wave of civic enthusiasm. According to Santana,
the "compulsive bi-partyism" of the past has been found wanting. He
places his bets on "fluid pluralism," the creation of forums involving popular organizations and NGOs in civic exchange and revitalized municipal
government. Like other authors in this collection, he suggests that international donor agencies have been infatuated with the central state and indifferent to local government.

Mexico's Difficult Democracy

Luis Hernández and Jonathan Fox trace the origins of Mexico's social
movements in areas of housing, women's issues, environment, rural development, and human rights. They analyze the relative primacy of social
movements over NGOs in Mexican civil society, noting the growth and
salience of producers' organizations in rural settings and of movements for
housing and other services in urban areas (many of these triggered by the
Mexico City earthquake of 1985). Until recently, such movements were
disconnected from Mexican NGOs, which have a much lower profile and
impact than in many South American countries. Hernández and Fox cite an
omnipresent state, less foreign assistance, and the mask of democracy as

external causes. They note that most Mexican NGOs specialized in education and welfare programs, and, until recently, they isolated themselves from social movements and from the mainstream of socially activist Mexican intellectuals. Since the early 1980s, some Mexican NGOs have contracted with government agencies to deliver services. A number of programs originating in NGOs were adopted or transferred to federal government agencies, especially in low-income and self-help housing.

Julio Moguel's case study of the city of Durango clearly illustrates a trend in Mexico toward collaboration between NGOs and social movements, although in the Durango case it is the social movement itself that created an NGO to provide technical assistance in a specific arena (housing and legal aid). In Mexico, social movements and producer associations have a higher profile than NGOs. During the administration of Mexican President Carlos Salinas, many producer and consumer organizations and some NGOs entered into bargaining and concertación with federal and municipal agencies. Several NGOs brokered debt swaps and increased their visibility at national and international levels during the past several years. The transition from confrontation to policy recommendation (from "protest to proposal") in Mexican social movements reflects greater self-confidence within the movements, their recognition that the state alone will not resolve problems, and that pragmatic solutions can emerge from the people.

Moguel underlines the permanence of clientelism and corporatism in Durango and the danger that NGOs and popular organizations—seeking allies within federal agencies to neutralize dominant local elites, caciques, and government party power-brokers—can become co-opted themselves. The Committees for Popular Defense in Durango, Mexico, illustrate the risks nicely; this social protest movement spanning over two decades evolved into an effective multiclass alliance on environmental issues, then unsuccessfully tried its luck as an alternative political party. The movement/party did not easily survive electoral failure.

Clientelism and co-optation are alive and well, though often in a more technocratic guise, as the Mexican presidency's National Solidarity Program (PRONASOL) creates a structure parallel to the declining apparatus of the Institutional Revolutionary Party (PRI). PRONASOL makes grants directly to "independent" NGOs, social movements, and local governments for social welfare and economic infrastructure projects determined locally from a set menu of options. (Some Mexican observers speculate that this program may evolve into a new political party, thus introducing a second party apparatus parallel to the PRI and linked directly to the state through the president.)

Peru: Myths and Utopias

Baltazar Caravedo has written a historical essay on the ties between NGOs, the state, and society in Peru. He analyzes the "myth and utopia of the

Benefactor State" that dominated Peruvian development aspirations in the 1960s and 1970s, to be replaced at the outset of the 1990s by a "neo-liberal myth and utopia." He examines the regionalization and decentralization of Peruvian public administration in recent years, a response to the inefficacy of the center and to the growing phenomenon of violence epitomized in Sendero Luminoso (Shining Path), while warning against pressing NGOs into an impossible role as guarantors of development and democracy. Political parties have lost credibility, and antipolitics prevails.

Who, then, are the key actors in development for the 1990s? Caravedo identifies the following four sets of social actors: (1) individuals struggling to survive in the informal economy (the microentrepreneurs celebrated by Hernando de Soto), (2) small and mid-size businesses, (3) NGOs, and (4) base organizations. He traces the changing role of NGOs through recent segments of Peruvian history—especially their importance in urban settings as municipal governments, beset by austerity, have contracted them for service delivery, technical skills, and administrative skills. While Peruvian NGOs number in the hundreds, with fifteen consortia or second-level federations pulling them together, Caravedo warns against fabricating yet another myth of NGO capacity to resolve the impasses of Peruvian development and democratization. President Alberto Fujimori's closing of Congress in April 1992 underscores the fragility of democratization.

Shaping Social Policy for Diversity

How can the social policy arena become more inclusive? What do country case studies in different countries teach us about making social policy environments more conducive to broader participation and better management of scarce resources? Let me suggest three fundamental challenges facing public policy managers and citizens, which have illustrative responses in this book: (1) managing a shrinking resource base, (2) rediscovering subnational political units and associations, and (3) debureaucratizing through flexible specialization.

One hard lesson of the "failed development decade" is that social equity and economic efficiency are challenged by a shrinking resource base. Monopolies and oligopolies, whether of the state or of the private sector, have seldom proven efficient. Smaller endeavors, on the other hand, may be highly competitive but equally ineffectual—Adam Smith's legions swamped by Charles Darwin's fittest. Quite apart from ideological preferences, both public and private ventures must seek ways to better husband scarce resources now that natural resources are more broadly recognized as finite and coping with austerity becomes an ingrained, if irksome, habit.

A second lesson is that vitality as well as efficiency exist, even flourish, beneath the national level. The fiscal crisis of Latin American cities has stimulated the rediscovery of subnational politics, stirred calls for administrative decentralization, and led to the discovery of an organized citizenry. Politics and administration are alive and well at many levels of the system, and leaders are learning to deal with diversity as well as austerity.

A third lesson is that effective management practice, public and private, turns increasingly to decentralization and to participatory approaches to the production of goods and delivery of services. "Flexible specialization" is celebrated as the model of the future for industrial production, with consumer satisfaction regarded as the hallmark of success. "Thriving on chaos" is the prescription for the 1990s marketed by North American management specialist Tom Peters, and Latin American public managers already recognize the symptoms, if not the cure.

If heterogeneity is the rule within and among Latin American countries, it is gospel among NGOs and social movements. The plurality of countries, cultures, resources, problems, and responses challenges development planners and democratic advocates alike. Residually pluralistic, NGOs pose dilemmas for government and development "social engineers"—if diversity is regarded as inimical to democracy and development rather than as an inherent element. NGOs have long served as laboratories in which mechanisms of participation and representation are tested and proven. Municipal politics survives, sometimes converted into a vital setting for democratic competition, capital accumulation, and equity. Few can quarrel with the incremental logic behind testing social policies and programs in small arenas before expanding them to the national level.

Given such variation, it may seem presumptuous to venture policy recommendations. In addition there are limits to cross-national generalization and comparison, for in the final analysis the results of a policy or "authoritative allocation of resources" must be measured against specific people in specific contexts with specific problems. Paradigms, like policies and programs, are in flux. If austerity and program cutbacks constrict the fiscal landscape, new horizons open with pragmatism, experimentation, and the changing identities of the local state and NGOs. Intergovernmental relations must include more than revenue transfers, just as extragovernmental relations must encompass NGOs and social movements. The final chapter of this volume will explore in greater depth the changing policy frameworks accompanying democratization. For now, let us review how Latin Americans are "muddling through the middle."

Policy: Macro, Micro, and Mezzo

If market forces and the organized interests of civil society increasingly intrude upon policymaking at the national level, how do they affect subnational politics? Decentralization and changing intergovernmental relations have dramatically altered the context of social policy in Latin America. The principle of subsidiarity has gained currency; "superior units should not do what is readily doable by inferior ones." The resources managed by local governments, traditionally based on transfers, increasingly will have to be generated locally. Local politics, usually associated with clientelism, may yet yield to more participatory arrangements, especially as NGOs and social movements grow more insistent about *making* as well as *taking* policy, proposing solutions as well as protesting problems.

A comparative reference may be useful to this discussion. For example, the democratic transitions of Europe and Latin America—usually compared only at the national level—are equally if not more relevant for analyzing local policy and subnational politics. First comes the question of the level of analysis. Lowi's classic distinctions between distributive, regulatory, and redistributive policies look different viewed from above than viewed from below. Revenue transfers by the center (redistribution) are often viewed as regulatory in the periphery. However, regulation by the center may be the only way distribution can occur in the periphery. For example, tied and targeted ministry funding for primary health care clinics in outlying urban *favelas* or villas offers perhaps the only vehicle by which services can be delivered in Latin America. From a comparative perspective, localism in urban Latin America, as in parts of Europe, may in the long run become an asset rather than a liability for democratizing central government. As Ashford noted,

> both ideological and administrative values may be reversed in subnational politics, that is, the sub-units may be bastions of radical opinion and protection for good governments in the system rather than conservative and corrupt strongholds. Political stability owes more to the "sotto-governo" (undergovernment)—competent administration and routinized competition at the local level—than to constantly changing ministerial actors (1976: 54).

In sum, the merging of frontiers between public and private sectors may contribute to strengthening participatory local government and lead to more inclusive, diversified social policy. Territory, like ethnicity and culture, has a way of resurfacing on political agendas from which it has long been banished. Negotiations, pacts, and compromise happen more readily through the propinquity principle; face-to-face encounters, while they may not guarantee good results, do require policymakers and policytakers to at least explore accommodation, for they will meet again tomorrow.

Faced by nearly overwhelming fiscal crisis, municipal governments are increasingly receptive to collaborative ventures in service delivery, often seeking to emulate NGO flexibility, innovation, client responsiveness, and programmatic effectiveness; they may contract for training and technical assistance or piggyback NGOs to obtain resources and fill service gaps. Reform and popular municipal governments are multiplying. New mecha-

nisms have been created to institutionalize participation and add a deliberative character to city government through neighborhood councils and associations. Not surprisingly, increased frequency of meetings and daily
exchanges on topics of mutual concern reduce distrust and open doors to
shared efforts between these public and private actors. In many democratizing settings, for example, reform leaders emerged from popular movements
and NGOs. They are known quantities (Loveman 1991).

What else do the NGO and social movements bring to the policymaking
table? What have they learned on their journey from protest to proposal,
and what more must they learn? Many have long experience in negotiating
grants with international donors. However, making pacts, contracts, and
deals with local and national officials is a relatively new experience for the
organized poor and their advocates. Independent research centers and think
tanks, another key set of NGO actors, supply social scientists and technical
personnel who can chronicle negotiations, assess trade-offs, and help accelerate the organizational learning curve. They encourage more systematic
and programmatic learning, identify technical problems, and formulate
alternative social policy. In the final analysis, the challenges confronting
policy and science are identical—for both are reduced to meeting humanity's needs as their ultimate measure.

Some clear messages for policymakers have emerged from these studies. Many of these recommendations are context specific. For example,
Mexican participants argued that membership organizations must make
pacts with federal technocrats in order to counteract local clientelistic
elites. Colombia recently celebrated local elections for the first time in its
history, and, despite a relatively decentralized tradition, observers there are
less concerned about neutralizing elite power at the local level. Chilean
NGOs contract with the health ministry to provide primary health care,
while Brazilians protest privatized (for-profit) health care that excludes the
poor—the protest more vehement where such health care was once more
readily available from the state, as in São Paulo.

Several current and former municipal and central government officials
commented on the chapters from their policy-implementing perspective.
Many of their recommendations for local government policy and donor
strategies have been integrated into this chapter. One participant, formerly
an NGO director and now a ministry of planning official, explained how her
perspective changed when "they" became "we," when opposition became
government. Another contrasted the outlook of officials who must deal
with massive numbers of competing claimants, of "new" as well as "old"
poor, against the perspective of NGO managers having a relatively circumscribed clientele.

Administrative efficiency and social efficacy challenge both NGOs and
local governments. The researchers cited many experiments and ideas for
promoting greater management skills in NGOs, finding more creative

domestic fund-raising strategies, opening more channels of communication to policymakers and policytakers using mass media, and easing NGO pilot programs more directly into the social policy stream. Given the need, it is time to celebrate even small victories. The environment of social policy is expanding to incorporate interests and actors previously excluded. Both the rules of the game and the number of players have changed.

During this research enterprise, a number of recommendations emerged that seem relevant to most countries for further expanding the social policy dialogue. These policy and programmatic recommendations fall into three groups: (1) those directed at NGOs and other organizations of civil society, (2) those involving the relationships between NGOs and local governments, and (3) those relating to the policy environment. The last set of recommendations is usually determined by central governments, although sometimes international or multilateral agencies are involved. Among the propositions and recommendations for NGOs and organized social movements (as well as international donors who support them), I emphasize the following:

NGOs

- Support enhanced technical, management, and analytical skills among NGOs, MOs, and GSOs.
- Stimulate more cross-fertilization, the transfer of ideas, experiments, and social technology within and across national boundaries.
- Promote greater NGO sophistication in information management, communications media, and formation of public opinion.
- Encourage NGO effort and creativity in *local* fund-raising to help stimulate domestic philanthropy or reorient it from charitable to development purposes.
- Respect heterogeneity of NGO communities and their determination of suitable timing and shape of second- or third-level association (federations, consortia, networks, etc.).
- Encourage greater programmatic focus within NGOs since holistic approaches are frequently utopian.
- Promote multiple-issue movements to obtain multiclass support.

NGO–Local Government Relationships

- Support NGO projects that feed into or give direction to public social policy.
- Stimulate NGOs to act as laboratories of social experimentation, technical assistance, and training for local governments; document the experiences.
- Generate more information on functions of local government and

examples of effective mechanisms for relating to civil society (neighborhood councils, associations, etc.).
- Recognize low skill levels and rapid turnover of local government personnel. Recognize also that, although often short on managerial and technical skills, NGOs tend to be permanent actors.
- Document successful tax reform, innovative transfer mechanisms, and those collaborative ventures that reduce the endemic fiscal weakness of local governments.
- Encourage NGOs to be more flexible and less doctrinaire, open to negotiating ties to the state at every level.
- Explore how NGO international fund-raising and technical assistance might be replicated by local governments, for example, intergovernmental lobbies, the International Union of Local Authorities, Sister Cities International, Partners of the Americas, and so on.
- Identify in each country the comparative advantage of public and private actors (for primary health care, housing, education, etc.). Who more effectively delivered what, to how many?

Policy Environment

- Pay more attention to state and local governments and to intergovernmental relations.
- Expand fiscal capacity of local governments, especially tax-gathering capacity.
- Permit NGOs autonomous space to function as mediating structures for the design and implementation of social policy.
- Simplify regulatory environments and procedures whereby NGOs are legally recognized and made accountable.
- Demonstrate where privatized social services effectively deliver services to the poor (rather than discriminating against or merely neglecting them).
- Experiment with mechanisms and incentives to make contracting, fees for service, and other types of private-public exchanges feasible and attractive.
- Design legislation and regulatory packages to distinguish those NGOs actually providing goods and services from for-profit ventures seeking tax shelters.
- Explore how NGOs can generate revenues abroad without unduly threatening sovereignty.

Conclusion

Latin American urbanization is irreversible (although democratization and development are not). According to the World Bank's *World Development*

Report 1992 urbanization figures for 1990, Argentina (at 86 percent) and Chile (at 86 percent) had higher proportions of their populations living in cities and towns than did the United States (at 75 percent). Brazil reached 75 percent in 1990, and Mexico, at 73 percent, is almost as urban as its North American neighbors. Colombia (70 percent) and Peru (70 percent) are not far behind. How are urban populations to gain fundamental goods and services? Where and how does their citizenship begin? Examining illustrative cases of NGO and local government conflict and collaboration, we will explore in this book how Latin American city dwellers are forging their own variations of de Tocquevillian democracy through the "art of association" despite growing "inequality of conditions."

Argentina offers a prime, if tragic, illustration of the spreading phenomenon known as the new poor, people formerly of the middle class who have seen their incomes erode through withdrawal of subsidies, suppression of public-sector jobs, and imposition of related policy reforms—all products of structural adjustment and conditionality. These new poor join the ranks of the old poor; both include migrant and native, recent arrivals and long-term urban dwellers. Our journey through six of Latin America's most populous countries begins in Argentina, a good example of a developing country that has reversed its progress.

2

State, Civil Society, and Popular Neighborhood Organizations in Buenos Aires: Key Players in Argentina's Transition to Democracy

MARCELO CAVAROZZI
VICENTE PALERMO

An Unstable State

For much of this century, political volatility has been a feature of Argentine life. The military coup of 1930 ushered in a prolonged era of political instability, which intensified with the overthrow of the first Perón regime in 1955. A lengthy period followed during which neither civilian governments nor military dictatorships managed to achieve any degree of continuity and legitimacy. For example, most of Argentina's presidents since the 1950s have been overthrown by successive military coups. Others, such as Aramburu in 1958, Lanusse in 1973, and Bignone in 1983, succeeded military governments that had been repudiated by the people and forced to relinquish power to civilian politicians.

Over the past several decades, two factors have weakened the Argentine state apparatus: first, the frequent turnover of leadership, and second, a series of economic and social forces that have subjected the country to sectoral pressures. Urban entrepreneurs (industrialists, builders, and service providers), unionized workers, agricultural producers of the *pampas,* and other groups have variously imposed their agendas upon the state—a course that has hindered the formulation and implementation of public policy. This capability to place the state in check has led many to a belief in a strong civil society as a counterpart to the weak state. Many argue, in fact, that a "weak" state and a "strong" civil society are complementary.

The interventionist state, part of the social and political framework that developed in Argentina from the 1930s, has been irreversibly dismantled over the last fifteen years. In raising the question of how this process has affected civil society, one must ask whether society has been strengthened—a hypothesis that could be assumed if civil society is seen as standing in opposition to the state—or whether it too has become disorganized as the state has weakened.

Origins of Popular Participation

In the 1930s, despite widespread political instability, Argentina entered a period of economic dynamism. During this decade, the country made successive strides in developing import substitution, structuring a semiclosed economy whose axis was the internal market, regulating the financial and labor markets, and moderating inflation (i.e., holding it at 20 to 50 percent annually). This economic model was one component of a state-centered social framework based on the operation of two mechanisms of equilibrium.

The first of these was the relationship between the market economy and the state (defined as the instruments for political regulation of the economy). Although private capital was the main agent of accumulation during the decades following the crisis of 1929–1932, it was subject to limitations and exposed to incentives designed and controlled by public agencies. Likewise, public capital participated actively in industrial and service enterprises. The processes articulated in the market and around the state were complementary, not antithetical. In other words, in the state-centered framework, political regulation of the economy helped to generate investment capital, to create externalities with dynamic effects, and to set limits on predatory behavior by entrepreneurs.

The second mechanism of equilibrium was the relationship between civil society and the state. The state, in this sense, should be understood as an organizer of the mechanisms of political-institutional and cultural control established over the social actors and their organizations. Since the 1930s, civil society has strengthened as public participation expanded, particularly in the urban popular sectors. This participatory process included the emergence and growth of workers' organizations and the urban poor, the rise (and subsequent decline) of social movements, and the modernization and secularization of social relations in daily life: family, workplace, school, and neighborhood. All this was reflected in the opening of doors that hitherto had been closed to the popular sectors.

Countering expanded participation, however, were control mechanisms implemented by the state or redefined through either legislation or informal practice. These combined the old and the new and included, among other things, the spread of clientelist practices (albeit refocused on the state), implementation of corporatist mechanisms, and inclusion of quasi-state political parties. Basically, participation and control grew in tandem, and the achievements of the popular sectors often appeared as concessions, or even gifts, of the state.

Peronist Influences

In contrast to other Latin American countries—such as Chile, Brazil, and Mexico, where similar mechanisms of equilibrium existed—articulation of the state-centered framework in Argentina included two distinct stages. This had a significant impact on the specific form of the relationship between state and popular sectors. During the first stage, which spanned the Juan Perón government of 1945–1955, the state explicitly and vigorously promoted greater participation by the popular sector. Actually, the creation of new channels of participation alongside existing ones was part of a strategy geared toward forging a political alliance that would be an alternative to the coalition that held power in the 1930s through electoral fraud and support from the business classes.

Although Perón failed in his effort to consolidate a stable political regime, the processes unleashed during this decade became partially autonomous from the movement that had promoted them; the participative mechanisms created during that period remained in effect despite the fall of the Perón government. Thus, the popular sectors continued to participate as they had during the Perón decade. Perón's fall did introduce a major change, however; for almost two decades after 1955, succeeding governments maintained a hostile relationship with the Peronist movement, which was banned from electoral participation until 1973. Since for the most part the popular sectors continued to identify themselves as *peronista,* those nondemocratic governments mustered no more than a precarious legitimacy since none of them could pass the test of free elections.

Nonetheless, the state maintained the mechanisms of control and remained the point of reference for participation; that is, demands and pressures continued to be directed to the state's institutions. Yet, because these institutions were controlled by individuals and currents hostile to *peronismo,* the nature of the relationship changed. Exchanges between the state and popular organizations came to be dominated by attempts to pressure and even blackmail successive governments with a view toward maximizing short-term benefits. The array of methods used to extract resources from the state became more sophisticated and took into account both the fragility of these governments and their status—whether civilian or military.

Perón's return to power in 1973 occasioned a paroxysm of these practices, first both to precipitate the final fall of the already weakened military government of the Argentine Revolution and then to demand immediate retribution from the new constitutional government. This moment constituted a key point of inflection that few noted at the time, as the state's long reign of regulation came to an end during 1974 and 1975 and civil society began to influence the state relatively effectively.

After 1974, political violence began to permeate all spheres of Argentine society, in part caused by the struggle within the Peronist movement over two issues. The first concerned power within the various state organs, the second, control over the organizations—political parties and others—linked to the popular sectors. This struggle depressed political participation markedly, whether individual or collective. During the last year and a half of the Peronist government, widespread fear and political exhaustion replaced the mobilization and activism that had grown steadily since 1968. In particular, this phenomenon was seen in unions and grass-roots workers' groups, in neighborhood associations, and in various organizations formed in the neediest sectors by progressive groups of "third world priests." As a result, only groups linked to the militarized organizations (i.e., the Montonero guerrillas and the parapolice bands created by the Peronist ultraright) and the most motivated activists continued to operate. The common folk distanced themselves from these processes, and their participation ceased.

It was in this context that the military coup of March 1976 took place, followed by intense and systematic repression that sought to wipe out guerrillas and alleged collaborators and to deactivate the associative practices of civil society. Five years of paralysis and inaction followed, during which the only significant manifestation of opposition and protest was that of the Mothers of the Plaza de Mayo. Not until the late 1970s did other human-rights groups organize effective protests.

Early Popular Organizations

Argentina's first stage of metropolitan urbanization, beginning in the late 1930s, occurred mainly within Buenos Aires. During this period, the principal dwellings of low-income residents were tenements (*conventillos*) inhabited primarily by migrants to the city. Beginning in the mid-1930s, however, the tide of internal migrations eased, and neighborhoods developed whose houses were built by self-help construction on low-cost lots outside the city. This settlement pattern fueled the growth of Greater Buenos Aires, as popular sectors increasingly came to reside in outlying areas. Lacking infrastructure, periurban lots were cheap; also, a certain amount of credit assistance was available for housing construction. These factors combined with the spread of motorized public transport to spur the city's expansion during the 1940s and 1950s in a radial pattern along the spokes of the transportation system.

At first, such housing was located in relatively low-density neighborhoods inhabited by middle- and lower-income sectors; together with the shantytowns (*villas de emergencia*), these neighborhoods formed an expanding ring that came to characterize the spontaneous and disorderly popular urbanization of Greater Buenos Aires. During this stage, also, urban growth coincided with increased siting of industries in suburban areas, which further expanded urban sprawl.

Until the mid-1940s, the creation of neighborhood-based popular organizations followed the pace of popular urbanization within the context of a limited state presence that provided services in the wake of neighborhood growth. Demands by these organizations for infrastructure and equipment from the state were significantly complemented by community participation in executing public works; for example, one type of popular organization—the neighborhood development associations (*sociedades de fomento*)—mobilized neighborhoods to contribute labor and money to supplement government assistance. In this way, local development associations helped to direct the resources of the state, which assumed only partial responsibility for providing infrastructure and services. When state offices earmarked significant resources to public works, it was relatively easy for the development associations to influence the redistribution of these resources in ways that partially corrected the tendency to spatially segregate low-income residents. In general, the intensity of neighborhood participation varied according to its collective requirements and tended to decrease as the neighborhood consolidated itself.

Specifically, neighborhood development associations focused on creating or expanding socialization among residents, developing the neighborhood's social infrastructure (generally in education and health), and promoting construction of physical infrastructure such as drinking water systems, residential gas installations, and paved streets.

Mechanisms used by these societies included *participation,* or mobilizing residents to attain certain goals; *management,* in which the core of leaders or activists took charge of the supply and administration of services; and *mediation,* in which the society became the main instrument for channeling residents' demands to government offices.

During the late-1940s, the state began to intervene in the life of the popular sectors, often absorbing activities hitherto managed by neighborhood associations. During this stage, the tendency for all demands to be put to the state intensified until this practice came to be seen as the principal and, at times, only type of collective action. At the same time, the capability for autonomous cooperative action weakened, greatly influencing the institutional culture of the associations, which then consolidated themselves as mediators. This was a role calling for a considerable degree of institutionalization, and one in which state recognition, required by laws and municipal ordinances, was necessary if neighborhood associations were to operate effectively.

With this role change, however, came a loss of autonomy and a greatly diminished ability to garner state handouts. As the neighborhood move-ment became further isolated from other urban social actors, the disaffec-tion of each socioterritorial stratum vis-à-vis the needier grew; collabora-tion gave way to horizontal competition for public resources. As a result, despite the heterogeneity of the social contexts in which the neighborhood associations operated, they tended to express relatively homogeneous demands. Such demands mainly sought a prompt and specific response within the context of a bilateral relationship between the individual organi-zation and a given state agency. As the vertical nature of such relationships led to tensions and competition among organizations from socially similar grassroots groups, it became harder to create public arenas in which to negotiate and reconcile opposing demands.

Contemporary Participation: Diminishing Gains

The collapse of the Argentine state, which began in 1975–1976, intensified in 1981–1982 as the dual effects of the external debt crisis and internal fis-cal crisis took hold; what had begun as a deliberate and systematic attempt to reduce the size of the state and disarm some of its main mechanisms became an uncontrolled and chaotic collapse.

With the exhaustion of the state-centered framework and the crisis of the prevailing model came serious consequences for the urban popular sec-tors. Employment became precarious, the networks covered by the social security system were significantly weakened, and real wages declined steadily after 1975. Also, state subsidy mechanisms (sometimes called the "indirect wage") linked to social services and infrastructure were dramati-cally reduced. Two of the most significant consequences were the deepen-ing of social segregation in urban development and a total halt in public works for the popular *barrios*. The most recent settlements, along the periphery of Greater Buenos Aires, were hardest hit by the combination of regressive factors. In La Matanza (west of the Camino de Cintura) and the Ninth Barracks in Lomas de Zamora, for example, infrastructure and equip-ment needs have yet to be met in 1994.

Within this context of economic and social disorganization, the mili-tary government fell, a collapse that had catastrophic effects both for the high-level officials involved in the handling of government affairs and for the armed forces as a whole. The military disaster of the war with Great Britain added to the economic and political failures of the authoritarian government.

For the last eighteen months of the military government, which spanned the period from the defeat in the Malvinas war to the transfer of power to authorities elected in October 1983, a virtual power vacuum exist-ed in Argentina. Circumstances during this period contributed to a significant erosion of state control mechanisms that, albeit spasmodically, had been in place since the 1940s. In addition, the transition from authoritarianism unleashed an unprecedented reassessment of democratic institutions and political parties, which, in contrast to Argentina's earlier transitions, had played a key role in the process.

With the unexpected rise of the Radical Civic Union (UCR) and the triumph of its candidate, Raúl Alfonsín, political pluralism broadened. (From 1946 to 1976, free elections in Argentina had been synonymous with Peronist victories.) The first national defeat of what had been the majority party instituted the notion of political party competition for the first time in contemporary Argentina; not only could the citizens vote against the authoritarian government in power, they could also choose among different political alternatives.

Party choice assumed special importance in the popular zones of Greater Buenos Aires that, since the appearance of peronismo in the 1940s, had always voted as a block for Peronist candidates. But in 1983, these areas—which remained distant from and hostile toward all non-Peronist parties for thirty years—voted in unprecedented numbers for the UCR. While peronismo barely triumphed in the poorest municipalities, such as Florencio Varela, Moreno, La Matanza, and Merlo, the UCR scored victories not only in the highest-income areas of the north and northwest, but also in traditional bastions of peronismo such as Avallaneda, Morón, and Quilmes.

Participation at the Neighborhood Level

During the final years of the military government, several mobilizations occurred around municipal and neighborhood issues. The high level of participation, as well as the apparent rise of new leaders, suggested the emergence of a new neighborhood movement. Enjoying greater autonomy from the state, this movement was geared toward broadening the agenda of urban politics and strengthening relations between local society and public authorities. As a response to the drastic change in the direction of state action during the military government, some grassroots associations had already gained greater involvement from community residents and had begun to develop certain forms of self-management to address worsening living conditions. Many believed that the confluence of these tendencies would be reinforced by the democratization of institutions and the disappearance of the political violence that ten years earlier had quelled any inclinations toward participation.

After just two or three years of the new democratic government, however, the fragility and ambiguity of popular processes in Argentina became evident. Around 1986, there was a turnaround in the trends toward greater participation and involvement in urban associative life as neighborhood associations encountered major difficulties in maintaining participation and began to head down well-trodden paths, abandoning innovative tendencies as they went. Older organizations failed to consolidate new styles of action and leadership, and new ones never developed characteristics of the emerging new neighborhood movement. Instead, grassroots organizations (*juntas vecinales*) and other forms of local associative life appeared to reverse their promising trends.

What happened to frustrate these processes so quickly? The truth is that since the very outset of the transition, popular endeavors were limited and fraught with negative characteristics not initially perceived by the analysts and organizations that tried to ride the participatory wave. To a great extent, such innovations as local self-managed economies and participatory institutional models took place largely in an artificial context. Although other weaknesses afflicted neighborhood associative life, a significant negative for popular organizations in Argentina was their vulnerability to state and political party intervention. During this period, politicians at both national and provincial levels and those from the Peronist opposition (which still controlled a great many municipalities in Greater Buenos Aires) continued to act as if the old forms of state-civil relations were still in effect, or at least easily rebuilt.

Low-Resource Clientelism

Particularly among middle- and lower-level functionaries and politicians, a resurgence of the old clientelist practices quickly impregnated the spectrum of exchanges around urban and neighborhood needs and the flow of resources to popular organizations and local institutions. In such a context, the "new institutionality" often touted by municipal managers turned out to be fictitious; in fact, announcements of municipal decentralization that allowed neighborhood associations to have effective involvement in government-generated expectations proved exaggerated, if not illusory.

This lack of substance was attributable not only to the politicians, but also to grassroots leaders and even local-level militants. Ultimately sabotaging their own interests, these groups adopted the return to clientelism, although initially the popular organizations had reacted with street protests when authorities stalled effective opportunities for institutional participation. These protests failed, however, and were costly as well, so most organizations eventually acquiesced to a renewal of traditional patterns of state and party action.

The return to old ways dealt a serious blow to the neighborhood movement. Because the new clientelism operated with fewer resources, an inevitable result of the state's fiscal bankruptcy, neighborhood associations found themselves obliged to redefine their objectives, activities, and modes of action. First, they abandoned their quest for improved urban infrastructure and focused instead on social activities. Second, they stopped promoting mobilizations of human and material resources from the neighborhood through participation, focusing instead on a core of activists specialized in the supply and administration of certain services (management, direction, administration, and initiative) and in articulating demands to state agencies. Increasingly, neighborhood demands began to reflect whatever the state chose to offer. Instead of challenge and pressure, the stance of neighborhood associations toward public policy became one of accommodation to state policies and to the limited involvement of the beneficiaries. As a result, these organizations competed among themselves for allocation of resources that were already earmarked for them.

In contrast to the past, these resources became fewer and fewer as municipalities abandoned their functions of building and maintaining urban infrastructure. Public works tended to appear as an "adjustment variable" of the municipal budgets, which means that most municipalities fully transferred the task of building and maintaining infrastructure to residents. Under this emerging self-management model, residents were also responsible for sustaining local implementation of social policies. The participation of private actors was guaranteed through various regulations; however, local organizations are experiencing problems: on the one hand, leaders specialized in mediation are sometimes co-opted by government officials who want to expand their political clientele; on the other, discouragement, disaffection, and disbelief on the part of residents has become widespread.

Essentially, the situation shifted from one in which these organizations articulated the relationship between state and neighborhood to one in which the state articulated the relationship between the neighborhood, represented or not by an association, and the private actors. Therefore, at present it is difficult for neighborhood associations to act as pressure groups. In order for them to do so effectively again, it would be necessary both to redefine the traditional style of demand directed toward the state and to reject political parties' clientelistic practices.

It appears that the participatory phenomenon following the collapse of the military government was too weak to survive. Discouragement and frustrated expectations, along with leaders' ambitions, created a climate that allowed a return to the old political-cultural orientations of traditional *vecinalismo*. The power of state and political party clientelism proved too capable of co-opting leaders, usually quickly, and placed the neighborhood associations in a dependent relationship oriented toward these forces rather than toward each other. Being thus weakened, they carried little weight in the municipal power structure despite the state's decreasing capacity to build and maintain city infrastructure and despite the fact that the resources needed for such work would come mainly from direct users.

Problems at the Grassroots

In the poorest barrios, neighborhood associations are greatly weakened by the state's diminishing resources. Often, such groups must discard any efforts that cannot be sustained by their neighborhoods—which often lack the means even to meet basic needs; thus, they reorient themselves toward smaller-scale, cheaper, and more accessible activities that the core of active members can manage. In such circumstances, community self-management sometimes degenerates into a very negative type of relationship in which neighborhood efforts focus on transferring responsibilities instead of creating new channels to improve living conditions. In the areas of public education and health, there is often a sort of trickle-down transfer of the responsibility for maintaining services. This transfer, however, does not increase the influence local organizations have on resource allocation or policy formulation. It is rare, for example, that popular organizations have an institutional counterpart in the municipal government to facilitate broader participation in decisionmaking; indeed, such organizations have little voice regarding the policies that directly affect them.

When providing infrastructure, the municipal government shifts part of the work to the neighborhood associations, which, limited in human and material resources, seek to share the costs with residents, charging a commission on the services provided. For their part, the residents' involvement in the services is practically nil, as the associations manage the services obtained and solve any problems that may arise with the official agencies (which often fail to carry out the modest promises they make). Such involvement takes up a substantial amount of local activists' time and energy, which curtails their efforts to expand the agenda of issues or to increase neighborhood participation.

As leaders and activists increasingly specialize in mediation and management, many distance themselves from the neighborhood. Often, leaders are co-opted by political party machines or by the weak municipal bureaucracy through the clientelistic growth of employment and the creation of new offices with the mission of "promoting" neighborhood participation. Many leaders choose to increase the prestige of their organizations by participating in a replication of the state pattern of resource allocation. In this instance, they collaborate with local party leaders (*punteros*), whose main function is to get members (i.e., votes for internal party elections). To some degree, these votes also translate into support for that party in local, provincial, and national elections.

The core of activists surrounding a neighborhood association leader focus their energies on the management and maintenance of equipment and services and on the organization's social activities. This internal distribution of functions expresses the implicit pact by which presidents count on the organization as the basis for their local outreach and the organizations count on their leaders as a relatively successful means of gaining access to public resources. Thus, there has been a shift from an initial structure in which leaders primarily focused on gaining benefits for their organizations to one in which these organizations now form a part of their leaders' framework of opportunities. This explains another paradox of local associative life in recent years; organizations have multiplied even as associative organizing in general has waned. Although levels of activism and participation have diminished, proto-organizations—converted into a fundamental part of the opportunity structures of their leaders—have been maintained.

In the wake of community disaffection and indifference, the various rings of community proximity to neighborhood associations have begun to disintegrate. Because leaders concentrated on the peripheries of their organizations (those areas involved in activities least appropriate for generating new members or pulling together a consistent and cohesive core of activists), the existence of these organizations is threatened.

Popular Organizations and Political Parties

A novel feature of the transition to democracy in the 1980s was the way in which local party politics unfolded in Greater Buenos Aires, in part because the elections of 1983 and 1985 broke the hegemony that the Peronists had maintained for several decades. Important as well was the democratization of the Peronist party itself, which now allowed party members to elect officers and candidates in contrast to their being handpicked (as Perón traditionally did).

In 1983, local parties began to play an increasingly important role in neighborhood politics, although their influence rarely spread to city politics. As the parties never became decisive articulators of exchange and negotiation among the social actors of the city, they contributed little to the rise of cooperative strategies for generating institutional and material resources. Furthermore, they did not promote real experiences of institutional reworking, nor did they formulate creative proposals for solving fiscal and urban crises.

One factor reinforcing the parties' exclusion has been the strategy of urban leaders. Operating immediately above the punteros, these individuals generally view their positions as a springboard to the post of provincial deputy—from which they may eventually climb to the national legislature. The main concern of these leaders is usually to obtain resources for "their" punteros or to woo punteros linked to their internal opponents; such resources, generally jobs or subsidies that the punteros then distribute among their clientele, serve as a lightning rod for energies that might otherwise be spent on broader concerns. At the same time, the issues around which local leaders structure their discourse and debate priorities are located not locally but at the national or provincial level. This circumstance, which in times of "normal" politics would not be too serious, in an exceptional period such as the present becomes an insurmountable obstacle to effective redefinition of local priorities and methods of government.

As party competition intensified, it became channeled into traditional forms that maximized short-term results and encouraged single-issue and exclusionary demands. This style of action, which subordinated efforts to have more cooperative exchange and more participatory institution-building processes, led to savage and corrupt party factionalism.

While in power, neither the UCR nor the Peronists responded in an effective way to the worsening conditions of the popular sectors and to the expectations that neighborhood associations held at the outset of the transition. Due to the inefficient and regressive nature of local fiscal policy, community control over revenues and expenditures became impossible. Although theoretically the community legislative bodies or deliberating councils could have formulated urban proposals that reflected social demands, they were unable to go beyond establishing insignificant regulations and attending to very particularist demands. Therefore, despite abundant and predictable rhetoric of decentralization and participation, the fictitious nature of the local political renewal was apparent from the beginning. Although many government agencies created offices for citizen and neighborhood participation, new ideas and new bureaucratic offices generally served the most immediate and prosaic needs of infighting among party factions. Many agencies charged with implementing social policies, such as the National Food Program, were inaccessible to opponents from other parties or from the same party. Thus, despite a fiscal crisis within the country, agencies that duplicated functions were sometimes created out of competition and ambition.

Despite these abuses, political parties escaped open challenges from the popular organizations. On the contrary, both new and old development associations and other new organizational forms (for example, the associations of squatters) adapted to the predominant clientelism and particularism without questioning the narrow opportunities for institutional and material participation that were reserved for them in public affairs. The local state set most policies without taking into account the neighborhood associations, which were merely beneficiaries of residual resource allocations in the form of "subsidies to the intermediate entities." These subsidies, most of them in the area of public health, were rarely granted according to optimal allocation; instead, they were directed discretionally to reward the compliant and penalize the unruly. In fact, one of the priorities of municipal authorities was to oppose efforts of neighborhood associations to develop autonomously and to organize initiatives. By adapting to the overall pattern of municipal resource allocation, these organizations helped legitimate such action by providing concrete support for certain decisions and by failing to mobilize opposition activities.

Often, neighborhood associations were co-opted by the political parties, particularly if the organizations were very new or had a discontinuous history with little or no tradition of activism and a minimal institutional density. They also often operated upon an extremely tenuous and atomized community fabric. Leaders who flourished in these organizations were those who more or less openly turned them into platforms for launching their own political careers in exchange for material benefits. In the organizations with a stronger institutional culture, more indirect forms of subordination came about, and internal administrative ritualism prevailed. Committee meetings might be held, for example, and a minimum of organizational life maintained even in the absence of long-standing members and leaders.

Leadership in Neighborhood Associations

As noted, association leaders often tried to take advantage of the existing state supply of services or to activate a latent supply, independent of their neighborhoods' direst needs. This was often due both to the leaders' self-interest and to local political dynamics. In the vast majority of cases, such leaders merely compounded their status as community activists, political party activists, directors of some other "public interest" organizations, and local notables with a wide range of contacts; the performance of these other roles often took precedence over their leadership of the neighborhood associations.

Acting as articulators between the association and the state/party and associative network in which it unfolds, leaders generally occupy their posts by virtue of the external source of power or prestige associated with their position in another local entity. Multiple memberships hold an implicit promise of greater access to resources, a promise that feeds leaders' ambitions for more prominent roles on the local political scene. The prevalence of activists with these characteristics is an indicator of the de facto dependency that afflicts neighborhood associations.

The leaders' need to seek an adequate context of opportunities helps to explain the apparent paradox of the coexistence on the one hand of many organizations, and on the other, of limited organizational structures and resources. Association leaders' practice of projecting themselves *from* their organizations, rather than as a part of them, contributes both to the low levels of organizing that neighborhood associations have manifested and to unoriginal and unimaginative demands. The only gambles their leaders take are those they believe will advance their own political careers.

Thus, activism and participation are declining, at times to minimal levels. Most remaining proto-organizations, having evolved into an essential element of their leaders' ambitions, are artificial. Preserving the organizational myth thus becomes a prime function of calculating leaders, who consider the neighborhood organization a base from which to launch political careers. While it is not easy to advance in a political party career, and parties rarely promote neighborhood association leaders by virtue of their status as such, there are at least well-known rules of the game and a discernible route of progress the limited associational horizon fails to offer. Hence, leaders often credit their personal success to the circumstance of being co-opted by the party machines or to holding offices in the local government. Some who have moved on retain a vague commitment, although the neighborhood movement rarely benefits because the leaders drawn into the government offices usually become disconnected from the neighborhood associations or fail to take them into account.

The co-optation process is particularly destructive to the neighborhood movement, since it decapitates the associations that give birth to neighborhood leaders. Under the appearance of participation, the organization actually becomes more dependent, and the activist is transformed into a "former member of the neighborhood movement." Precisely because specialized mediation is often the substance of the exchange between leaders and those who elected or supported them, a leader's exit from the scene is very costly for the neighborhood association, since there usually has been no organizational learning process. One characteristic of specialized mediation is its lack of openness. A leader's desire to maintain exclusive contacts, handle all information, and control the organization following retirement work against the development of the membership. Thus, a marked discontinuity ensues when that leader leaves.

Association leaders generally attract new active members from among their own peers—friends, next-door neighbors, and relatives. Such a course guarantees relations based on trust, facilitation of control, and a particular placement within the neighborhood stratification. Because of this recruitment mode, it is fairly uncommon to find a dynamic of internal conflict within neighborhood associations that reflects the social heterogeneity of their formal radius of action (usually set by the municipality).

The "Apoliticism" of Neighborhood Associations

Frequently, leaders and activists assert that "what we do here is not politics." Local development is defined a priori as apolitical; politics is seen as something dirty that divides and causes conflict. Thus arises the paradox of association activists distrusting the appearance of parties on the scene, while these same parties are led by former neighborhood activists. "Apoliticism" predominates to a greater extent in the older associations, which reject party politics and embrace a pragmatism evident during the period of military authoritarianism. This combination leads them to attribute neutrality to the state spheres with which they establish linkages; even so, these linkages may be operated by party leaders in their status as formal authorities of the neighborhood associations or articulators of informal channels. The ambiguity of such a relationship is evident by such comments as: "It doesn't matter who provides benefits, the development association or the neighborhood, just as long as politics are not dragged in," and "In the development society, there is no talk of politics."

This "not talking about politics" is actually a way to avoid speaking of urban issues that have a decisive impact on association actions. As a result, only the most immediate demands are discussed. While recognizing that the allotment of scarce municipal resources reflects strictly party aims, neighborhood leaders go along with the fiction that submitting to state political action without actually expressing support for the governing parties guarantees their organizations' autonomy. In reality, the antiparty and antipolitics discourse become the necessary complement of the very adaptive instrumental orientation that is eroding the autonomy of neighborhood associations.

The ambiguity of the antiparty discourse is evident in the internal tensions that affect these associations. In many, an informal yet clear division of labor exists between the leader—specifically dedicated to the tasks of mediation—and the activists, who accompany the leader, second his opinions, and take charge of managing the services provided by the association. Even if the leaders are relatively successful, there remains a muted questioning on the part of the activists. This sort of persistent murmuring reproaches the leader's preferences for activities "outside" of the association and for frequent absences. The leader is quietly accused of preferring party politics to the supposed responsibilities of a "true *vecinalista*."

What is the significance and function of this murmuring, beyond its obvious incongruence? It is seldom translated into open and formal questioning because it does not call into question the basic parameters of the leader's performance. While there are complaints that the current forms of action are unsatisfactory, alternatives are rarely proposed. Such murmuring, however, is useful because it maintains a substratum of dissent upon which the activists may draw when, for whatever circumstance, the delicate equilibrium between instrumental pragmatism and subordination of the neighborhood associations to the dictates of party politics is broken. At that point, the questioning ceases to be "background noise" and becomes protest.

The tendency, however, is for dissent to become explicit only when the extreme of protest is reached, and the rupture that usually follows rarely contributes to the organization's learning. The consequences are usually costly. In voluntary associations such as the development associations, exit is much easier than expressions of disagreement because dissident members rarely have the tools to force or induce association leaders to change their behavior. Most likely, the dissidents themselves will eventually become discouraged and drop out. This outflow in turn makes it more difficult to turn conflict situations into opportunities for learning that produce lasting changes in organizational behavior. In the few cases in which learning did occur, it happened through trial and error, which may be costlier than preventive reorientation.

Gloomy Prospects for Genuine Participation

By 1987, politics in Argentina had begun to lose its content; mobilization and participation in representative institutions were perceived as a heavy burden, and most people had begun to distance themselves from politicians and to oppose calls for participation. Such appeals increased the public's distrust of those in the "political class," who, from the collective perspective, had not only failed to solve the economic crisis but had also sought to involve citizens strictly to justify their own positions and to retain increasingly unpopular corporatist advantages.

A key feature of the period ushered in by the elections of 1987 was the appearance of a new type of personalism in Argentina. In contrast to the *personalismos* of the past, the new leaders established a sort of "structural complicity" with the masses who, after suffering a dramatic decline in living conditions and real incomes, wanted to "get things done" without having to participate beyond the ritual act of the election. Indeed, the exhortations to mobilize directed to the masses were viewed with skepticism and distrust. For their part, the leaders promised to "deliver the goods," signaling that it was unnecessary for the masses to organize.

The partial exhaustion of the democratic mechanisms and parliamentary institutions that occurred in Argentina affected the local level to a considerable degree. It began the perception of political participation as an exercise in futility, a view particularly prevalent in the suburban zones of Greater Buenos Aires in 1987 and 1988 when this fieldwork was carried out. As inflation, a shrinking public sector, and a deteriorating economy lowered living standards of both old and new poor in the late 1980s, inflated political discourse, fiscal impotence, and clientelistic leadership diminished the scope and salience of participation through popular organizations in Buenos Aires. The experiences of neighborhood associations in Buenos Aires are significant (although atypical) for other major capital cities in the world; the neighborhood associations were too close to power, yet far from efficacy.

3

Negotiated Interactions: NGOs and Local Government in Rosario, Argentina

Roberto Martinez Nogueira

The Actors

In recent years, widespread unemployment and rampant inflation have plunged many of Argentina's citizens into deep poverty. Few cities have suffered more than Rosario, now one of Argentina's principal centers of social conflict. Here, for example, was the epicenter of a wave of looting that shook the country from May 1989 to February 1990 and was a factor leading to Rosario's change of municipal government in 1989.

Among the initiatives growing out of these desperate circumstances were three that attempted to foster community organization by (1) setting up community centers, (2) supporting neighborhood participation and self-direction, and (3) promoting cooperation with municipal government. Both economics and politics affected the way these projects unfolded in Rosario, compelling a redefinition of their objectives and testing the abilities of NGOs and the commitment of neighborhood associations. This chapter examines relations among the four actors involved: NGOs, neighborhood organizations, local governments, and political parties.

NGOs

In analyzing the evolution and recent development of Argentine NGOs, one must first examine the growth of society and the simultaneous spread of poverty within the country. For many decades during the twentieth century, most Argentine citizens viewed rising mobility as an automatic condition; few of them faced long-term unemployment, and widespread poverty was simply not an issue. The state had expanded as a result of its own initiatives and in response to social demands and corporatist appropriations. Between society and the state were many mechanisms of inclusion and control, among them trade unions and service providers for the popular sectors, most of whom were wage earners.

Deindustrialization and the collapse of the state, however, led to a sudden and substantial change. No longer was the state a service provider (in the manner of a premature "welfare state") but, instead, had become a distributor of privileges from which those lacking the protective shield of corporatist organizations were excluded. As unemployment increased, unions could no longer complement the state, and the number of citizens with no linkage to the public sector and minimal social benefits grew quickly. Structural unemployment became a key issue in Argentina, provoking the dramatic expansion of poverty and the withering of long-standing memberships and loyalties.

Within this context, the urban NGOs emerged. Theirs was not an easy road, as they had little to guide them; rural NGOs, for example, were weak and few in number. Moreover, there had been no demand for NGO services from active urban organizations, and the NGOs were not integrated into a political movement. Most were formed during the transition to democracy (in this regard, Argentina's experiences differed from those of its neighbors).

Encompassing technical personnel from the public sector or former party activists with some prior experience in grassroots work, these organizations began to carry out projects with support from international cooperation. The NGOs gained little political strength during this period, involving themselves only to a limited extent, if at all, in political action and likewise failing to win social legitimacy to any significant degree. (As late as 1990, there were still relatively few NGOs operating in Argentina.)

The number of Rosario NGOs working in promotion and development is likewise small (ten, according to a 1990 survey), and they are relatively new. For example, two of the three NGOs that will be described later in this chapter emerged after 1983. Thus, they have but limited collective experience in planning and implementing projects and in extracting the lessons learned.

Neighborhood Organizations

Rosario's territorial organizations assumed two basic forms: social clubs (*clubes de barrio*) and community development associations (*sociedades de fomento*). Such clubs became a major social phenomenon with the urban growth of the early twentieth century. Founded in the homogeneous setting of the neighborhood, they served as recreation centers and as places for encouraging local identity and intergenerational contact; they constitute a surprisingly well-developed institutional network. The community development associations served not only as social clubs but also as a means for bringing demands before the municipal government, which has sometimes delegated functions to them (Herzer and Pirez 1988).

The development associations function in other ways, as well, pressing claims vis-à-vis the local authorities, providing services, and creating spaces in which to gather with neighbors. By promoting solidarity and generating a sense of collective identity based on common needs, these groups integrate their participants, who often differ in status, class, political preference, and so on (Milofsky 1988). The profiles of these organizations vary depending on the degree of neighborhood consolidation; in the older neighborhoods, for example, the traditional development movement was geared toward obtaining services; in the newer ones, community members want water and sanitation infrastructure and health services; in the squatter settlements (*villas de emergencia*), the main problems are title to the lands residents occupy and the threat of relocation. Within the discourse of neighborhood organizing, neighborhood action is seen variously as a means of providing services, an alternative to the local government, an arena for political-party organizing, and a catalyst for mobilization around issues that transcend the neighborhood.

To fulfill these roles, community development associations walk a narrow line that, on the one hand, develops state mechanisms of control and, on the other, guarantees results that stimulate citizen participation. Neighborhood organizations exist in large part due to recognition by the state; they are a means of gaining access to the state, and they are perceived as an appropriate instrument for meeting needs. However, authoritarian regimes restrict, compartmentalize, and channel the action of these organizations; often, resources from the state are either granted as rewards or withheld as punishment based on the political behavior of organization leaders and neighborhood residents. For their part, political parties see the neighborhood organizations as recruiting grounds and as a seedbed for clientelism. Together with the heterogeneity of situations and the competition for resources, these factors lead neighborhood associations to forge stronger relations with the municipality than with other neighborhood associations.

Local Government

In Argentina, municipalities traditionally lacked substantive political functions. Authorized only to provide minor services yet charged with expanding and maintaining the urban infrastructure, they limped along with weak tax bases and heavy dependence on transfers from the provincial governments. In this subordinate role, municipalities enjoyed virtually no access to the national scene.

However, the widespread deterioration of infrastructure and services and economic hardship have turned these local governments into implementers of social policy because of the withdrawal of national and provincial organizations from territorial jurisdictions. The lack of programs to create a "safety net" for those hardest hit by adjustment policies and by poverty and marginalization obliges municipalities to address a growing number of demands with dwindling resources, insufficient administrative structures, and inadequate mechanisms of articulation with social organizations.

Political Parties

Rosario traditionally provided a strong base of support for the Peronist movement. Its large working population from the industrial belts, railroads, inland port, and flour mills made trade union organizing the mechanism for political participation. Historically, *peronismo* gained absolute predominance in neighborhoods with large working populations, whether these were well-established neighborhoods or periurban settlements created through internal migrations. Local *caudillos* flourished through clientelism and the channeling of state welfare policies but played only a peripheral role in the life of social movements.

The middle-class vote was sought by the Radical Civic Union (UCR) and the Progressive Democratic Movement, a small national party based in the city. Although the UCR has an extensive organizational network reaching many neighborhoods, other smaller groups—such as the Communist Party and the Popular Socialist Party—were competitive in specific areas (neighborhood organizations, cooperatives, the university) but had no neighborhood meeting places for militants and activists.

In recent years, political parties have undergone major changes aided in part by deindustrialization, which helped weaken occupation-based organizational mechanisms such as trade unions. Considerable intraurban mobility took place, as well, brought about by the growing impoverishment of many sectors and the general deterioration of living conditions and housing. New contingents, expelled from their places of origin by recurrent flooding of the Paraná River, joined the migrations. The UCR began to emerge as the party with a competitive edge in the popular sectors, winning the municipal elections in 1983. It was, however, defeated by the Popular Socialist Party (PSP) in 1989. The PSP is a highly centralized party with a student and professional base and a history of successful struggles in the university union movement; it had, however, virtually no presence in provincial and municipal politics prior to the elections.

The City

Rosario has become significant because of its social conflicts, being the scene of the most critical incidents in the widespread looting that broke out in late May 1989, some weeks after the national elections (in which the governing party was defeated). Another episode of looting took place in 1990. No rigorous studies have yet been done of these events, which stemmed from a series of structural and short-term factors: the narrow concentration of wealth, rampant unemployment, and galloping inflation (W. C. Smith 1991). Existing information and observations reveal a dramatic and confused situation that led to uprisings by the poor. On both occasions, the upheaval persisted for several days.[1] At first, little law enforcement took place, however this interval was followed by an intimidating police presence and an eventual stage of siege.

The social response to Rosario's uprising was to try to help the neediest, an effort that received little state support. These events left a profound mark on the collective memory and have had a lasting impact on promotional activities organized in the popular barrios and villas.

Urban Development

Rosario's spectacular growth from 1870 to 1930 was spurred by its status as a rail hub and marketing point for much of the agricultural production in the *pampas*. Located in the province of Santa Fe, Rosario was for many years the country's second-largest city and the busiest inland port in Latin America (Cragnolino 1990). Yet its economic significance was never reflected politically; for example, Rosario is four times larger than the provincial capital, which is highly suggestive in a country whose political units have been created around urban centers that radiate power through their administrative apparatus. This circumstance has marked its history, created continual tension with the provincial capital of Santa Fe to the north, and give Rosario its unique pace and identity.

The city began industrialization early, gearing its first manufacturing plants toward agriculture, processing produce and constructing and repairing farm machinery. As in other urban centers, light industry began to expand in the 1930s—first into metallurgy and textiles, then into chemicals and petrochemicals. These endeavors drew large numbers of internal migrants (Castagna et al. 1990; Bonaparte 1990). Import-substituting investment strategies broke down in the late 1960s, and the outlook for industry was discouraging. Signs of stagnation, inefficiency, and obsolescence abounded, and agricultural production began to lose its original dynamism. In the 1970s, major changes overtook the productive structure; the number of establishments and jobs in manufacturing declined by 20 percent, and employment became more difficult to secure, more people were employed in services (Toutoundjian 1988), and the informal sector expanded notably.[2] This twenty-year process pushed unemployment to historic highs, putting Rosario on a par with urban centers having no tradition of industry.[3]

Social Configuration

Rosario, with approximately one million inhabitants, is home to neighborhoods of striking diversity. Ringed with middle- and upper-class neighborhoods, the downtown business, administrative, and cultural center enjoys good services and social infrastructure. These localities are in turn surrounded by a larger area of low population density, partial or inadequate community services, little infrastructure, poor housing construction, and large undeveloped tracts. This is where most of the villas are to be found, many of them dating back to the 1950s and early 1960s.[4] Their inhabitants are mainly internal migrants with no legal title to the lands they occupy and little or no involvement in the productive apparatus, as they are mostly unskilled and confined to uncertain employment and low incomes. Maintaining a lesser institutional presence than more consolidated neighborhoods, villas develop or attract few organizations—with the significant exception of the Catholic church and evangelical groups, who both compete for members.

The popular organizations are diverse both in their territorial links to the city and in the unusual differentiation that emerged as they developed. First were the cooperatives, spawned by nearly a century of tenant farmers converging on the city. (Cooperative and associational initiatives are often short-lived, however, varying according to community incomes and employment.) Second came the wave of unionization that accompanied expansion of the rails, the port, and industry. Next to rise were the voluntary associations established and developed by generations of immigrants—especially Spaniards, Italians, and Jews—which became a major force in their communities. Fourth were the clubs and social protection agencies that clustered around Rosario's strong occupational cultures. Finally, there was a proliferation of neighborhood organizations arising from the mosaic of identities created by this city's history and topography.

Politics and Neighborhood Organizations

Throughout its history, Rosario's location in the province has led to the rise of many groups claiming to represent the city's specificity and proclaiming the need for a change in its institutional status. In addition, political behavior has been atypical provincially and in the city. Santa Fe was the first Argentine province in which the Conservatives held power in the early stages of the country's modernization, and Rosario was the only interior city to spawn a national political party, although electoral outcomes here are highly variable. Finally, Rosario has experienced a level of combativeness and violence unseen in the rest of the country.

Dating back to 1931, Rosario's first neighborhood organizations focused on obtaining and providing services, particularly in health; some of these groups provided vital assistance. Their spheres of activity were determined not by the city's jurisdictional boundaries, but by the barrios themselves—anchored in the collective identities and perceptions of their neighborhoods and thus difficult to demarcate. As a result, neighborhood organizations have no clearly delineated zones within the barrio; this legitimatizes the mediating and regulating role of the municipal government, which judges each neighborhood organization's territorial realm of action and determines its functions and attributes.

With Argentina's return to democracy in 1983, the UCR gained control of the municipal government, while the Peronists triumphed in provincial elections. Rosario's mayor was a man of great energy, and his administration carried out several public works projects. His management style, however, involved considerable personal oversight and very little consultation. During this period (1983 to 1989), civic participation was reflected solely among certain elements of the local government. However, municipal involvement was instrumental in specific activities generated by the neighborhood organizations.

In December 1989, the PSP gained control of the municipal government, a victory that reflected the influence of a local issue and a widespread rejection of the promises made by the major parties.[5] The PSP took power shortly after the social upheaval and looting and provided food to Rosario's neediest, drawing resources from the party itself and from provincial and national sources. The strategy of this government has been to forge direct links with neighborhood organizations, avoiding confrontation and trying to win a base of support (although it has faced competition in this strategy from the large political parties and from smaller parties traditionally involved in neighborhood organizations). Inspired by its exposure to neighborhood organizations, the municipal government adopted new attitudes and behavior. For example, it divided the city into decentralized administrative units to address local problems and promote participation; it then convened neighborhood organizations to identify priorities and to discuss the programming and coordination of activities. Several of these organizations entered into agreements with the government as partnerships that explored new urban-management models. The government granted legal recognition to the neighborhood organizations and implemented in-kind subsidies to support them.

Not everyone agrees with these new policies, and some criticism has arisen over initiatives that certain observers believe to be aimed at generating mechanisms for political recruitment and for new forms of clientelism. Some observers believe also that the government's consultations with neighborhood organizations have no real impact on government decisions, reflecting instead a desire to facilitate administration. Increasingly, therefore, the subordination of neighborhood organizations to the decisions of municipal authorities is being challenged.

This issue is particularly important in view of the opposition some of these organizations are raising toward permanent location of squatter settlements within the perimeter of their jurisdictions, a position that entails frequent confrontations and eviction requests. Indeed, there are few neighborhoods in which any integration has taken place between the two populations; only rarely have neighborhood organizations included villa residents in their activities.

At present, an organizational process is underway within the villas, which, by their location outside the city's boundary, are not recognized by the municipal government. Lacking legal representation, the villas find themselves also lacking social or political representation. Emerging villa groups adopt a variety of organizational models, the most common being mutual aid societies and cooperatives that facilitate a wide array of activities such as housing construction and income generation. The Community Movement for Popular Habitat (MCHP), a coalition of such cooperatives established in seventeen villas and settlements, hopes to become a mechanism for their political representation. In this capacity, the MCHP is working to obtain title to the lands its members occupy, promote housing projects supported by European NGOs, and help the villas gain access to national and provincial programs. One such program is the Lot Plan, whose objective is to legalize ownership of land upon which the villas de emergencia stand.

The Projects

Following is a description of three community development projects undertaken in Rosario. Each project undertook the construction or modification of a community center hoping to promote community organizing and self-direction. All three projects involved community participation.[6] (See Tables 3.1, 3.2, 3.3, 3.4, and 3.5 for population and project characteristics.)

The implementing NGOs had certain attributes in common: a limited institutional history, technical personnel with prior experience in the public sector or in academia, a "professional" approach to the task, and the explicit objective of testing models of action transferable to the state. From the outset of the projects, these NGOs gained visibility in the city because of their institutional profile, because they had engaged in systematic activity, and because they had adequate financing and multiple linkages to social organizations and the local government.

Table 3.1 Population

Population	Unión y Parque Casas	La Esperanza	La Paloma
Settlement type	Consolidated neighborhood	Villa relocated and new housing units constructed	Villa
Community size	Large	Small	Diffuse
Population type	Heterogeneous; predominantly working class	Wage workers and informal sector	Homogenous; predominantly informal sector
History	Distant conflicts; little recent activity	Land purchases and initiatives to obtain housing	None
Prior relationship with municipal government	Through services (cultural and health workshops)	Close ties with housing service	Use of municipal soup kitchen

Table 3.2 Nature of Neighborhood Organization

Neighborhood Organization	Unión y Parque Casas	La Esperanza	La Paloma
Organization prior to project	Long-standing	Group not formalized	Did not exist
Leadership	Established	Established	Did not exist

Table 3.3 Project Characteristics

The Project	Unión y Parque Casas	La Esperanza	La Paloma
Size	2,500	150	1,500
Direct beneficiaries	—	150	—
Objectives	Community center	Community center	Community center
Organizational objective	Strengthen	Strengthen; obtain legal recognition	Create and strengthen; obtain legal recognition
Type of organization anticipated	Neighborhood association	Mutual aid society	Civic association

Table 3.4   Project Execution

Project Execution	Unión y Parque Casas	La Esperanza	La Paloma
Relationship with government	Limited independence	Very close; joint work	Municipal government provided locale; independence
Agency involvement	Secretariat of Planning; Secretariat of Culture	Public Housing Service	Secretariat of Social Promotion
Conflict over leadership	High; renewed at election	High; split at the beginning; constant tension	None
Attitude toward crisis	Distance	Solidarity	Solidarity
Attitude toward disturbances	Rejection at first; then helped form soup kitchens	Distributed food; aided soup kitchens	Set up a nighttime soup kitchen
Central services provided	Health, culture	Day care, health, culture	Food, day care, health, culture
Usage of locale	High	High but declining	Increasing
Horizontal linkages	Formal; through zones of the municipality	Low; not recognized as neighborhood organization	High; linked with *villero* movement

Table 3.5   NGO Characteristics

The NGO	Unión y Parque Casas	La Esperanza	La Paloma
Nature	Research center	Group of professionals	Professional association
Involvement with project	Partial	Total	Partial
Institutional orientation	Academia	Public sector	Profession-specific
Continuity in technical team	Growing differentiation within the center	Full	Separation and creation of new NGO
Conception of the task (basic aspiration)	Horizontal relationship	Transfer for public policies	Group work
Primary objectives	Development of actors; urban articulation	Impact on public agencies	Recycling of buildings
Action model	Working groups in the neighborhood organization	Action committees; division of labor with the municipal government	Interinstitutional and working groups
Reorientation activities	Organizational development	None	Social promotion

Unión y Parque Casas

This project sought to revitalize an old neighborhood organization that had declined over the years as participation dwindled and the capacity to mobilize withered. Many urban neighborhood organizations share this status, therefore, an effort was made to test a replicable model of action to keep such organizations alive. This particular neighborhood at one time boasted three, whose activities vanished as the economic situation deteriorated.

Unión y Parque Casas is an old area that has fallen into decline because of cutbacks in public investment and its inhabitants' impoverishment. Despite its poverty, however, the neighborhood is served by a certain degree of urban infrastructure, and its social makeup is quite heterogeneous. This area has expanded as people migrated from the core of the city to the periphery, a reflection both of lost employment and of a decline in real wages. Now, about two thousand families live in the neighborhood, for the most part blue-collar and clerical workers employed primarily by the railroads and small metallurgical shops. Residents live in single-family housing, built mainly by themselves. Two villas are nearby, both viewed by the people of the barrio as threats.

Of the area's many problems, those posing the greatest hazards are unsafe drinking water, limited health services, and the lack of flood control. Additional problems include insufficient transportation, unpaved streets, and the isolation of neighborhood sectors.

Created in 1958, the neighborhood organization has a long history of collaborative service provision. It cooperated, for example, with the municipal government and the university for medical and dental care, job training, and recreational activities for children and youth. At one time, the organization included three thousand members, but this number has dropped to around seven hundred. Past years have seen political turbulence within the organization, and it has had radical leaders who left their mark on many participants' memories.

The cooperating NGO, the Social Science Research Center of Rosario (CRICSO), emerged through the initiative of researchers, most of them professors at the local university. Socially committed, pluralistic, and democratic, CRICSO brings together a major group of the city's social scientists. Initially serving as a forum from which working groups emerged for exchange and theoretical development, it began to carry out action-research in education, labor relations, political science, and urban development. Its cooperation with this particular neighborhood organization began early, but the project agreement was formalized only after several years of joint work began to overcome the neighborhood's distrust of CRICSO's technical team.

CRICSO's neighborhood work had two aims: to explore alternative interventions for public policy and to help neighborhood organizations identify needs before shaping and channeling their demands for alternatives. CRICSO's experience in this area was extremely limited as the project in Unión y Parque Casas was its first systematic effort along these lines. Encouraged by the experience of other NGOs, however, CRICSO's team members gradually became advocates while testing new forms of organizational work. This particular project was to include the remodeling, expansion, and outfitting of the community center locale and the formation of working groups to plan health and recreational activities. An effort was also made to develop linkages and exchanges with other community organizations.

During the first project stage, the participants held workshops to identify and rank problems and to determine various courses of action; CRICSO also mediated with the municipal government and helped draw up the needs assessment. Unfortunately, the project began only a few days before the wave of looting, and community meetings had to be suspended for a period. The project could not have begun under more difficult circumstances and found itself in the exceptional and uncomfortable position of having financial resources while surrounded by impoverishment and desperation. Nevertheless, the neighborhood organization decided not to carry out any activity related to the emergency and declined to participate in or support the soup kitchens organized in the area. The organization defended this decision with the argument that it could thus avoid the social stigmatization that affects the poorest of the poor. The consequences were immediate and profound, operations came to an abrupt halt, project materials were stolen, young people who had played a vital role in certain activities began to distance themselves. At the same time, competing initiatives were launched in the barrio calling upon neighbors and community members to join in solidarity.

Throughout this difficult period, CRICSO provided staunch support to the project's steering committee, which operated in a tense and depressed context. Hoping to revive motivation for the resumption of project activities, CRICSO technical personnel participated in the steering committee's meetings. This reactivation attempt was successful, and the neighborhood organization began to collaborate with other institutions.[7] Eventually, a new dynamism emerged, ushered in by new committee leadership that asked CRICSO technical staff to absent themselves from committee meetings. After assessing the new situation, CRICSO agreed to stand back.

When inflation took an upturn, CRICSO thought it best to hasten construction so as to avoid a drop in the purchasing power of available resources. This meant however, that the participatory processes originally planned were bypassed; as a result the building, intended to become the fruit of a process of organizational development was actually its beginning. Although meetings were held to evaluate alternative architectural designs, it was clear that community members subordinated design considerations to speed and ease of construction. This stage involved a consolidation of relations between CRICSO and the neighborhood organization; project-related construction was marked by an openness in procedures, and the barrio gained a better understanding of its own situation.

When the economic environment grew abruptly worse in December 1989, it dealt a harsh blow to those who had managed to weather the previous inflationary outbreak. By then, however, the attitude of the organization's leadership had changed, and this time it persuaded the provincial food assistance program to distribute packages of food to the neediest families, which the neighborhood organization helped identify and register.

During the construction period of the new center, all other activities of the center on the existing lot had to be curtailed. Its completion crystallized many of the initiatives then surfacing, including workshops in drama, ceramics, music, sewing, and plastics. In addition, other neighborhood groups used the center to set up a community radio station and an agreement was reached with pensioners for their use of the facilities.[8]

Construction was completed as the steering committee's term drew to a close, whereupon a loosely formed group arose that questioned the activities undertaken, demanded additional health services, and criticized efforts made to improve neighborhood infrastructure. In its struggle for leadership, this group attacked the project's limited consultation with community members, its overall process and its handling of resources. The CRICSO team had warned that project activities might become too closely identified with the outgoing committee (whose chairman was autocratic and controlling) and had raised the question of implied support: At what point did project activities carried out during the electoral period strengthen the position of those who occupied leadership positions? To clarify the picture, the CRICSO team held public meetings with opposition candidates, an approach criticized by the outgoing leadership.

During the leadership of the Radical Civic Union (1983–1989), the project gained the municipal government's interest. It showed support for the project by paying the salaries of workshop trainers, which they in turn donated to the neighborhood organization. As the crisis worsened, however, their donations ground to a halt, and a conflict arose about whether these trainers should continue, as the community was beginning to question their solidarity. After the UCR's defeat in 1989, relations between the community and city hall became more regular and fluid; this facilitated municipal support for new recreational activities for youth and greater collaboration in the health services area.

Project results. The project attained a considerable degree of success, most significantly in the scope of project activities, which drew in major participation by women, young people, and the elderly. Problems encountered related to the project's design and methodology and also to the nature of the activities undertaken. Although CRICSO included neighborhood leadership in discussions of the project, it required them to provide few tangible resources to the project; instead, CRICSO offered external resources and technical support to the community at no cost. Thus, although community participation was solicited and accepted, it was not incorporated as a self-sustaining practice. Also, internal factors combined with economic considerations to diminish both the opportunities for community deliberations and the quality of those encounters. In the end, neighborhood initiative was limited to nonessential aspects such as helping to choose the architectural design and determining how to use the new building.

After undergoing a period of reflection and self-evaluation as a result of project experiences, CRICSO gained a better sense of its role and adopted new tactics. Of particular note was its recognition of the importance of flexibility in its operations, the need to avoid precipitating social processes, and the importance of networking and of creating spaces in which individual needs could be expressed as collective demands.

This project highlighted the ease with which socio-organizational factors yield to construction imperatives. Centered upon a physical goal, the project had to consider construction issues such as labor and materials, costs, schedules, and technical requirements. These preoccupations soon held sway over the group process, which was subordinated to the need to follow through on commitments made and to preserve the value of the resources at stake. Thus, what had been intended as a means for organizing and participation became an end in itself. CRICSO also learned that despite having made a major effort to assess the neighborhood's situation, it did not fully grasp the dynamics of community life—the conflicts and differing perceptions of power, politics, leadership, and neighborhood identity and cohesion.

La Esperanza

This project was conceived as a way to help a "new" community maintain and reorient the participation arising from its relocation and rehousing through the city's Public Housing Service. It was feared that the community organization might weaken and wither away upon completion of the construction, as had happened several times in housing projects. The action model tested in La Esperanza was expected to yield useful lessons for other NGOs and government organizations.

Formerly a sprawling villa de emergencia, La Esperanza later divided itself geographically for reasons having to do with land tenure, seniority of the settlements, and the degree of consolidation of the housing units. The project being described was begun for 150 families in La Esperanza Norte, a 2.5-acre maze of precarious housing. Around 1983, a group of neighbors began to purchase land within the neighborhood, using the housing service as intermediary. Once the purchase was completed, the neighborhood was included in the Progressive Housing Program of the national Ministry of Housing.[9] In 1989, land titling and property transfers began, after which the Ministry of Health and Social Action granted a subsidy to help cover the cost of the housing units. These units were to include an initial module that could later be expanded and refined. While such a design could not completely satisfy the housing needs of each family, these modules provided a certain flexibility and could be built quickly.

With the purchase of land and the construction of housing, an interesting organizational process unfolded during which an informal neighborhood organization coalesced around the process of legalization and construction. By the time the NGO became involved, the neighborhood organization had already developed a certain ability to negotiate with the state and had carved out a space for itself in the neighborhood. For example, this organization made it possible to tear down the villa's precarious housing to make way for the new construction; it also took responsibility for construction supervision and provision of guards, completion of the infrastructure, demarcation of the lots, and distribution of materials, paint, and so on. Later, residents took charge of maintaining the neighborhood and finishing the common areas.

The leader of the neighborhood organization in La Esperanza Norte played a key role in the entire process. Competing with leaders of the southern sector, he won support from the housing service for his sector, though both had been trying to purchase the land. When the NGO entered the neighborhood, however, the conflict between North and South eased, Esperanza Sur came into the program, and the leader of the neighborhood organization stepped down.

The cooperating NGO was the Center for the Support of Local Development (CEADEL), an organization that has promoted innovative local planning and public policy since 1986. CEADEL made its first contacts with La Esperanza via the housing service, which had discovered it lacked funds to build the day-care center included in the construction plans. In discussing various needs the project could meet, CEADEL and the neighborhood organization discovered that all of these needs required a space for collective use. Thus was born the idea of a community center; complementary actions included legalizing the neighborhood organization, training its leaders, facilitating negotiation with the state, and supporting the implementation of production projects.

The project was closely coordinated with the municipal government, whose project arm—the housing service—adopted a working system based on community participation. The strategy was first to develop a process of social organization and only then to move on to construction issues. As the tasks got underway, a new dynamic emerged in the barrio; members of La Esperanza Sur joined the effort, and tensions erupted in the neighborhood organization, whose leader voiced opposition to the style of work adopted.

The leader resigned, proclaiming his skepticism and his desire to dissociate himself from the project. A neighborhood assembly accepted his resignation and designated a "support group" for the project that, when the association became formalized, became its board of directors. Working groups were soon formed for construction and became sources of frequent conflict, as their participatory mechanisms made it possible to socialize information and contacts, explicitly criticize authoritarianism, and identify possible courses of action.

Once construction was completed, the neighborhood organization turned its attention toward increasing the participation and organization of neighbors within the community by establishing issue committees as channels. Social promoters helped with role definition and coordination, a process during which participants generated initiatives and structured the work. At times, technical personnel mediated between barrio factions in an effort to maintain work continuity. The neighborhood organization gained a great deal from the organizing process, implementing by itself such activities as a sewing shop, kindergarten, barrio bulletin, and community radio programs. It also arranged for training and recreational activities. To support these activities, the neighborhood organization initiated accessory construction of a radio station and ball fields and expanded the dispensary.

The organizing effort matured during a slow process of adaptation and learning that culminated in the formal inauguration of the neighborhood organization. This transition from informal entity to legally established mutual aid society (*mutual*) was marked by advances and setbacks, fear and uncertainty, delays and demands for greater technical assistance and training, and competition among subgroups for control.

During the most critical period of hyperinflation and emergency, the mutual organized a community soup kitchen, obtaining food donations and distributing the food; this group carried out its activities and channelled social energies during a very difficult time. However, despite strengthened involvement within the barrio, some signs of disintegration were seen in the form of broken commitments (gardens neglected because the community failed to clean the plots) and competition for remunerated work (such as the work in neighborhood construction, etc.). The withdrawal of CEADEL and housing service technical staff upon project completion meant the loss of external support, a loss aggravated by conflicts between the mutual president and members of certain working groups. Without mediators, the organization failed to democratize its functioning and to integrate openness into decisionmaking processes. As a result, external relations, political contacts, and credit-grabbing for community achievements continued to be the bases on which leadership was sustained.

Project results. The project attained its objective of gaining formal status for the neighborhood organization; it also helped constitute specialized realms of participation. In addition, the project provided training and worked to strengthen the barrio's institutional organization. These positive actions were clear to all actors involved, as were the results during construction. Later, however, some of these gains were offset by experiences after the departure of the technical personnel when it appeared that the community did not consider these advances their own. This attitude hindered sustainability. With the new administration in 1989, the municipal government considered its task concluded, and the housing service once again concerned itself mainly with the technical and construction aspects of public housing; it also changed its form of community promotion.

The project in La Esperanza called upon CEADEL to implement a theoretical model of action and adapt it to difficult circumstances, an important learning experience. For the municipal technical staff, the experience of working with NGOs provided continuity, resources, methodologies, and professionalism, as well as a space to contain the influence of political-party pressures.

La Paloma

In La Paloma, the goal was to enlarge the site and scope of a municipal soup kitchen (*comedor*), turning it into an organization that would obtain legal title to the lands upon which the villa sat and to improve housing. The villa is poorly organized, suffers from a difficult economic and social situation, and receives very few services. Its 1,500 residents live in shanties they have built with nonconventional materials. At the time of the project, a total of 450 people visited the comedor in two shifts, nearly all of them children. Most of these were children of single mothers or from disintegrated families, all of whom lived in extreme need due to unemployment or underemployment that permitted only basic survival. The area had only two neighborhood commissions, both with a limited presence in the villa, therefore the residents lacked associative mechanisms of their own.

The NGO executing the project was the Rosario Architects Center, a well-established and respected institution with support from members of the profession. The center formed a working group to advise on popular housing for social-promotion purposes, using its visibility and capacity for dissemination to obtain and channel public resources. As it unfolded, the project became a source of debate within the NGO: How advisable were certain project activities, how autonomous should the NGO project team be, where and how does one obtain financing, and should the NGO be engaged in organizing and fostering popular participation? These issues were part of an internal struggle to control the NGO, a struggle that adversely affected relations between the team and the municipal government and between the team and the community. Eventually, the NGO's project team formed a new NGO, the Rosario Community Studies and Technical Assistance Center

(CREATS), which took charge of continuing the work and encountered all the difficulties one would expect in transferring responsibilities and funds.

The project plan called for the community center (which was to be built on the foundation of the comedor) to provide a variety of services and generate development and subsistence projects. It was expected originally that additional resources would be mobilized from the municipal government, the university, and the National Mortgage Bank, but these funds were not forthcoming. The Inter-American Foundation provided a grant, but it included no resources for physical works.

As designed, the project would revolve around community participation, and a working group would include representatives of the participating organizations. This group, which was to take part in both programming and execution stages, came together during the first semester of project implementation. It later became the neighborhood organization, consolidating itself as the representative of the neighborhood and undertaking actions not initially considered for the project (safety, infrastructure upgrades, children's activities, etc.). The neighborhood organization joined the Community Movement for Popular Habitat not long before the looting, an indication of its desire to improve the neighborhood infrastructure. However, the chaos of 1989 interrupted the institutional process and the reorientation of activities; the organization was forced to focus on the food emergency and put off refurbishing the comedor premises. The organization channelled food to the neediest, served a night shift at the soup kitchen with its own resources, and tried to start community gardens and a fishermen's cooperative. It also improved the children's comedor and provided a room for evening health care; a proposal to install training workshops for adolescents, however, yielded to the need for a day-care center to facilitate mothers' access to the job market.

With the change of municipal authorities in 1989 came the need to renew ties with the local government. This was done, and with municipal endorsement the neighborhood organization obtained a subsidy from the Ministry of Health and Social Action to carry out the first stage of construction, although this grant actually contributed little toward the building costs.[10] (The task continued with financing from CEADEL.) Later, however, the municipal government repealed the previous administration's decree declaring a public interest in refurbishing the comedor, an action that ushered in a new period of negotiation with city hall.

Project results. In June 1991, the center was inaugurated, with somewhat more modest installations than had been anticipated. The neighborhood organization operates on site with a conditional authorization from the municipal government, providing lunch and a snack out of the comedor. There is also a drawing workshop, partially supported by the municipal government, and a community radio station linked to the neighborhood organization. In addition, the building houses a legal office staffed through an agreement with the local bar association (*Colegio de Abogados*). Municipal literacy teachers offer regular courses, and the dispensary will soon be installed.

The project's most important achievement was the development of the neighborhood organization, which has demonstrated a significant administrative capacity now channelled at involving the villa in municipal plans for obtaining legal title to the land on which it is sited. (On this issue it faces resistance from barrio organizations that wanted the villa relocated.) Project activities advanced by virtue both of the NGO's efforts in building ties of solidarity and commitment and of the neighborhood organization's persistence and continuity. The project served as a catalyst for actions other than those foreseen, such as the incorporation of the Community Movement for Popular Habitat. A project that began with modest aspirations—to make new use of a public building through popular participation—thus had a significant impact, albeit indirect, on a nascent actor in the life of the city, the villa movement.

Project Issues

Despite their differing venues, circumstances, and goals, all three projects shared certain design considerations. One of these was the extent to which community participation took place as activities unfolded. Originally viewed as the linchpin of each project, full participation yielded to other concerns, and neighborhood solidarity and project sustainability suffered to some degree thereby—despite notable gains. Another significant element was the stance of each collaborating NGO toward its project partners, particularly the neighborhood actors. Often, NGOs found themselves obliged by circumstances and events to modify a preferred approach. Following are discussions of these and other elements from the perspective of project experiences.

Community Participation

What is a workable definition of community participation? If technical personnel are the ones who play a structuring role, if the call to participation corresponds to a scale of needs that can easily be reconstructed, and if solidarity actions take place within the framework of a rationality that is enhanced by individual involvement but drops off when this benefit is diluted, participation can be considered a complex process replete with ambivalence, ambiguities, and preferences that are not readily discernible. For example, in La Esperanza certain group tasks were remunerated. When the project drew to a close, however, participation dropped off; payment contaminated the motivation to participate and had a negative impact on the sense of solidarity.

Participation is also specialized. In the three cases a stratification of participation can be identified, with a primary leader, a handful of subleaders, and a core group of several dozen activists occupying concentric circles. The participation of the rest of the community members is geared toward specific activities; rarely do people shift from one working group to another. Only the members of the leadership group have an overall sense of the organization, which in turn is conditioned by the leader's monopoly over outside contacts and information. His or her overall vision results more from interest and insertion in the community than from any formalization of procedures. This being the case, participation is not a dimension that takes place in a wholesale manner. Rather, it is a behavior and an attitude shaped by various factors, each of which is associated with specific mechanisms of activation and incentives. When neighborhood organizations address the question of food, for example, they draw not only upon physical facilities but also upon community points of reference, mechanisms for mobilizing the population, and institutional realities that people recognize, even though at times they may not use them. The three case studies show how the emergency caused a temporary rollback of solidarity efforts while the most basic needs were addressed; the question of meeting such needs moved quickly from the private to the collective. Although the soup kitchens were rejected at first in Unión y Parque Casas, when hunger affected the whole neighborhood, the neighborhood organization decided to deemphasize sociability and health care and transform itself into a basic resource for survival.

While participation is specialized, its growth can be achieved by expanding the number and variety of activities and services. It has been stressed, however, that participation becomes unspecialized when needs become urgent and cannot be put off, in which case there is greater commitment and less susceptibility to formalization. For the NGO, the challenge thus becomes to harmonize dimensions that appear to operate in a dissociated manner, institutionalizing forms of behavior and at the same time promoting less specialized participation that encompasses goals and activities relevant to survival and development.

How is this integration best accomplished? According to one social action model, the causes, significances, and consequences of the objective situation in which a particular population or social category finds itself may be beyond its understanding (or awareness). In such a case, an outside actor (a vanguard, or organic intellectuals) gives meaning to the situation, formulates the strategy, and takes initiative in carrying out actions. Under such a model, NGOs would play a similar role vis-à-vis the social movement, whether it be one already in existence or one to be constructed. According to another, more realistic, model, the grassroots understands its "felt" needs perfectly well and the NGO *facilitates* the process aimed at meeting the need by providing inputs that the grassroots organization can appropriate. Rather than one party becoming subordinated to the other, this model allows both to benefit from shared power and complementary knowledge.

In each of the projects, a consistent sequence emerged from the relationship of NGO and participants:

- As the NGOs gained legitimacy they were seen as neighborhood resources.
- The communities assumed greater responsibility as the traditional leaders' abilities to play benefactors gradually declined.
- Relations with the municipal government changed after it ceased to be the sole supplier of a locale or resource. Instead, it became an interested party—one more claimant seeking credit for the project.
- The NGOs reinterpreted their role and reassessed some of their aspirations and program methodologies.
- The neighborhood organizations transformed their image as they responded to emergencies, expanded the scope of projects, or mobilized community members.

In the cases considered here, it would seem that the NGOs' most significant contribution lies in the increased confidence and capacity that participants developed through their association with the projects. In situations of growing complexity they found themselves identifying problems, discovering and assessing alternative solutions, recognizing capabilities and limitations, and questioning leadership styles. Perhaps most important, they acquired and polished negotiating skills to use among themselves and in their dealings with the municipality. They can use these new skills to initiate new actions outside of the project and outside of the neighborhood organization.

Ranking Needs

Deteriorating economic circumstances required that the neighborhood organizations frequently adapt their programs and accommodate to both old and new poor. For example, subsistence and survival issues led people to establish a hierarchy of needs: food, work, land, housing, health, community infrastructure, recreation, and cultural activities (in order of importance). With greater deprivation, members of the neighborhood organization directed their efforts toward meeting needs at the top of the list. However, as economic and social resources became available and emergencies were overcome, participation was motivated by items farther down the list.

Community members set up programs for those at greater risk, especially children and the elderly, with food, health, or even recreation programs. Day-care centers for children and activities for the elderly are services often demanded of community centers and have become the primary channel for women's participation. The projects tested the flexibility of the NGOs and their commitment to grassroots groups, but they also yielded a particular lesson: Effective projects presuppose an existing social process. Even when no formal organizations exist, as in La Paloma, residents have an identity, shared interests, and histories of collective action. While projects may be generated from outside, the sine qua non for their effectiveness is recognition and understanding of the community reality.

Welfare, Development, or Negotiated Interaction?

Relief and development do not occupy mutually exclusive compartments. During Rosario's emergency, for example, some NGOs reluctantly carried out actions typical of the relief model, which they feared would create dependency and undermine autonomy, self-reliance, and skill transference. But because hyperinflation had led to a postponement of the development projects and community mobilization was for a time viable only around urgent needs, these relief activities had an unexpected integrating effect on the communities. Despite the neighborhoods' extreme economic distress, group and family initiatives took place and institutional continuity was ensured, benefits that might not have occurred had original project designs been rigidly followed. During the emergency, NGOs were forced to reconcile relief and development roles.

All three projects required negotiated interaction between NGOs and community participants. To that interaction, each NGO brought some resources (techniques, information, contacts, etc.), and each neighborhood organization its own institutional identity, project needs, and financing. In this dynamic of accommodating expectations, of continually redefining legitimacy, and of testing skills and leadership, a project crystallizes but does not exhaust the relationship between the NGO and the community. Daily crises, leadership struggles, and competition for resources are the elements that shape the negotiated interaction.

The Projects and Local Issues

The Rosario projects have had some effect on the political decisionmaking processes. From the intervention in La Esperanza, which mobilized public investment and tested a model of joint action, to the contributions of the project at La Paloma, which made it possible to combine relief work with an arena for community expression, new options for service delivery were created and brought to the attention of municipal government. During the UCR regime, municipal policy focused on assisting neighborhood initiatives, providing personnel to complement these efforts and the work of the NGOs without thus assuming the leadership or taking credit for the achievements. It was a distant yet open administration, noninterventionist but willing to support grassroots initiatives. In a climate of enthusiasm for the return to democracy, this policy made it possible to awaken the grassroots social organizations and redefine relations between them and the municipal government. Thus, the local government's position was propitious, as NGOs could count on support without compromising their autonomy or identity and without having to face competition from the municipality.

Politicizing the Neighborhood Organizations

With the change of municipal administration in 1989, however, came a substantial change in municipal outlook. The government of the Popular Socialist Party, which claimed to place greater priority on neighborhood issues, resuscitated inactive neighborhood organizations, called zonal meetings, and established an organic communication channel. Nevertheless, no additional initiatives were generated with the neighborhood organizations, municipal contributions continued along the lines set forth by prior governments, and in some cases municipal technical personnel were withdrawn. Thus, although the PSP administration appears to be closer to the world of the neighborhood organizations, it has been narrower in the ways it supports them. In such a context, the NGOs' task often becomes more difficult, as they must deal with situations in which collaboration is sometimes replaced with competition.

In general, one sees a greater recognition of the role of neighborhood organizations as legitimate representative mechanisms. Thus, expectations are rising concerning the future development of such mechanisms for linking demands and solving disputes—another contrast with the prior administration. In the beginning, the PSP government tried to increase its influence by officially recognizing neighborhood organizations with no real leadership, precipitating a struggle between the PSP, other political parties, and the communities for controlled access to these channels. Since those neighborhood organizations tended to be organized along party lines anyway, the potential conflict between the two realms of participation and representation were eventually reconciled. The question remaining was whether a party-oriented organization would dilute the neighborhood's sense of action and ultimately sabotage the municipal government's objectives.

This process brought to light just how intertwined political party issues have become with actions that local governments carry out within the neighborhoods. Throughout Rosario's two most recent administrations, relations between the government and neighborhood organizations have been based more on "instrumental interests" (i.e., meeting some basic need or carrying out a fundamental task) than on shared values. The two administrations have differed, however, in the thrust of their interest. During the UCR administration, interactions addressed specific needs connected to particular activities and resources rather than to policies; the relationship was neither systematic nor organic. With the change in government, the interests that structured the relationship were more "strategic," that is, by facilitating regular information and consultation, they established potential long-term political relationships (Davis 1991). Thus, during the UCR government, relations were more administrative, while in the PSP period they were more "political," even though the discourse tended to emphasize efforts to "depoliticize" municipal management and diminish the extent of clientelism.

This contrast helps to clarify a point with respect to the usual analyses of relations between NGOs and local governments, attributing a model of action "from below" to the former and a "top-down" model to the latter. The projects analyzed show the reality to be more complex. Two of them sought to change public policy through the demonstration effect of their actions, which were directed toward government officials and technical personnel. While these efforts did not succeed in changing policies, they did cast light upon possible actions that were included in the debate on municipal government.

All three projects made clear the potential for fruitful collaboration between outside actors and neighborhood organizations, and efforts are already underway among certain sectors of the municipal government to replicate the NGOs' work style. Such a course will likely lead to some competition between the local government and the NGOs. The change in municipal authorities presents other challenges as well; efforts have been interrupted, relations must be redefined, intentions must be clarified. All of this indicates that the NGOs' function is not fully accepted, even while their political content is explicitly recognized.

Inevitably, a tension exists around what NGOs say, what they do, and how they are perceived by politicians. Nevertheless, these organizations will continue to support the rise and consolidation of new social actors to accompany them down the road that leads from raising demands to articulating interests, from protest to social movement, from sporadic events to sustained action, from resource transfers to skill generation, from isolation to collective action, and from discourse to action—all in a context in which structural constraints are daunting and strategic options are few. These sometimes tenuous linkages—variously binding the organizations of civil society to one another and, increasingly, to municipal governments—hold the key to democratization and sustainable development.

Notes

1. In May, June, and July of 1989, inflation stood at 78.5, 224.5, and 196.6 percent, respectively. In 1990, the first three months saw inflation figures of 79.2, 61.6, and 95.5 percent. Other factors contributing to the disturbances were the perception of a power vacuum, the repeated announcements that these events would occur (acting as a self-fulfilling prophecy), the actions of paramilitary groups that incited violence, and great uncertainty as to the country's political and economic situation. It should also be noted that in the days leading up to the disturbances, distribution of the food packages from the National Food Program had ceased. Events were particularly virulent in the province of Santa Fé, where from May to July 1989 there were 231 lootings (accounting for 35 percent of all such events nationwide, with 1,283 persons arrested, or 42.5 percent of the national total). These episodes were repeated in February and March of 1990, with the epicenter in the city of Rosario; this time, provincial arrestees accounted for 63 percent and 80 percent, respectively, of the national figure. These data are based on estimates from the July 1989 and March 1990 reports of the Center of Studies for a New Majority.

2. According to the 1974 census, Rosario had 4,892 establishments that employed 46,702 people. In 1985, these figures fell to 4,054 and 37,994, respectively. In May 1990, the figure for economically active residents was 455,974 of a total population of 1,194,836, or 38.2 percent. The city's composition by occupational category reveals a clear predominance in the services sector, which in May 1990 accounted for 65.5 percent of employment, both private and public. Although industry had accounted for 35 percent of total employment in 1974, by May 1990 the percentage had fallen to 21.3 percent, the lowest point during the period.

3. In May 1990, unemployment was 8.8 percent in Greater Buenos Aires, 7.4 percent in Córdoba, and 10.8 percent in Rosario (Center of Studies of Participation and Development 1990).

4. There are several estimates of the number of villas de emergencia and their population. A 1987 survey estimated the total number at 72, with approximately 120,000 inhabitants. According to the Center of Studies and Agrarian Promotion (CEPA), an NGO based in the city, there are 89 settlements, while the municipal government survey puts the figure at 105. Estimates of the current population of the villas put it at 20 percent of the city. New efforts are underway to come up with more precise estimates. For example, the municipal government is undertaking a new survey, this time with participation by the population. CEPA has also advanced in this direction, as has the Community Movement for Popular Habitat, which has collected basic data on the settlements where it is working.

5. The Popular Socialist Party is a small national party whose strength lies primarily in the city of Rosario; it draws more heavily upon strong local personalities than upon ideological affiliations. In the 1989 elections, the PSP elected its first national deputy, from the province of Santa Fé. The PSP is part of the Socialist Union, an alliance with the Democratic Socialist Party and the Socialist Party of the Chaco. In addition to Rosario, the party controls a few other municipal governments.

6. Rosario's projects were part of a portfolio of projects supported by the Inter-American Foundation that promoted independent self-construction, construction with mutual assistance, and rehabilitation of tenement dwellings. Although not geared toward solving the housing problem, community centers helped facilitate attempts to improve housing quality and to promote popular organization.

7. As a result of these collaborations, the neighborhood organization was able to offer dental services to barrio residents.

8. An older neighborhood, Unión y Parque Casas has an elderly population estimated at between 30 and 40 percent of its total residents.

9. The neighborhood organization participated in this process. In addition, in 1984 it began tasks of common interest such as neighborhood clean-up; ditch cleaning; obtaining medicines, notebooks, and school supplies; and helping to solve family problems.

10. Inflation was such that the amount originally requested in australes, equivalent at the time to U.S.$33,000, was equal to only U.S.$770 when the disbursement was ordered and to a mere U.S.$70 when the disbursement was actually made.

4

Brazilian NGOs in the 1990s: A Survey

RUBEM CESAR FERNANDES
LEANDRO PIQUET CARNEIRO

This chapter reports on a survey conducted during the first national assembly of Brazilian NGOs, held in Rio de Janeiro in early August 1991. A landmark even for Brazilian NGOs, the assembly led to the formation of a national association, thus ending years of hesitancy toward formalizing the networks. Data from the survey, which was conducted as the conference opened, were immediately shared with the participants, an example of how rapidly research results are available in this electronic age.

Serving as respondents were the directors of 102 leading Brazilian NGOs, who provided a broad range of information about themselves and their organizations.[1] This was the country's first national-level survey of NGO leadership and thus far its results have received scant dissemination in Brazil or abroad. Some of the material provides a useful backdrop to Chapter 6 in this book on NGO-municipal collaboration on urban environmental problems in Brazil and to Chapter 5 on relationships among local health administrators, NGOs, and social movements in São Paulo. From a comparative perspective, Brazilian NGO leaders' attitudes toward government contrast rather sharply with Chile, where many NGO leaders played a major role in the *concertación* government (see Chapter 7). In Mexico (Chapters 10 and 11), "independent" social movements and NGO leadership have chosen a middleground between Brazilian and Chilean cases, alternately accepting and rejecting invitations and support from the Mexican government—with much of the waltz (or "to-ing and fro-ing") danced around the government social development program, PRONASOL (National Solidarity Program).

NGOs in Brazil

Brazilian NGOs embody a new type of organization that combines the tension of large and small, public and private, in a curious way. Although small and private, and lacking the representational function of other types of institutions (trade unions, political parties, and neighborhood associations), they nonetheless act as though they were large and public. Each NGO speaks only on its own behalf and in this way these organizations resemble private citizens; at the same time, their expansive vision of social action leads them into larger processes and broader contexts. Thus, NGOs might be thought of as "supercitizens."

NGOs have inherited much of their capacity from the Catholic Church, thought of as "a universal party," and from those Marxists who have striven to represent all of society. Confronted with ever changing realities, NGOs have maintained their legacy while radically modifying their means. Although diminished in size, they continued to be spurred on by vast horizons. NGOs are rather like the Lilliputians besieging Gulliver on all sides. Where they differ from Swift's fantasy, however, is in the source of their power, which lies not only in their numbers but also in their flexibility and in their role as social catalyst. The whole is articulated not from the top, like church or state, but from the bottom or grassroots level on a local and situational basis.

The first NGOs in Brazil were established during the authoritarian period of 1964 to 1985, when the shutting down of politics was partially offset by modest and low-profile projects carried out locally in civil society. NGOs continued to grow as a delayed microinstitutional response to the dictatorship during the subsequent transition to democracy, multiplying in the 1980s. Other processes and dimensions also contributed to the rise and spread of Brazilian NGOs. For example, countless nongovernmental associations and cooperatives sprang up in response to the social and economic differentiation accompanying modernization in Brazil. International cooperation was undergoing worldwide expansion at much the same time.[2]

According to a recent study of records (shown in Table 4.1) in Rio de Janeiro and São Paulo, over 60 percent of the civic associations registered were founded between 1971 and 1987 (dos Santos 1990).

NGO Leadership

A brief look at the leadership of Brazilian NGOs may add perspective to the information presented on the NGOs themselves. For one thing, the high level of education is striking: 85 percent of the NGO leaders surveyed have college diplomas, and 39 percent have graduate degrees. Few careers nationwide have such a high percentage of graduate-degree holders, all the more impressive since a college degree is not a formal requirement for employment with an NGO. Many leaders studied abroad, as can be seen in Table 4.2.

Table 4.1   NGO Founding Dates

Founding Date	De Facto Founding		Official Founding	
	Number	Percentage	Number	Percentage
1991-	—	—	1	1.1
1985–1990	26	27.4	37	38.9
1980–1984	22	23.0	20	21.0
1975–1979	13	13.7	11	11.6
1970–1974	11	11.6	10	10.5
1965–1969	5	5.3	6	6.3
1960–1964	1	1.1	3	3.2
1955–1959	2	2.1	—	—
Did not answer	15	15.8	7	7.4
Total	95	100	95	100

Source: Questionnaire sent by organizing committee to participants in the "First International Meeting of NGOs and UN System Agencies."

Table 4.2   Countries Where Education Received

Germany	19.0%
France	14.3%
Canada	9.5%
Italy	9.5%
Great Britain	9.5%
The Netherlands	4.8%
Other	33.4%

Source: Questionnaire sent by organizing committee to participants in the "First International Meeting of NGOs and UN System Agencies."

NGO work has become a serious matter in Brazil. Of the respondents, 78 percent stated that working with NGOs is their main professional activity, while only 17 percent defined it as secondary. Of those who practice some form of religion, 57 percent are Catholics, 13 percent Protestants, 10 percent Candomblé, 7 percent Spiritists, 5 percent Umbanda, 3 percent Jews, and 5 percent other. Of these, 30 percent worship at least weekly. A total of twenty-six respondents (about 25 percent of the sample) indicated support for "Catholic Action/Progressive Christianity."

A majority (75 percent) stated that they identify with a political party, and of those, 89 percent identified with the Worker's Party (see Table 4.3). The remainder divided their support among five other parties. More than half of the respondents are party members, 39 percent participate in party management or work regularly as party trainers or advisors, and 47 percent work in election campaigns.

The violent repression during the 1960s and early 1970s affected many NGO leaders directly. In our sample alone, two had their citizens' rights suspended, eleven were haled into court, six were fired from their jobs, seventeen were imprisoned, seven were tortured, six were exiled, and

Table 4.3   Party Identification

Party	Number	Percentage 1 (Base=102)	Percentage 2 (Base=80)
Worker's Party	71	69.5	88.8
Brazilian Social Democratic Party	2	2.0	2.5
Brazilian Communist Party	1	1.0	1.3
Democratic Labor Party	1	1.0	1.3
National Municipalist Party	1	1.0	1.0
Green Party	1	1.0	1.3
Did not answer/Do not identify	25	24.5	3.8
Total	102	100	100

Source: Questionnaire sent by organizing committee to participants in the "First International Meeting of NGOs and UN System Agencies."

Note: Percentage 1 column represents party members and Percentage 2 column represents those who identify with a party but are not members. Parties that do not appear include the Party of the Brazilian Democratic Movement, Brazilian Socialist Party, Communist Party of Brazil, and National Renovation Party.

seven chose voluntary exile. Such figures reflect the collective memory of Brazilian NGOs. It seems that most of this generation of NGO leadership was spawned at the intersection of university researchers, popular pastoral workers inspired in liberation theology, and Marxist dissidents resisting the dictatorship. With this in mind, let us take a look at where these activists work.

Geographic Distribution

The largest numbers of NGOs are found in the Southeast and Northeast, followed by the South, the West-Central region, and the North. The concentration in the Southeast reflects the general distribution of the country's resources: São Paulo and Rio de Janeiro have the largest shares, Espíritu Santo almost none. The concentration in the Northeast reflects the NGOs' "preferential option for the poor"; for the generation educated in the 1960s and 1970s, the Northeast provides the images emblematic of the country's poverty. Within this area, Pernambuco appears to have the largest share of NGOs, followed by Bahia. The South is quite weak in NGO development, considering the wealth and social complexity found in Rio Grande do Sul and Paraná; however, factors related to the regions' political culture and legacies of the populist past have inhibited the rise of NGOs there. In the North and West-Central regions, NGOs have increased with the growth of environmental awareness and activism.

NGO Services

According to this survey, advisory services are far and away the leading type of service that Brazilian NGOs provide. Forty percent of the respondents stated this as their main activity. A very generic term, "advisory services" expresses less a specific activity than a linkage established between advisors and advisees. On the one hand are the intellectuals; on the other, the social organizations or movements. By means of this relationship requiring mutual trust and a certain affinity of purpose, expertise can be shared. However, this relationship does not imply a hierarchical bond between the parties—differing in this regard from the linkages obtained through consulting firms, political parties, and church pastoral work. Other services offered are Table 4.4.

Table 4.4   NGO Services

Service	Main Activity
Advisorship	40.0%
Research/Documentation in Social Services	13.7%
Popular Education	12.6%
Technical Advisorship	10.5%
Leadership Training	10.5%
Technological Research/Development	6.3%
Training for Unions	2.1%
Economic Production Projects	2.1%
Communications	1.1%
Training for Agents	1.1%
Total	100%

Source: Questionnaire sent by organizing committee to participants in the "First International Meeting of NGOs and UN System Agencies."
Note: Base = 95.

In a sense, NGO services in Brazil could be described as intellectual support for the popular movements, as almost all survey responses named advisory services, research, or education/training. Oddly enough, communication was mentioned as a priority service by only 1 percent, an interesting omission considering all the written and audiovisual materials that NGOs have produced. Generally, however, such support is meant to be used on a face-to-face basis; few NGOs provide training or education to explore using the mass media.

A broader NGO function is to work for a changed society. According to the survey, half prefer to define their action as an "alternative project of development"; 36 percent define themselves in more particular terms as contributing to the development of "alternative public policies"; 28 percent see their first priority as mobilizing society to participate in politics. Only 16 percent think of themselves as pressure groups for attaining specific objectives. About 8 percent aim their action directly at specific problems, independent of overall policies.

Brazilian NGOs operate mainly among the poorer classes, where marginality is growing exponentially in Latin America. In a sense, the NGOs themselves are marginal from the large official structures, given that NGOs emerged and developed at a distance from the state. As part of their working agenda with the marginalized sectors, NGOs often focus on education and training (as shown in Table 4.5) as a way to help people move from marginality to full citizenship. Many of them also stress productive and economically profitable activities that either generate income or help people to stretch their own incomes further.

Table 4.5 NGO Program with Marginalized Sectors

Priorities	First Priority	Second Priority	Third Priority
Training for Citizenship	73.5%	89.2%	91.2%
Support for Productive Activities	14.7%	50.0%	69.6%
Affirmation of Values	7.8%	23.5%	50.0%
Recovering Popular Religiosity	1.0%	13.7%	34.3%
Recovering Philanthropy	1.0%	2.0%	6.9%

Source: Questionnaire sent by organizing committee to participants in the "First International Meeting of NGOs and UN System Agencies."
Note: Base = 102.
The question asked was: "How would you define a work agenda with marginalized sectors of society?" (In order of first, second, and third priorities.)

Among Brazilian NGOs, the service provided is rarely defined by the client (in a commercial sense); on the contrary, NGOs provide "moral services" representing freedom, truth, democracy, world peace, and environmental equilibrium. In this sense, they are like other types of institutions such as those found in politics, art, religion, and science that also eschew entrepreneurial logic. Most NGOs deny that they are welfare-oriented or paternalistic, claiming instead to be providing a public utility, or public service. It could be said that they are part of a modern type of charity—or, better still, that they practice what remains of charity after it has passed through the critical sieve of leftist political thought and after it has become professionalized in a society based on the market economy.

The logic and charitable spirit that conditions NGO programs and practices operates according to a simple formula: receiving resources from some in order to provide services to others. In most cases, beneficiaries cannot pay for these services; in fact, being unable to pay is an implicit condition for becoming a beneficiary. Paradoxically, to survive in this system the NGOs must train themselves to provide a service needed by a group of people who are unable to pay for that service. In so doing, NGOs operate in counterpoint to traditional market trends.

Impassioned Pragmatism

Brazilian NGOs have learned the language of "projects," in the process absorbing the pragmatic virus that defines actions in terms of singular objectives and controllable timeliness. While they may resist this context, they cannot escape it and so tend to make a virtue of necessity. Thus, they are driven more by visible ends than by utopian dreams. Nonetheless, they maintain the visionary style of their origins, and this is the paradox from which they derive their strength, the transformation into projects (with timeliness) of seemingly impossible tasks. In so doing, NGOs are serving as a small vehicle for great causes.

NGO Budgets and Personnel

Just how wealthy are these NGOs? Judging from the respondents' combined annual budgets (approximately U.S.$28 million), not very—particularly when one considers that the survey included most of the larger NGOs in the country. That sum, a pittance compared with the total worth of the state or the private sector, reveals the impracticality of NGOs assuming the state's role in addressing social problems. It would be impossible to think of an "NGO welfare nonstate" in Brazil with such limited funds. Nor is it a significant amount in relation to the scale of international cooperation.

A more positive view of the equation is this: Although there may not be much NGO money, it is very productive. Take the sum of ten thousand dollars, for example. It might be spent in a single business trip by an executive; whereas, the same ten thousand applied to a microproject in a *favela* can generate a complex of activities over an entire year! NGOs pay relatively modest salaries to staff and mobilize a certain number of volunteers, giving these organizations a high labor-to-dollar ratio. Also, most NGOs are small, which may allow them to be more flexible and efficient than larger structures. See Tables 4.6, 4.7, and 4.8 for more information.

Table 4.6   NGO Annual Budgets

Annual Budget	1990	1991	1995[a]
Less than U.S.$30,000	23.53%	8.82%	0.98%
U.S.$31,000–100,000	30.39%	32.35%	9.80%
U.S.$101,000–500,000	23.53%	26.47%	34.31%
U.S.$501,000–1,000,000	3.92%	5.88%	11.76%
U.S.$1,001,000–2,000,000	5.88%	6.86%	5.88%
U.S.$2,001,000–3,000,000	0.98%	—	1.96%
Over U.S.$3,000,000	0.98%	0.98%	0.98%
No response	10.79%	18.64%	34.33%

Source: Questionnaire sent by organizing committee to participants in the "First International Meeting of NGOs and UN System Agencies."
Notes: Base = 102.
a. Projection.

Table 4.7   NGO Staff Size

Number of Permanent Employees	Number of NGOs	Percentage
1 to 5	29	30.5
6 to 10	23	24.2
11 to 15	14	14.7
16 to 35	15	15.8
36 to 60	0	0.0
61 to 90	3	3.2
91 or more	6	6.3
Did not answer	5	5.3
Total	95	100

Source: Questionnaire sent by organizing committee to participants in the "First International Meeting of NGOs and UN System Agencies."

Table 4.8   NGO Volunteers

Number of Volunteers	Percentage
1 to 5	30
6 to 10	13
11 to 15	3
16 to 20	4
21 to 25	3
26 or more	5
Do not have volunteers	42
Total	100

Source: Questionnaire sent by organizing committee to participants in the "First International Meeting of NGOs and UN System Agencies."
Note: Base = 95.

Forging Cooperative Links

Brazilian NGOs are small organizations, "microarticulators" that mediate relationships between their clients and beneficiaries and the major institutions of society. Like small craft, they navigate under the sway of larger ships such as the state, churches, political parties, universities, social movements, the private sector, the mass media, and so on.

Judging from the survey results, NGOs place a high priority on relationships with social movements. Of the respondents, 31 percent evaluated the actions of the social movements as "very positive" and 59 percent as "positive." None considered them unimportant, and only 2 percent held a negative view. Such a broadly positive view is intriguing; it is as though the NGOs saw in the social movements their ideal partners, perhaps because the movements have a multiplier effect in the public arena, where they are many and segmented and do not imply hierarchical subordination.

Historically, NGOs represent an innovation in the institutional culture of the Brazilian left, although this does not mean that all NGO leaders are on the left. Indeed, NGO relations with the political left vary. Many, for example, look favorably on the actions of those parties in their respective areas of work, while others believe them to be irrelevant to effective NGO activity. A few Brazilian NGOs reject political parties entirely. Nevertheless, these origins are seen in many NGO goals today. Based on their generic political discourse, many NGO leaders sound little different from various leftist sectors in Brazil. Where differences become apparent are in the specific type of work done by the NGOs, whose general goals are to strengthen social movements and to build civil society.

Worthy of special mention is this: Although 78 percent of NGO leaders surveyed identified themselves with a party, only 63 percent have a positive view of party performance as it applies to work with NGOs. Some NGOs (19 percent) favor a political relationship that contributes to the building of a party that could bring together popular demands (and thus, we inferred, also unify the NGOs); a similar number (18 percent) stated that they prefer to act independently. A larger group (28 percent) believes it is correct to continue placing priority on political-party organizing, while defining themselves in dual terms—for example, as a "political front" motivated by "a democratic development project." Furthermore, another group of equal weight (26 percent) stated that they prefer to maintain channels of discussion with several parties around matters of specific interest to their NGO or to the social sectors with which they work. In sum, the sample was split down the middle, oscillating between the two poles of political identification and virtual indifference. It is an issue—a tension—running through the hearts and minds of most NGO leaders.

Many NGOs have established formal cooperative ties with church organizations, often through the pastoral commissions and Christian base communities; of these, the Land Pastoral (*Pastoral da Terra*) is most important, as 38 percent of the NGOs surveyed had worked with this group. There is also considerable cooperation with the church hierarchy at the diocesan and national levels. Of the major national institutions, the Catholic Church has no doubt been the most successful in drawing on NGO services, but relations with the Protestant (or evangelical) churches are also significant. Primarily, NGOs provide their church "partners" with a form of social mediation—helping them establish linkages with secular social movements, for example. NGOs interact with Brazilian universities to some extent, frequently through seminars but also through joint projects and formal agreements. Among the NGOs, there appears to be a growing interest in developing social or technological research centers of university-level academic competence.

The relationship between Brazilian NGOs and the state is complex and ambiguous.[3] In a country where institutions (including private businesses) are so dependent on the government, NGOs are notable for their independence of public resources. Much of their funding, for example, originates in countries of the North. Nevertheless, most NGO leaders expect a great deal from the state (see Tables 4.9 and 4.10). Nearly half of them participate or have participated in government-supported projects at the municipal, state, and federal levels (with a slight predominance of municipal government involvement).

Table 4.9 Government-NGO collaboration

Have collaborated with government at different levels	43.2%
Have never collaborated with government	55.7%
Did not answer	1.1%
Total	100%

Source: Questionnaire sent by organizing committee to participants in the "First International Meeting of NGOs and UN System Agencies."

Table 4.10 NGO-Government Collaboration by Level

Municipal	36%
State	34%
Federal	30%

Source: Questionnaire sent by organizing committee to participants in the "First International Meeting of NGOs and UN System Agencies."
Note: Multiple answers were allowed.

The ambiguity between a state-centric political vision and a nongovernmental function is evident when we consider the example of public health: What role should NGOs play in addressing the country's declining health levels? Most NGOs look to the state to resolve such problems; perhaps then, NGOs should work to transform the state. A significant minority, however, prefer to turn to civil society; these NGOs seek to act as a catalyst for mobilizing human and material resources to confront social and economic problems. A third perspective proposes to formulate alternative policies for the sector, thereby avoiding the radical opposition between state and civil society.

Although each NGO has its own form of organization, direction, and working guidelines, a spirit of mutual cooperation is growing. For example, of the NGO leaders interviewed in this survey, 56 percent said that their organization performs some regular function with another NGO. Participation in NGO networks is an almost universal practice, and a national association of NGOs has evolved, as well. This association appears to be the culmination of a long and slow developmental process during which the NGOs tried many approaches. It may be argued that their support for the association reflects NGOs' desire for institutional affirmation; beyond the services they provide, they want to be recognized as entities in and of themselves.

Many Brazilian NGOs have found support within the system of international cooperation, becoming partners of institutions geared to addressing the complex dilemmas of development. On any workday of the year, at least one NGO is either receiving a counterpart from another region or sending out a representative of its own. Indeed, the NGO circuit is one of the most internationalized parts of the local society. See Table 4.11.

Table 4.11   Brazilian NGO Relations with International Donors

Donor	Country of Origin	Number of Brazilian NGOs
1	Germany	57
2	The Netherlands	53
3	United States	42
4	Great Britain	31
5	Canada	28
6	Switzerland	20
7	France	17
8	Ireland	14
9	Belgium	10
10	Italy	10
11	Sweden	9
12	Austria	7
13	Denmark	4
14	Spain	4
15	Portugal	3
16	Finland	3
17	Norway	2
18	Luxembourg	1
19	Scotland	1

Source: Questionnaire sent by organizing committee to participants in the "First International Meeting of NGOs and UN System Agencies."
Note: Base = 95. Many NGOs draw on multiple funding sources simultaneously.

In an effort to attain greater coordination, some partner agencies have promoted meetings with the NGOs they finance (their counterparts) in Brazil. These seminars, held to debate priorities, lines of work, types of relations, and so on, provide an opportunity for communication and clarification by all sides. Of the cooperating countries, Germany, the Netherlands, the United States, Great Britain, and Canada lead in the number of their Brazilian NGO partners. The position of the Netherlands is impressive, just behind Germany in its activity and well ahead of the United States. Of the NGO leaders surveyed, 63 percent plan major fundraising drives in Europe, and only 43 percent intend to turn to North America. This suggests that Europe will continue to play the leading role in cooperation with Brazilian NGOs. A small amount of fundraising is planned in Asia.

Protestant (both evangelical and ecumenical) funding sources figure prominently in the budgets of 45 percent of the organizations surveyed; for Catholics, the figure was 25 percent, a curious inversion in view of the predominance of Catholicism in the NGOs financed. This may reflect a liberal and ecumenical spirit within the large Protestant churches of the North.

Prospects for the 1990s

NGO leaders, when invited to speculate on the future, foresaw major transformations in the forms of cooperation. Most believe that resources from governments, multilateral agencies, and private foundations will increase, with most nongovernmental resources remaining at about the same level. There is some pessimism, however, regarding Catholic sources, as some leaders believe these will diminish their levels of cooperation. (See Table 4.12.) The experiences already undertaken with cooperation have generated major enthusiasm for working on a multinational scale, whether with NGOs from the North and South, with the United Nations Development Program, or with the World Bank.

Table 4.12   Anticipated Resources in the Coming Decade

Agencies	Will Increase	Stay the Same	Will Decrease	Can't Evaluate	Don't Know
Governmental	29.4%	17.6%	14.7%	7.8%	30.5%
Multilateral	26.5%	12.7%	11.8%	13.7%	35.3%
Private Foundations	23.5%	17.6%	10.8%	13.7%	34.4%
Ecumenical/Evangelical	23.5%	70.6%	29.4%	21.6%	—
Nongovernmental	18.6%	37.3%	19.6%	3.9%	20.6%
Catholics	9.8%	31.4%	22.5%	10.8%	25.5%

Source: Questionnaire sent by organizing committee to participants in the "First International Meeting of NGOs and UN System Agencies."
Note: Multiple answers were allowed, so vertical totals exceed 100 percent.

By contrast, expectations of national resources are slim, with NGOs anticipating very little from the state. Only 14 percent of those surveyed indicated an intention to submit funding proposals to the federal government. This figure falls to a mere 6 percent relative to state governments but rises slightly, to 7 percent, for municipal governments. Considering that nearly half the NGOs have entered into contracts with governments at some point and that both they and the governments assessed the experience positively, this low expectation may reflect general pessimism regarding the short-term financial potential of the Brazilian state.

Brazil's Catholic Church, as well, is no longer seen as a source of financing; in fact, it appears to be seeking services itself. These diminishing prospects are leading some NGOs to consider major fundraising efforts with Protestant and ecumenical agencies in Brazil, with private foundations, and with local private businesses. Independent of the state, running against the grain of the market, and distanced to some extent from what limited local philanthropy exists, some NGOs have begun to generate resources for themselves by selling services (consultant services and technical assistance) and products (videos and books). In this way, they are discovering the potential (and perils) of self-financing.

A Vision of the Future

In the 1970s, human rights and popular education were the key words for NGOs. What will be the dominant issues of the 1990s? Perhaps a wider range of issues will evolve during this decade; the environment, democratization, civil society, internationalization, development, and cultural diversity are all likely areas for NGO activity as we approach the next millennium. See Tables 4.13 and 4.14.

Table 4.13   Where to Concentrate Imaginative Efforts in the 1990s

Civil Society	78.4%
Culture	46.1%
Politics	39.2%
Economy	21.6%
Science	19.6%
Ethnicity	7.8%
Religion	4.9%
Other Themes	3.9%

Source: Questionnaire sent by organizing committee to participants in the "First International Meeting of NGOs and UN System Agencies."
Note: Multiple answers were allowed.

Brazilian NGOs are in the midst of a major transition. New key words and new trends in cooperation indicate an enlarging NGO arena, autonomous and distinct from the logics of private enterprise, political parties, and churches. The creation of the Brazilian Association of NGOs appears to be a step in that direction. The institutional weight of NGOs is growing, their professionalism is rising, their scope of action is broadening, and their expenditures are increasing. Heavyweight partners, such as government and multilateral agencies, are entering the circuit. Some NGOs have

Table 4.14 Most Important Themes for the 1990s

Ecology	47.06%
Democratization	43.14%
Civil Society	34.31%
Economic Development	23.53%
Internationalization	28.43%
Cultural Diversity	19.61%
Human Rights	18.63%
Violence	13.73%
Popular Education	12.75%
Women	10.78%
Symbolism	9.80%
Ethnic Groups	6.86%
Other Themes	3.92%

Source: Questionnaire sent by organizing committee to participants in the "First International Meeting of NGOs and UN System Agencies."
Note: Multiple answers were allowed.

begun to sell services and products, often to subsidize the activities they value most. These are profound transformations, opening up a broad array of positive alternatives for civil society in the future.

Notes

1. The sample group of respondents included a large number from NGOs that provide services to the popular movement, fewer from women's organizations or black organizations. In addition to the data collected through the specially designed questionnaire, the survey administrators drew upon information provided on the conference registration cards.

2. The last (and only previous) survey of Brazilian NGOs dates from 1988 (see Landim). According to the information gathered at that time, there were approximately 447 agencies or organizations providing services to the popular movement, 196 women's organizations, and 565 black organizations—a total of 1,208.

3. Decidedly unambiguous, however, is the NGO position regarding the Collor government. Almost all NGOs oppose it, although a few favor specific elements such as environmental policy and computer policy.

5

NGOs, Social Movements, and the Privatization of Health Care: Experiences in São Paulo

Amelia Cohn

Public Health in Brazil

Despite improvements in the quality and accessibility of Brazilian health care, overall public health is declining. Not only are diseases striking more often, they are also striking more people in their spread to new geographic areas and populations. Hardest hit by the worsening health situation are the urban poor living on the fringes of Brazil's largest cities, people whose poverty restricts them to settlements that often lack sanitation and potable water as well as other basic public services. Such settlements are a symptom of Brazil's rapid urbanization and industrialization in recent decades, which have led also to the country's declining health levels. These in turn reflect the close relationship between environment and disease. To comprehend the magnitude and complexity of Brazilian morbidity, the reader need only reflect upon the following statistics:

- In 1987, there were some 460,000 new cases of malaria, a threefold increase over 1985 figures. This figure is linked to expanded settlement and gold prospecting in the Amazon, where 97 percent of all malarial cases are concentrated.
- Chagas' disease now affects people in nineteen states. Typically a rural illness, it has spread to major urban centers in a mirror image of rural-to-urban migration patterns. Estimates suggest that 500,000 of the 8 million people suffering from Chagas live in São Paulo and Rio de Janeiro, the largest urban centers in the country.
- Thirteen million Brazilians are carriers of schistosomiasis, and in

recent years high rates of diphtheria, polio, tuberculosis, and
Hansen's disease (Brazil accounts for 80 percent of leprosy cases in
Latin America) have been reported (Cohn 1988).

As for overall mortality, in the mid-1980s the leading causes were diseases
of the circulatory system, cancer, and infectious and parasitic diseases,
while respiratory infections and perinatal and parasitic diseases were the
main causes of infant mortality. Violence has also become one of the leading causes of death in large Brazilian cities.

Public health care in Brazil not only suffers from complexity but also
from the manner in which it has been addressed. For one thing, the health-
provision model has shifted its emphasis somewhat in recent years, moving
from primary health care toward a technology-oriented treatment mode.
Correspondingly, medical professionals have emerged as central figures, to
some extent displacing primary health personnel formerly associated with
the Brazilian health-care model.

Other changes have occurred as well. Health care is now seen not as a
universal right but as the outcome of a contractual relationship involving
compulsory contributions (social security payments) from the *employed* in
exchange for access to (private) health care. Such a view reflects the state's
privatist policy toward medical care, a policy that became radicalized in
Brazil from the 1960s to the 1980s. In transferring this primary role to the
for-profit sector—serving the wealthy and the formally employed—the
state itself theoretically becomes responsible for the millions who fall
through the cracks—the poor, workers in the informal economy, and the
unemployed. However, the social welfare system (formerly the main service provider and principal source of financial investment in the health sector) is undergoing its worst crisis in recent decades, as the state adopts
orthodox economic measures in its struggle to deal with the fiscal crisis.
Thus, public health care has become a responsibility the state cannot bear
alone. Unfortunately, few groups appear able to move into the breach.[1]

Another problem lies in a pattern of health-care distribution that heavily favors urban areas.[2] Much of this imbalance occurs because of the system's financial dependence upon social security contributions. Geared primarily to the formal labor market, social security is largely concentrated in
urban areas. State action also tends to be subordinated to the rules of the
market, as are medical professionals and, to a certain extent, public-sector
professionals (Mello 1977). Whether of the private or public sector, both
groups are therefore drawn to work in urban areas. Market-driven influences such as these have led to overwhelming health-care inequalities in
Brazil.

To the problems of unequal access and shifted emphasis from primary
health care to treatment for illness there are two immediate consequences.
First, the community-medicine model becomes an inviable mechanism for

extending universal health care to the underprivileged—that is, those bordering on absolute poverty, who, according to optimistic estimates, number 40 million. Second, the predominant medical model shapes public expectations and demands, since this is now the *existing* pattern of health services. Combined, these two factors effectively bar millions of Brazilians from the health care they need and deserve as citizens.

Current Health Policy Trends

Since the mid-1970s, the question of health has mobilized certain sectors of Brazilian society and stimulated intense debate. The conflict lies in these dilemmas: privatization *or* nationalization of health services, centralization *or* decentralization of their organizational structure, and universalization of *or* selective access to services as a way to render viable the constitutional precept according to which "health is a right of all and a duty of the state."

The Brazilian health-care system can be characterized as follows:

- *Highly centralized.* Sectoral guidelines and priorities, including those related to financing, are prepared by the national executive. States and municipalities have a limited degree of autonomy; however, their role is more to implement guidelines drafted at the federal level than to formulate their own policies. As a consequence, the care provided often fails to reflect the real needs of local citizens.
- *Excessively privatized.* Increasingly, individual medical care is provided by the private sector (some 80 percent) and paid for by the state through social security contributions.
- *Progressively distant from genuine health needs.* Specialists in social medicine agree that the vast majority of health problems in Brazil could be solved with primary care. However, the existing health-care infrastructure is complex and relies on highly technical equipment; also, there is no integration or ranking of services based on technological complexity. As a result, available services correspond less to need than to the logic of the market and the dictates of profit.
- *Divided between public and private sectors.* The public sector covers collective care—control of communicable diseases, measures against epidemics, and so on—and more recently, medical care for the unemployed. It is also responsible for certain types of high-cost treatment. The private sector, on the other hand, takes charge of profitable and for-profit care.
- *Discriminatory and inequitable.* Formally employed Brazilians— those linked to the social security system—have access to more diversified health care (generally private) than do those in the infor-

mal sector. Lacking social security, and thereby access to the private system, the neediest must look to the public sector, which suffers from low state investment in health.

• *Profoundly distorted in its financing.* To the extent that the bulk of care is under social security, access to medical care becomes a "paid" right through a compulsory contract with social security. Such an arrangement largely relieves the state of any financial responsibility for health and denies access to the unemployed and informally employed.

In recent decades, these characteristics have turned the Brazilian health system into one both distorted and costly. It is also extremely vulnerable to economic crises because of its grounding in a social security system built upon the wages and revenues of Brazilian firms. In the mid-1970s, public health physicians (from the public health network), university professors specializing in social medicine and public health, progressive and leftist political parties, and a wide array of NGOs and popular movements sought to reverse this situation and to democratize health care. Because of limited grassroots participation, however, these efforts did not meet the expectations and demands of the popular classes and cannot be considered as effective social mobilization. In fact, this and many similar experiences of popular health movements lead one to question whether health issues can effectively mobilize popular sectors into sustainable movements or whether they provide only a short-term organizational stimulus.

In contrast to several Latin American countries, Brazil has seen little NGO activity in the provision of local health care and very few joint ventures between the public and private sectors. Even in the 1980s, successful health endeavors came about primarily when social movements and organized sectors pressed demands upon the state, rather than when they looked for ways to collaborate. Nonetheless, some experiences in São Paulo do indicate a degree of collaboration between the public health sector and popular support and mobilization groups in efforts to gain health services tied to needs.

São Paulo Today

São Paulo is the major industrial and financial center of Brazil and home to its principal trade union organizations and federations. Here the modern coexists with the archaic, paralleling the disparities found nationwide. In effect, São Paulo serves as a microcosm of the inequities and contradictions in Brazilian society. This is clearly evident in the health arena.

If the municipality is viewed as a series of concentric circles, public health displays a radical dichotomy between the more central areas and those on the periphery. In the center, for example, problems of infrastructure and health services are quite similar to those in industrialized countries, as are profiles of morbidity and mortality and available medical care; the situation in the periphery, however, is the opposite. Here, one finds serious health problems—epidemiological indicators comparable to those of much less developed societies, combined with a deteriorated health infrastructure. In line with the rest of present-day Brazil, São Paulo has a two-tiered system of medical infrastructure—high-tech equipment for the advantaged, poorly maintained and less-sophisticated equipment for the rest. There is an estimated deficit of over 130 outpatient units, especially in the periurban areas, and São Paulo's outdated public hospital network has too few beds. Of all hospital beds in the municipality, 29 percent belong to the public sector and 71 percent are private. Thus, even though São Paulo has 3.2 hospital beds per 1,000 population, a ratio quite close to World Health Organization recommendations (4 per 1,000), their distribution relative to area is out of balance: 8.3 per 1,000 in the center, 2.8 per 1,000 in the intermediate area, and fewer than 1.8 per 1,000 in the periphery (where in some areas it falls as low as 0.2 to 0.6 per 1,000 persons).

Diseases strike São Paulo's 10 million residents unequally. The incidence of cardiac diseases grows among the well-to-do, while gastrointestinal and pulmonary infections plague the poor. Infant mortality, despite a downward trend from 76.98 per 1,000 live births in the 1970s to 35.14 per 1,000 in 1988, is also markedly different. On average, the risk of death before one year is about three times greater in the periphery than in the center of the city.

Basic sanitation in São Paulo compares well with the rest of the country; for example, water supply and refuse collection networks cover 93 percent of the urban population. These services, however, are distributed unequally. Residents in the center are well served, but 700,000 people on the periphery lack safe drinking water and 3.9 million have no access to solid waste systems. Moreover, sewage systems reach only 60.5 percent, a worrisome statistic given the increase in cholera throughout Latin America.

Some attempts have been made to meet the health needs of periurban residents. The following two examples are taken from accounts about health-care movements in São Mateus and Jardim Nordeste, written by Pedro Jacobi (1989) of the Center for Contemporary Culture Studies in São Paulo, and describe interaction in the early 1980s between popular health movements and state and municipal health officials in these two communities. Both accounts describe the progression from protest to collaboration and give a flavor of the dynamics and tension between these often opposing actors, whose exchanges set the stage for the participatory neighborhood health councils that have become the norm in the early 1990s. Jacobi chronicles the emerging consciousness and organization of these health movements, which are almost invariably led by women, to reveal the financial, geographical, and human resource constraints to providing health care to São Paulo's periurban residents.

São Mateus

Community organizing in São Mateus dates from the early 1970s, when progressive Catholic priests and laypersons helped residents organize to make bulk purchases of food and other staples. In 1975, the health movement began with state inauguration of a health post, where one thousand local children were registered in the first six months. However, community health needs far surpassed available care and led residents to organize under the direction of the Pastoral Health Commission (PHC).

Over the next four years, health commissions were established in various neighborhoods, health demonstrations were organized, and a research project detailing the area's health problems and precarious health-care situation was completed. At that time, the infant mortality rate was 115 per 1,000 in São Mateus, whereas São Paulo registered a rate of 74.8 per 1,000.

In May 1979, the movement gained recognition with its first assembly meeting—promoted and organized by one of the PHCs and attended by the new state health secretary and a representative of the city. These representatives toured the area and listened to residents' demands for a health council to oversee the health centers, for improvements to existing centers and construction of new ones, and for the establishment of a public hospital and outpatient clinic run by the social security agency, National Institute of Medical Assistance and Social Welfare (INAMPS).

This meeting marked the beginning of interaction between the health secretariat and the popular movement. By September 1979, the São Mateus project was formalized with full participation by local residents. Monthly meetings drew representatives from established and newly organized commissions to track project progress. Toward the end of the year, the government announced its support for health councils in each center, improvements in six health centers, construction of new centers in thirteen of the twenty-two neighborhoods, and construction of one emergency clinic.

After nearly six months construction had begun on only one of the centers, and competitive bidding for the other centers was still underway. Patience wore thin, and in December 1980, a year after the project had been announced, six hundred adult residents and their children boarded buses to protest directly to the secretary of health. Here is what transpired, in the words of a leader of the São Mateus movement:

> We made banners and posters depicting the neighborhood's problems and we demanded that he come . . . because we wanted to have a public hospital in the region and an INAMPS outpatient clinic. We also demanded a meeting with the three secretaries and the municipal, state, and the

regional superintendents of INAMPS, because otherwise they would just be passing the buck. Dr. Adib, the state health secretary, promised that within three months he would give an answer. . . . In those three months we waited; when we went there, he always said that the superintendent of INAMPS was travelling, that he couldn't meet. So we decided ourselves to organize an assembly and invite all three.

At this assembly both Dr. Adib and the INAMPS superintendent, Colonel Camanho, were present. Taking advantage of this situation, we pressed our grievances, calling for improvements to the existing health center and immediate installation of provisional health centers. We requested public confirmation that the hospital would be built by the end of 1981, along with the outpatient clinic staffed with specialists. We called for a council elected directly by the people of the neighborhood. We can't leave it up to the judgment of the government, as they'll choose entities that already exist in the neighborhood, and so it's not going to be worth our while to work so hard. We want the council chosen directly from where we live, where we work. When Dr. Adib told us that *he* would choose the members of the health post, we refused. We wanted the chief of the post to participate with the people in the meetings to make known to the population the problems of the health center and public hospital, so that the people could exercise oversight (Jacobi 1989, 102–103).

Over the next couple of months, the community organizers received assurances that work would proceed on schedule and that, by June 1981, the health posts would be operating; that the hospitals would be opened within two and a half years; and that the election of the health councils would be approved.

The movement spurred more community participation as grievances were voiced. Other periurban neighborhoods began to press for improved health service, and inspectors were dispatched to determine the actual health situation. Eventually, the secretary of health affirmed the legitimacy of their demands and agreed that the situation was indeed precarious.

Six months passed, however, and little government action took place. This led to more protests. Demands for services at the existing health posts increased to include distribution of powdered milk and medicines; specialized care from physicians, public health experts, and nurses; vaccination campaigns; emergency care; and expanded hours of operation. The government responded that it had insufficient funds for these services and that physicians and public health experts were reluctant to stay at the posts for more than an hour and a half due to the low salaries. The residents continued to press their demands.

By 1982, the government had built twelve health centers in São Mateus. However, pressure in response to this continuous the movement for better health care did not stop nor lose its momentum. In July 1982, residents sent further demands to the new secretary of health—that more staff be hired at the clinics because there were few practicing physicians, that pending promises be kept, and that services be expanded. Again, they took their requests directly to the secretary, who stated his commitment to improving health care. The slow pace of government response led to a period of strained relations between the state and municipal health secretariats and the local population. By the mid-1980s, however, the situation improved through the successful establishment of municipal health councils, first begun in the Jardim Nordeste neighborhood on the edge of São Paulo.

Jardim Nordeste

In 1974, residents of Jardim Nordeste initiated the first of many calls for a health center. Their movement gained momentum in 1976, when many community children contracted measles. During this crisis, the children had to be taken to Tatuapé, 15 kilometers away, because there were no health posts in Jardim Nordeste.

In response to the emergency, a group of medical students provided outpatient care at a local church. During these contacts, the students and residents discussed neighborhood problems and identified health as a priority. A health commission was formed to pressure the government for the construction of a health clinic. In 1977, the secretariat agreed to lease a small house for use as a health center. Upon its inauguration, residents installed a plaque that read "a conquest by the people" (*uma conquisto do povo*). Residents assumed administrative oversight for the center as soon as they realized the law gave them this right. Their initiative came not a moment too soon because, as one public health expert in the region noted:

> What the people saw was that to a certain point most of the health centers were established based on political, clientelistic criteria. After this one was installed, there was only one nursing auxiliary and at most, one physician. . . . That same day, the people began circulating a petition demanding that improvements be made at the center, since it was already clear that the services would be very precarious (Jacobi 1989, 108).

In October 1978, the neighborhood commission presented the secretariat with a petition, signed by 3,760 people, that demanded assurance that the center would provide adequate coverage. A week later, the regional health office promised increased medical personnel (and improved registration procedures), vaccination programs, and nursing services. Although nurses soon appeared daily, the government dragged its feet on the other services, and residents realized that the mere existence of a health post would not solve health problems. This became painfully clear when residents discovered that the center's only physician rarely stayed longer than an hour at the center, often leaving before waiting patients had been treated.

A new round of mobilization efforts began, organized primarily by women, to protest a decree directing that community councils in the centers be chosen from among the local elite: delegates, regional administrators, school principals, and politicians. Faced with an energetic campaign to place such elites on the councils, the women decided to form a council of mothers since they considered themselves the most knowledgeable about neighborhood health problems. Thirteen women ran for council posts, and twelve were elected in March 1979 when the eight communities of Jardim Nordeste voted. Their impact was immediately felt.

> The post began to function just right; the physician began to stay for more time and the staff attended the people better. We raised people's awareness so that they would go to the center more and not blame the staff for the lack of resources and infrastructure. . . . Later, through monthly meetings with the physicians and auxiliaries, we were able to get somewhat improved services and to have everyone work their full schedule. But our principal achievement was the reform of the existing center and the construction of an adequate building next year. The council was our security and a way to continue struggling for better medical care (Jacobi 1989, 110).

The official duties of council members as stated by law were "to verify whether people are being well attended [and] to make sure there is no lack of drugs and milk, staff, etc.," and "to inform the people [and] monitor operations of the health center on a day-to-day basis" (Jacobi 1989, 112).

The Jardim Nordeste health movement led to routine communication between residents, health center staff, and the health secretariat. The council's supervision led to swift responses to problems, and community pressure hastened the secretariat's allocation of funds.

Communities like São Mateus studied and eventually adopted the Jardim Nordeste health council approach. In September 1985, when elections were held to choose health councils at state and municipal health posts, over 140,000 residents of 37 neighborhoods in the region chose 838 council members; of these, the majority were women.

The health movements in São Mateus and Jardim Nordeste spotlight both combative and cooperative relations between community members and public health authorities. Concerned residents were unceasing in their demands for access to broader and better health care services. As elected health council members, representatives of these same residents acquired quasi-policymaking roles and improved their ability to shape the overall health picture. No doubt, the mobilization experiences in São Paulo's peri-urban communities helped pave the way for the municipal government's health reforms in the early 1990s.

The São Paulo Joint Venture

A recent municipal endeavor in São Paulo is instructive as a model to correct distortions in the country's health system. The administration of Labor Party Mayor Luiza Erundina (1989–1993) sought to promote participation and extend decision-making power to organized "management committees" by initiating a health management program that would give decisionmaking autonomy to the municipality's ten administrative regions, thereby enabling hospitals and clinics to run their own programs. The program also provided guidelines for upgrading employee qualifications and working conditions. Has it been successful? To a promising degree, yes. However, the process of turning the popular-participation goal into a reality advances unevenly; older and more organizationally sound social movements have set up health management committees more quickly.

The management committees are tripartite with membership drawn from medical/health administration, government, and clients—the first two totaling 50 percent, and clients or consumers, the other 50 percent. These committees represent their constituencies before the municipal executive, specifically the health secretary, through a municipal health council that is deliberative in nature and composed of sixteen client representatives. In the current administration's municipal health councils, representatives of social movements predominate; of the sixteen representatives, eleven are from popular movements, two from employer and trade union associations, and three from associations of patients and/or disabled.

Of a total of 196 projected health posts to be installed throughout thirty-two health districts, 39.4 percent have been established as of this writing, many with active management committees. By instituting channels that allow organized groups to participate in health management, São Paulo demonstrates the viability of this model. It is one that aspires to create an efficient health services division and demonstrates that social movements and the state can forge a mutually beneficial relationship without co-optation.

Ultimately, interdependency is established when the movements effectively voice customer demands and when the state, responding to this pressure, channels greater resources to the health sector and receives legitimacy and support for confronting corporatist and/or private interests. São Paulo's municipal health councils and management committees play an important role in the fruitful relationship developing between the executive (the administration) and the social movements.

As a result of this relationship, the health sector has gained significantly more resources, from 11.1 percent in 1988 to 16.2 percent in 1991. (It is noteworthy that when the legislature voted on the budget, various associations joined together in a lobbying partnership.) Other changes have occurred as well. For example, the pursuit of greater efficiency of services now reflects the broader view of social movements, which through their representatives on the management committees have come to understand and accommodate interests of health workers—including their attitudes toward working hours or assignment far from downtown São Paulo.

Reforming Health Policy

If the Brazilian health system is to shed its present inequities in both law and practice, health care must become *universal* and not dependent solely upon employee contributions. The Constitution of October 1988 and its enacting legislation took a step in that direction by setting forth objectives in support of a single, universal, and equitable health system. Two key proposals are to decentralize the public health sector and restructure its financing.

Under a decentralized system, each level of government would designate one person to oversee health matters, but local authorities would have relative autonomy in defining health policy and controlling finances within national and state guidelines. Putting such tools directly into the hands of municipalities would improve health care accessibility and also enable local populations to obtain the care they need. In theory, it would also provide greater flexibility in adapting available equipment to demand. The public health sector would be strengthened, also, by added investments via automatic transfer of social security resources. Current financing distortions would be overcome as all three levels of government would contribute a portion of their budgets to this general health fund. At the same time, public financing of the private health sector would be prohibited and strict mechanisms put into place to ensure quality care and monitor technical-financial operations.

Intruding upon this rosy picture, however, are major obstacles that stand in the way of the constitutional objectives. First, despite announcements that the government aims to substantially increase spending, public investment in health continues to shrink. Second, because health policy has received so little priority over the past two decades, Brazil's health-care system has deteriorated technically and professionally to the point that it now may be labelled a "junked" (*sucateado*) public health system. Third, strong private-sector opposition to public oversight has kept health out of the political institutional framework. Finally, neoliberal ideologues throw their weight against organized pressure groups, rich or poor, to selectively assist the poor as individuals. Their economic proposals "deorganize" society, while shrinking the state to a minimal, clientelistic, social welfare role.

How then can participation be encouraged? Can NGOs promote community participation in health care policy? Can they serve as effective advocates of public policy, and health policy in particular, when state support for local needs is shrinking? The next section discusses ways that NGOs and social movements may be able to brighten Brazil's prospects for a functional and equitable health care system.

The Role of Brazilian
Social Movements and NGOs in Health Care

In forging a new model of health care, the goal should be a system that is efficient, rational, characterized by different levels of technological complexity, and geared to primary, preventive health care as well as to treatment of illness. What role can NGOs play in the evolution of such a system? Alone, perhaps a limited one because Brazilian social movements are generally more involved in the health arena than are NGOs. The involvement of social movements, however, is often difficult to sustain. In general, social movements emerge when underserved or ill-used people mobilize to seek recognition and press claims vis-à-vis the authorities. Such movements maintain a spasmodic existence, constantly struggling to keep the mobilization alive beyond the point at which their demands are met or ignored.

Generally speaking, social movements are specialized by sector—health, housing, education, and transportation, among others—and rarely unite in common struggle. As economic conditions deteriorate, competition for survival often displaces solidarity. Along with NGOs, social movements are often targeted by a wide range of political organizations, particularly progressive political parties advocating a strong state presence. In the health sector, this has translated into calls for statization of all health services. Given an ineffective state, however, progressive parties and militant social movements generally prefer community-based health care to none at all.

Because decentralization has been discouraged in Brazil and the state has controlled social services and infrastructure, NGOs have thus far played a minor role in health activities. The central government assigns itself the role of involving the community and promoting access to services (albeit on a limited basis for the impoverished sectors), sometimes relegating NGOs to such areas as provision of direct services. Many NGOs, however, have resisted or refused the role of service provider. Those programs that are undertaken for the most part serve the disabled, children with special needs, and people seeking family planning services. Relatively few outpatient medical clinics are operated by NGOs; of those, most are religious and usually Catholic.

Several factors contribute to the absence of Brazilian NGOs from the health-care sector. One is the traditional view that the state has principal responsibility for solving the needs of the underprivileged. Yet, the state is often discredited and distrusted because it either fails to address or only partially addresses popular demands. Another issue is the overemphasis upon "technical knowledge," assumed to be indispensable in the delivery of health services. Again, the state plays the lead role as it delegates the task of *solving* health problems to those with this technical knowledge (government health bureaucrats) while relegating social movements and NGOs to auxiliary roles (identifying problems and pressuring the state to meet needs). Or, to use a health-care analogy, NGOs and social movements are allowed at most to make diagnoses while others prescribe and administer the required therapy. A third issue is the impact that NGO involvement in the health sector may have on NGO autonomy vis-à-vis the state and politics. Is co-optation a danger? Many would say yes, although when the organization and/or health movement is more consolidated, the risk of co-optation appears to be lower.

Effective mobilization depends largely on well-informed community members, therefore information must be made readily available. NGOs and social movements may come to play an increasingly important role in providing both information and training on health issues. However, current studies indicate a need for funds to cover the costs of producing and disseminating such information. NGOs and social movements view dissemination as a two-way street, receiving information from their bases and promoting greater awareness of health issues among the people. It is here that NGOs and social movements for health often find common ground—both reject the role of service provider in place of the state and instead assume the role of identifiers and articulators of society's health needs. Occasionally, however, NGOs provide health services in addition to making demands. Even within São Paulo, strategies and tactics of NGOs and social movements vary considerably.

In societies afflicted with inequalities and social injustice, the withdrawal of the state from such fundamental public responsibilities as health care should not doom society to the extreme of either statization or privatization. Rather, the issue must be one of providing equitable health care that meets popular needs and does not exclude private health-care providers. This requires a developmental process in which the division of responsibilities between public and private sectors is not predetermined but evolves in such a way that it draws upon all available resources. If these Brazilian experiments have yet to show a major impact on relationships among NGOs, social movements, and the state in health care, they do demonstrate how some of the "assisted" have become citizens, with rights and responsibilities thrashed out in public debate. Health issues alone do not sustain mobilization, but they are vital elements of the struggle for social justice.

Notes

1. Brazil's weakening state is already affecting groups that once undertook collective measures to gain access to health care. They are severely hampered by the lack of resources and by their diminishing capacity to pressure the government. Often excluded from the productive process, these groups are largely excluded from the health-care system as well.

2. This pattern is seen both in the regional distribution of private and public hospitals and in the distribution of medical services. In the mid-1980s, for example, the urban-rural ratio for hospitalizations was about 49:1 and for medical consultations about 40:1. (The urban-rural population ratio was approximately 2:1 during this same period.)

◆◆

6

Making Cities Livable:
Local Initiatives in Solid Waste
and Public Transportation
Management in Brazil

SILVIO CACCIA BAVA
LAURA MULLAHY

Stagnant Services and Underserved Populations

Like many cities of the developing world, São Paulo confronts problems relative to its scale: overcrowding, declining public health, environmental pollution, inadequate public services, and growing violence. Overwhelmed by these growing pains, the municipality of São Paulo has made little progress in two vital areas: public transportation and solid waste collection, yet both are intimately bound to the quality of urban life. The urban poor, eking out an existence on the outskirts of the city and on the margins of society, are the most seriously affected by the lack of these two services.

Such is the case in São Paulo, whose outer edges reflect realities common to many Latin American cities. Brazil's *favelas,* Peru's *pueblos jóvenes,* and Chile's *poblaciones* are all versions of the shantytowns housing millions of low-income Latin Americans. This explosion of squatter settlements has paralleled the unprecedented population growth and urbanization of recent decades. Residents of these marginal settlements live in makeshift shacks constructed from cardboard, corrugated iron or aluminum sheets, and packing crates. Often, these dwellings lack water, electricity, and sanitation facilities.

For most shantytown dwellers (and for countless residents of established neighborhoods), the only work possibilities require a lengthy commute to the city center, where they might have a full-time job or be employed mending clothes, shining shoes, or selling everything from used auto parts to lottery tickets.

A typical favela resident must begin her journey around five o'clock in the morning to arrive on time for such a job. Leaving her tiny house, she descends the rough hillside paths leading to the bus stop on the main road. Her route passes alongside the favela's colossal garbage pile composed of household and industrial waste that looms above the favela shacks. Even more dramatic than its physical prominence, however, is its stench. As seductive to insects and rodents as it is repellent to humans, the odor attracts creatures that burrow and nibble or hover about the pile. Making her way down the path, the senhora glances at the garbage pickers, yet another type of "visitor" to the pile. The pickers are early risers who rummage through the heap for any scraps to salvage and process.

Reaching the main road at last, the senhora joins the people waiting for a bus to take them downtown to work. She consults no bus schedule for none exists. Instead, she and her companions wait interminably for a bus that arrives at random times—when it arrives at all. Favela residents are accustomed to this, however, for every morning and evening they must wait for an overcrowded and overpriced bus if they are to get to and from work. They wait—despite the cost, the crowding, and the time lost each day—for they have no alternative. They are captives of a system that, although undependable and inefficient, is nonetheless their sole route to a paycheck.

Other residents remain close to the shantytowns. Some of them work as garbage pickers whose workday unfolds on the dumps. Ecological disasters, these vast piles nonetheless provide subsistence to the pickers, who glean their booty from other people's trash.

Moldering garbage dumps stand in mute testimony to São Paulo's inability to handle its citizens' refuse. Similarly, the absence of reliable public transport attests to another seriously flawed urban policy. Both problems highlight an institutional deficiency common to many developing countries, whose central governments consider refuse management and public transportation to be "fringe" issues. These services remain low priorities, particularly during the redemocratization process after long periods of nondemocratic rule. In Brazil, these urban challenges provide opportunities to another level of government: local or municipal managers who, because of the decentralization wrought by the Constitution of 1988, are charged with certain responsibilities for education, health, and public transport.

Rising Voices for Change

The much heralded return to electoral democratic systems throughout the continent, while sounding an optimistic note for the future of Latin

America, simultaneously increases expectations and demands on central governments. In the aftermath of elections and power transfers, new societal groups have joined the traditional cast of actors in demanding their due from "the system." In part, this increased mobilization is an expression by the people of their rediscovered associative capacity. However, some of society's claims on new governments seek vindication for the marginalization suffered during less democratic periods.

Latin America's typically centralized governments cannot satisfy the myriad demands made upon them, particularly when escalating expectations coincide with the tremendous challenges of the transition to democracy. The delivery of effective governance and representation is in itself a monumental task; to do so while redefining both state and party roles and inching along the economic tightrope toward growth and equity presents an overwhelming, perhaps insurmountable, challenge. Yet, the times call for heroic efforts because the social costs of the structural adjustment imposed upon Latin American countries include a high rate of unemployment, which has brought urban poverty into alarming relief throughout the region.

As demonstrated by a number of cases in Latin America, local governments and NGOs are likely problem solvers for these times in which societal demands overwhelm government supply. Local governments can make a difference if they approach the basic needs of society with a more appropriate and convincing response than central authorities have thus far produced. Their potential is particularly noteworthy in Brazil, a country of spatial and demographic dimensions exceeding those of any other Latin American nation.

Brazilians are captives of a system that views the creation of wealth, rather than social welfare, as its primary aim, and they are begging for equitable government. Moreover, they have learned of the positive effects of such governance elsewhere. Yet, an eclectic executive branch whose programs have frequently proven inconsistent, self-contradictory, and heavily weighted toward elites continues to make the majority of policy decisions in Brazil. Recognizing the potential of local governments is the first step toward breaking the traditional pattern of subordination to state government and ending the crisis of administrative centralism.

Pólis: Rallying for Local Self-Determination

Brazilians and other Latin Americans who foster collaboration between nongovernmental organizations and local government might find inspiration in the experience of the Institute of Research, Training, and Advisory Services in Social Policy (Pólis), a pioneering São Paulo institution founded in 1987. A nonprofit, nonpartisan grassroots support organization (GSO), Pólis has succeeded by combining an overall problem-solving outlook with a specific municipal focus. Its nineteen-member staff of sociologists, urban planners, anthropologists, documentalists, lawyers, and economists reflects Pólis's multidisciplinary focus.

In response to Brazil's complex urban reality, Pólis strives to provide expert assistance to urban community groups and to encourage awareness among civil society. It concentrates its efforts on problems characteristic of Latin America and other developing areas: poverty, inequitable public policies, and inadequate public services.

Functioning as both an information clearinghouse and a consulting center, Pólis conducts several learning-oriented activities to promote the idea that democracy leads to a strengthened civil society. This GSO urges a rise in public consciousness to bring about not only the democratization of society but also a better standard of living and civil and political rights for all Brazilians. Pólis promotes the "acculturation of Brazil's cities," referring to an assimilation of groups and peoples with different norms and values, by studying the values and behavior surrounding the integration of urban residents.

One of Pólis's specific objectives is to establish a solid reputation as a mediator for informational exchange. This ambitious goal involves interactions with popular groups and grassroots movements, NGOs, city governments, and other entities formulating social policy. Its urban focus, combined with its willingness to collaborate with government and grassroots efforts alike, places Pólis in a special category of GSO.

Pólis activities fall into four general categories: (1) courses and seminars, (2) publications, (3) consulting and technical assistance, and (4) information collection and dissemination. Since its establishment, Pólis has organized and conducted workshops, forums, debates, and special training courses for public leaders and administrators. Increasingly, the organization collaborates with local and regional NGOs on joint publications and seminars, and on technical assistance programs for popular movements.

Combined efforts such as these have enabled Pólis and other NGOs to achieve a profound level of integration with popular movements and municipal governments. For example, its NGO collaborations allow Pólis to broaden its impact and avoid duplication of efforts, while its involvement with local authorities increases the pool of available material and financial resources. These successful partnerships fill the leadership void when popularly elected officials prove lacking in experience and managerial skills.

Pólis publications cover a wide range of topics. During 1991, for example, its documents addressed urban reform and citizens' rights, tenement housing, low-cost housing construction, and environmental issues such as pollution and soil use. One publication series initiated that year highlights what are hailed as "pioneering experiences in democratic management," calling attention to the diverse methods of public policymaking evidenced in four Brazilian municipalities (Pólis 1991).

An issue dedicated to the city of Lages, in the southeastern state of Santa Catarina, describes how this local community has flourished under its "Celebrate Your Neighborhood" (Viva Seu Bairro) program, initiated in the 1970s. This program helped foster popular participation in government decision making through the creation of neighborhood organizations—particularly as related to low-income housing and community agriculture. Lages's successful programs exemplify the effective use of local management.

The commitment to identify, and subsequently disseminate, this and other creative solutions to urban problems led to the Pólis publication *Inovação Urbana*. Produced trimesterly since 1990, the series is distributed among principal Brazilian municipal administrators. By highlighting innovative techniques in municipal management, Pólis hopes to inspire their replication in other locations. The *Inovação Urbana* series began with an issue highlighting creative ways to address urban Brazil's waste problem. The experiences related in that issue, entitled "The Selective Collection of Garbage," provide a lesson in effective and innovative problem solving.[1]

Inovação Urbana issues try to stimulate the formulation of public policies based on certain fundamental values: democratic decision making, social equality, better use of public resources, and ecological preservation. Its emphasis on dissemination of exemplary experiences in municipal governance stems from Pólis's conviction that an unbreakable link exists between public awareness and government accountability. Pólis aims to help municipal administrators regain respect for basic democratic values.

Burying the Garbage Problem

A key item on municipal agendas in developing countries is the treatment of solid waste, one of the most critical problems in Latin America today. Faced with the rising tide of trash accompanying urban expansion and congestion, city managers must resolve a critical dilemma: how to manage a product that is inseparable from humanity, yet seriously threatens both its health and its environment. Despite the considerable funds devoted to the problem of solid waste management—an estimated 30 to 50 percent of municipal budgets according to the International City Management Association (1992)—refuse collection in Latin America remains largely inefficient and inequitable.

> No issue affects the urban poor with such direct irony as that of solid waste, which is simultaneously a source of income and of endangerment in Third World cities. Urban parts of the Third World produce nearly 700 grams [about 1.5 pounds] of solid waste per person per day. By the turn of the century, urban areas in Latin America will produce 370,000 tons per day—almost an 80 percent increase over present levels. Only about 60

percent of this total is collected, and less than half of the collected amount is disposed of in an environmentally sound manner (Campbell 1989).

Until recently, the staggering volume of refuse generated in large metropolitan centers such as Brazil's São Paulo has led municipal leaders to contract with private companies for garbage collection in preference to adapting their own collection infrastructure. However, São Paulo had too few resources to pay for the amount of collection and processing needed; thus, vast depositories of garbage (*lixões*) abound in vacant lots, in stream beds, and on hillsides at the city's edge, unleashing a chain of serious environmental and sanitation problems. Not only do these piles contaminate the water supply, attract rodents and insects, and spread disease, they also emit a host of hazardous and toxic emissions from untreated waste material (Campbell 1989). Assaulting both humanity and environment, urban lixões serve as a potent reminder of the magnitude of Brazil's refuse management problem.

The country's conventional forms of solid-waste processing include landfills, composting plants, and incinerators, all of which have limited success. Composting plants and incinerators can process only materials that meet a predetermined grade of "purity." Incinerators have an additional disadvantage, as the resulting ash ends up in landfills. In its effort to tackle the monumental problem of solid waste management, Pólis has compiled information on alternative strategies. Its findings, published in the *Inovação Urbana* series, describe processes similar to those adopted in the United States and several European nations, including "selective collection" (pickup and sorting) and recycling of garbage. Pólis urges individuals, private residences, schools, businesses, and other establishments to become involved in recycling by calling attention to its multiple benefits (ecological, economic, social, and political).

The "Selective Collection of Garbage," published in October 1990, documents three exemplary Brazilian initiatives in solid waste treatment: Curitiba, a city that has traditionally claimed the title of the "environmental capital of Brazil," and two areas of São Paulo—Vila Madalena (a middle-class neighborhood) and Monte Azul (a favela where, until 1989, a single dumpster was allocated for the refuse of its 400 residences). Together, these case studies represent a broad spectrum of management and cooperation strategies.

Curitiba

Curitiba is the capital of Brazil's southern state of Paraná, and, until 1989, the city lacked an effective system of solid waste management. Despite Curitiba's reputation as an environmental pioneer, it had no adequate treatment for the 1,070 tons of garbage generated daily. In 1989, however, the city government began to develop a comprehensive plan for treating urban solid waste.

The plan was a multifaceted project involving construction of recycling plants, compost factories, and incinerators to process the different types of waste (i.e., recyclable, organic, and inorganic). Sanitary landfills were constructed—using clay and plastic liners to prevent seepage—for items rejected by the other refuse-treatment processes and for all nonrecyclable materials. By making full use of these facilities, city authorities anticipated that they could lower by over 400 percent the amount of garbage left at landfills daily—from 700 tons to 147 tons.

A second aspect of the Curitiba experience was the development of two new systems for household-refuse collection, both incentive-based and designed to appeal to the public. The "Purchase of Garbage" project is unique in its provision of a token, good for a free bus ride downtown, in exchange for each bag of trash delivered by favela residents and members of neighboring squatter settlements. Perhaps this system's greatest virtue is that it extends regular trash collection to areas where no such services previously existed. Begun in January 1989, the "Purchase of Garbage" system met with noteworthy success during its first months and served over 16,000 families by mid-1990. The second program developed in Curitiba illustrates the vital importance of educating the public about the environment. The "Garbage That Isn't Garbage" project began by providing environmental education to students in the municipal school system. Volunteers costumed as trees visited the city's 110 schools to encourage children to participate in the recycling effort. An illustrated primer, describing the advantages of selective collection, was distributed in the community. Building on this foundation of enhanced public awareness, a dual-strategy collection system for recyclable materials was introduced in October 1989. Recycling bins were installed in supermarkets, where a company then "purchased" the garbage with vouchers valid for use in the supermarkets. Meanwhile, weekly door-to-door collection was instituted using bright green trucks inscribed with the slogan "Garbage That Isn't Garbage."[2]

Today, Curitiba can feel deserving of its reputation as Brazil's "environmental capital" because the city recycles over 100 tons of its trash every day. An even more impressive statistic is the number of residents (over 70 percent) who regularly participate in recycling efforts. When compared with New York, where only 10 to 15 percent of the population recycles consistently (Pedreira and Goodstein 1992), Curitiba shows itself to be not only a "local hero," but also an international precedent-setter.

Vila Madalena, São Paulo

In megacities such as São Paulo, vast urban sprawl has severely hindered the construction of new sanitary landfills. After a frustrating search for alternate solid-waste destinations, São Paulo's Secretariat for Services and Works (a branch of the city government) began a pilot project for selective collection in 1989. This project, which attempted to prolong the life of existing landfills, was identified as a compromise measure. The Vila Madalena neighborhood was considered an appropriate test location for two reasons. First, it is a community recognized for the environmental awareness of its citizens; second, it is located near an old trash incinerator that was due to be deactivated.

Municipal officials in Vila Madalena launched the pilot project by meeting with neighborhood associations and creating a Selective Collection Commission. They enlisted the participation of both residents and municipal representatives. As in Curitiba, information dissemination and public education efforts figured prominently in the project. In July 1989, the commission began a newsletter to publicize the collection effort. Subsequently, a pamphlet (printed on recycled paper) was distributed throughout the neighborhoods. Both publications described the procedures to be adopted in the project and emphasized the importance of citizen contributions to environmental protection.

Vila Madalena's pilot project met with impressive public support and enthusiasm. Over 80 percent of the neighborhood households joined the selective collection effort—a rate comparable to the outstanding environmental programs initiated in Switzerland. Popular receptiveness extended even to community members living beyond the established collection circuit. Residents in these areas joined the effort voluntarily and delivered their household refuse directly to the recycling center. Some residents even volunteered to sort the different recyclable materials.

Vila Madalena's positive results encouraged the city government not only to continue the project bit to extend it to other São Paulo neighborhoods. As it expanded, the project incorporated other arenas; for example, the city government developed subsequent collection and recycling systems for favelas, schools, public offices, and commercial areas.

Favela Monte Azul, São Paulo

A single dumpster in Monte Azul, too small to hold the trash of four hundred households, was located far from the majority of favela residences. A stream flowing near the dumpster became the final resting place for most waste, leading to unsanitary conditions and interrupting water flow.

In February 1989, after consulting with members of the pioneering collection and recycling program in Niteroi, Rio de Janeiro, the São Paulo city government implemented a garbage pickup and recycling project in Monte Azul. The inaugural event was a one-day cleanup of the favela that brought together residents, city government members, and personnel from the Monte Azul Community Association. A door-to-door promotional strategy targeted the fifty residences closest to the target area. During these visits, members of the project team emphasized the importance of cleanliness, hygiene, and public health and explained how the collection process would work before making their appeal for participation.

Households choosing to participate in the selective collection system received plastic receptacles donated by a pharmaceutical company. Participants deposited their household trash into these containers, then took them to a nearby shed and dumped the contents into the larger collection barrels stored there. (Weekly door-to-door pickup of recyclable materials took place in certain areas outside the favela.)

During its first year, the project in Favela Monte Azul enjoyed great success, with over two hundred households participating regularly in selective collection. Moreover, cleanup of the surrounding land and stream improved conditions markedly; for the first time in recent memory, no flooding occurred during the rainy season. An additional, if indirect, achievement of selective collection in Monte Azul was the development of other social and environmental activities, such as the creation of an Office of Artisan Paper, which recycles some of the paper materials collected in the favela.

Integrating the Informal Sector

A common element of these three Brazilian experiences is an effort to incorporate the informal economy, that phenomenon of the Latin American workforce generated by the escalation in urban migration during the recession of the 1980s. As increasing numbers of poor people arrive in the city only to encounter few available jobs in the formal economy, they must devise their own sources of income. Many join the "informal" sector, engaging in unregulated production and employment to survive. This rapidly growing sector provides many of the cheap goods and services essential to the economies, businesses, and consumers of Latin American cities.[3]

One of these services is trash collection. In most Latin American countries, some level of trash collection and recycling has traditionally been carried out by members of the informal sector. In Brazil, these people are called *catadores*. Local governments, overwhelmed by the multitude of problems facing them, have ranked solid waste disposal low on the list of needed public service improvements, thus giving informal-sector operations ample opportunity to collect, sort, recycle, and sell refuse recovered in large cities (Campbell 1989).

For many of Latin America's poor, survival and urban waste are inextricably linked. Informal-sector activities are carried out by small-scale (often family-owned) enterprises that are highly competitive. Those involved in refuse collection are organized in two ways: by "turf"—each person's position on the dumps or in city streets—and by the material he or she collects and recycles. Control of the informal garbage business lies in the hands of established buyers of bulk materials who, in effect, define the work and income opportunities of the poor.

Environmental movements are making concerted efforts to coexist and cooperate with the catadores, working toward the common goals of recycling and reducing garbage. For example, cities limit their collection to a relatively low percentage of total refuse, an arrangement that complements the catadores' activities rather than competing with them or replacing them. A more dramatic tactic has been taken in Vila Madalena by giving legal status to the profession of the catador. This is a significant step, and one that diminishes the possibility that conflicts will erupt between the catadores and municipal garbage workers. By regulating the activity of the catadores, the potential for rivalry and resentments is substantially mitigated.

In designing and implementing new environmental efforts, local planners considered the informal sector in other ways as well. In Vila Madalena, for example, municipality-sponsored efforts have steered clear of the catadores' turf in the local commercial district. This recognition of one group's unofficial, yet clearly established, territory communicates a degree of respect and cooperation crucial to successful and sustained environmental projects.

In Curitiba, all materials collected by the "Garbage That Isn't Garbage" project are donated to the Rural Foundation for Education and Integration (FREI), an agency providing social assistance. FREI recruits indigent persons to take part in the sorting, refurbishing, and sale of the various recyclable materials. Labor-intensive recycling of this kind is an effective way to improve the productive potential of the poor. It also demonstrates ways in which conventional waste collection and disposal methods used in industrialized countries may be modified to address the social dimensions of the waste problem in Latin America.

In observing these new Brazilian developments in solid waste management, one finds an interesting parallel between the recycling of refuse materials and the "social recycling" that occurs with the incorporation of the catadores and other groups operating outside the official economic system. An educational side effect of these initiatives has been an increased use of materials previously undervalued by consumers. For example, in Monte Azul, wheat bran—a product traditionally used solely for animal feed—is the staple ingredient in a highly nutritious bread distributed to participants in selective collection programs. The production of this bread is an attempt to avoid waste. Likewise, the importance placed upon working with the informal sector, street people, and garbage pickers demonstrates a conscious effort to avoid the devaluation of human potential.

The focus on interaction reflects a new way of thinking about Brazil's marginal residents. It acknowledges that these sectors are not exempt from environmental problems—instead they are being called upon to help resolve them. Nor should they be excluded from the benefits that result from combined efforts of this kind. Actions such as the legal recognition of Vila Madalena's catadores demonstrate a disposition for problem solving and a recognition of the need to pursue creative solutions.

All three of the Brazilian projects described demonstrate successful appeals to voluntarism and encouragement of wide popular participation— a resource long ignored by government authorities. Promoting grassroots democracy begins with the invention of new mechanisms to address deep lingering problems, such as garbage.

Shared Responsibility, Greater Mobility: Brazil's "Transportation Fee"

One of the most significant issues facing all urban centers of significant scale is how to design an urban environment that will not demand that we use automobiles as the principal basis for transportation, yet at the same time will meet the need for mobility in those environments.

—*Robert Yuhnke*

A System in Need of Change

In recent surveys evaluating the performance of the mayors of Brazil's state capitals, citizens consistently named inadequate public transportation among the three most serious urban problems. Many factors have contributed to the progressive decline of mass transportation in Brazil. At the forefront is the intense urbanization since the 1970s that has concentrated 60 percent of Brazil's population in metropolitan areas. Brazil has paid a high price for the accelerated expansion of urban centers and for indiscriminate modernization. Regrettably, urbanization was not accompanied by the investment to improve, or even maintain, the marginal quality of transportation services.

A 1987 São Paulo study of the distribution of daily travel revealed a disproportionate reliance on cars and buses, each of which accounted for about 42 percent of daily transportation use. (Secondary forms of transportation accounted for a far less significant amount of total daily travel: trolleys, for example, were used in just 0.7 percent of trips, trains in 4.4 percent, and subway travel in 7.6 percent. The remaining 3.3 percent of daily trips encompassed all other forms of transportation, including taxi, jitney, and motorcycle.) The countless vehicles on the road contribute to Brazil's frustratingly high incidence of traffic jams. Gasoline, diesel, and alcohol emissions intensify the environmental deterioration of metropolitan areas. Clearly, pollution from cars and "dirty" mass transit poses a steadily increasing threat to the quality of life in Brazilian cities.

The overreliance on cars has other consequences on the quality of urban life. To congested roads must be added gasoline shortages and parking and insurance costs—all burdens to automobile users, whose ranks are growing in response to the lack of reliable public transportation. More and more vehicles are entering circulation, many being driven farther than ever before. Unfavorable traffic conditions—backups, jams, and other roadway crises—hurt producers as well by causing slowdowns in the industrial, commercial, and services sectors.

The country's mismanaged and inequitable public transportation system exacerbates Brazil's urbanization and traffic problems. Brazil's highway system consistently receives greater federal investment than do the train and bus systems, resulting in the progressive decay of suburban rail systems, rolling stock, and other equipment. No help can be expected from bus-fare revenues, which today barely cover operating costs. Thus, subsidies must often be drawn from overstressed municipal treasuries, since underemployment and inflation make further fare hikes impracticable.

Users of mass transit are the real victims of this biased policy, which is aggravated by transportation companies' focus on profit maximization. Typical of the abuse riders encounter in São Paulo are overcrowded public buses, which during rush hours carry thirteen people per square meter, an area comparable to the interior of a phone booth. Daily, Brazilian bus riders must submit to conditions almost inconceivable by standards in industrialized countries. Dissatisfaction and frustration among Brazilian public transportation patrons frequently manifest themselves in violence.

Deficient mass transit negatively affects the entire Brazilian economy. In São Paulo, some workers must spend over four hours per day traveling to and from work, a tremendous waste of citizens' time. By reducing the time employees can spend on the job, this protracted commute between home and workplace undercuts the production and circulation of goods and shrinks the labor pool. It also jeopardizes the safety of its patrons by obliging them to commute at late hours or in dangerous areas. In addition, public transportation is very expensive relative to the cost of living and average take-home salaries of Brazilian families, an imbalance aggravated over the past several years. Between 1980 to 1986, bus fares in São Paulo represented about 10 percent of the minimum wage. However, during the national recession (beginning in 1987), minimum wages dropped sharply while bus fares rose. By January 1988, fares claimed about 35 percent of the minimum wage. After a brief decline, a second steep increase occurred during 1990, bringing the percentage back to above 20 percent.

Although users of public transportation live virtually at the mercy of an inefficient and unreliable system, it is the only option for millions. Without it, countless urban and suburban residents would have no access to employment, commercial areas, and social activities.

Planting the Seeds

During the past few years, several Brazilian municipal governments have reached the conclusion that the public transportation system is unsustainable in its current state. Seeking to reverse decades of neglect, these governments have developed new transportation management plans that prioritize collective, rather than individual, modes of transportation. These new policies build upon a vision of mass transportation advocated by Pólis: that of an essential public service—a *right* implicit in the concept of citizenship. As such, mass transport should be assessed not solely on a criterion of profitability, but also in terms of its efficiency, quality of service, and attention to users.

The municipalities designed a set of measures for a process called the "Municipalization of Collective Transportation," whose goals included improving regularity and reliability of bus services, standardizing services and fare schedules, increasing fleet size, balancing profitability among the companies involved, integrating the various systems, and modernizing management of the companies. Further, the "municipalization of transportation" process proposed to direct additional resources to the transportation sector.

Pólis Spearheads the Effort

Pólis agreed that Brazil's public transportation system is rapidly approaching collapse and urged a response that would improve the quality of transportation service while also developing programs for cost sharing. To reach these goals, Pólis identified new financing sources for the growth and improvement of municipal mass transportation systems. One such source is the "transportation fee," a concept developed by Pólis. Designed to distribute the cost of public transportation in a more equitable fashion, this fee incorporates an innovative cost-sharing arrangement between the public and private sectors. In essence, businesses pay a special fee (whose amount varies depending on several factors) to the municipal government, which uses this revenue to help maintain and restructure local transportation activities.

The rationale for the creation of a transportation fee rested on the argument that public bus service represents a production input for economic infrastructure, as do water, electricity, and similar public utilities. Thus, Pólis argued, it is only fair that business establishments located in the municipality should share responsibility for improving and expanding services.

The transportation-fee project drew inspiration from a similar initiative undertaken in France during the 1970s, when economic activities in the greater Paris area generated such demand for mass transportation that new investments by the state became necessary (Caccia Bava 1991). Because contributions from the commercial, industrial, and services sectors were insufficient to support the concomitant rise in maintenance costs, French citizens' tax payments were, in effect, subsidizing private enterprise. A new fee (the *versement transport*) was proposed to remedy this distorted situation, giving the region's entrepreneurial sector joint responsibility for investments in transportation. Calculated according to a percentage of company income, revenue from the versement transport was invested primarily in infrastructure and equipment that would improve the metropolitan transportation system. As a desired standard of quality was attained, the fee would be gradually redirected to subsidize fares.

Brazilian planners and technocrats had taken interest in the French fee since its introduction in the 1970s. However, not until the Constitution of 1988 could the mechanism be replicated in their own country. Provisions of the constitution empowered municipalities to establish new taxes for the first time, placing exclusive responsibility for public bus services in the hands of municipal administrators. It was declared a municipal obligation to "organize and provide, directly or by issuing licenses or permits, public services of local interest, including collective transport" (Caccia Bava 1991: 2). Although the new constitution allocated a 30 percent boost in resources for Brazilian municipalities, a host of other responsibilities fell to them simultaneously—leaving insufficient funds to significantly upgrade the bus system. Another obstacle to swift reform were the needs of other long-neglected and more traditional public service areas, such as health and education, that competed for municipal attention.

Although it understood the extent of these difficulties, Pólis also recognized that the enhanced authority of municipal governments after 1988 created an opportunity for change. After undertaking feasibility studies, Pólis arrived at an adaptation of the French versement transport model that would suit Brazil's national context, yet remain consistent with Brazilian legislation.

The transportation fee, proposed in 1989, is a charge for transportation services levied upon legally recognized entities in each municipality. Applied to organizations from the business, industry, and services sectors, the fee varies according to the number of employees in each company. (Those companies with fewer than ten employees are exempt, as these account for a very small segment of the urban labor force. This exception reduces administrative expenses for fee collection and regulation.)

Since the overall project must fit the specific needs of each municipality, Pólis undertakes special social and economic studies to determine the amount charged to each local business. Such studies clarify the ability of individual companies to pay based on the size of their payrolls and sales totals, in order to make the fee as easily absorbed as possible.

One of the most valuable aspects of the transportation fee is that its revenues may be used only to improve and expand the municipal bus system. In this sense, these funds are tied; they cannot be transferred to any other area, despite the priorities established by the municipal government. The transportation fee project specifically stipulates that its revenues should be fully applied to three areas: (1) infrastructure (i.e., roadways, terminals, vehicle storage, signs and traffic lights, and equipment procurement); (2) planning and management, including a program to conserve gasoline and to gradually convert to a methane-burning fleet; and (3) ongoing inspection and monitoring of the system.

By establishing these areas as priorities to be financed by the transportation fee, Pólis created a comprehensive instrument that could radically transform the mass transit system. The city of Campinas offers an idea of the substantial resources that may be garnered through the fee; revenues there were estimated at U.S.$8 million in 1991.

A final provision of the transportation fee, designed to expand democratic participation in municipal administration and to ease potential conflicts, was the establishment of a Municipal Transportation Council. This council brings together workers, entrepreneurs, public transportation users, and representatives of the mayor's office to analyze and deliberate on the use of revenues from the fee. The establishment of this council was intended to guarantee that both present and future municipal administrators will involve civil society in the planning and monitoring of public transit services.

Pólis enlisted the support of several municipal administrators who were willing to test this adaptation of France's versement transport. As expected, implementation of the taxa transporte was controversial and involved confrontation with the opposing private-sector lobbies. Members of the affected businesses vehemently objected to this new fee, the burden of which would fall largely on their shoulders. Unable to deny the social significance of the project, they argued that the bill proposing the fee was unconstitutional. A legal battle ensued between these business interests and the alliance of organized popular groups and municipal administrators.

The dispute over the fee continues today; however, Pólis has assumed an active role in the negotiations that will determine its future. Pólis holds periodic meetings with municipal authorities, labor unions, neighborhood associations, and industrial and business interests throughout Brazil, using consciousness-raising as its primary weapon in the struggle to implement the taxa transporte. Pólis's goal is to convince employers that they have a considerable stake in improved public transportation and may, in fact, benefit more than their workers.

Pólis remains optimistic that the transportation fee will enjoy greater acceptance in the future, noting that resistance and skepticism are currently exacerbated by Brazil's deep recession. The country's roughly 4,500 municipalities provide ample ground for experimentation with this innovative mechanism.

Despite the controversy, several municipalities introduced legislation during 1990 in favor of the transportation fee. Bills were approved in Campinas and Diadema, where the fee now functions as law, and fell short of approval by just one vote in Santo André. The two approvals set a precedent, paving the way for other municipalities to present similar legislation. The transportation fee has also sparked discussion in Brazil's National Public Transportation Association.

Pólis argues that the potential advantages of the transportation fee extend well beyond its initial objective of expanding resources for municipal mass transit. The fee also serves as an instrument through which financing for the transportation sector may be revamped. It enables the reallocation of public resources earmarked for the sector by drawing a distinction between resources for investment and those to be used for subsidizing fares. According to Pólis, even currently recalcitrant business interests will profit from the transportation fee. Once it has established a system of regular contributions by members of the affected sectors, the fee will expand the radius of labor recruitment and improve accessibility for both consumers and suppliers.

To help stimulate improved transportation service, Pólis recommends that municipalities provide incentives to businesses in the form of benefits, or "preferential treatment." For example, Pólis suggests fee discounts to firms that reduce rush-hour traffic by offering flexible work schedules. Also rewarded would be businesses that provide their employees with housing at or near the work site, thus reducing the flow of bus riders during peak commuting hours. These discounts, negotiated directly between city mayors and firm representatives, can reduce individual fees by up to 20 percent.

Polis's pragmatism and adaptability were fundamental to its development of the transportation fee. If its involvement in the dissemination of creative environmental initiatives through *Inovação Urbana* demonstrated Pólis' role as an "information broker," its more direct participation in the transportation issue highlights its importance as an advocacy unit.

The transportation fee also points to the value of adapting ideas and technology. While France's versement transport could not be duplicated precisely, it provided the necessary groundwork for what was to become a distinctly Brazilian mechanism. Throughout the adaptation, Pólis performed the indispensable role of "bridge-builder," identifying a valuable experience and adjusting it to the national context. Ideas and technology are abundant; by adapting, revising, and "recycling" those that are successful, administrators and planners can effectively address certain of their own problems.

Pólis's activities, combining the close monitoring of governmental actors with attention to public awareness, exemplify the way GSOs can bridge the gulf between government and civil society. Informed citizens are more likely to hold government accountable for services and attention. If collaboration between government and civil society takes root, citizens' expectations from authorities should likewise increase. Perhaps we can look forward to a time when government accountability will become less of a rarity and more of an expectation in Latin America.

"Think Globally, Act Locally . . ."

In downtown Washington, D.C., Rio de Janeiro, and Mexico City, bumper stickers, banners, and T-shirts emblazoned with this slogan make a unified, dramatic appeal. They urge greater public recognition of the fact that local crises—garbage piles in São Paulo, dilapidated buses in Campinas, smog in Mexico City and Los Angeles—are symptoms of a critical situation. Democratizing countries can best address these issues through parallel efforts at national and local levels.

Latin America's central governments must assume responsibility for the redefinition of economic and environmental goals and priorities. Truly sustainable development will begin only with the generation of positive incentives for change. The state must also provide the infrastructure necessary to deliver organizational, economic, and technical options to confront the critical challenges affecting each country individually and the region as a whole.

As national governments work toward a worldwide environmental consensus, local authorities must assume equal responsibility for protecting the health of their own citizens and ecological systems. Certainly, the proximity of local entities to the sources of ecological destruction gives them a stake in finding solutions to these problems. A local environmental campaign should take advantage of existing resources. For example, international instruments for the control of air and water contamination remain to be implemented locally. A global-to-local adaptation of these instruments would reinforce their validity at all levels.

Brazilian joint ventures in solid waste and transportation management suggest that the global-local dialogue should work both ways. We might, in fact, try inverting our bumper-sticker exhortation as we consider the options available to policymakers in democratizing Latin America. Perhaps global thinking, paired with local action, should not be our sole strategy. Thinking and observing locally might also provide new ideas and instruments through which global actions can be undertaken in a more responsible and effective manner. The Pólises of the world, in the business of moving ideas in and out of contexts, are teaching us that "global" and "local" are best thought of as complementary spheres of action.

Much can be learned from local-level initiatives such as those promoted by Pólis. Their example is not only valid for other countries' local managers but may also be understood in a broader context. One of the most valuable lessons to be drawn from Brazil's pioneering solid-waste initiatives and Pólis's transportation fee is the value of partnerships and associations.

Associations can be formed at many levels, bringing together spheres often considered adversarial, such as "public" and "private." In the transportation sector, for example, the purchase of buses is frequently a private-sector function. Yet, buses must operate according to standards set by the public sector. Genuine coresponsibility between public and private will involve private entities accepting public-sector rules of operation and monitoring.

Through the creation of partnerships between the public and independent sectors, efforts to save the environment or to improve public transportation might serve concurrently as instruments by which to strengthen democracy. One instrument conducive to this cooperation is the establishment of local councils. These serve as forums where local authorities, representatives of the business community, government organizations, and interested citizens can meet to work together on global and local problems. By expanding the network of concern for such issues, associations of this kind can play a key role in the adjustment of priorities and the redistribution of vital resources.

Finally, civil society has a significant role to play in building associations, and local authorities should be encouraged to pursue relationships at this level. Municipal governments are best positioned to foment the public participation essential to sustained development. The solid-waste initiatives in Curitiba, Vila Madalena, and Monte Azul show how local officials can stimulate environmental consciousness.

Effective community mobilization already exists in Latin America. Membership organizations, cooperatives and neighborhood associations, and social movements of the poor work toward the evolution of a new ethic. Along with Pólis, they emphasize shared responsibility for local conditions and heightened expectations from government. Public authorities at all levels should recognize and value the energy, vitality, and innovative capacity of independent groups and organizations. If these forces can be channeled in a productive way, civil society may prove to be a key contributor to democratic policymaking.

It may be some time, however, before favela residents feel a trickle-down effect from these new forms of collaboration. Willingness to trust and accept input from Latin America's poor is still only a glimmer in the distant future. However, new associations and joint ventures are beginning the process and, at the very least, serve as a reminder that justice and equity are within reach of all Latin Americans. The possibilities for progress and constructive change are endless when different perspectives, outlooks, and priorities unite in a common interest.

Notes

1. Paulo Sergio Muçouçah's article, "A coleta seletiva do lixo" (*Inovação Urbana,* no. 1, October 1990), provided a comprehensive assessment of the solid-waste initiatives in Curitiba, Vila Madalena, and Favela Monte Azul, and was indispensable to the research for this chapter.

2. Curitiba's current mayor, Jaime Lerner, was one of a group of Brazilian urbanists who brought environmental consciousness and balanced development to the fore during the early 1960s—deviating from the trend toward construction of tall buildings, highways, and subways. The numerous programs implemented during Lerner's three-term administration demonstrate his philosophy of linking environmental and social policy. Among his achievements is an efficient and rapid bus system, featuring a system of express lanes exclusively for buses, which has dramatically reduced automobile use and traffic congestion.

3. The "informal sector," a term originally elaborated in International Labor Organization publications from the early 1970s, was popularized in Hernando de Soto's study of the underground Peruvian economy, *The Other Path: The Invisible Revolution in the Third World* (1986). The term is now approaching common usage in the study of Latin American social sciences. For further discussion of the informal economy, see de Soto as well as Alejandro Portes' *The Informal Economy: Studies in Advanced and Less Developed Countries* (1989).

◆◆

7

Chilean NGOs: Forging a Role in the Transition to Democracy

BRIAN LOVEMAN

State and Society in Chile

Throughout most of its political history Chile has been a highly state-centered society, with the direction, character, and limits of private initiative defined by government policies. Wealth and power converged in Santiago, the nation's political capital and principal metropolis, despite the fact that Chile's principal exports and main economic activities were generated elsewhere—the central valley, the southern agricultural provinces, and the deserts of the north.

Over time, an expanding political and administrative system also concentrated social and economic opportunities in Santiago, especially for professionals, academics, technicians, and political elites. Even entrepreneurs and business executives depended on government-created opportunities and policies. Financial, agricultural, and industrial activities responded to a panoply of government subsidies, loans, currency manipulation, and protectionist tariff policies.

In such a climate, public enterprises and those financed or stimulated by government programs played an ever larger role in Chilean economic life. By 1970, the public sector accounted for some 70 percent of all investment in Chile; government policies in the form of tariffs, multiple exchange rates, subsidized credit, tax credits, and other nonmarket interventions structured the shape and composition of the Chilean economy.

From 1970 to 1973, a coalition government headed by Dr. Salvador Allende, Latin America's first elected Marxist president, attempted to take Chile down the Chilean road to socialism. Theirs was a comprehensive program of political, economic, and social change intended to transform the fundamental character of Chilean society. Three years under Allende's

119

Popular Unity coalition intensified the central role of the state in Chilean daily life and led to extreme political polarization. Finally, government and opposition forces, finding themselves unable to patch together even a short-term truce, propelled Chile toward a political and human catastrophe of tragic dimensions, the military coup of 1973.

The Coup

In mid-September of 1973, claiming that politics and politicians had betrayed the Fatherland and allowed Marxists to gain control of the Chilean state, General Augusto Pinochet, who gradually consolidated his personal control over a new Chilean dictatorship, affirmed that "reality has laid bare the inadequacy of the concept of liberty as understood by classic liberalism" and that it was essential "to deny the enemy access to the control of the mass media, universities, [and] trade unions" and to recognize that "human rights . . . are, without exception, subject to the restrictions imposed upon them by the common good" (Loveman and Davies 1989).

During the next three years there followed a systematic attack upon persons, organizations, institutions, and political traditions—a *junta* tactic to destroy the "vices of the past," construct a new political order, and "banish forever the inveterate habits which are an inevitable consequence of the excesses which Chilean partisanship brought down upon itself during various generations" (Loveman and Davies 1989). The attack upon ex–Popular Unity supporters, other opponents of the military junta, and the institutional apparatus of liberal democracy took the form of wholesale murder, imprisonment, mistreatment and torture of detainees, "disappearances," and political exile, among other manifestations of state terror and intimidation.[1]

The new regime "legitimated" these patterns of personal and collective repression with a series of decrees, institutional innovations, and "constitutional acts" that, taken together, eliminated the possibility of legal/organized opposition to the military government. As conventionally understood, democratic participation was to a great extent outlawed: political party activity was banned or suspended, and the activities of unions, community organizations, and many other associations were controlled or repressed by the government. The network of NGOs, however, gradually expanded.

Chilean NGOs: History and Development Prior to 1973

Although the NGO sector mushroomed in response to junta policies after the coup, important historical and institutional foundations for such pursuits already existed in Chile. These strong (if not extensive) foundations provided a basis for the initial NGO activity after 1973. Likewise, the experience of pre-1973 NGOs in rural areas and among the urban poor offered personal and institutional contacts, models for charitable and development programs, and a certain *legitimacy* for social-action projects that preceded the conflicts of the late 1960s and early 1970s.

Since colonial times, religiously inspired NGOs had played a vital but limited role in Chilean society; charitable, emergency, health care, and educational institutions of the Catholic church were a common feature of Chilean life. In the first decades of the twentieth century, newly founded institutions dedicated to informal education, technical assistance, and service provision among the rural and urban poor served as precedents for the rapid NGO expansion after the mid-1970s.

Generated by initiatives of the Catholic church around 1915, and to a lesser extent by a variety of Protestant missions (for example, Methodist Rural Missions in the 1920s), worker and peasant cooperatives, mutual aid societies, small centers for popular education, and more politicized adjuncts of labor and political parties were woven into the Chilean social fabric—in both countryside and urban areas (Affonso et al. 1970, and Landsberger and Canitrot 1967).

It is difficult to overestimate the role of the Catholic church as a social and political force in modern Chilean history. This is particularly true in the formation of intellectual and political elites committed to social change in accord with emergent church social doctrine. In these efforts were spawned some of the first NGOs and GSOs; these same efforts forged the resistance to dictatorship in the 1970s and the NGO umbrella of the 1980s.

In 1915, the Reverend Julio Restat and two students, Eduardo Cruz Coke and Emilio Tizzoni, founded the National Association of Catholic Students as an elite group to study and incorporate the social gospel into Chilean life. Parallel development of study circles on social themes presaged similar study circles at the Academy of Christian Humanism supported by the church after 1976.[2] By 1928, under the influence of Oscar Larson, these organizations formed a cadre of Catholic-inspired leaders who would become dominant figures in Chilean political life, first in the Conservative party and then within the Christian Democratic party.

In the midst of the political and economic crises accompanying the depression of the 1930s, the church founded Catholic Action—ostensibly following the dictates of Pope Pius XI's encyclical "Ubi Arcano Dei" (1922). Catholic Action gained its inspiration from social catholicism and fear of socialism and absorbed earlier church organizations such as the study circles. It also created new GSOs through its secretariats, including the Secretariat of Social and Economic Activities. Over time, this church agency provided support and orientation for youth, worker, and peasant organizations and for organizations, dedicated to finding solutions to the "social question."

By the 1930s, Conservative party landowners were protesting the activities of a small number of priests who had formed agricultural unions. Industrialists, who decried church support for worker organizations, also objected. Nevertheless, small-scale church involvement in GSOs continued, if with setbacks and controversy. In the late 1940s and early 1950s, a rural union organization called Chilean Sindical Action gained the support of church leaders in Talca province and provoked a regionwide strike that culminated in a march on Santiago in 1953. A year earlier, the Chilean Conference of Bishops had decided to create a separate entity, Catholic Rural Action (ACR), as a response both to increased Protestant penetration into the countryside and to expanded political activities by the Chilean left. ACR established small centers in rural towns and farms to promote "community development."

In 1955, as part of this effort, ACR established the Institute for Rural Education (IER), a prototype NGO that has survived to the present. Since its founding, the IER has been a dominant force in training leadership cadres for peasant unions, cooperatives, and production centers, carrying out a wide range of formal and informal education and technical support activities. The IER publishes technical and doctrinal materials, engages in educational radio broadcasting, and, more generally, acts as a multifunctional rural-oriented NGO. Through the years, it has received financial and other support from international agencies, from entities of the U.S. government, and from the church. The IER has also sought cooperation from progressive landowners to support education services among the rural labor force.

In many respects, the IER was a forerunner of future church-supported and secular NGOs working in the countryside and/or researching rural issues. In 1963, Cardinal Raúl Silva Henríquez and Bishop Manuel Larraín Errázuriz sponsored the Institute for Agricultural Promotion (INPROA), which carried out experiments in land reform, agricultural cooperativism, and technical assistance in the rural sector. INPROA continued its work from the 1960s through the period of military dictatorship to the present day and expanded its activities to include a wide range of extension and direct-assistance programs among rural workers and smallholders. Unlike the Institute for Rural Education, INPROA relied entirely on private donations and external assistance, thereby avoiding allegations of subordination to the Pinochet government due to financial dependence (Barria and de la Cuadra 1989; and Thiesenhusen 1966).

Cáritas/Chile, another church-related NGO, also carried out rural-oriented programs during this period. However, in the rural sector as in most other areas of work, the NGO/GSO was a relatively rare entity in Chile prior to the 1960s. Thus, Sergio Gómez (1989) reports that only eight NGOs of the sixty-one working in rural areas in 1988 were established prior to 1973. A similar pattern prevailed for the 123 NGOs working in social action and urban-development programs in Santiago, Valparaíso, Concepción, and Iquique studied by Irene Agurto and Carlos Piña in 1988, and for the 107

NGOs with health programs studied in 1989 by Judith Salinas, Carlos Vergara, and Giorgio Solimano (Salinas 1989).

The Catholic church and church-related entities also supported formation of the most prominent nongovernmental research and research-based social action centers in the 1950s and 1960s. These included the Jesuit Belarmino Center, Institute of Christian Humanism, Center for Social Development in Latin America, Center for Educational Research and Development, Corporation for University Promotion, and Latin American Institute for Doctrine and Research. Most other serious research took place in universities and certain government agencies prior to 1973. While precedents existed for NGO activity in secular research organizations, such facilities were rare. However, the military coup and the repression that followed would change this social reality and stimulate a dramatic expansion of Chilean NGOs.

Private Organizations and the Coup

Political and armed resistance to the dictatorship, although never entirely suppressed, could not overcome the new regime or force it to modify its radical policy initiatives. However, complex patterns of personal and organizational adaptation emerged and gave rise to important networks of subsistence and community organizations among the urban and rural poor. Likewise, there evolved a web of private (nongovernmental) associations dedicated to a variety of socioeconomic "development" functions.

Grassroots Organizations

After sixteen years of dictatorship dedicated to purging Chilean life of "politics," the ultimate failure of the military junta's policies and programs in the political sphere could be seen in the fact that not only had all significant existing political movements and organizations survived the repression of the dictatorship, but also new political forces and a multiplicity of new *types* of organizations had come into being. Among these were a vast array of grassroots efforts focusing upon issues of daily subsistence—nutrition, health care, employment, and housing—and supporting projects such as community kitchens, cooperative purchasing, urban gardening, and various forms of informal cooperation among poor households. Researchers in Chile identified five general types of subsistence organizations:

- Small production units
- Associations of unemployed looking for work and/or relief
- Consumer organizations that included buying cooperatives and cooking and eating collectives

- Housing associations (groups seeking shelter, housing, and housing services)
- Interest groups (organizations seeking to provide or improve basic services such as health care, education, and local recreational opportunities)

By 1986, one study of the Santiago metropolitan region had identified some 1,400 "subsistence organizations" (Razeto 1983; Sánchez 1987; Jansana 1989).

Generically called popular economic organizations, these grassroots associations buffered urban and rural poor people to some extent from the impoverishment that accompanied the military junta's radical restructuring of the Chilean economy. As local organizations that brought people together to meet common needs and solve urgent human problems, the popular organizations inevitably went beyond carrying out narrow functional tasks; in some cases, they served as the only "legitimate" social outlet for people subject to economic misfortune and political repression.

Community and neighborhood associations, including the subsistence organizations, formed a basis for new social and community networks. They also represented potential bases for alternative political responses by poor people within the context of a dictatorship prohibiting party, union, and other associational life. Frequently, they depended upon material and organizational support from development organizations or grassroots support organizations linked to the Catholic church, other religious organizations, or other nongovernmental organizations.

NGOs

The "first generation" of postcoup NGOs (1973–1976) emerged to support these subsistence and community organizations and to work in the area of human rights. From 1974 to 1976, a small number of academic research centers, typically sheltered and/or supported in part by the church, emerged as well and initiated a number of activities. Of these centers, the most important was the Academy of Christian Humanism, created in November 1975 with the support of Cardinal Raúl Silva Henríquez. The AHC ultimately served as an umbrella for a variety of research and action programs.

Between 1976 and 1979, a second generation of human-rights, academic, and action-oriented NGOs arose that tested the limits of junta tolerance and experimented with organizational forms, financing alternatives, and programmatic focus. It is significant that most of the pre-1973 NGOs—including institutions like the Institute of Rural Education, the Institute for Agricultural Promotion, Cáritas, and Evangelical Christian Assistance—adapted to the changed circumstances of the period from 1973 to 1980 and maintained or enhanced support programs for urban and rural poor.

A third generation of NGOs appeared and rapidly multiplied after adoption (1980) and implementation (1981) of the new political constitution. Taking advantage of the regime's "opening" of the economy and emphasis on privatization of social and economic programs, this third generation diversified the functional, programmatic, and geographic reach of the Chilean NGOs (Abalos 1987; Jiménez et al. 1989). Third-generation NGOs included new human-rights organizations, academic and research centers, and GSOs whose services included health and nutritional education, technical assistance in rural and urban settings, and training for union leadership.

From 1983 onward, many NGOs also served informally as nuclei of more overt political opposition to the Pinochet government, thereby occupying temporarily part of the "political space" historically reserved to political parties and movements, voluntary associations, and trade unions—all of which suffered repression and restriction by the military government.

NGOs multiplied as professionals, intellectuals, technicians, former government officials, and (ultimately) returned political exiles created literally hundreds of research institutes, extension and educational "firms," and more specialized purveyors of technical and human services. In some cases, groups of academics or former government officials reconstituted entities that had been cast off from the universities or public sector.[3] In other cases, institutions previously supported by international organizations were transformed into "national" NGOs out of political necessity.[4] During these years, international agencies such as the Economic Commission for Latin America, the International Labor Organization, and other United Nations or regional entities also sheltered Chilean professionals and political refugees who would later return and participate in the NGO community during the 1980s.

Usually, however, like-minded professionals or academics formed new research and social action entities that sought to establish a thematic, methodological, and programmatic niche within the expanding NGO universe. Ideological affinity coupled with professional and technical training tended to define the individual NGO—although an important lesson of the 1970–1973 period and of the harsh times that followed was the value of pragmatism and efficacy.

A significant number of NGOs were dedicated specifically to improving the immediate or long-term living conditions and opportunities for the poorest sectors of Chilean society. These groups constituted an NGO subsector that might be labeled, following L. David Brown (1979), as "private voluntary organizations dedicated to development" or, less formally, as "grassroots support organizations." While sharing many attributes of traditional charitable and/or relief agencies or organizations dedicated to social action programs, the NGOs and GSOs in Chile after 1973 tended to have other specific characteristics:

- They were formed as private-sector firms, nonprofit organizations, or semiautonomous, church-related research centers or action agencies, or as cooperatives financed to varying degrees by donations from national or international agencies.[5]
- They were staffed by paid professionals and technicians seeking alternative employment that provided scope for their dedication to social action and community development while allowing them to make a living within the context of the dictatorship's persecution of opposition intellectuals and party leaders.
- They planned and implemented research or action programs and/or projects intended to improve the living conditions of Chile's urban and rural poor and to encourage long-term socioeconomic development.
- They served as "bridge" organizations and catalysts in development programs linking groups of urban and rural poor to national and international financial-support networks; they served, also, as providers of concrete goods and services. (In some cases, this meant filling gaps left by government repression directed at political parties, labor organizations, and other local community groups.)

Notwithstanding these temporary functions, the NGOs do not claim to represent their constituents or clientele as a traditional political party or to make demands upon government and nongovernment actors (e.g., business) as a lobby, labor union, or interest group. (Exceptions to this general rule would be NGOs working in human rights and legal services, or entities dedicated to influencing the content and implementation of public policy while conducting research or providing services—for example, environmentally focused NGOs.) Unlike religious organizations, NGOs do not typically seek converts.

Viewed with hindsight, a certain irony characterizes NGO evolution during this period because those working in the areas of human rights and charitable relief, as well as with the early academic centers and the later GSOs, were largely staffed by people who had favored a state-centered, government-directed transformation of Chilean society. Most of the early post-1973 organizations were formed out of desperation to confront government repression or official policies—momentary responses to the available political space and to the reality of human needs unmet by public-sector programs. The NGO was a tactical instrument adopted as a survival strategy, with little theoretical rationale or long-term commitment to nongovernmental response to the challenge of socioeconomic development.

Only later did the survival strategies generate a more reasoned and permanent commitment to the NGO role, premised on theoretical arguments regarding democratic development and local initiative, as well as on the diverse practical experiences of the years after 1973. Committed socialists and revolutionaries, as well as Christian Democrats and "nonpolitical" religious, viewed NGOs as a way to ameliorate the effects of government policies and to adapt to enforced privatization schemes and the reduction of government programs.

From these experiences participants gained a conscious recognition of the importance and potential of private initiatives in social and economic development—particularly in local and community settings. The freedom from bureaucratic regulation, the need for creativity, spontaneity, and efficacy, and the consequences of failure—for themselves and their clientele—conspired to produce a heterogeneous pattern of pragmatic adaptations and socioeconomic experiments in neighborhoods, communities, rural areas, and (less frequently) entire regions. Professionals and intellectuals who had previously looked to the state as *the* appropriate agent to direct socioeconomic development now defended private action, local initiative, and diversity and experimentation in preference to their former reliance on centralized policy and administration.

What followed constituted a complex privatization of social and economic development experiments, popular education, and social welfare programs—as well as an elaborate network of private agencies and firms previously of limited significance in Chile. By 1990, as General Pinochet's regime neared its end, Chilean civil society was more complex, more variegated, and in many respects more talented, specialized, competent, and innovative than at any time in Chilean history.

Human Rights NGOs

Certain NGOs, usually those associated with the Catholic church and other religious organizations, constituted a significant response to the brutal repression that followed the coup of 1973. Inasmuch as the military government sought to avoid an explicit break with the church, organizations that were associated with the church or were part of the church's own networks escaped some of the formal restrictions on meetings and the censorship of publications applied to unions, political parties, or community organizations. Although this did not mean freedom from harassment or persecution, it did provide a unique, if ambiguous, political space within the authoritarian regime that allowed a small number of human-rights groups and other NGOs focused on social action and relief programs to operate during the early years of the dictatorship.

By the end of September 1973, a group of Protestant organizations had established the National Committee to Aid Refugees to assist foreign nationals in Chile who were affected by the coup.[6] In October of that year, the Committee for Cooperation for Peace (COPACHI) was inaugurated under the formal leadership of two bishops, one a Lutheran and one a Catholic (the auxiliary Bishop of Santiago). These organizations, both of which later changed their names and expanded their functions, provided legal assistance, shelter, and economic relief to victims of government repression.

COPACHI encompassed a highly ecumenical membership and constituency, both religiously and politically; eventually, government attacks and accusations of Marxist influence led to arrest and harassment of religious and lay personnel and, ultimately, to COPACHI's "dissolution" in 1975. General Pinochet involved himself directly in the attack upon COPACHI, revoking Lutheran Bishop Frenz's residency permit for Chile and communicating directly to Cardinal Silva Henríquez the government's anger at COPACHI's activities.

To replace COPACHI and bring its legal, socioeconomic, and "relief" activities under closer church control, Cardinal Silva created the Vicariate of Solidarity in 1976. The vicariate became one of Chile's leading moral and political forces in the area of human rights and in the support of organizations delivering health, nutrition, informal education, and legal services.

With the departure of most foreign refugees and the fulfillment of its mission, associates of the National Committee to Aid Refugees (CONAR) created the Christian Social Assistance Foundation in 1975, which received support from the World Council of Churches and was linked with the United Nations High Commissioner for Refugees. The Foundation assisted exiles, victims of political repression, and their families; it initiated pioneer studies and psychological services for political prisoners, torture victims, and their families and extended financial assistance to refugee and detainee families. These human rights organizations stood as a somewhat permeable umbrella raised by the church and other allies to shelter Chileans during the early years of the reign of terror.

After 1976, a number of new NGOs dedicated to human rights appeared, each with a unique focus and objective. These organizations included the Service for Peace and Justice, founded in 1977 as a Chilean affiliate of the overall Latin American organization; the Chilean Human Rights Commission (1978); Protection of Children Affected by States of Emergency (1979); the Committee for the Defense of the People's Rights (1980), a more politicized and leftist NGO; the Center for Treatment of Stress (1986), which provided assistance to victims of torture,[7] and the Latin American Institute for Mental Health and Human Rights (1988).[8]

Certain specialized membership organizations also evolved during this period, acting as traditional interest groups or "lobbying" organizations, given the limitations of such a term within the context of radical authoritarian regimes. These groups included the Association of Relatives of Political Prisoners (1974); the Association of Relatives of Detained and Disappeared (1975); the Association of Relatives of Political Executees (1979); and the Sebastián Acevedo Movement Against Torture (1983). These latter organizations, lacking the professional mission and organizational formality of most of the NGOs, tended to appear or expand their activities in the early to mid-1980s as limited political spaces opened up within the political system.

Academic-, Research-, and Development-Oriented NGOs

The junta established military control over the universities (including the Catholic University) after targeting them as centers of Marxist and leftist ideologies and thus dangerous sources of opposition. Thousands of students and hundreds of professors were expelled and, for survival, forced to seek refuge in nonacademic endeavors. Many were detained or jailed; some were murdered, executed, or "disappeared," while others fled into exile.

As he did for the human rights NGOs, Cardinal Raúl Silva Henríquez played a central role in establishing a limited sphere of "protected" action for small numbers of academics confronted by loss of employment and professional freedom. In November 1975, the Cardinal established the Academy of Christian Humanism (AHC) as a response to military intervention in the Catholic University. The Academy provided employment and protection to selected academics, encouraged research in the social sciences, prevented the flight or exile of certain leading Chilean intellectuals, and focused on policy problems stemming from military rule—particularly in the areas of education, nutrition, health, housing, and the economy. Funding came first from the Ford Foundation and later from a large number of external donors that included the Inter-American Foundation, International Research Development Centre (Canada), Swedish Agency for Research Cooperation with Developing Countries, Netherlands Organization for International Development Cooperation, and Institute for Iberian-American Cooperation (Spain), as well as other European governments and private donor agencies.

The AHC commenced operations with three small programs and a handful of investigators; by 1989, the individual NGOs associated with the AHC employed almost two hundred professionals, maintained many high-quality research and extension programs, and published numerous books, magazines, technical bulletins, newsletters, and educational materials. Some of the NGOs maintained important linkages with subsistence organizations and with other NGOs as well (see Table 7.1).

Over time, the AHC became affiliated with a number of preexisting research groups—for example, the Interdisciplinary Program for Educational Research, one of the most important groups working on educational research in Chile.[9] Other programs evolved out of AHC-sponsored study circles—seminar groups focused on particular topics or policy areas such as health, women's issues, and the environment. Still others were newly formed but typically reunited small cadres of investigators who had worked with the same themes or in similar programs during the Popular Unity years.

Table 7.1   Number of Researchers at the Academy of Christian Humanism
(1981–1987)

Program	1981	1982	1983	1984	1985	1986	1987
Center for Contemporary Studies (CERC)	—	—	6	13	16	22	21
Agroregional Studies Group (GEA)	7	6	6	14	15	22	34
Agrarian Research Group (GIA)	19	19	28	22	25	35	22
Labor Economics Program (PET)	11	13	17	16	25	30	28
Study Circle on the Condition of Women	16	16	26	10	—	—	—
Interdisciplinary Program for Educational Research (PIIE)	19	14	22	15	21	25	17
Human Rights Program (PDH)	3	7	5	3	3	11	8
University Bulletin Project	2	2	2	2	2	—	—
Latin American Faculty of Social Sciences (FLACSO)	21	21	24	29	29	29	29
Transnational Institute of Latin American Studies	5	5	12	14	17	11	11
Total	103	103	148	138	153	185	170

Source: Memoria de Actividades AHC 1981, 1982, 1983, 1984, 1985, 1986, 1987. The data not include research assistants and students. After Maria Teresa Lladser LL, in José Antonio Abalos and Rodrigo Egaña, *Una puerta que se abre,* Taller de Cooperación al Desarrollo, 1989.

The AHC served essentially as an institutional umbrella, with each NGO program seeking its own funding and maintaining relative organizational and programmatic autonomy. Internal conflicts were not always avoided, and ideological or programmatic differences between church authorities and study circles could lead to breaking of ties. For example, the Study Circle on the Condition of Women lost its AHC sponsorship in 1984 over issues relating to abortion, divorce, and sexuality. Divisions within this circle gave rise to two separate NGOs: the Center for Women's Studies, which remained more research oriented, and the Women's House (*La Morada*), which assumed the character of a Chilean feminist group.

This pattern in some ways typified the growing NGO universe after 1981, with new organizations defining themselves according to spheres of action (urban or rural); policy areas (health, nutrition, environment, housing, labor, artisan production, and education); subjects of study or target populations (women, youth, and ethnic minorities); or dominant activities (research, technical assistance, and health services).[10]

To some extent, donor pressures for more action-oriented "development" projects pushed NGOs to expand their activities beyond the earlier emphasis on research. Growing specialization, refinement of organizational niches, and competition for resources and recognition came to characterize the NGO network. Thus, Arteaga's study of NGOs working on women's issues found eighty-seven NGOs dealing with "women's issues" and seven NGOs composed of "women that work almost exclusively with women" (Arteaga and Largo 1989). These organizations ranged from essentially academic research centers such as the Center for Women's Studies to groups working with subsistence organizations and delivering technical training, marketing assistance, and organizational support to production cooperatives in poor neighborhoods. After 1981, all of these NGOs were created as independent organizations (Arteaga and Largo 1989).

In the late 1980s, as Chileans anticipated an end to the Pinochet regime, the AHC was transformed formally into a small university independent of the church, and some of the NGOs went their own way. Academic and research NGOs appeared after 1981, as well. By the end of 1988, at least eighty-two research centers and research-based social action programs operated in Chile (Lladser 1989). Thus encouraged and protected by the church and international donor agencies, the academic and research NGOs (along with NGOs emerging later) formed centers of intellectual ferment and political resistance to the dictatorship. They also provided the most important ongoing technical assessments of the impacts of Pinochet's government. In the post-1983 period of so-called "political opening," the writings and research of NGO staff proved a key factor in forging opposition consensus; research groups also provided "legitimate" forums for contacts among leaders of the various leftist and centrist political forces that sought to create a unified opposition to the dictatorship.

Perhaps most importantly for Chile's future after 1990, these NGOs fostered diverse international support networks, encouraged professional advancement and training that created groups of skilled researchers, developed staff with expertise and experience in policy studies, and served as the base of the "policy commissions" that developed the platform of the Democracy Alliance for the 1989 elections. The alliance (or *concertación*) was a multi-class, multiparty coalition of actors and organizations united in opposition to Pinochet and in favor of revitalized civic and political activity. These NGOs also provided key personnel to the first post-Pinochet administration. Indeed, in the cases of the Economic Research Corporation for Latin America, Latin American Faculty of Social Sciences, Center for Educational Research, Center for Developmental Studies, and Labor Economics Program—among the most obvious—high-ranking staff and ministers have been associated with these NGOs for many years. In this sense, not only academic and professional elites, but also key political elites, emerged from the NGOs of the 1970s and 1980s.[11]

The Role of External Funding

Whether religious or secular, and whether focused on charitable activities, emergency relief, education, technical assistance, or provision of other types of services, Chilean NGOs have depended upon significant *external* support, which frequently has influenced their programs, budgets, and orientations.

Indeed, a key precedent for Chilean human-rights NGOs (and other

NGOs, as well) was established by the support of many international and bilateral donors to these programs, especially in the case of the Committee for Cooperation for Peace and the Vicariate of Solidarity. Private U.S. foundations (e.g., Ford Foundation) and also the Inter-American Foundation (IAF) played critical support roles in the early years. The IAF, an agency of the U.S. government, became a source of particular concern and anger to General Pinochet and his supporters. In early 1978, government security forces confiscated documents outlining the IAF programs in Chile, and the conservative newspaper *El Mercurio* blasted IAF support for dissidents and "communists."[12] Only concern about alienating international financial agencies and the U.S. Congress prevented the Pinochet government from curtailing many IAF-supported programs in Chile.

By 1990, some seven hundred private organizations relied upon external financing for their Chilean operations; perhaps three to four hundred would be classified as NGOs or GSOs for our purposes herein. Thus, in a sense, the military regime's repressive policies and its measures to reduce the public-sector role had at least three unintended consequences: an array of nongovernmental organizations sprang up to provide employment and income for displaced professionals and political opponents of the regime; a new sociopolitical influence was felt in Chilean life; and a socioeconomic transformation took place during those years.

Ironically, the NGO universe enlarged considerably as a result of junta policies that forced international organizations, foreign governments, and private donor agencies to rethink their relationships with the Chilean government and to reevaluate their ongoing programs in Chile. Unwilling to be perceived as supporters of the military junta, yet anxious to ameliorate the impacts of the government's policies and to continue long-term commitments to Chilean development, many external agencies and foreign governments looked to the private sector to provide alternative channels for charitable and development assistance.

In other cases, foreign governments, political parties, trade unions, and donor agencies also sought ostensibly "nonpolitical" counterparts through which to assist opponents of the military regime—even if these had to be created parallel to the repressed Chilean political parties and labor organizations. In such cases, the donor agencies clearly intended to support the *political* role of certain NGOs but preferred, for reasons related to internal politics or the niceties of international relations, to support less explicitly "political" institutions such as NGOs.

The Search for Points of Entry

Pinochet's emphasis upon privatization of social and economic activities previously reserved to the state, or predominantly carried out by the state, created multiple opportunities for far-ranging NGO initiatives in education, health care, nutrition, microproduction, and marketing. The expansion of private research and private secondary and university education also offered new niches for NGOs. Organized as voluntary nonprofit organizations, church-linked, quasi-autonomous agencies, private consulting firms, or purveyors of other services, NGOs took advantage of the government's liberalization of trade, financial flows, and currency exchange to finance their activities with funds and resources from international donor agencies.

Provided the NGOs did not overtly engage in politics, the neoliberal model that underlay government policies sanctified their activities as part of the principle of subsidiarity and the movement toward privatization. When NGO personnel crossed the ambiguous line separating politics from business, consulting, or charity, however, harassment, raids on work centers, or repression and incarceration of NGO staff quickly followed (Lladser 1989). Particularly prior to 1981, the small number of active NGOs and their focus on human-rights issues, combined with their work in the poorest urban neighborhoods or with rural laborers and peasants, made them obvious targets of regime repression—even with the partial protection provided by the Vicariate of Solidarity or other religious affiliations.

Since the NGO universe also replicated the centralization of Chilean life more generally (some two-thirds of the NGOs were based or worked exclusively in Santiago in 1989), the Pinochet regime was understandably sensitive to efforts by political partisans or union leaders to shelter opposition politics in the capital under the NGO umbrella. Inevitably, this created a certain level of self-censorship, dissimulation in project design and language, and obscurity in organizational behavior—some of this for the benefit of donor agencies, some for public legitimation, some for constituents, and some (perhaps clandestine or at least unadvertised) intended to forge long-term development alliances and political bases. The extent of such activities varied over time among and within the NGOs, depending upon immediate personal as well as institutional circumstances.

Although antagonism characterized much of the interaction between NGOs and the Pinochet government, this pattern was not universal. A few NGOs collaborated with government programs while working with urban community groups (e.g., health and nutrition programs) or in rural towns and agricultural regions (organic farming, informal education, agricultural extension programs) or, more generally, in local "community development" programs. The Institute for Rural Education, one of the oldest NGOs working in rural Chile, was severely criticized for what other NGOs and opposition political elites perceived as its support for government policies in the countryside.

In some instances, local and provincial officials named by the Pinochet government sought quiet cooperation with selected NGOs. A combination of local needs, NGO talents and resources, and pragmatic mayors or government officials led to isolated experiments in NGO-government collaboration (Jiménez et al. 1989). Although limited both by the unwillingness of most NGO personnel to become a municipal political arm of the Pinochet government and by government distrust of the NGOs' long-term intentions, these experiments nonetheless demonstrated the potential utility of NGO-government collaborations in the provision of community services. This is particularly true in the area of *local* government, given the relatively small size and resource base of most NGOs, but could also be extended in certain program areas to larger communities and regions. Chile's transition in 1990 to a more democratic system created new and broader opportunities for NGO-government cooperation at various levels (Jiménez et al. 1989).

NGOs and Municipal Government Under Pinochet and Aylwin

Prior to 1974, Chile was divided administratively into twenty-five provinces, with each province subdivided into departments, subdelegations, and districts headed by administrative officers serving at the pleasure of the president. Administrative reforms introduced by the military government reorganized the country into twelve regions, in turn subdivided into fifty-one provinces and over three hundred communes. While in theory the military rulers advocated decentralization and administrative rationalization, in practice these reforms tended to intensify the centralist political tradition.

As part of a package of policy initiatives collectively labeled "the seven modernizations," the Pinochet government drastically modified the role and structure of municipal government in 1980–1981. For example, immediately after the coup of 1973, municipal government no longer functioned through elected mayors and councilpersons; all mayors were designated by the military junta according to Decree Law 25 (22 September 1973). Decree Law 573 (12 July 1974) defined internal administration and local governance as "intimately linked to order and internal security of the country." The "autonomous" municipality thus became a local territorial administrative unit of the national government, with a mayor selected by the junta.

Local politics and local government disappeared. At the same time, administrative decentralization assigned new and more diverse functions to the municipal authorities. In many cases, retired or even active-duty military officers or police assumed mayoral positions. Local administration became the level of government surveillance and control at which new policies of the military regime were implemented. Thus, the junta's decentralization of administrative tasks reinforced the centralist, statist tradition of national politics as the "decentralized" administration implemented the policies imposed by the national government.

Modifications to this scheme came about through the 1980 Constitution implemented in 1981 and also accompanied the earlier Decree Law 1289 (1976) and Decree Law 3063 (1979), which increased municipal revenues. The municipality remained an integral component of the "internal administration of the state," however, leaving the country with no elected regional or local government and no means of direct citizen participation in the formulation and implementation of municipal public policy.

Nevertheless, municipalities assumed responsibility for educational services and administration of previously national-level welfare and employment programs. Under this scheme, the appointed mayor became the unique source of local authority and was responsible for administering government programs within the municipality. Important differences in programmatic emphases and administrative styles depended on the idiosyncracies of the local mayor: personality, political ideology, family and friendship networks, business interests, professional training, and technical skills. This reality provided both opportunities and dilemmas for NGOs wishing to carry out programs within particular municipalities or to cooperate with local government officials in designing and implementing socioeconomic development programs.

The organic law (Law 18605) regulating municipal government, adopted by the military government in 1988, vested authority for municipal government in a mayor and a municipal development council. Under this law, the mayor was named to a four-year term by a regional development council, itself composed of governors of each province within the region, a representative from each of the armed forces and from the Chilean police force, five government officials from specified state or semipublic enterprises, and representatives of "the principal private-sector groups with activities in the region" (60 percent of the council membership). An exception to this rule was provided for sixteen municipalities—Arica, Iquique, Antofagasta, Valparaíso, Viña del Mar, Santiago, Conchalí, La Florida, Las Condes, Nuñoa, Concepción, Talcahuano, Temuco, Puerto Montt, Coyhaique, and Punta Arenas—where the mayor was named by the president of the republic and removed at presidential discretion. In short, the law dictated a complex form of corporative and indirect "representation" of interests within regions, provinces, and municipalities. No conventional democratically elected officials figured in the scheme of internal administration at any level.

In contrast to the limited role of municipal government prior to 1973, however, the new municipal regime provided a broad scope of political and administrative functions: urban planning and administration, public transportation programs, housing and public utilities, sanitation, and municipal development. In addition, municipalities had discretionary authority in the areas of social welfare, public health, environmental protection, education and culture, adult education and employment development, sports and recreation, tourism, urban and rural road maintenance and development, public housing and urban infrastructure, emergency planning and relief, and the development of activities of common interest at the local level. In order to carry out any or all of these discretionary activities, the municipalities were authorized to charge fees, grant concessions, enter into contracts with private or public enterprises, acquire, manage, and transfer or condemn property, and *grant subsidies or make direct grants to nonprofit institutions* that collaborated directly in carrying out municipal programs. Thus, while the internal organization of municipal government was highly detailed by the organic law and its constitution highly undemocratic, great potential existed within the authority of local government for collaborative programs with NGOs.

In the first months of its administration, the Aylwin government sent proposals for democratization of municipal government (essentially for elections of mayors and councilpersons) to the Congress. Congressional approval of reforms, followed by municipal elections in 1992, altered the political basis for local government. During the interim, mayors and municipal development councils in a number of localities took advantage of the previous legislation to incorporate NGO skills, resources, and energies into selected public programs. The extent to which this occurred had much to do with political decisions made by government officials and with the creativity of NGO leaders, less to do with legal or administrative impediments. Personal and political constraints or lack of awareness on the part of NGO and municipal leaders of mutually beneficial possibilities constituted more serious dilemmas than did legal or administrative obstacles.

For example, in the first months of the Aylwin government the NGOs tended to focus their attention on municipalities where President Aylwin had designated mayors, hesitating to begin initiatives in other municipalities. Recognizing the limitations of this trend, some NGOs had begun to test the water elsewhere by June 1990. Meetings between mayors, municipal officials, and NGO personnel working in nutrition, health, housing, child care, recreation, and microenterprise generated both enthusiasm and skepticism but identified potentially constructive program initiatives. If NGOs can diversify the spatial scope of their activities to match the functional and budgetary expansion of municipal government introduced by the Pinochet regime, they may help to bring about important long-term changes in local politics.

Some Constraints

Democratization of municipal government after March 1990 presented a short-term political dilemma for the concertación, requiring a visible definition of the relative political strength of its numerous members. It was one thing for party activists to join in fashioning a campaign against the general; it was quite another for former political rivals, after years of political inactivity, to reveal their strengths and weaknesses at the local level to potential competitors. Such an explicit repoliticization of local government had the potential to stress the Aylwin coalition, reignite historical animosities and personal quarrels, and create tension between the national government and local coalitions. While such developments were inevitable as democratization proceeded, they did complicate the initial phases of the transition.

In its first year, the Aylwin government proposed limited reforms of municipal government, focusing on restoring elected mayors and city councilpersons. The proposed reforms slightly expanded the authority of municipal government to operate public enterprises but scarcely altered the basic functions and internal operation of the municipalities themselves. Nor did they address the dominance of mayors in local government, to the exclusion of an authentic legislative role for municipal councillors.

To replace appointed mayors with elected officials threatened local political machines and the bastion of patronage of the opposition parties. Thus, the political right resisted municipal reform, seeking to delay municipal elections and using its veto power in the senate to block constitutional amendments for municipal government that the Aylwin government proposed in its first year of office (March 1990–1991).

This meant that NGOs working as GSOs in urban and rural communities had to preserve their capability for autonomous action, seek some collaborative relationships with the municipal authorities bequeathed by the Pinochet regime, or take the initiative in collaboration with the mayors appointed by the new president in the sixteen exceptional municipalities. As democratization at the national and municipal levels proceeded after 1992, interactions with community groups, political parties, unions, and the Aylwin government itself also required NGO attention.

Indeed, during the presidential election campaign the concertación leadership had already raised the issue of the NGO role in post-Pinochet Chile. During the discussion it became evident that competition for external financing, the desire to channel foreign assistance into programs identified by the new government as priorities, and the intention of some Aylwin supporters to "coordinate" NGO activities represented a serious challenge for NGOs after March 1990. Some NGOs perceived the new Fund for Social Solidarity and Investment, created by the government to mobilize programs to eliminate "extreme poverty," as a potential competitor for donor funding. Similar concerns were voiced in regard to the influence or control over NGOs that might be exercised by the new Agency for International Cooperation within the new Ministry of Planning and Cooperation, established shortly after Aylwin assumed the presidency.

NGOs and the Concertación Program

The concertación elites recognized that NGOs had played a key role in the *political* contest against the Pinochet government, as well as in designing alternative policies and programs, which led them to explicitly consider the NGOs in the concertación program. Inasmuch as staff from a variety of NGOs elaborated much of the program, this should not have come as a great surprise; however, never before had such an issue surfaced in a Chilean presidential election. In October 1989, the concertación's "NGO Working Group" issued a background paper on the NGOs, with a preliminary estimate of the number of active NGOs by policy area: 40 academic; 45 agriculture or rural sector; 73 dependent on the Catholic church (across policy areas); 135 urban social action—for a total of 293. Later estimates raised this total closer to 400.

In late November 1989, the working group circulated a document titled *Concertación Policies vis-à-vis Private Development Corporations and NGOs.* This document recognized that the proliferation of Chilean NGOs was paralleled by similar developments in other parts of Latin America, as well as in Asia and Africa, and that "these private development corporations and NGOs have earned themselves a role as effective instruments to support development, a manner of fortifying civil society, and to encourage popular participation." It noted further that the NGOs, supported by important levels of international cooperation, had contributed to the redemocratization of national life.

With this in mind, the Working Group defined its "policies toward Private Development Corporations and NGOs" in this document as follows:

> The Concertación recognizes the value that these organizations have in the promotion of development. Therefore, it promises to respect their autonomy, to support their institutional development and, in those areas where it is possible, to establish working agreements so they may cooperate in the implementation of public policy.
>
> Likewise, the Concertación promises to support and expand upon the successful experiments of these types of entities that favor the development of the popular sectors and which, in the framework of the social policies of the future government, motivate popular participation.
>
> In implementing its government plans, the Concertación visualizes diverse areas—in the fields of economic, social, and cultural development—in which it will be possible to count upon collaboration between public-sector entities and NGOs and private development corporations. The Concertación commits itself to finding adequate and expeditious means to operationalize this collaboration. This may take the form of working agreements, contracts for research, experimental programs, etc.
>
> In reference to international cooperation, the Concertación specifically recognizes the nongovernmental pipeline as a way to channel international cooperation. It affirms that their views, procedures, manners of

operation, and independence in relation to government action will be respected so long as legal norms and democratic conviviality are not violated. The Concertación desires that present programs be maintained and, to the extent possible, that they be expanded. Given the economic situation facing the country, it cannot be expected that the resources obtained by the NGOs during these years can be replaced with national resources.

. . .

The Concertación of Parties for Democracy recognizes the role that NGOs have fulfilled in the past years in establishing the so-called informal diplomacy, whereby solidarity ties have been created with many organizations from friendly nations. It is hoped that in the democratic [government] these entities continue to fulfill this role as members of civil society, assuming a coresponsibility in the forging of international relations. This role will be seen as distinct, but complementary, to that exercised by the government in the design and conduct of the country's foreign relations (2–4).

This conceptual formulation of government-NGO relations in both domestic and international spheres was unprecedented in its specific recognition of the potentially important role of NGOs in Chilean socioeconomic development and in linkages to foreign governments, foreign NGOs, and foreign donor agencies. It was also unprecedented because it recognized, and ostensibly rejected, the temptation of a new government to regulate NGO activities with the rationale of "coordination" of national development programs. At the same time, *if sustained,* the concertación declaration on NGOs represents a modified intellectual vision of Chilean society and politics, founded upon diversity, that harbors an enhanced role for private and local initiative and a new faith in political pluralism.

Just prior to the elections of December 1989, a summary of the policy commissions established by the working group to formulate proposals for various policy areas showed near consensus among commissions that NGOs should be incorporated into policy development and implementation. Also mentioned was the possibility of granting public subsidies for certain NGOs—for example, those working in the health field—as well as contracting with NGOs for service delivery in other fields of action. Under such a scheme, the National Agrarian Development Institute might contract with NGOs providing services in agriculture or the Ministry of National Resources with NGOs providing research or services in environmental affairs.

These possibilities, however, hold risks of further NGO politicization and of "domestication" as transmission belts for implementation of government programs, with a consequent loss of autonomy, initiative, and capacity for critical assessment of government policies. Inevitably, government contracts or subsidies involves competition among NGOs and a reluctance to bite the hand that feeds.

These risks are not merely theoretical. During the 1989 election campaign, for example, some NGOs dedicated more resources and energy to the elections and policy commissions of the working group than to their formal programs; these priorities created conflicts with certain donor agencies, and sometimes "accounting dilemmas," as well.[13] Given the lure of the concertación government, the personal and professional relationship of NGOs with appointees to the new administration, and the desire to make a difference after seventeen years of dictatorship, many Chilean NGOs face difficult tests in retaining key personnel, autonomy, and credibility in the post-1990 milieu.

The transition to a more democratic political system also provided opportunities for NGO staff to return to the university, church, labor union, political party, mass media, or other place of origin or to yield to the lure of jobs in the public sector. A natural flow of professionals, technicians, and academics to normal activities was to be expected.

Other sorts of challenges accompanied the transition to more democratic government. NGOs began to face increasing scrutiny from donor agencies who no longer felt a protective or survival urgency with the transfer of the presidency to Aylwin; the sloppy accounting procedures, slack internal administration, and poor use of resources that afflicted some NGOs became less acceptable than in the past. Overcoming these deficiencies, which have affected individual NGOs to a greater or lesser degree, will require organizational reforms.

NGO Prospects

Several days before taking office in March 1990, the concertación scheduled a meeting with donor agencies and NGOs in Santiago. President-elect Aylwin and other soon-to-be officials of the new government reaffirmed the commitment to NGO participation, autonomy, and diversity as earlier provided in the election platform.

Among the government's first initiatives was the creation of a Ministry of Planning and Cooperation, which would house the newly established Agency for International Cooperation (ACI) and Fund for Social Solidarity and Investment (FOSIS), established to implement the government's international and domestic programs. The ACI would coordinate the complex network of agreements and partnerships with foreign government agencies and private donors; FOSIS would be charged with channeling investment into projects specifically designed to overcome poverty and marginality, working *through* community organizations, NGOs, municipal governments, and other public agencies.

The government signaled its awareness of the need to formalize NGO-government relations by appointing the editor of an important book on

NGOs (*Una puerta que se abre,* 1989) and an active participant in a well-known NGO himself (the Labor Economics Program) as the ACI's executive secretary. The appointment of professional staff from other prominent NGOs to key positions in FOSIS underscored the message.

These appointments also signalled to NGOs the immediacy of other challenges they would face: loss of staff to the government, competition among NGOs for government posts and contacts, and tension between government and NGOs as foci of policy initiatives. These tensions will persist and intensify as certain NGOs form close associations with government agencies and obtain government support while others find themselves less favored. The extent of these dilemmas was not fully apparent when taking into account only formal appointments, inasmuch as many NGO staff were also called upon as consultants, part-time employees, and informal advisers in a number of government agencies. The tendency for most NGO staff to take leaves of absence rather than to resign from their respective organizations may provide some optimism regarding the long-term intentions of those temporarily leaving for government service.

From July to August 1990, six meetings between NGO staff and the Ministry of Planning and Cooperation, organized by a facility dedicated to the study of NGOs and international cooperation, examined the challenges and opportunities NGOs face in the democratic transition. Included on the agenda were the rising concerns in some quarters over government competition with the NGOs for donor resources, as many feared that FOSIS and the ACI might disrupt existing relations between donors and NGOs. Concerns were raised as well about the potential for politicization of the ACI and FOSIS and about a range of other thorny issues.

Most of these issues were openly discussed at a meeting attended by NGO personnel and government officials at Punta de Tralca in October 1990. As the Aylwin government entered its second year (March 1991–1992), NGOs continued their efforts to create more formal relations among the NGOs—for example, national and regional federations—as a way to increase collaborative projects and information sharing. They also continued their efforts to clarify government-NGO relations. One of the challenges facing NGOs in their transformation from antiregime institutions to institutions supporting the elected government was that of retaining their character as nongovernmental, autonomous, and innovative elements in grassroots development.

In the short run (1990–1993), a probable shaking out in the NGO sector seems likely to result in redefinition, refinement of roles, pressures for internal efficiency, and more professional personnel administration. This process may be accompanied by a reduction in the number of NGOs and/or further specialization—although new NGOs will appear as the emergent political situation presents new opportunities and new challenges.

To survive, most NGOs will need to streamline their internal operations and present a clear definition of their role in the democratic transition to donor agencies. Some will benefit from government contracts; others will continue to rely fundamentally on external or church resources. Still others may find new, if partial, forms of self-financing although limits to this option for most GSOs seem rather severe given the poverty of their clientele. Less handicapped in this regard will be the business interests, former officials and supporters of the Pinochet government, and NGO entrepreneurs who are already making use of the NGO format to channel national and external funds into more conservative think tanks and social projects.[14] Divisions within existing NGOs will also spawn a number of new organizations.

Notwithstanding the challenges and inevitable disappearance, amalgamation, or reduction in size of some NGOs, the socioeconomic experiments they initiated, the leadership they generated and nurtured, and the diverse and critical approaches to public policy dilemmas they offered ensure them a significant role in the complex social web of Chilean society for the foreseeable future. Relationships among NGOs and between NGOs and political parties, trade unions, religious groups, and other social movements and organizations (for example, the subsistence organizations, neighborhood improvement associations, and women's production cooperatives) will make the NGO role both controversial and politically significant across the ideological spectrum of Chilean politics.

These relationships will also offer opportunities to devise and implement experimental solutions to the most pressing socioeconomic problems facing Chile at the neighborhood, local, and municipal levels—and to expand upon successes achieved as partial responses to the overall socioeconomic challenges facing the country. Some opportunities may also exist on a broader scale, but the NGOs alone will not solve the complex, long-term dilemmas facing Chilean society nor will they replace the need for government policymaking to confront national issues. The very characteristics that contribute to NGO success in small-scale projects and experiments—face-to-face relations, informality, flexibility, personal commitment of staff, sense of urgency, ideological or religious motivation—are inherently difficult to replicate or sustain in large-scale, more bureaucratic enterprises.

Nevertheless, the NGOs may prove key actors in formulating options, experimenting with technical and institutional innovations, and encouraging grassroots initiatives. Recognizing both the limits and the capabilities of the state, local government, and NGOs in a dynamic setting may permit Chile's traditionally state-centered society to evolve gradually toward authentic political democratization, decentralization, and grassroots development.

Notes

1. "Disappearances" refer to persons who were not officially arrested or detained but were thought to be kidnapped or murdered by security forces.

2. Unlike research programs, study circles consisted of seminars and sessions of reflection on a variety of topics during a period of harsh repression by the military government. Participants were unpaid professionals directed by selected academy/church staff.

3. For example, the Center for Planning Studies (CEPLAN) was detached from the Catholic University and became the Economic Research Corporation for Latin America (CIEPLAN), a leading private center of predominantly Christian Democratic academics who would significantly influence the course of Chilean politics in the 1980s and provide key ministers and other high-ranking officials to the government of President Patricio Aylwin after March 1990.

4. In the case of the Latin American Faculty of Social Sciences (FLACSO), the Chilean government failed to renew the international accord with UNESCO that had allowed FLACSO to become a leading research and teaching institution in Latin America. After 1979, FLACSO was transformed into a private research center affiliated with the Academy of Christian Humanism. Former officials of the Popular Unity government, "socialists" of a variety of orientations, and other anti-Pinochet academics made FLACSO a much more "national" institution as foreign researchers left Chile and international accords with the Pinochet government were abrogated or simply not renewed. Like CIEPLAN, FLACSO provided a number of key appointees to the Aylwin administration, including members of the presidential staff and technical personnel and consultants in education, international cooperation, the Ministry of Justice, and agriculture.

5. Many NGOs adopted the legal status of professional societies, which, by definition, are profit-seeking entities. (However, in practice or in their internal reputations, the NGOs' nonprofit character was made clear.) This legal tactic was adopted as a response to government-imposed difficulties in chartering "foundations" or "nonprofit corporations" as provided in Section 33, Book I of the Chilean Civil Code. In accordance with Decree Law 1183 (1975), the military government imposed significant obstacles on and repressive financial and political control over nonprofit corporations. Applications for such charters were routed through the intelligence agencies and the secret police for "clearance," a ploy that discouraged most NGOs from pursuing this route. CIEPLAN, however, obtained a legal charter as a nonprofit entity prior to implementation of Decree Law 1183.

6. It is estimated that approximately 13,000 Latin American political "refugees" were in Chile at the time of the coup. Many were detained by the military government and taken to the National Stadium or other detention centers, and a public campaign against "foreign subversives" was carried out by the new regime. This situation precipitated the formation of CONAR.

7. This NGO was initially sponsored and financed by the Research Center Against Torture in Copenhagen, Denmark.

8. The Latin American Institute was created by a group of mental health professionals and psychologists who had worked in the Christian Social Assistance Foundation. It combined research, therapy for victims of repression and torture, and collaboration with human rights organizations in other Latin American nations.

9. The staff of the Interdisciplinary Program for Educational Research included researchers who had helped make education policy during the Allende government. After March 1990, a number of them joined the Aylwin administration as Ministry of Education staff and as educational consultants.

10. Illustrating this trend was an inventory of approximately seventy private institutions (mainly NGOs) providing support of some kind to small businesses in June of 1990. Less than one third of these entities had existed in 1981. The pace of change in the NGO sector was reflected in the fact that some of the programs listed had already disappeared, while other NGOs providing support for small businesses and *talleres* were not listed in the inventory (Pardo 1990).

11. NGOs helped shape the Aylwin government to a considerable degree, as former NGO staff have served in the Bank of Chile and the Ministries of Labor, Justice, Finance, Economy, Agriculture, National Resources, and Treasury, among others.

12. See "La Inter-American Foundation y sus Programas en Chile," *El Mercurio,* 25 January 1978. While the article exaggerated the funding level for IAF projects in Chile, it identified some twenty-one projects between 1973 and 1977— most of which were church-affiliated. Cited in Brian Smith (1982): 329.

13. In some cases, donor agencies had implicit understandings with NGOs that permitted "political overhead" or direct channeling of funds to political parties or labor organizations. A small number of NGOs were essentially adjuncts of political parties. Some European donor agencies fully intended to support opposition political movements in Chile with their grants but necessarily preferred to disburse funds formally to NGOs rather than to more obviously political entities. In other cases, however, NGO staff diverted their energies and resources to projects not specifically included in their agreements with donor agencies.

14. A minority of NGOs, staffed by persons sympathetic to the general outlines of the Pinochet government's neoliberal policies—if not to the repression—have added a more conservative sector to the network of Chilean NGOs (for example, the Kast Foundation and the Private Development Foundation). Even within the network of human-rights NGOs, a pro-Pinochet group called National Pro-Peace Defense Corporation (CORPAZ) was created to denounce acts of terrorism and provide reparation to police, military personnel, and other victims of terrorism. Unlike most other NGOs, CORPAZ apparently operated almost entirely with national financial resources prior to 1989. With the opposition victory in the December 1989 elections, new conservative NGOs emerged that included groups associated with leading former government personalities—presidential candidate Hernan Büchi, for example. After March 1990, a number of such NGOs were created, along with other regional NGOs stimulated by legislators in the recently reopened congress as a way to promote development in their legislative districts. By 1990, the NGOs' demonstrated organizational flexibility and political utility appealed to politicians across the ideological spectrum as well as to entrepreneurial professionals and academics.

8

Chilean Health NGOs

JUDITH SALINAS
GIORGIO SOLIMANO

State and Society Policy

For many decades, Chilean social policy has been closely linked to the state. Sometimes the state has played a benign role, as in the late 1930s, when Chile began a slow but steady democratization that extended to the general population goods and services previously available only to a few. These gains included significantly broader education coverage, a newly created housing and urban development infrastructure, labor legislation aimed at protecting workers, complex systems for social security, and a network of public health services that eventually extended nationwide.

The state played a fundamental role in this progressive democratizing process; not only did it provide resources for the system to operate, it also established public bureaucracies and controlled the formulation, management, and administration of social policy. Until roughly the end of the 1960s, the division of social functions was quite clear: citizens channelled their demands through the political system (via political parties), and the state provided the goods and services called for.

It was a special time. The country was growing at a reasonable pace, external assistance was generous, and there was a relatively established social demand (with ample resources for social investment). Furthermore, mediation between the state and civil society was grounded upon parliamentary debate of the budget. No intermediaries intruded between citizen and state in the formulation of social policy. That time passed, succeeded by a long period of authoritarian rule after the military coup of 1973. The economic recessions of 1976 and 1982–1983 were followed by profound transformations in the definition of social policies and in the internal organization of the state apparatus. At the same time, the external debt crisis imposed severe restrictions on investment potential in the social sector, making the shortage of resources a serious problem.

With political party activities prohibited by the Pinochet government, the channels of representation and mediation between citizens and the state disappeared; the loss of their political voice and the dramatic deterioration in living conditions led countless Chileans into popular organizing. For its part, the state withdrew as a principal actor in the distribution of resources, giving the market a major role in such allocation. Additional reforms granted local government a major role in designing and carrying out social policy. Elements such as these illustrate the profound changes that took place after the coup. Out of this context arose a wide array of NGOs dedicated to serving popular needs, many of them related to health.

Given democratic reconstruction now underway in Chile, social policy models in general must be rethought. For example, what role should nongovernmental organizations play in formulating and implementing such policy? This question requires serious reflection and review, both of the social capital NGOs represent and of their work during the military dictatorship. In analyzing the experience of over one hundred health NGOs in Chile, their contribution to meeting emerging popular needs, and their innovative contribution to social policy, the authors identified six NGOs that, as a whole, illustrate the heterogeneity and rich experience of all. These six appear as case studies later in this chapter.

Public Health: The Changing Role of the State

Prior to the military regime, a strong and centralist state took charge of health care for most Chileans—providing, in addition to universal plans and programs, preventive actions for health. During the military government, however, the state assumed an increasingly subsidiary and decentralized role; health policies depended more on the market as a regulating mechanism than on a policy to help those with fewer resources. Such changes represented an abrupt break with the historical development of a health care system whose roots go back to the early twentieth century.

The process that led to creation in the 1950s of the National Health Service for workers and the indigent corresponded both to a widespread sentiment recognizing the right of low-income people to health care and to the political leadership exercised by public health experts. Influenced by modern epidemiological thinking and social medicine, the evolution of public health ideas at the time contributed significantly to professionalization and modernization of the health sector. The health service was also a response to pressure from social movements demanding that the state respect citizen rights to health care and social security.

The National Health Service operated through tripartite financing: funds came from the state, through general revenues; from workers, through social security payments; and from employers, through contributions proportional to wage payments. During the 1950s and 1960s, however, health care became more discriminatory with the introduction of graduated stratification between white-collar office employees and blue-collar workers. This free-choice system (National Medical Service of Employees) later helped to legitimate the stratified health care installed by the military regime.

The so-called modernization of health care and social security that resulted from the military regime's neoliberal economic model brought with it profound changes in administrative structure and financing mechanisms. When the National Health Service was dismantled in 1979, its functions were transferred to the Ministry of Health, which implemented a new administrative structure involving twenty-seven regional health units. Together, these regional units made up the National System of Health Services, which (although decentralized administratively) remained under the control of the central government.

To these changes were added private (for-profit) institutions to provide retirement plans and health care to the middle- and upper-income population. In turn, the annulment of employer contributions provoked a dramatic reduction in the state's matching contribution to public health that had to be offset by a large increase in the wage-earners' contribution to 7 percent of taxable wages. Another significant change occurred when the military regime placed responsibility for primary care in the hands of municipal governments. By positioning medical offices under the mayors, who represented the military government, local health care became politicized as medical professionals yielded to political administration. Added to the mix were problems of loss of funds labor instability, and the increasing complexity of health care.

These transformations, designed to force health care into the neoliberal model, polarized the system around two axes: one, an expensive and sophisticated private system for the small upper-income segment of the population; the other, an underfunded and deteriorated state system for the rest. Accompanying the public sector's weakening health role were major social transformations. For some, exclusion and poverty produced resignation and desperation; for others, it sparked a collective search for responses to the day-to-day problems of survival. This search expressed itself in a variety of organizational forms and in a variety of innovative experiences directed toward assistance and promotion. Many of these were church sponsored.

Popular Organization in Health

A study done by the Labor Economics Program (PET) found that approximately 20 percent of the marginal urban population of greater Santiago participated in popular organizations, one-third of which were geared toward solving health problems (see Table 8.1) (Hardy 1989). In 1990, the Metropolitan Coordinator of Population Health Groups reported the existence of some three hundred health groups.

Table 8.1   Self-help Health Organizations (greater Santiago)

Type of Organization	Number of Organizations	Number of Active Members
Soup kitchens	201	4,191
Community kitchens	20	269
Cooperative buying	223	4,700
Family gardens	67	1,757
Community bakeries	25	501
Health groups	137	1,538
Total	673	12,956

Source: C. Hardy.

These forms of popular organization and self-help, many of which arose during the military regime, are expressions of the effort and creativity with which popular sectors address their basic needs.

Given their variety, it is difficult to establish a schematic description of the popular organizations today; for example, many are but one component of other functional or neighborhood organizations with broader objectives. In addition to these, a large number of organizations oriented toward consumption also undertake health actions. As well, the multiple membership of women in different self-help groups and organizations makes it especially difficult to gain a full view of the scope and extent of the popular organizing that occurs around health.

It is possible, however, to indicate some elements common to these organizations. The first is their marked heterogeneity of experience, in terms of the type of support provided, group work style, and participants' sociodemographic background. In general, their initiatives are carried out among the dispossessed, both urban and rural, who have few opportunities for access to an increasingly privatized health system. Initiatives often integrate a variety of elements, combining an economic component, for example, with health-related activities and social, educational, and personal development or combining group development with political and pastoral action.

Another feature common to many grassroots organizations that include health activities in their program is the self-management that guides their activities; each member is encouraged to participate actively in making decisions, carrying out tasks, and in promoting cooperation, reciprocity, and mutual aid. As noted, a very significant aspect of these organizations is that most of their members are women, especially those involved in the leadership and management of these organizations.

Chilean Health NGOs

Nongovernmental organizations are not a new phenomenon in Chile; some NGOs date from the early years of this century. Although the installation of the Pinochet government led to important changes in many NGOs, their development accelerated and multiplied after 1973. Estimates indicate that at present there are approximately three hundred NGO initiatives in health and social action, bringing together some two thousand health and social science professionals. Despite their diversity, health NGOs generally share certain characteristics:

- They are private and independent of the state apparatus, with no permanent public financing.
- They operate on a nonprofit basis.
- They are made up of interdisciplinary technical teams heavily weighted toward health and the social sciences.
- They carry out actions geared mainly toward the popular sectors and seek to respond to the most urgent health needs and problems.
- They take as their point of departure comprehensive and participatory approaches to health, and they develop dignified and humanized models of medical care.
- They develop practices that generate relatively permanent links with the popular sectors at the individual, family, and organizational levels.
- They operate primarily through local programs and projects in the areas of direct action, research, and training, placing heavier emphasis on the quality of actions than on the number of beneficiaries.
- They constitute areas of application of a broad concept of primary care and a local development strategy.

Many Chilean NGOs arose as a response to the direction health policy took under the military government and to the critical lack of care affecting most of the country. These problems were worsened by the country's growing impoverishment, the ever more precarious living conditions of its people, and the notable and sustained deterioration of state health-care systems. Adding to an increasingly desperate situation was the significant damage to the country's mental health from seventeen years of military repression.

About 20 percent of Chilean health NGOs function as assistance or charitable organizations; often, these are groups predating the military coup of 1973. Other NGOs functioned originally as charitable institutions, then reoriented their focus after 1973 to respond to emerging health-care needs. Of the health NGOs newly established after 1973, most have developed solidarity programs emphasizing comprehensive and participatory approaches to health. Most employ permanent technical teams drawn from two groups: professionals and/or public employees relieved of their posts and younger people actively committed to working with the popular sectors. Church membership is significant; about 40 percent of those staffing the NGOs studied belonged to churches, of these, Catholic NGOs were the most numerous. A significant concentration of NGOs operates in the Santiago metropolitan area (65 percent), although some of these have extended their work to other parts of the country.

Table 8.2 shows the distribution of institutions studied according to the period in which they began their activities.

Table 8.2   Initiation of Activities

Period	Number of Health NGOs	Percentage
Before 1973	25	23.4
1973–1978	14	13.1
1979–1981	9	8.4
1982–1984	29	27.1
1985–1988	30	28.0
Total	107	100.0

These NGOs carry out heterogeneous activities geared predominantly toward solving urgent health problems of the dispossessed, although more are solidarity organizations than are assistance agencies. Many are centers for applied research and training, whose main orientation is academic. In recent years, however, some academic NGOs have carried out successful exchanges with various worker groups, generating a process of communication and mutual learning. Health NGOs are arranged by orientation in Table 8.3.

As illustrated in Table 8.4, a large percentage of NGOs (80 percent) focus their actions on solving health problems the state has not addressed, such as primary health care, mental health problems and the effects of human rights violations, health education, and the struggle for food subsistence.

Table 8.3 Orientation of Sample NGOs

	Number of NGOs	Percentage
Assistance	12	11.2
Solidarity	82	76.6
Academic	13	12.2

Table 8.4 Activities of Sample NGOs

	Number of NGOs	Percentage
Primary health care	23	21.5
Mental health and human rights	22	20.6
Support for organizing and education	22	20.6
Subsistence and food	18	16.8
Specific problems requiring secondary and tertiary care	9	8.4
Research and training in public health	13	12.1
Total	107	100.0

As for the type of actions implemented, a considerable number of NGOs gear their work toward health promotion from a participatory perspective (44.9 percent, as seen in Table 8.5). Health education has been a top priority for many, along with training for participation and work with grassroots organizations, health leaders, and health monitors.

Table 8.5 NGO Approach

	Number of NGOs	Percentage
Treatment	24	22.4
Health promotion	48	44.9
Comprehensive	35	32.7
Total	107	100.0

One of the most significant NGO contributions has been their support for processes of social participation combined with innovative methodologies appropriate for the popular culture. A large number of the NGOs studied worked with and for popular health organizations that cropped up during the military regime.

In Table 8.5, the first category of NGOs includes those providing assistance in the form of curative responses to health problems. The second category emphasizes health promotion, carrying out mainly promotional and preventive tasks. Their work involves education, training, and support for popular organizing and for community and social participation in health. NGOs of the third type carry out comprehensive actions, combining health care programs with promotional activities and participatory education. Representing 32.7 percent of the total, these NGOs account for nearly one-third of the experiences examined.

Most of the NGOs studied maintain no formal relations with the public sector, through either municipal agencies or the National System of Health Services. In local microexperiences, however, informal mechanisms of collaboration between NGO professionals and municipal primary-care teams have sometimes arisen out of practical need. Table 8.6 demonstrates the distribution of health NGOs studied according to the status of their relations with the public sector.

Table 8.6   Relations with the Public Sector (percentage)

Nature of Actions	Yes	No	Total
Assistance	7	16	23
Mixed	12	34	46
Promotional	9	22	31
Total	28	72	100

Note: Base = 67.

Case Studies

In selecting the case studies to be presented, an initial criterion was that the NGOs emphasize direct social action in health. The six experiences selected (see Table 8.7) illustrate two important elements: (1) the diversity of expressions that emerge from the interaction between state institutions and private organizations and (2) the particularity of local movements and contexts. Each experience was analyzed from the perspectives of the state and social policy and of the NGO's future prospects.

Table 8.7   Case Study NGOs: Categories of Classification

	Relationship with Public Sector	
Nature of Actions	Yes	No
Assistance	Hogar de Cristo (pre-1973)	CIASPO (post-1973)
Integrated	CODEIR (post-1973)	SOINDE (post-1973)
Promotional	Pirque (post-1973)	INFOCAP (post-1973)

Christ House

The health of the poorest and most abandoned of society. Founded in 1944, El Hogar de Cristo is one of the oldest institutions in the country and one with the broadest reach. Its objective is to provide shelter and health care to the needy. Both emergency and ongoing assistance is available, oriented toward comprehensive health promotion and primary care. Christ House promotes ties of solidarity in the community as a way to help foster greater social justice.

The beneficiaries of its health actions are homeless men and women, children and youth at risk, and sick persons covered by neither state nor NGO health services. To pursue its objectives, Christ House maintains polyclinics, hospital facilities, outpatient centers, hostels, and homes throughout the country. In 1990, over seven thousand people benefited from its services, 81 percent of them in Santiago.

The health program provides education, comprehensive medical and dental care, and medicines. At the same time, it addresses the critical problems of nutrition and mental health that afflict a large number of poor families. In recent years, its work with drug-using children and youth has taken on special importance.

Since its launching, the health program has grown steadily—particularly since 1984. Such growth is explained largely by the deterioration in health and living conditions among the poor and by the worsening lack of state social services. In addition, however, the organization now directs its fundraising efforts toward the private sector and donor groups with more resources.

The experience. The relationship of the Christ House with the state has been open and varied, depending on local realities. It has cooperative agreements with health professionals and programs of the various metropolitan health services, and its work enjoys the formal recognition of the Ministry of Health.

One of the organization's top priorities has been to win the support of as many organizations as possible, both public and private, and to promote joint tasks. Thus, the Chilean Association for Protection of the Family provides Christ House with professionals and equipment, and Cáritas donates some of the food it receives from abroad. During the military regime, however, the organization limited its relationships with other NGOs, relying more on staff relationships with colleagues in other institutions and autonomous agencies.

Christ House supports popular organizing through regular food deliveries to solidarity groups linked to parishes. (Community kitchens are one destination of such deliveries.) Thus, the military government viewed Christ House in a positive light due to the charitable nature of its activities, its efficiency and apoliticism, and its orientation toward the neediest. Christ House enjoys widespread social legitimacy.

Plans and prospects.   To the extent that state health services improve the quality of medical care, Christ House plans to orient its midrange work toward health promotion and primary health care rather than medical treatment. In so doing, the organization proposes to devote itself to its main vocation, that of trying to solve the health problems that all have abandoned and no one wants to address. Its work with the sick in prisons and with drug addicts reflects that purpose, which could expand to encompass work with AIDS patients in the near future.

Christ House has articulated the need to provide more educational support to consumer solidarity groups as a way to help them strengthen themselves and reorient their work so they do not disappear as urgent situations of hunger are overcome. To strengthen its own program, however, and to meet one of the main challenges posed by the country's democratic process, this NGO must begin to cooperate with local health authorities and municipal governments.

Corporation of Respiratory Patients (CODEIR)

Solidarity and creativity to overcome the crisis.   CODEIR, formed in 1984 by a group of professionals and patients, contributes to the rehabilitation of chronic respiratory patients, wages preventive campaigns against smoking, and supports research in this field. At present, the organization has over six hundred members, most of them respiratory patients and family members. Its interdisciplinary team of part-time professionals includes a physician and nurses, social worker, teacher, kinesiologist, and engineer—most of whom donate their services. Overall direction is in the hands of the patients, although there is also an advisory technical committee that, to all intents and purposes, has assumed the role of technical direction.

CODEIR's priorities are education and training of monitors; research on appropriate technologies, and research on smoking and air pollution. As well, it provides low-cost drugs, a significant contribution to homebound respiratory patients' daily struggle for survival. CODEIR also delivers oxygen to patients, although coverage is limited due to high costs.

The experience.   During the military regime, health authorities agreed to collaborate in some of CODEIR's activities (once distrust was overcome). One fundamental gain was the home-oxygen program, implemented jointly by the Thoracic Hospital (in Santiago) and CODEIR. As advances became increasingly evident, health authorities provided more support and collaboration. The ambulance obtained for the program is one example. However, authorities ignored CODEIR's repeated requests for a headquarters. Eventually, CODEIR found support in a parish that provided an office.

CODEIR's strategy—to gain technical validation through communication of its experience and its results—helped overcome much of the skepticism of a specialized clinical milieu. Its relations with other NGOs have been irregular and based largely on interpersonal relations. However, several professionals of the corporation have participated in meetings and training activities in the area of education, and coordination meetings have occasionally been held with environmentalist organizations.

The program was established on the assumption that a client group, given the necessary technical support, can consolidate, find responses to urgent problems, and interface with the state. In practice, however, this initiative has some limitations. As one of the program's physicians put it, "the initial idea was to put organizational initiative in the hands of the sick, with our role being that of an external technical-support group. But the difficulties and limitations of an organization of the sick who get sick has overwhelmed us, and today we are debating the scope of its work once again."

Plans and Prospects. At present the prospects for relations among members, technical staff, and hospital in the new democratic context is a matter of debate. One line of argument proposes that health projects such as carried out by this NGO be directed by public-sector professionals, who would plan with CODEIR the tasks to be undertaken. Another option is to prioritize educational and promotional work over direct assistance. Yet another line of activity relates to the local dimension of this type of organization and its possible linkage to other participatory endeavors at the neighborhood or community level. CODEIR also plans to strengthen its relationships with municipal governments as a way to increase its social legitimation.

CODEIR sees its short-term challenges as strengthening its organizational work and systematizing its activities to identify lessons that can be drawn upon by other regions of the country. However, all of its plans—short and long range—represent efforts to address the hospital crisis in a rational manner, while proposing alternative policies and programs for the chronically ill that recognize NGO contributions and autonomy.

The Pirque Program

Health management in the community. In 1982, a health program was initiated in the rural community of Pirque based on its mayor's request for five government rural health posts for the municipality and a new clinic in the center of the town. In general, the program set out to implement the concept of comprehensive health and to promote community participation in health management. Thus far, education and research have been its priorities in such fields as school health, women's health, and child and adolescent health. These priorities reflect the demands of the population, as well as the sociopolitical context of the program. The professional team divides its workday between the project's outreach activities, which include training for community groups, and those carried out at the municipal clinic.

Financing for the program has come mainly from the outside, with the municipality contributing varying degrees of support in the areas of infrastructure, equipment, and honoraria for health personnel.

The experience.   Surrounded by an ambiguous brew of crises and ruptures, political mistrust, and genuine support, the program has weathered shifting political events and the policies of four different mayors. Its relationship with the municipal administration (designated by the military government) has been complex, to say the least.

The program's participatory strategy for primary care, implemented from the municipal clinic, was variously perceived as a threat or outright attack by the established authority. On occasion, this perception brought about the removal or resignation of a mayor; it also forced the team into a learning process that included adjustments, setbacks, and redefinitions. Support from health authorities at the local and central levels has been crucial; sometimes the Ministry of Health had to pressure a particular mayor to stop harassing the program or to honor agreements for joint work with this NGO. From the standpoint of program relations with the public sector, a "legalistic" strategy was chosen, which was reflected in such agreements.

A fundamental aspect of the Pirque program has been the relations developed between the program team and other groups of professionals. As one physician noted: "We need to complement one another in the different areas with our skills and competencies; none of us can claim to be self-reliant." Work with academic NGOs and with organizations dedicated to direct action, formal agreements with the Catholic University, rotations of medical and social work students—all have helped form the broad array of relationships established by the Pirque program. Interactions with government and municipal representatives of other public services have been important as well. Initiatives implemented include a program with teachers, a "school for parents," and activities with sports clubs—linking such work with the General Directorate for Sports and Recreation.

Plans and prospects.   The program's most prominent challenge has been its own learning process; at each stage, questions arose that needed to be examined in greater depth. Systematization and evaluation are ongoing tasks, both for the feedback learning requires and for their contribution to other local experiences.

Considering the challenges during the government's transitional period, the program team considers that its role should be one of helping to bring health services in line with the nation's health needs and demands. In the words of the program coordinator, the challenge is "to articulate the local with the national so that we can go beyond the local circuit and move on to the national dimension."

The Center for Research and Action in Popular Health (CIASPO)

A center where health and freedom are human rights. CIASPO was founded in late 1985 by medical and health professionals returning from exile and focuses on models for alternative health systems. In its activities, the center, which describes itself as democratic and pluralistic, emphasizes solidarity and respect for human beings. Its purpose is to carry out health activities that promote community participation and thereby strengthen community members' ability to organize and take charge of their own well-being.

At present, CIASPO's work is organized around seven interconnected programs: general medical care, pediatric care, adolescent care, women's care, community medicine, occupational health, and community development. Since its inception, CIASPO has worked with some 120 popular organizations of various sorts. Most of its health-care activities are carried out through agreements with labor, union, community organizations, and, to a lesser extent, private patients. As revenues from the health care program are minimal and cover only part of CIASPO's costs, the organization depends largely on external agencies of cooperation.

The experience. The military government's repression of the popular sectors made CIASPO's work difficult and at times generated tension within the team. During its early years, the center forged few outside linkages; its interaction with public organizations has thus far been limited to referral of patients to public health establishments. Interaction with other NGOs has been sporadic, as well. In 1989, however, CIASPO and other health NGOs held a meeting to develop mechanisms to deal with such difficulties as institutional jealousies, competition for financing, and the fear (during the dictatorship) of making known one's activities.

CIASPO's approach toward grassroots organizations has been increasingly educational and supportive of their autonomy. There has been growing cooperation, with a goal of attaining joint direction. The center's relationship with interest groups and political parties has been translated into a fluid exchange within the framework of support for popular organizing. In addition, CIASPO has initiated cooperation with a private university so that psychology students can do their professional training at the center. As well, an applied research program is being implemented that responds to the center's needs and makes it possible to contribute to the discussions and analysis within other organizations in the health field.

Plans and prospects.   One of the main challenges CIASPO faces is to broaden its scope, now mainly local, to include state participation. The center is interested in helping itself and other popular organizations gain access to state agencies and develop working relationships with them.

Medical care continues to be one of CIASPO's priorities: "The medical center is part of our identity; we cannot imagine a future without medical care," according to the assistant director. However, the center plans to increase its emphasis on health promotion and community participation. CIASPO believes that such participation helps the community to become aware of its right to health and to begin defending this right as part of the struggle for self-determination.

At present, CIASPO is designing a viable health care model that integrates coverage, efficiency, and educational action. Another area of interest is popular participation in the design and implementation of local policies and in intermediate health bodies. Thus, CIASPO seeks to democratize local government so that it respects the autonomy and freedom of action of non-governmental organizations.

Interdisciplinary Society for Development (SOINDE)

A community clinic as a technical-political project.   The SOINDE clinic in Conchalí was established in 1984 by a group of health professionals who, working closely with local community leaders, defined their priorities and lines of work. The project coordinator recalls that "we had been talking about promoting health and education, but the people didn't want that. . . . The social context did not allow it." What the community wanted, instead, was a medical center to provide care for cases of acute illness.

The Conchalí clinic (located in a neighborhood of northern Santiago) based its services on health assessment done by the users themselves, who denounced the deficient primary health care provided by the state. "SOINDE is a service that has been created to support and consolidate [community] social organizations," in the words of the coordinator, which it does by spurring organized community involvement in democratized and participatory health action.

The organizations participating in the initiative chose representatives, mostly women, to do outreach work for the clinic; their tasks are to provide first aid within the community, diagnose health problems, and refer patients to the polyclinic. At present the clinic's work includes three dimensions: community health, medical treatment, and mental health.

The experience.   From its origins SOINDE gained a close relationship with popular organizations and political representatives at the community level. These relationships were very useful during SOINDE's developmental stages, as the resulting input helped to guide the definition (and redefinition) of roles and the distribution of the health team's work.

SOINDE worked hard to maintain a straightforward relationship with the state health system and, after overcoming distrust and other obstacles, gained authorization to operate as an independent clinic and pharmacy. SOINDE understands the value, also, of relationships with private individuals and groups. Socialization of its experience academically and with other NGOs has been one of its priorities.

Plans and prospects. For SOINDE, a fundamental task is to continue promoting communication between popular organizations and the local government as a way to aid the process of democratic transition. According to the coordinator, "We will be at the service of the political structures of the social pact . . . contributing our experience and also our view of health and of the processes of community participation." In the short term, SOINDE plans to place greater emphasis on health promotion and identification of specific areas in which to develop educational activities that complement the work of the state.

Institute for Popular Education and Training (INFOCAP)

A comprehensive educational practice in local health. The INFOCAP health program was formed in 1984 to provide training to interested organizations and community members in the areas of health, nutrition, and family well-being. In general, INFOCAP works to develop the technical and personal capacity of individuals who wish to receive such training, thereby facilitating the emergence of a society that can organize itself to control its own destiny. INFOCAP offers a set of technical study programs as well as popular education programs; most of its action takes place in the Western Zone of Santiago.

On several occasions, the INFOCAP program has been reoriented and adjusted to better fit the perspective of the community and its participation in health. The program addresses problems related to infant malnutrition, family food subsistence, and general health. In other words, it seeks to cover health needs of the family and the community. At present, INFOCAP has various spheres of action: it delivers training to women, both individually and in organizations; it provides technical and other support for popular organizing in health; it helps develop coordination among local NGOs; it produces educational materials; and it systematizes and disseminates its own experience as an institution.

The experience. INFOCAP made no major efforts to hook up with other groups in its first years, although it responded to educational demands from the community. However, the new sociopolitical opportunities and the need to increase a sense of community both among NGOs and between NGOs and the public sector pose new challenges. INFOCAP's response has been to promote meetings of primary care groups working in the Western Zone. Despite initial mistrust, resources have been brought together, and technical capabilities have been recognized. Also, the team has participated in calls to action and coordinating networks generated by other NGOs.

The INFOCAP team also participates in grassroots community health groups and in communal and sectoral coordinating bodies. In addition, its close and permanent contact with the university world, including academics and students in training, provides a permanent source of feedback for the team.

Plans and prospects.   The program's permanent task is systemizing its knowledge and learning from experience. In the immediate future, INFOCAP believes it must multiply replicable programs, health strategies, methodologies for community work, and educational materials. One priority is local-level training and coordination, both for nongovernmental groups and for the state. Likewise, its work with clinics and grassroots leaders (monitors) is considered essential in the new democratic context. "We are working to bring about a genuine democracy in the sense that the issues are issues not only of the governments, but also of the entire population. The problem of health, like so many others, should be assumed by society as a whole; to this end, we will seek ways of cooperating with the state," says INFOCAP's director, who also believes that "integration should be from the grassroots, from the local reality."

Prospects for Partnerships

Many challenges confront Chilean health NGOs and municipal governments as they work to shore up and expand the country's health care system. The vital question is, will they be able to seize the opportunities created by democratization and decentralization to forge a health-care mechanism that draws upon the strengths of all sectors? In other words, what are the odds of successful public-private collaborations in health-care delivery?

Health NGOs as Potential Collaborators

First of all, many NGOs understand the importance of participatory and comprehensive approaches and methodologies in strengthening local capacity for initiative and organization and in broadening democratic spaces. NGOs have also demonstrated a great capacity for addressing specific health problems at the local level; they have developed technological innovations of considerable scope, especially in health education and promotion, and have designed health-care models from a family and community perspective. NGOs have provided key support for popular demands for better public health policies and programs, policies and programs moreover that include popular input. These demands can be satisfied only to the extent that points of articulation bring together the largest number of local actors—NGOs, popular organizations, public service institutions, local government, and others.

NGOs have proven themselves capable of promoting innovative practices in local health work, and they are very familiar with current needs and the processes of social organization, including community and social participation. Their successes are facilitated by their flexibility and commitment and by their distance from the costly state bureaucracies. NGOs have demonstrated that they are innovators in primary health care.

Research and training NGOs have contributed significantly to reflection and debate, generation and systematization of knowledge, and policy formulation. For example, many of their staff members actively participated in preparing the programmatic bases of the concertación and assumed public posts when the current transitional government took power. The technical-political role that NGOs played during recent years vis-à-vis social development, public health, and popular organizing calls for medium- and long-term strategies for action. It should be noted that the NGO role is primarily that of providing spaces for experimentation and of validating innovative proposals to address emerging health problems from a comprehensive and social outlook.

The practice of interaction with the public sector, with grassroots social organizations, with political parties, and with other NGOs has been rewarding for some NGOs, but for others such interaction is practically nonexistent. This is certainly the area of decision and change during the current transition. Within this scenario, the NGOs are asking themselves many new questions: What guarantees their viability? Their institutional accreditation? Their technical specialization? Does knowing how to relate with one another contribute to determining and meeting social demands in public health? NGOs will also be asking themselves to what extent their technical-political capacity may guarantee their permanence in a democratic transitional government. Much uncertainty surrounds the role of NGOs in a democratizing Chile.

The Government as Potential Partner

A promising field for collaborative endeavors is primary health care, which is one of the new government's priorities. Preventive and participatory, such an approach to health care goes beyond curative actions alone, assigning great importance to local participation in planning and implementation.

The government has recognized the role of NGOs and has committed itself to implementing mechanisms of communication and dialogue with the nongovernmental sector, while preparing the bases of a policy that links both public and solidarity sectors around social issues. For example, an office for NGO-government liaison has been set up in the Ministry of Planning and Cooperation to define and maintain channels of cooperation with the NGOs.

In the area of health, a first step has been to initiate a dialogue and implement a plan for technical and financial cooperation with the NGOs. This plan, supported by contributions from international donors, facilitates collaborations on specific primary health-care projects. The process, generated from the ministerial level, features decentralized management through local agreements for the clear purpose of improving the health of groups most vulnerable to disease or at greatest social risk. Important elements of this process are direct action against prevalent problems and a health-care presence in the country's poorest neighborhoods.

Impediments to Overcome

Many obstacles have slowed the progress of this initiative and have threatened the promotion of a participatory strategy for health that includes NGOs and other social actors. These difficulties stem from a combination of the rigidities of the public system itself, the country's recent history and technical-political ambience, and the limitations of the NGOs. Political and bureaucratic tensions create problems for the public system, as do financial restrictions. NGOs, for their part, sometimes lack clear technical leadership in health and social participation and tend to favor *medical* approaches over primary health; the fears and frustrations of the NGO health teams also work against participatory initiatives that respect the autonomy and identity of different groups.

There is still a great distance between the political will, that is, the public commitment shouldered by the authorities, and the operational measures that facilitate the process of linkage and cooperation between government and health NGOs. This gap is particularly noteworthy in priority areas that contribute to the attainment of national goals and to a public health mentality.

On the positive side, however, a process of communication has begun throughout the country. Thanks to the NGO's capacity to respond and to the warm reception from primary care departments, more and more projects favor the establishment of mechanisms for local coordination. The risks are that certain NGOs may not advance beyond the single-project stage, that they may become worn out or achieve only partial results, and that they may fail to have an impact on policy formulation and program design. These are valid concerns, as NGOs have limited themselves in certain ways.

Rarely do NGOs move beyond conditions and possibilities offered by the government when considering collaborations. Also, their national coordination networks have been weak; it appears that most energies are devoted to local-level coordination and to addressing specific problems.

Thus, a qualitative leap is needed for NGOs to expand their vision and their spheres of activity. To meet today's challenges, NGOs must make the transition from shelter institutions to institutions that play a leading technical and policy role, overcoming isolation and dispersion and establishing distinct alternatives of association and cooperation based on autonomy and on the participation of individuals and organizations in social policy-making.

9

Local Governments, Decentralization, and Democracy in Colombia

Pedro Santana Rodriguez

Decentralization as a Tool for Democracy

Territory and politics have been intertwined for as long as people have debated political systems. Ancient Greeks saw their small cities as the setting for discussion and resolution of civic issues, a pattern that survives in many countries. Indeed, the Western democratic political tradition developed around the concept of the *polis,* or city, as habitable space.

Recent debate on political systems, especially democracy, continues to emphasize territoriality, reinforced by social movements seeking decentralization and autonomy—in both older and newly democratized states (the former Soviet Union is a compelling example). Territory is at the core of concentric identities at local, national, and international levels. Globalization and interdependence squeeze national identities and sovereignty from above, even as regions and municipalities grow more assertive and make claims from below. Increasingly, decentralization is becoming a tool for promoting both administrative efficiency and political participation. Besides strengthening local identities and protecting territorial interests, it could contribute to introducing or salvaging full citizenship and popular sovereignty.

Citizenship, however, requires participation. Political parties sometimes provide a genuine vehicle for such participation. Over the years, political parties have arisen to represent diverse interests and ideologies, if not utopian visions, for organizing society. Some of these parties have lost their political legitimacy over time, finding their ties to civil society weakened to the point that today many citizens fail to vote in elections. As a result, elective officeholders often represent a minority of the voters.

The emergence of modern grassroots movements was a clear sign that political parties failed to represent many interests. In fact, numerous groups decided not to work with political parties at all, turning instead directly to the state. Social movements coalesce around a variety of issues. Some radically question the consumer society's way of life and relationship to nature; others challenge the domination of certain groups over others, or of a centralized state over lesser-ranking entities. Still others concern themselves with social welfare issues and public services.

Like political society in general, political parties are currently undergoing a process of transformation aimed in part at putting their relationship with civil society on a new footing. Party changes have been spurred by the emergence of grassroots movements and by changes in production and communications (whether robots or microcomputers). Latin American political society today has experienced a profound change leading to the rediscovery of civil society and recognition of movements previously disdained or repressed by the state. This transformation affects not only the political parties—their external relations and their internal systems of organization—but also the state.

Colombia's Crisis of Centralism

For over one hundred years, Colombia endured a centralist state. Its legislative and judicial branches were subordinate to the executive branch, its public administration to the logic of war and internal confrontation—a logic under which human rights were considered a subversive ideology posing grave dangers to the state. The centralist process reached its peak in 1968 with the adoption of constitutional reforms placing national executive authorities over all others.[1] As political-administrative centralization unfolded, centralization of public finances took place as well. This process was reflected in departmental and municipal finances (and in the ratio of regional to national tax revenues). In 1931, for example, total departmental and municipal taxes accounted for 46 percent of total public revenue; in 1976, however, they accounted for only 16 percent (Office of the Presidency 1991).

The centralization of public finances in the national government led to across-the-board bankruptcy of departmental and municipal treasuries, which furthered the social crisis as those governments lost the resources to provide public services. Departments and municipalities all but disappeared as governmental entities capable of making investments. Although the largest share of departmental and municipal revenues went to cover the expenditures of these bureaucracies, they could carry out almost no functions.

During the late 1970s, studies undertaken by various agencies recommended a rollback in the centralization process and the adoption of a decentralization policy. At the same time, a groundswell of local and regional social movements arose (civic strikes, guerrilla movements, marches, peasant demonstrations, regional strikes demanding economic and political resources for public investment, etc.). Worker movements and popular demands for better living conditions also came into play.

Social Movements

Among workers, movements often develop when their wages lose purchasing power due to inflation or other factors that increase the cost of living. Such was the case with the trade union movement in Colombia, which became an axis around which sectoral interests expressed by other movements could coalesce. The recently created Central Workers' Union, for example, has come to play a major role not only in the realm of wages and economic conditions, but also in the nation's social and political life. The union has spoken out on such issues as human rights and violence; the need for substantive economic and social reforms; mechanisms and policies that the government should implement to address political violence; renegotiation of the external debt; and the need for a plebiscite and a national constituent assembly. Its somewhat privileged position is due to two fundamental factors: first, it represents over 70 percent of all unionized workers nationwide; second, it is an institutionalized part of civil society, with legal recognition, drawing much of its strength from capitalist accumulation.

A second type of movement in Colombia includes those growing out of the urban and regional crisis. Known as popular civic movements, these comprise organizations such as local and regional civic committees, centers for promotion, and community and neighborhood associations, which generally unite around urban and regional demands and to protest crime, violence, and repression.

As noted, some movements have participated in civic strikes, which often bring a halt to production and transportation as well as to administrative, educational, and commercial activities on a local, or even national, level. Plagued with inadequate and/or highly priced water supply, sewerage, electricity, waste disposal, and urban public transport, citizens join these movements as a way to maximize the effect of their protests. Movements organized around the public-services issue take on different characteristics depending upon whether they form in a small town, a medium city, or a large city. In a small town the demand is generally associated with a civic strike, since it is thought to be the only way to call state attention at the departmental or national level. From 1978 to 1986, there were over two hundred civic strikes in Colombia. Information collected on 105 of these strikes reveals that thirty-five were directed at the national government level, thirty-nine at the departmental level, twenty-seven at municipal governments, and four at private companies.

In medium and larger cities, protest may take a broader and more varied form. The capital cities of the Atlantic Coast region (aside from Cartagena and Barranquilla) also experienced civic strikes in the 1970s to protest major public services problems. In those cities, routine activities ground to a halt, as strike actions included marches, roadblocks, and takeovers of government offices. Larger cities (such as Bogotá, Medellín, Cali, and Barranquilla) witnessed similar actions during civic strikes—marches, blockades, and takeovers. In Bogotá, sectors of the city have been paralyzed.[2] During the past fifteen years, such strikes have become the preferred instrument for demanding investment from the central state in basic public services not funded by municipal or departmental governments. The regions made similar strikes protesting the exploitation of natural resources and the lack of investments in the economic infrastructure.

By the early 1980s the crisis had spread to all corners of the country, raising concerns about eventual guerrilla involvement. At this moment of truth, the Belisario Betancur administration (1982–1986) responded with several projects for modernizing and democratizing the political regime. Two of these were crucial for the country: first, Betancur began a process of dialogue and negotiation with the guerrilla groups;[3] second, the administration undertook a political opening, whose most novel aspects were decentralization and municipal reform, that began the process of dismantling Colombia's old political institutional arrangement.

Reforms of the 1980s

The political-administrative reform (begun in 1983) that aimed to return power to the municipal governments was consolidated with the approval in 1986 of several pieces of legislation covering three broad areas: local treasuries, duties and powers of municipal governments, and new mechanisms for citizen participation. The first category of laws strengthened municipal treasuries by stipulating that locally raised revenues would now be paid directly into the municipal treasury, where they would remain. Assessments were updated, and a new tax was created for financial institutions. Fiscal decentralization policies also included an increase in the transfer payments made from central government finances. In this regard, the sales tax and value-added tax were restructured to increase revenues collected by the central state, which then increased the share of these taxes earmarked for the municipalities. From 30 to 50 percent of the tax was earmarked for transfer to subnational government units, and the municipalities' share increased from 25.8 percent (1986) to 45.3 percent (1992). Municipalities with populations under 100,000 receive a special share, which in 1986 accounted for 0.4 percent of the total and was expected to rise to 16.8 percent in 1992. At the same time, the law introduced the concept of "fiscal effort" (i.e., more efficient property-tax collection) into the municipal transfer payment. An effort was made, as well, to motivate public investment as a way to diminish the operating costs of the municipal bureaucracy.

A second area of reform enhanced the administrative powers of municipalities, assigning local governments new responsibilities in urban planning, public services (water supply and sewer systems, power, refuse collection, etc.), housing policy, agricultural technical assistance, schools, primary health-care services, and municipal transport. In addition, the jurisdictions gained powers hitherto reserved for national agencies, such as a degree of control over development plans, housing policy, municipal land banks, and land management in periurban areas.

A third area of reform broadened the social base of political institutions and generated new channels to represent community interests as a way to deal productively with civic strikes, peasant marches, and related popular manifestations. Legal mechanisms for broadening citizen participation may be summarized as follows: returning electoral power to local communities, establishing local referenda, including representatives of civic organizations on the boards of directors of municipal public enterprises, allowing municipalities to contract projects and services from community organizations, and establishing local-level administrative units and citizens' advisory boards to assist in providing and administering the best possible public services.

As local forms of autonomy are being recognized, municipal and regional governments are assuming new roles and citizens are taking direct legislative initiative. Through these transformations, government legitimacy lost or at least called into question is being regained. Such reforms, combined with new trends in state restructuring—including privatization and reorganization of public agencies—forge new ties between the state and civil society. Because of the state and political restructuring mandated by Colombia's constitutional reforms of the 1980s, the state has been brought into closer contact with its citizens. This reorientation, combined with a reformation of political parties, has created a new dynamic in which the parties can mediate between civil society and the state.

Bogotá: A City Trying to Cope

The capital city of Bogotá is a microcosm of the political and administrative problems and challenges affecting all of Colombia's cities. Its political system is weak economically as well as politically; public social investment is low; administrative systems are in disarray. The local political system is weak, also, insofar as authority and social representation are concerned.

Bogotá's city administration has always found ways to fragment popular organizations. Here, emerging urban movements encounter an institutional vacuum, and few citywide organizations permit poor people to effectively advance their interests. One such organization, the Federation of Communal Organizations, emerged from efforts three years ago to set up zonal associations; there are now seventeen of these, which represent 1,060 neighborhood associations with some 600,000 members. However, many citizens (including the leadership of the neighborhood organizations) lack full understanding of how they might organize to defend their interests. When they do organize protests, they tend to press immediate demands rather than to mobilize for long-range goals that would require continuous effort. Many communities, for example, still view public works as "favors" from certain groups or certain political leaders. Only a few are aware of public issues. This lack of awareness may be the worst political-cultural legacy of past governments.

An examination of Bogotá's municipal government reveals other problems that impede effective collaboration between citizens and administration. One is that the municipal administration covers only part of the city's populated area, leaving many periurban residents in an administrative limbo. A second problem is that, although the main city is subdivided into twenty districts, each with its "minor mayor," there are no decentralized administrative structures to speak of. Such an arrangement cannot possibly provide effective channels of popular participation for the more than 5.5 million people living in Bogotá.

Understandably, the neighborhood organizations complain that there is no effective decentralization of power and decisionmaking and no real space for citizen participation. To permit such participation, Bogota's administrative apparatus would have to be substantially reformed, as the city is governed by structures established thirty years ago. At that time, the population was less than half its current size, and the city's social problems were not so overwhelming. Today, unemployment stands at over 12 percent; at least 40 percent of Bogota's residents are unemployed, underemployed, and/or in the informal sector; public health services are in a state of permanent crisis; and the number of public school teachers has been frozen for over ten years. The citizens and government of Bogotá now confront a number of challenges, which include:

- Finding ways to break up current patterns of urban segregation
- Inventing new forms of urban planning that combine technical skills with popular participation
- Creating incentives for building the city in all its dimensions and through all available avenues, i.e., not relying exclusively upon traditional capitalist approaches to ensure productive urban processes, but instead facilitating the myriad efforts of the poor in self-help construction, self-provisioning of services, and income generation through the informal economy and regular employment

- Adapting urban policies to better fit their context:
  — All of Bogotá's neighborhoods should fall under municipal administration
  — Housing and services should be provided for all
  — Urban mass transit must be a priority
  — Controls must be placed on land speculation
  — More public parks should be developed
  — Laws and statutes that fail to reflect the reality of informal and underground economies must be revised
  — Current urban legal codes must be revised to grant full citizenship benefits to all

Colombia's Decentralization Process

In Colombia, municipalities lost much of their autonomy from 1886 to 1988, a period during which municipal authorities were appointed by political bosses based on clientelistic considerations rather than the public will. Mayors held office not to solve local problems but to ingratiate themselves with the "political godfather." During that century, a network of clientelistic services was woven that endures despite the reforms of 1986.

The popular movements described previously pushed for municipal reforms, as did many of the guerrillas. Although it is still early to tell, it appears that the main effect of these reforms is to strengthen municipal finances and expand their administrative attributes and competencies; they also seek to respond to civic and popular mobilization by creating new opportunities for citizen participation (elected mayors, local administrative boards, and consumers as board members of municipal public enterprises). A start has been made, but violence stands as a major obstacle to the democratization of municipal life and of the country in general. During the last two years, hundreds of mayoral, municipal council, and departmental assembly candidates have been assassinated.

Nevertheless, Colombia's municipal reform thus far has been bold and comprehensive, encompassing both municipal finances and citizen powers and forms of participation. Although many people believe that decentralization is simply a matter of laws or legislation, decentralization is a complex process involving beliefs, customs, and ways of life. It involves local, regional, and national authorities, and a number of actors associated with municipal life: political parties, local unions, social organizations, community associations, sectoral organizations, academic and professional centers, and municipal authorities and agencies, among others. However, the linkage of the actors to the process varies depending on the processes of assimilation and the commitment to decentralization. Not everyone is in favor of decentralization; many oppose its development and implementation.

Organizations differ in their level of support for the process: popular organizations are generally more enthusiastic than are professional, economic, and academic associations. Not all political parties uniformly support the decentralization processes, and some state agencies are supportive while others actively oppose decentralization. Thus, for example, some municipal councils, which were to transfer their functions to local administrative boards, are not doing so, and popular organizations are struggling for control of these functions (and resources) on behalf of the local administrative boards, which are much closer to the community.

Overall, decentralization has strengthened Colombia's municipal governments. It would be no exaggeration to say that the process is recreating the municipality. Communities may now have a direct impact on the type of works financed by municipal governments; already, there are a number of organizations and citizens participating in local debates over municipal budgets. In some cases, community organizations have presented draft budgets for discussion.

With reform, a process to restructure municipal governments has begun in most municipalities. Payrolls, budgets, and direct and transfer revenues are being systematized. Municipal enterprises have been created to deliver public services and to perform the functions entrusted to the municipal governments by the constitution and the law. This modernization is slow, however, and encounters major obstacles in the traditional political class, which is accustomed to the abuse of power, graft, and corruption.

Municipal institutions are slowly winning legitimacy; today, more people vote in mayoral elections than in congressional and presidential elections. Mayors are generally responsive to community pressures and to the major problems of their municipalities, among other reasons because of the political toll that poor management will take on their parties and movements. Earlier fears that mayors would take a militantly populist line or that public monies would be pillaged have been unfounded; on the contrary, municipal governments are increasing investments while reducing operating expenses.

Institutional mechanisms of participation are being established in many municipalities, although some mayors have undertaken few internal processes to democratize municipal life. Many mayors and municipal councils appear to fear that decentralization will diminish their power. In large and intermediate cities, *comunas* and *corregimientos*—new organizational forms to be implemented in cities of 50,000 to 100,000—have barely had their regulations spelled out (over five years after these groups were created). Local administrative boards have been elected in thirty cities nationwide, accounting for about 40 percent of the population, but in almost all cases, they have no clear functions nor local economic resources. Thus, decentralization has had to rely heavily on popular organizations that, together with the local boards, have developed ways to gain resources. In some municipalities this struggle has been successful, and citizen participation is growing (Fundación Foro Nacional por Colombia 1991).

While gaining certain functions and competencies, municipal governments have also lost ground to newly established national and regional institutes. Activities that local governments no longer perform include popular housing, electricity, and adjudication and definition of urban public transportation routes. Municipalities often find themselves trapped in a web of national and departmental state institutions that, although providing an impressive network of vital public services, remains centralized. Dozens of public entities operate within a single municipality with little, if any, coordination, and their policies are often at odds with those of the municipal government.

Clearly, decentralization is a process that advances slowly and confronts many ideological as well as cultural and political obstacles. For over a century, the Colombian people were distanced from municipal authorities, believing they had no voice in affairs of state and that such questions could be dealt with only by professionals and bureaucrats. Municipal governments became increasingly aloof from their populations. Only now is the process reversing itself.

Another challenge is the relationship of local elites to the regional and national authorities. As others have noted, local society is not merely a small-scale replica of the national society; rather, it is a very specific and concrete amalgamation, the outcome of historical processes, of the interplay of various local actors and forces, and of the influence exercised by the regional and national powers. In Latin America, local society is often identified with its more traditional and antidemocratic sectors, particularly in localities with a predominantly rural social and economic base.

Traditionalist tendencies linger in Colombia as expressed in clientelist practices, irrationality, lack of planning, and delayed municipal reforms. Planning becomes a means of participation and negotiation when a participatory methodology is adopted; traditionalist tendencies can be combated when power rests at the local level.

It is possible for grassroots organizations to gain a presence in local institutions; the proximity of such organizations to their social bases makes involvement a form of genuine citizen participation. This participation may be channeled through instruments such as the local referendum or, as has already occurred in some Colombian municipalities, may involve groups in government councils that allow the municipal mayor, grassroots organizations, interest groups, and sector-based organizations to meet and discuss the allocation of municipal resources. Such councils also facilitate the contracting of social organizations to develop and implement local programs—constructing schools and community centers, paving streets, collecting refuse, developing educational programs to foster citizen participation, and so on.

In Colombia, the municipality has become an arena in which traditional and antidemocratic interests confront those seeking to create democratic and participatory localities. The major tendencies that find expression in the regional and national organs of power confront one another at the local level. It is here, also, where relations between civil society and the state are concentrated, and participatory practices are possible. Municipal governments are better positioned to become true schools for democracy, although they can do so only if local actors help promote genuinely participatory processes. Local regions offer certain favorable conditions for democratic modernization, but, for this process to become a reality, many social sectors must become involved.

Local Governments, Popular Organizations, and NGOs: Are Joint Projects Possible?

Authoritarian and dictatorial regimes, which have kept most Latin American countries under their sway, are on the wane (although whether temporarily or definitively is unclear). Accompanying the rebirth of national democracy is the reestablishment of democratic institutions, accompanied by the rapid rise of social movements calling into question old forms of organizing power. In most Latin American countries, the processes of redemocratization or political opening have included regional and, particularly, municipal decentralization. Commonly, such decentralization invests local regimes with powers, resources, and processes for relegitimating local authorities based on direct election (or in some cases indirect election). This has been the case in Colombia, with recognition of local autonomy and popular election of departmental governors and assemblies, mayors, local administrative boards, and municipal councils; recognition of mechanisms for citizen action; and the dismantling of certain organs of power in the central bureaucracy. As well, popular-sector social organizations have increased throughout the continent; political parties are no longer the sole intermediaries for citizen claims and rights.

These changes have transformed an array of social and political actors with relations and interests in the municipality. Popular organizations, for example, are changing their outlook vis-à-vis the state and its decentralized levels. To the extent that both national and local political authorities are open to the interests and concerns of these organizations, it will be possible to undertake cooperative programs that extend beyond sporadic collaborations around specific actions. Popular organizations that press the state to meet basic community needs are now open to joint programs with other actors such as local governments and NGOs; they also see the need for their organizations to shape programs that go beyond presenting challenges and pressing immediate demands.

NGOs are changing as well, finding that not only must they preach democratic transformation (which in large part is already happening), they must also promote projects whose experiences can later be replicated by popular organizations reaching further into the communities than do the NGOs and by political organizations whose role is to promote democracy. NGOs are changing their relationship to the state and, within a context of greater openness, involving the state in various local projects. Municipal projects offer the advantage of their proximity to the social base, the people and their organizations. Such projects play an increasingly important role in NGO activities.

A few international cooperation agencies are beginning to perceive the nature of the changes that have occurred. Most have yet to comprehend the process underway in Latin America and to gear their actions to municipalities that have been or are being democratically recreated. The most solid bases for development in Latin America are the local communities, and democracy is more an idea than a reality. Yet, local democracy plays a vital, irreplaceable role in development efforts, as local investment is proving more efficient and direct than investment from agencies of the central government. Also, popular organizations have proven themselves capable of promoting development and finding workable solutions to build more democratic societies. Projects involving the participation of local governments, popular organizations, and NGOs have become a reality and should be supported by international cooperation agencies. This support should take the form of action and resources that are both bold and creative and that elicit local participation in battling poverty and marginality.

The Colombian Experience

Collaborative projects involving municipal governments, popular organizations, and NGOs, although made legal in 1986, face certain difficulties in Colombia. Notwithstanding the economic advantages such programs offer through pooling efforts and resources, until now there have been relatively few experiences and projects involving all three actors. Those undertaken tended to focus on aspects such as local planning, health services, housing, and dissemination of reform regulations. A few projects have stressed food outlets and popular supply, and there are some programs and projects in the area of production and services, including the formation of cooperatives for refuse collection and recycling. A solid waste collaboration keeps clean the city of Bucaramanga (population, 500,000), and it is now being extended to Manizales, a city of 400,000.

The greatest difficulties in developing and extending projects involving municipalities and NGOs lie in the limited support that such projects receive from local, regional, and national governments, and in the sluggish pace of policy change in development cooperation agencies. Because no data banks on municipal projects exist, there is little dissemination of information about successful projects in health, education, housing, soup kitchens, food supply, microenterprises, cooperatives, and so on. Nevertheless, changes in the popular organizations, NGOs, and state have resulted in joint efforts and novel projects.

A new characteristic of popular organizing in Bogotá is the link between popular organizations and the development of self-managed projects in production, consumption, health, and so on. Several recent experiences merit special mention. The first, in 1986, involved four sectors: (1) popular organizations, in the form of three communal associations (Suba, Ciudad Bolívar, and Santa Fe); (2) NGOs (including the Center of Research and Popular Education, the Social Foundation, and the National Forum for Colombia); (3) city government, through the Secretariat for Social Development; and (4) international cooperation agencies, in the form of the United Nations Development Program. In Santa Fe, five projects were undertaken, among them a shoemakers' association and handicrafts and brick production. Besides promoting coordination among the sectors involved and spurring community participation, these projects helped spread involvement to new areas. For example, the communities began to demand participation in debates on the city budget and funding allocations and in drawing up the city's development plan. More than two thousand people took part in the committees and meetings related to this program. In Ciudad Bolívar, kindergartens were organized, and a transportation cooperative was launched to address the acute lack of public transport in this part of the city. Although the supporting program was abruptly suspended, a community movement had arisen that demonstrated that community participation was linked not only to bringing demands before the state, but to community self-management to confront problems in their locality.

The experience just described was the basis for a communal movement to begin a series of self-managed projects linked to and directed by the popular organizations. In the past two years, ten community stores have been built in different parts of the city; one such store was organized in San Antonio Norte. Although at first the store offered a stock of only eighty basic items, after seven months it offered over four hundred products and had monthly sales of some U.S.$25,000 and a monthly net profit of U.S.$2,000, which was used to strengthen community organizing. Initially, these stores enjoyed little institutional support; their only support came from the Institute of Agricultural Marketing, which furnished credit for a stock of basic consumer items—and from the community organization, which contributed economic and human resources.

In light of this successful experience, and pressured by popular communities that had no community stores, the Bogotá city government decided to support the program. By the end of 1991, the experience involved some seventy community stores. Some problems have arisen from clientelistic attempts to take advantage of the support, but the program has been successful and has helped strengthen democratic self-management in the communities.

Another example is a seven-community meat market that distributes meat at prices 40 to 45 percent below those of commercial outlets. It manages this feat by deleting eight intermediaries that intervene in the commercial distribution of such products. The meat market distributes 3,000 to 4,000 kilograms of meat on a weekly basis. A fourth experience is a drugstore in Usaquén that operates alongside a health center and sells drugs at a 40 percent discount. Previously noted is the transportation cooperative in Ciudad Bolívar, an enterprise with over seventy vehicles that provide transportation services to an area underserved by private companies.

Projects are unfolding in which communities contract with public agencies. Three zonal organizations—in Usaquén, Ciudad Bolívar, and Suba—have contracted with the Institute for Urban Development to have the streets in their neighborhoods paved. The popular organization of the Santa Cecilia barrio has done the same and now has thirty square blocks of paved streets.

These are some of the endeavors that popular movements, together with NGOs and local governments, have undertaken in Colombian cities. The experiences are novel and significant for the development of initiatives that attack the problems of the country's neglected social sectors. Decentralization and fiscal reforms are redefining local government clout and capacity. Pushed by social movements and occasionally pulled by NGOs providing services, social policy appears to revolve increasingly around communal associations and an unfamiliar but promising exercise of citizenship.

Notes

1. Among the 1968 reforms were measures defining the departmental and municipal regimes. Here again, the role of the executive was strengthened to the detriment of state legislatures and municipal councils. For example, henceforth only mayors and governors could initiate public spending; their exclusive powers extended to the administrative and financial management of their respective jurisdictions.

2. During the last fifteen years, protests in Bogotá (259 in all) have been motivated principally by discontent over service and costs for water supply and sewerage, electricity, and domestic fuel; public transportation; and solid waste collection. Housing- and labor-related problems have also given rise to demonstrations of protest. Of the 259 local stoppages organized from 1970 to 1985, however, 55 percent grew out of demands related to electrical coverage, water supply, and sewerage.

3. This initiative, the most important until that time, enjoyed considerable success. Some of the guerrilla groups later disarmed and returned to civilian politics.

◆◆

10

Mexico's Difficult Democracy: Grassroots Movements, NGOs, and Local Government

Luis Hernandez
Jonathan Fox

State and Society in Mexico

Mexico's democracy once seemed like an oasis amidst the desert of Latin America's dictatorships. Abroad, the Mexican government's benign image was reinforced by many of the nation's most distinguished intellectuals and, more recently, sophisticated public relations firms. For many Mexicans, however, this oasis of democracy was a frustrating mirage. Conditions were not as they appeared from abroad for those without privileged protection from the arbitrary exercise of governmental authority. The glowing image of Mexico's political liberalization concealed a reality of citizens whose names were deliberately erased from the voting rolls or whose charred ballots could be found floating in its rivers.

The unexpected explosion of political opposition in 1988 put electoral democracy at the top of the political agenda, but the issue is hardly a new one. Since the beginning of the twentieth century, Mexico has produced a wide range of popular movements for democracy. The revolution of 1910 began with the call for "effective suffrage"—for the rights of citizens to choose their rulers. Since that time, movements for political rights have risen and fallen, with the most recent wave traceable at least as far back as the 1960s, a decade marked by failed attempts to democratize the ruling party and by the bloody repression of the 1968 student movement. Diverse movements for social and economic rights dominated the 1970s, and the call for political democracy filled many of Mexico's principal plazas during the 1980s.

The 1985 earthquakes marked a turning point. The impressive citizen response to the disaster contrasted sharply with the government's initial incapacity, and new social actors became legitimate players under new rules of the game. By the late 1980s, broad sectors of Mexican society from across the political spectrum—including important segments of the ruling party—agreed that Mexico had to begin a transition to democracy.

Contending national political parties and leaders are but one part of the story. The democratization process becomes more complex as one takes into account a broader range of actors, many of whom do not fit the frameworks designed for analyzing national political elites. This chapter analyzes the interaction between three key actors in this process: grassroots social movements, local governments, and nongovernmental development organizations.

Mexico's political and social life has long been shaped by the heavy hand of the state, which lacks the checks and balances that accompany the separation of powers; the legislative and judicial authorities are under the effective control of the executive branch, in general, and of the president's initiatives and proposals, in particular. In spite of partial electoral reforms, political choices are still limited by strict government controls on alliances between opposition political parties. The country has been governed by the same party, the Institutional Revolutionary Party (PRI), since 1929. Because the electoral process remains under government control with no effective channels for independent citizen oversight, fraud is a serious problem.

The government's human-rights record is both bloody and, until recently, invisible due to official bias in the broadcast media. Human-rights publicity has thus far been limited to the tiny minority of Mexican society that reads newspapers. By the late 1980s, however, independent human-rights groups had begun to monitor and document violations of basic human rights systematically. Perhaps the first such organization was the Mothers' Committee, founded in 1978, and followed by the National Front Against Repression. The most frequent victims of abuse are those whose voices are weakest in Mexican society—the indigenous peoples who make up at least 15 percent of the overall population and the majority of the rural poor. As of 1991, reformist currents within the state were still unable to challenge the impunity of human-rights violators deeply embedded within the state apparatus (Americas Watch 1991). It should be noted, however, that the Mexican government grew increasingly sensitive to international pressure on human-rights issues during the course of 1991. It remains unclear whether this is the beginning of a long-term, sustained commitment or a short-term reflection of concern for the government's image during the delicate negotiations for a North American Free Trade Agreement.

Most social organizations such as trade unions, peasant organizations, or business associations have long been controlled by the government. Membership is often obligatory, and the leadership is chosen from above. Although many different social groups have challenged this official monopoly on representation over the past few decades, results have been mixed. While the central state's capacity to control local political and social life has always been uneven, the Mexican state retained near total control over the channels to civil society from the top down with corporate controls at the national level even into the late 1980s. Among the many diverse groups that make up Mexican society, only the Catholic Church has succeeded in sustaining a powerful autonomous national organization.

Integral to the Mexican state's "success" is its skillful use of the carrot-and-stick technique. Typical government responses to popular movements for social reform and democracy have combined partial concessions with repression, conditioning access to material gains on political subordination. Nor does the state always wait to be pressured; its remarkable capacity for preemptive measures continues to surprise seasoned observers. One cannot understand Mexico's longstanding relative political stability without looking at both sides of the coin. The state does sometimes give in—to some people, some of the time—although usually with strings attached. Some of Mexico's rulers specialize in such bargaining, operating, however, in the shadow of their colleagues' capacity for fierce repression if the negotiations break down. This camouflage is a key component of what Mario Vargas Llosa (1991) called "the perfect dictatorship."

In spite of these constraints, the Mexican state has opened more political space than existed twenty or thirty years ago. The challenge to society has been twofold: to weaken the most authoritarian elements within the state and to develop strategies that are politically appropriate to each historical moment. Today's efforts toward local democratization build on a wide range of past experiences in the social as well as political arena.

Perhaps most significant is the shift from an exclusive emphasis on protest to one that includes efforts to build concrete social and political alternatives. Since the 1970s, Mexico's social movements for reform and democracy have been making the transition from confrontational opposition (*contestación*) to the construction of positive alternatives (*proposición*). In the process, a new sense of citizenship has emerged, combining community-based self-organization for socioeconomic development with a political push for accountable government. Although these two streams of social change followed separate paths in the past, they began to come together in the late 1980s. Social movements that had previously abstained from electoral politics began to assist in the often frustrating process of widening small openings in the state at both local and national levels.

Local Government

Mexican history has long been marked by political conflicts between central and local authorities. State governors were once highly autonomous actors, some of national importance; since the consolidation of the central state in the 1930s, however, they have tended to represent regional elites to the national state.[1] In theory, the United States of Mexico is a federation, and state governors have long considered themselves to be the sovereign authorities within their domains. In practice, however, ruling party candidates for governor can be named by the president, taking into account the balance of forces within the state. Governors can also be summarily deposed by the president, especially if they directly challenge him or are considered unable to contain political pressures within their domains. When the presidency changes hands, there is sometimes serious friction between the new central authority and his inherited subordinates (because of staggered electoral calendars), but these are conflicts within the ruling "revolutionary family" rather than expressions of democratic initiatives from below.

In Mexico, "municipalities" refer to cities, towns, or rural counties. Many municipalities include both urban centers and surrounding smaller towns and rural areas. As is the case in many countries, most of Mexico's political activity takes place locally. The status of the municipality, the smallest territorial politico-administrative unit, has risen and fallen often since independence. Not until the founding of the postrevolutionary Mexican political system was the municipality's status formally recognized. For example, even though the Spanish conquerors founded the township of Villa Rica of Veracruz as early as 1519, the municipality was not fully incorporated into the Mexican political system until the Constitution of 1917 (Elías Gutiérrez 1987). As the third level of government, after state and federal authorities, the municipality is a key arena of conflict between civil society, which tries to occupy this space, and the central state, which treats it as the bottom layer in the regime's vertical hierarchy.

Local autonomy and decentralization or "free townships" was the cry of the people throughout the Porfirian dictatorship (1876–1910). Embedded in the 1910 revolt for electoral democracy and the return of community lands, it resonated again with Zapata's revolutionary demand for "land and liberty." One of the first modern campaigns for municipal democracy took place in Acapulco, where widely shared grievances against authoritarian local elites combined with anarcho-syndicalist ideas left over from the revolution to launch a mass movement for local democratization. The Acapulco Workers' Party actually won the 1920 municipal election, although local merchants soon brought in the army to violently eject the victors from the town hall (Taibó and Vizcaíno 1990). Another key modern political campaign for municipal democracy emerged in 1946, led by the Civic Union of León—an electoral alliance of the National Action Party (PAN) and the Popular Force Party in the state of Guanajuato. Even though the Civic Union defeated the official candidate by a clear margin, the state government refused to acknowledge the victory and repressed the protests that followed. Such abuse of power continues to this day. At least two important contemporary regional movements for democratization (San Luis Potosí and Guerrero) trace their roots directly back to struggles of the late 1950s.

There are 2,378 municipalities in Mexico, distributed very unevenly throughout the thirty-one states. (The Federal District has a special status, since it is ruled directly by the executive branch.) Oaxaca, for example, is made up of 570 mostly small, rural municipalities whereas North and South Baja California have only four apiece. Each municipality's access to resources varies greatly, but not in proportion to either size or population. Most municipalities depend largely on discretional revenue sharing from state and federal authorities, which creates major obstacles for dissenting local governments, whether inside or outside the official party.

The government's National Indigenous Institute (INI) considers 28 percent of the nation's municipalities to be predominantly indigenous. These municipalities, mainly in southern Mexico, are far from the world of Western public administration, combining the juridical forms of the nation-state with traditional forms of self-government and community participation. These traditions reflect the imposition of Spanish colonial influence upon preexisting authority structures. Indigenous forms of governance incorporate a mix of civic-religious hierarchies based on rotating community responsibilities (*cargos*). This system involves a high degree of community political autonomy because after a traditional community chooses its authorities, the official political system often recognizes them as its candidates. Through a delicate bargaining process, the government cedes de facto local autonomy in exchange for a free hand in state and national politics. In this context, political party labels are quite superficial.

In regions where indigenous rights movements have grown, autonomous villages have united at the regional level, as in the cases of the Assembly of Mixe Authorities and the Assembly of Zapotec Authorities. As Mixe leader Floriberto Díaz Gómez put it:

> In our experience, political parties end up trying to divide us, to turn us into "yes men," or simple paper pushers. If our communities reject political parties, it is because we know that only all of us, together, can make the most important decisions that affect us, about land, justice, and government (1988).

In indigenous communities where social differentiation is sharply delineated and the poor have developed some degree of autonomous organization, the first phase of conflict for control over local political power often involves a struggle to control the representation of the official political party, the Institutional Revolutionary Party (PRI). In some municipalities, such as Yalalag in Oaxaca's Sierra Juárez, communities have managed to defeat the *caciques* (local and regional political bosses) and wield local political power from within the ranks of the PRI. In other cases this has not been possible, and communities have taken advantage of the official registries of opposition political parties.

Within regional centers—towns designated urban by the census but often quite rural in reality—another arena of conflict involves the municipal center and its satellite agencies or village-level branches. In many regional centers, rural community movements may be strong enough to democratize the agencies but not the urban center itself. These conflicts rarely appear as political party competition, but they involve key issues such as locally accountable police.

Two factors condition the degree of local autonomy: first, the economic importance of the municipality—the richer the town, the more likely the official party will have established a permanent presence there; second, the community's organizational consolidation—the greater its skills of unified mobilization in defense of village and ethnic rights, the less likely the official party will be able to penetrate. In these cases, the official party presence is often limited to local elites and their clients.

In the rest of Mexico, movements to democratize municipal governments began to spread more quickly in the 1980s, especially after the 1983 political reform permitted some degree of proportional representation in city and town councils (Meza and Padilla 1991; López Monjardin 1986). Two different political streams came together during this period. First were the civic movements against political bosses, often multiclass movements without sectoral demands. These movements were often led by professionals or businesspeople under the banner of the PAN. Many were relatively nonideological campaigns for "good government" that had their greatest success in provincial capitals far from Mexico City.[2]

At the same time, however, some of the emerging municipal democratic movements came not from the conventional world of political parties, but from the effervescence of grassroots social movements. Although largely outside of the electoral arena, neighborhoods and villages had long been organizing against local caciques—who might be landgrabbers, moneylenders, hit men, crop hoarders, or unresponsive local bureaucrats. By the mid-1980s, many of these urban and rural social movements had turned their attention to the possibilities opened up by the government's partial political reform. The precursor of many of these efforts was the Coalition of Workers, Peasants, and Students of the Isthmus of Oaxaca (COCEI), which began contesting elections in Juchitan, Oaxaca, in 1974 and won the municipality in 1981, then again in 1986, 1989, and 1992.

For urban social movements, winning the city or town hall meant gaining access to resources, both to deliver public services and to reinforce political legitimacy. For example, selective control over access to drinking water and electricity is a pillar of both urban and rural cacique power. Local police power is especially important, particularly when municipal authorities ally with landlords and use the police to push peasants or urban squatters off their land. As López Monjardin (1988) put it, "often peasants are not in the position of 'opting' for electoral struggle, rather they are obliged to get involved because the key to the social vise which grips their region is locked in the town hall."

Until the late 1980s, many civic movements for good government took place within the official party. Although closeted behind closed doors, conflict around the selection of official candidates was often quite real. What sometimes appeared to be factional conflict within the ruling party reflected genuine community conflicts, including struggles against local caciques. When losing factions were unable to express themselves through compensatory mechanisms, they sought refuge under the banner of one of the existing opposition parties—whichever had some local reputation or offered access to a line on the ballot (until recently, only nationally registered parties could run candidates, even at the local level). The local expression of most Mexican political parties thus had little to do with real programmatic competition.

Behind the Opening: Cracks in the System

Many of Mexico's contemporary social movements trace their roots back to the late 1960s when, after the 1968 student movement, many activists went to the neighborhoods, factories, and villages. New grassroots movements were born, and older movements were revived. Some survived into the 1990s, while others proved ephemeral. Some won key demands and were pacified, while others were dismantled by repression. But aside from their varying fates or political approaches, many shared two key characteristics; they tried to tackle social problems that directly affected their constituencies and, in doing so, tried to establish their autonomy from the state. Some, however, in the process of trying to "deliver," sacrificed their political autonomy in exchange for material benefits. Of the social movements of the 1970s that defended their autonomy as a matter of principle, many shared a third characteristic—the attempt to build new forms of participatory democracy.

This power-seeking process was marked by a sharp divergence between socioeconomic movements and political-electoral participation, a gap that has long frustrated the construction of citizenship in Mexico (Bartra 1992). Movements emerged to promote socioeconomic *or* political and civic rights, but rarely did movements manage to sustain efforts on both fronts. Three factors aggravated this tension: first, strong pressure from the state, which threatened social movements with repression and loss of access to possible concessions should they turn to overt political opposition; second, the extreme distrust many social movements felt for existing political parties, and the fear that their needs would be used for purposes beyond their control; third, the inability of most social movement leaders, long accustomed to electoral abstention, to create their own new ways of articulating social and political participation.

Since the founding of Mexico's postrevolutionary social pact during the Cárdenas administration (1934–1940), most social demands have been processed through corporatist organizations. (In some regions, however, caciques never bothered to convert their political machines into branches of the official mass organizations, leading to an uneven presence throughout the country.) These organizations, and the bureaucracies that administered them, served simultaneously as communication channels between the official party and its social base and as the channel for much of the national social welfare budget. For three decades, popular groups had limited opportunities to sustain autonomous leadership and find solutions to their problems outside of these official channels. However, possibilities for autonomous organizing were greater among urban community groups than among industrial workers or smallholding peasants, whose livelihoods depended more directly on political obedience. When, by the 1970s, a wave of social mobilization overflowed the boundaries of the official groups, certain sectors of the government were willing to bargain with these new social actors, but only if they did not get involved in electoral opposition.

Little by little, these "social left" organizations consolidated themselves in several cities (Moguel 1987; Nuñez 1990). Although often outside of the official system of legal recognition, their capacity to mobilize their bases and their ability to channel social energy toward the solution of concrete problems combined to permit these groups to negotiate with the state. Conservative elements within the state combined co-optation with repression, while reformists saw these community-based groups as safety valves for urban discontent—effectively regulating extralegal access to land for self-built housing, for example.

Community groups with the most staying power were those whose leaders gained bargaining power and legitimacy by taking advantage of elite conflicts within the system. Just as important, however, was knowing not to push too hard when the ranks of the powerful were closed. By the 1980s, the veteran social organizations of the urban poor, largely comprised of those displaced by rural poverty and rooted in the informal economy, had become key protagonists of a new "informal politics."[3]

In the end these groups were limited to small urban and rural enclaves in spite of sustaining their autonomy and experimenting with new participatory decisionmaking processes, often gaining the government's de facto recognition in the process. The combination of their own classist ideology and the mass media campaigns mounted against them isolated them from other social sectors. These small islands of "plebian democracy" were seen by others as lands of savages, protectors of criminals, and sources of disorder. Ironically, what really happened within these communities was exactly the opposite: order reigned, including the establishment of neighborhood guards, grassroots judicial systems, campaigns against alcoholism, and protection for women against domestic violence. The idea was to create a new sense of security. Unfortunately, two images had by then arisen; those outside saw these communities as the new barbarians, those within saw the outsiders as hostile, politically "damned," and beyond salvation.

Many grassroots organizers of the period reacted against the dominant political culture, which in their eyes combined the official conditioning of social demands on electoral clientelism with the tendency of opposition parties to sacrifice social movements in their secret bargaining with the state (with the exception of the PAN).[4] Convinced that electoral politics were inherently corrupt and useless as a path to change, these leaders of the social left preferred to build independent poor-people's organizations based on radical ideas of direct democracy. Members made decisions collectively in assemblies, held their representatives accountable, and combined negotiations with mass direct action to demand the government address their problems. For the increasingly politicized segment of the urban poor, these groups began to create a social counterpart to the informal economy.

Many of these movements were born in the course of broad civic mobilization for accountable government (Moguel, this volume). After these issue-oriented movements crested, winning what could be won at the time, the core activists became more class oriented, emphasizing the consolidation of poor people's organizations. As past tensions between movements for socioeconomic versus civic rights rekindled, general democratic demands failed to sustain poor people's participation, and the focus shifted to immediate survival issues. In the process, these organizations lost their capacity to lead multiclass civic movements for democracy.

The political reality of isolation stubbornly challenged these social left groups to find new styles and forms of organization in order to grow beyond their enclaves. Until they did, the best they could do was to extract partial material victories from the state and thereby to administer some of the demands of their members. In some cases, key activists withdrew to private life or joined the long march within the institutions of government. Some learned important lessons from their grassroots experience, leading them to design innovative public policies for confronting Mexico's perennial problems of entrenched poverty. The philosophy of coresponsibility between state and society that inspired the government's rural food-distribution program and urban self-built housing programs of the 1980s drew on this tradition, and these largely successful antipoverty efforts later inspired the Salinas presidency's National Solidarity Program (PRONASOL).

In some regions, political isolation led to internal decomposition. The new forms of assembly-style democracy showed weaknesses. While mass meetings may have been effective forms of popular representation during the movement's ascent, assemblies represented only the most active as mobilization ebbed. Leadership factions learned how to prevent assemblies from leading to unexpected outcomes. In some cases, however, organizations responded by developing creative new combinations of representative and direct democracy. The Popular Defense Committee of Durango, for example, began a process of neighborhood referenda on key issues, as well as the direct and secret vote for citywide leaders (Moguel, this volume; Haber 1992).

At the same time, changes occurred not only in the independently organized sectors but in society as a whole. Urbanization increased and access to education broadened during the 1960s and 1970s. More and more citizens rejected traditional state tutelage, especially after the post-1982 economic crisis limited the state's capacity to divide and rule with clientelism and subsidies. Broad sectors of the middle class, especially in the North, began to channel their discontent through the PAN's mass electoral campaigns.

The electoral success of the right wing took autonomous social movements by surprise. Efforts by these organizations and the political left to organize the growing popular discontent in the early 1980s through civic strikes failed (Carr and Anzaldúa 1986). When the PAN swept the 1983 municipal elections in the state of Chihuahua, it became clear that a wave of popular *civic* discontent was on the rise. The PAN won city halls in municipalities accounting for 70 percent of the state's population, which provoked a debate at the highest levels of the federal government about whether to recognize such defeats in the future. Those who sought to transform PRI defeats into victories, the "alchemists," won, leading to conflicts across the north that culminated in massive fraud in Chihuahua's 1986 gubernatorial election. The civic protests that followed were among the most extensive at the state level so far.

The PAN had become a key channel for business dissent, which exploded after the government's abrupt 1982 nationalization of private banking. The party also gained broad popular support because of its long-standing civic tradition of electoral opposition to single-party rule. Still bound to their strong proabstention position and their contempt for electoral and party politics, the autonomous social organizations were late in understanding the depth and breadth of popular sentiment in favor of real electoral democracy.

New Directions for
Grassroots Movements and Local Politics

The principal form of alliance building in the popular movements of the late 1970s and the 1980s was the sectoral network, or *coordinadoras,* which became umbrella groups for urban popular organizations, agrarian groups, and dissident trade-unionist teachers. By the end of the 1980s, however, it became clear that the national coordination of local sectoral politics was far from sufficient to affect the balance of forces at the national level. New autonomous social organizations began to bypass the veteran groups of the 1970s. For example, after the 1985 Mexico City earthquake, the National Coordinating Body of the Urban Popular Movement (CONAMUP)—once the leading force—became one among three, as the Union of Earthquake Victims and the Neighborhood Assembly developed creative organizing strategies and outreach styles (Hernández 1990; Moguel 1990).

Similar events occurred in the peasant movement, as the most promising arena of organizing shifted from land rights to production and marketing issues in the early 1980s. The National "Plan de Ayala" Network was unable to change with the times. Divided by internal political conflicts, it lost its leading role to more pragmatic groups that carved out a relatively autonomous political "gray area" that broke the past dichotomy between "independent" and official. A new national network, the National Union of Autonomous Regional Peasant Organizations, began to fill this political space, managing the difficult transition from contestation to proposition.

Challenged also by the rise of the PAN, many in the coordinadoras began to rethink their approach to electoral politics. As the 1988 wave of Cardenista sympathy swept their rank and file, even leaders who came late to this process had to rethink their antielectoral positions. Official political reforms had changed the rules of the game, both permitting and imposing the institutionalization of the informal politics inherited from the 1970s.

Regional social organizations that managed to consolidate themselves were faced with the challenge of municipal power. Where the leadership chose to abstain for ideological reasons, the rank and file sometimes chose to vote for political parties whose success led to a short circuit of the move- ment. One of the clearest examples of this was in the northern industrial city of Monclova, where for many years workers at the largest steel mill in the country had been organizing for union democracy. Together with left- wing allies, they managed to defeat the corrupt bureaucracy and win con- trol of their local, but the same bureaucracy still controlled the city hall. The workers wanted to exercise their citizenship rights and vote against their enemies—but did so by voting for the right-wing PAN candidate for mayor (Bizberg 1988).

Few popular organizations proposed electoral participation early on. The attempt to bring together social demands with political democratiza- tion was pioneered by the COCEI, which was the first independent leftist group to win an important city hall. In the early 1980s, the COCEI was active in both the "Plan de Ayala" Network and CONAMUP, since its base included both urban poor and neighboring peasants. Based in and around Juchitán, Oaxaca's second-largest city, the COCEI was built through a combination of class demands and emphasis on its ethnic Zapotec identity, articulated through mass protest and an electoral struggle for municipal democracy (Rubin 1987, 1990). From there, the coalition went on to participate in federal congressional elections. Between the municipal electoral victory of 1981 and the state government's violent takeover of the town hall in 1983, the COCEI pursued its class and cultural project, in the process building an influential series of national alliances. The COCEI's persistence and strong grassroots legitimacy permitted it to regain the city hall, first through a partial power-sharing arrangement in 1986, and then completely in 1989. In the process, the COCEI showed other grassroots organizations what could be accomplished through flexible tactics and alliances. The COCEI was an example for other Mexican social movements of what many smaller Oaxacan communities had long pursued by other means—proving that grassroots movements could win municipal democratization, even though the election laws required them to ally with national political parties that remained fundamentally foreign to local politics.

The narrow social base and confined outreach of most left-wing opposition political parties limited the options of community-based movements interested in making the transition from sectoral and economic lobbying to direct participation in local elections. This left a vacuum that eventually forced some social movements to act as electoral parties. In some cases, as in Juchitán, the regional organization was powerful enough to gain access to the electoral registry of a national party, creating an unusually balanced political alliance. The national political reform of 1977 had made such alliances possible by broadening the officially recognized party spectrum, but it also limited options by allowing the registry of national political parties only (Middlebrook 1986).

Like Zapata's guerrillas during the 1910–1917 revolution, who served as part-time soldiers and as farmers (going home to their fields during planting season), some of these regional organizations had to wear several hats, acting at some points as leaders of antiauthoritarian resistance, at other times as development agencies, and at still other moments as political parties. In this process, alliances with intellectuals have often been crucial.

Linkages Between Intellectuals and Social Movements

Encounters between critical sectors of the intelligentsia and popular sectors followed five main paths that encompassed the universities, government rural-development agencies, "organic intellectuals" bridging different movements, political parties and protoparties, and NGOs.

The first path, Mexican universities, experienced many waves of reform efforts since the 1960s by students, workers, and teachers. These movements tried to strengthen the linkages between the universities and the poor. Thousands of students fulfilled their social service requirement and ended up becoming advisors, organizers, and leaders of grassroots movements. The university offered both political and logistical shelter as the classrooms opened to social movements. Entire academic departments developed grassroots-support programs, such as housing programs, legal services, adult education, and health services. Over time, some of these activities became increasingly consolidated and integrated into the regular activities of the university, as in the state universities of Guerrero, Puebla, and Sinaloa. Others grew apart from their alma maters, launching private nonprofit service agencies or outright social organizations, as in Oaxaca and Zacatecas.

The second path consisted of government rural-development programs, which, since the early 1970s, played a key role in shaping what eventually became autonomous smallholder movements. By 1981, a comprehensive survey of regional producer organizations found that two-thirds had been founded through the initiatives of government agencies, and that most of the rest were connected to the official peasant organization. The outreach programs of a wide range of agricultural, credit, and marketing agencies penetrated deep into the countryside. Especially during the 1973–1976 agrarian reform revival and the 1980–1982 food-policy reform period, thousands of social-service-oriented, university-trained promoters worked in projects to increase productivity, broaden access to credit and funding, and organize subsidized food-distribution outlets for the poorest of the poor, leading to the creation of a wide range of new organizational forms. By no means all of these outreach workers saw their tasks as linked to the broader goal of democratization, but many did—in striking contrast to their bureaucratic superiors. Their main obstacles were not only the local caciques, but also the inertia and corruption of their own agencies. By the late 1980s, these various organizing efforts had had an important feedback effect, both on the character of the peasant movement and on national rural-development policies as well (Fox 1992b).

The third main path involved "organic," community-based intellectuals who built horizontal links between movements, such as the relationship between rural teachers and peasant movements. In Mexico, rural teachers usually come from humble backgrounds and are often highly politicized. Since the 1920s, they have played a strategic role in supporting and leading local peasant movements, linking them to one another and helping them to "scale up" in dealings with the state. Throughout the 1980s, teachers in Mexico's poorest rural states combined their own efforts for trade-union democracy and higher wages with support for peasant rights and municipal democratization. The cases of Oaxaca and Chiapas were the most successful (Cook 1990). In addition, other examples of organic intellectuals' bridging roles include urban community organizers who went into trade-union organizing, especially in the early and mid-1970s.

Linkages between intellectuals and popular movements through political parties have been much more limited than those forged by the first three paths. This fourth path has usually been indirect, as party-linked support agencies offered needed services to existing movements in an effort to gain political clientele. This indirect relationship was due to the parties' political isolation and big-city, middle-class character, as well as to the movements' persistent wariness about being used by the parties.

The fifth genre of linkage between intellectuals and grassroots movements is through nongovernmental development organizations. The first Mexican NGOs were closely linked to the Catholic Church, which directly or indirectly managed many welfare and educational institutions. By the 1950s and 1960s, the church's Social Secretariat played a crucial role in founding NGOs that worked in the areas of revolving credit funds, popular education, food distribution, health, and urban problems. Nevertheless, it was not until the spread of liberation theology and the emergence of Christian base communities that these institutions mushroomed. By the 1970s, many foundations and centers were set up to accompany and finance efforts at *concientización,* developed as part of the progressive church doctrine of the "preferential option for the poor." NGOs appeared in communities in Morelos, Veracruz, Jalisco, and Ciudad Nezahualcoyotl. Through NGOs, hundreds of Catholic youth were involved in grassroots movements.

For many years this family of NGOs concentrated their efforts on popular education. Inspired by the pedagogy of Paulo Freire, they emphasized "consciousness raising." Any kind of service activity could serve as the entry point for this higher goal: literacy, basic education, health and hygiene, housing cooperatives, small-scale artisanry, or food distribution. In the discourse of the time, the prevailing goal called for the poor to discover their oppression and find a path to liberation. Within this context, NGOs offered a variety of services along the way, although their overall goal was educational.

This "promotional" approach quickly showed its virtues and its limitations. To begin with, many of the production-oriented projects did not become consolidated. Economic projects were limited by the egalitarian approach of the promoters, who were very distrustful of any activity that led to class differentiation, a condition presumed to interfere with consciousness raising and to encourage shortcuts along the path to social change. In addition, this overpolitization of organizing work led to repeated cycles of desertion by the promoters themselves, many of whom turned either to opposition political activities or to the less frustrating arena of private and professional life.

This approach was also limited by its emphasis on the formation of small nuclei, while most mainstream grassroots organizers stressed mass mobilization. Many of these small groups were parish-based and depended on charismatic leaders. Some of the popular education promoters, secular as well as religious, were distrustful of the mainstream popular movements, perhaps fearing that an alliance could lead to a loss of influence over their community groups. At the same time, many of the key regional and national social movements, such as those involved in the coordinadoras, had serious reservations about many of the NGOs. They resented the NGOs' access to funding and the power that came with it. Most NGOs were seen as outside the movements, provoking suspicions that NGO staff wanted to take them over. Some NGOs, like the National Center for Social Communication, opened their doors to grassroots movements, organized press conferences, and denounced government abuses, but they were a minority with little strength to change the dominant tendency.

The mainstream grassroots movements of the social left and the progressive church emerged at the same time, sharing a concern for directly addressing the needs of the urban and rural poor, as well as the need to combine educational work with survival demands. The distance between them grew because of a struggle over the leadership of the movements, aggravated by some church activists' rejection of what they considered to be an overly economistic orientation that involved bargaining with the state. In the process of separation, the social left ended up with most of the movements and the religious NGOs ended up with the relationships with foreign funders. As in any divorce, the terms of the separation marked both partners for years.

Groups from all sides tried to bridge this gap. In the social left, groups like the Union of Popular Neighborhoods in Mexico City recruited Christian youth and worked closely with NGOs. On the church side, the Jesuits' Social Commission played an outstanding role in encouraging regional social movements. An NGO, the newly formed Equipo Pueblo, worked directly with the coordinadoras during the 1970s, opening up relationships between cutting-edge grassroots movements and international development agencies. Professionals from the nominally apolitical secular private sector also got involved in both rural development and urban small business, especially through the Mexican Rural Development Foundation and the Micro-Enterprise Development Foundation.

It was not until much later—the early 1980s—that more secular, technical, and politically oriented professionals began to set up NGOs in large numbers. Analysis, Decentralization, and Management (ANADEGES) was a pioneer in the late 1970s, bringing together a significant network of over twenty regional or sector-specific NGOs staffed largely by professionals who had left the public and private sectors. They consciously deprofessionalized themselves, raising international NGO and public-sector funding to put their skills at the service of community-based groups. In some cases, ANADEGES affiliates developed innovative policies through contracts with the public sector. For example, in 1983, the Committee to Promote Rural Development Research launched a program called "Solidarity Funds for

Peasant Development," which they carried out under contract with the state government of Guerrero (then relatively liberal). These revolving "on-your-word" credit funds did not require low-income peasant producers to put up collateral. After 1988, within the context of sharp cuts in conventional farm credit, the Salinas government's Solidarity program began to carry out a similar program nationwide, reaching many producers with essentially symbolic amounts (U.S.$100 per family).

Mexican NGOs and Social Movements

Most NGOs in Mexico are issue-specific in focus, although many work in both urban and rural areas, and quite a few deal with several issues at once. Mexico is only just beginning to develop coherent NGO networks within specific sectors, not to mention a more comprehensive set of alternative development policy–oriented alliances.

Housing

The earthquakes that shook Mexico City in 1985 spurred a qualitative leap in NGO development, both in their linkages to social movements and in their networking with each other. Foreign relief and development funding sky-rocketed, although it was overshadowed by the magnitude of the devastation and the massive display of volunteer citizen action. Dozens of new NGOs appeared alongside the more established agencies, while new social organizations emerged independently to face the challenge of reconstruction.

One of the government agencies whose track record inspired the postearthquake style of relatively pluralistic bargaining with social movements was the Fund for Popular Housing, which in turn was strongly influenced by NGO experiences in supporting self-built housing. In the process, the housing NGOs developed some of the most important sectoral networks in Mexico, including the Inter-Institutional Network and the Habitat International Coalition. Mexico's oldest housing NGO is the Operational Housing and Settlement Center, founded with church support in 1963. This NGO gave birth to the Housing and Urban Studies Center in 1979. Both organizations played important roles in the partial reorientation of government low-income housing policy in the early 1980s. Policy changes included the aforementioned Fund for Popular Housing, a new agency that broke with tradition by dealing with the urban poor in a relatively more equitable, efficient, and less clientelistic way (Aldrete Haas 1990; Annis and Hakim 1988).

Not only did the earthquakes bring down buildings, they shook the foundations of the established structures of social and political control and representation—including the social left organizations of the urban poor. Until then, CONAMUP had been the principal force defending the demands of urban homesteaders and low-income tenants. CONAMUP leaders had pinned their hopes on NGO funds, hoping to receive enough to develop their own reconstruction project and avoid dealing with the state. They were disappointed and lost their leadership role in the process. The Union of Earthquake Victims emerged to fill the resulting vacuum between the state and key sectors of the urban poor. The Union proved itself quite adept at combining mass mobilization with negotiations, obliging the state to make major changes in its original reconstruction policy. The most important policy changes allowed residents to remain in their original neighborhoods and stopped government expropriation of thousands of buildings. While some groups emphasized bargaining over the terms of government reconstruction aid, others developed close ties with NGOs and pursued more community-based building strategies.

The resources garnered by these NGOs were much less, however, than those obtained by the Catholic Church and the federal government. The utopian idea that NGO funding would permit the creation of social spaces completely autonomous from the government could not be "scaled up" beyond a certain point. Material constraints frustrated those for whom self-built housing was to be the foundation of grassroots autonomy, especially in the densely populated central city. Government contractors built or repaired over 44,000 housing units in record time, compared with at most a few thousand built by NGOs.

Once the Catholic hierarchy decided to make a pact with the federal government, most grassroots organizations had little choice but to deal with the state themselves. With the signing of the Democratic Concertation Agreement (by a multitude of actors),[5] which regulated temporary housing, provided low-interest construction loans and infrastructure, and suspended evictions, a new path opened for conflict resolution between state and society. That open-ended pattern continues to develop today. Unlike past populist welfare programs, this accord (or *concertación*) did not require community groups to give up their political autonomy. Through a creative combination of mobilization, negotiations, and alternative policy proposals, reconstruction aid increasingly became more a citizenship right than a clientelistic political favor. This "positive-sum" bargaining experience between the state and autonomous community groups paved the way for the more democratic official discourse associated with PRONASOL, the Salinas government's National Solidarity Program.

Women's Development

The popular response to the challenge of reconstruction provoked a major increase in women's participation in the development process (Schteingart and Massolo 1987). But autonomous women's organizing in the urban pop-ular movement had already made a qualitative leap between 1983 and 1985, with the formation of CONAMUP's Women's Regional Network. Women had long formed the backbone of the movements, but their forma-tion of an autonomous political space from which to identify and defend gender-specific demands was unprecedented. This process unfolded largely without input from existing feminist organizations. Key NGOs providing support services for women's movements included Women For Dialogue, a popular education group of religious origin that worked primarily in rural areas, and the Women's Team for Social Action, which also carried out popular education work. One of the first experiences with women's centers was carried out by Mexico's first female governor of the state of Colima (Velasco Rocha et al. 1988).

The principal challenge facing grassroots women's support efforts was the gap between middle-class feminist intellectuals and urban poor concen-trating primarily on domestic survival. Not only did they differ in their con-ception of the interaction between gender and class issues, they differed in their approach to the state. The women active in urban popular movements challenged the state to meet their material needs, which necessarily involved a pragmatic, apparently nonpolitical combination of mobilization and negotiation focused mainly on subsidized food programs. However, in the process of their struggle with the male-dominated leadership of the urban popular movement, increasing numbers of women pushed their gen-der boundaries further. Both intellectuals and grassroots activists began to bridge the gap with the emergence of a new popular feminism that respond-ed directly to the daily realities faced by urban poor women (Maier 1990; Stephen 1990).

The organizing efforts of Mexican peasant women have received less attention than those of their urban counterparts. The state has provided some support with its promotion of Women's Agroindustrial Units in the agrarian-reform sector. While many of these have followed the pattern typi-cal of top-down government projects, the Units have also permitted com-munity organizers to launch some modest but precedent-setting self-man-aged development efforts (Fox and Hernández 1989; Stephen 1991). NGO efforts have been small in scale, and few of the most consolidated regional peasant organizations have made women's projects a priority.

Environmental Defense and Sustainable Development

Most environmental NGOs are of relatively recent origin, although the Mexican ecological movement dates back to the late 1960s. Through the 1970s and early 1980s, most environmental groups were urban, middle-class membership organizations rather than NGOs in the sense of grassroots support organizations. Even now, most are still weak and narrowly based—

although some groups of "notables," such as the Group of One Hundred, have gained important access to the media to criticize official policies. Even though two national networks exist—the Pact of Ecological Groups and the Mexican Conservation Federation—as well as some regional and sectoral networks, none appear sufficiently broad or consolidated to represent the movement as a whole. Most environmental NGOs that work closely with social movements are either in the antinuclear power movement[6] or are involved in sustainable rural development work with peasant organizations. The Environmental Study Group, for example, has a history of working with peasant organizations (Alatorre and Aguilar 1990).

One of the rural development efforts with the longest track record involved close collaboration between university-based ecologists and the mountain community of Alcozauca, Guerrero, long a bastion of opposition political activity. Its democratic municipal authorities worked closely with the ecologists and some of the more open state and federal agencies in an innovative series of community-based agroecological projects (Carabias, Toledo, and Caballero 1990). Another innovative example of collaboration between an NGO and movements for community control over natural resources took place in the highlands of Oaxaca. The movement against a large paper company to recover indigenous community control over forestry resources began in 1967, and Rural Studies and Consulting has played a key support role since the early 1980s (Szekeley and Madrid 1990).

In several regions of intense but endangered biodiversity, NGOs are working with community leaders, government agencies, and international NGOs on regional conservation plans. Some of these groups have shifted their approach from traditional conservation, which tended to exclude community participation, to more responsive, sustainable resource-management programs, as in the conflictual Chimalapas region along the Oaxaca-Chiapas border.

There is one especially unusual case of an urban community movement which spun off its own environmental protection NGO. In the late 1980s, the Popular Defense Committee of Durango (CDP) broadened its support beyond its urban-poor base and developed new alliances among government reformers and local notables as a way to increase its leverage against hard-line local and state elites. The CDP formed the Ecological Defense and Preservation Committee (CDyPE) in 1988, which focused on the health and production effects of water pollution, moving from contestation to broad-based multisectoral consultation combined with technically solid alternative-policy proposals. Beginning with an Emergency Program that cooperated with community groups to reclaim and protect seventeen local springs, CDP scaled up to develop regional water management proposals (Moguel 1991).

Rural Development

In the general area of NGO and rural development work, two main tendencies came together in support of peasant-managed economic development projects. The first was that some of the more traditional religious and secular promotional groups changed their approach, with several becoming more active in their support for development efforts linked to autonomous peasant movements. The cases of SEDAC (an adult education service) in Hidalgo and Save the Children in Sonora are notable examples.

The second tendency was for rural development activists to form NGOs that offered the more professionalized support services required by the peasant movement's increasing level of economic organization, especially in the areas of credit, marketing, and technical assistance. One of the most outstanding examples is the Center for the Support of Popular Movements in Oaxaca, which has provided key assistance to one of Mexico's most important autonomous organizations of small-scale coffee producers. The Maya Rural Development Institute has also played a strategic support role for peasant-managed economic development initiatives, especially in the state of Guerrero. Unlike traditional NGOs, these groups were formed by experienced activists and leaders from the grassroots movements themselves.

The ANADEGES community economic-development network combines characteristics of both tendencies and is especially active in central and southern Mexico. As yet, no national network exists to unite rural development groups oriented toward peasant movements, although some collaboration has occurred in specific areas, such as alternative credit policies (Juárez 1990).

Two of the most promising technical support agencies are the new national networks of regional peasant-managed credit unions and fertilizer distributorships, which emerged to fill the gap left by the rollback of state agricultural enterprises. The National Association of Social Sector Credit Unions and the National Association of Social Sector Fertilizer Agents, both created by the regional peasant organizations themselves, have been struggling to keep up with demand (Myhre 1991).

Human Rights

Mexican citizens have long struggled against political persecution and police abuse, but only after the arrival of political refugees from South America did those efforts coalesce into an organized human rights movement. Previous generations had fought to free political prisoners, especially after waves of repression in 1959 and 1968, but these efforts did not call themselves a human rights movement.

The first organizations began to form in the late 1970s to defend the rights of political prisoners taken in Mexico's counterinsurgency campaigns of the early and mid-1970s. The human rights movement began to grow in the early 1980s, in part through the defense of the rights of large waves of political refugees fleeing military violence in El Salvador and Guatemala. By the late 1980s, at the same time as awareness of and protest against electoral violence and police abuse grew sharply, the movement began to spread and broaden its presence throughout the country.[7] From a mere four human rights NGOs in 1984, the number had grown to sixty in 1991. As one of Mexico's leading human rights activists put it, "We now have many allies and constitute what the sociologists call a 'social movement.' We have moved from protest to proposition" (Acosta 1992).

Of all the NGO sectors, the human rights network is one of the broadest based, including many church-oriented groups and spanning the political spectrum. At the national level, the Mexican Commission for the Promotion and Defense of Human Rights, the Mexican Human Rights Academy, the "Fray Francisco de Vitoria" Human Rights Center, and the "Miguel Pro" Human Rights Center are perhaps the most prominent groups.[8] Recently, the first broad-based national network of democratic lawyers was also founded.

Increasingly, democratic-minded professionals are forming their own local commissions at the city and state level, taking personal risks of retribution by police officials. The degree of organizational consolidation that the human rights movement has attained at the local level remains uneven, however. Important advances have taken place in the Chiapas highlands under the auspices of Bishop Samuel Ruiz, a staunch defender of human rights and social justice in one of Mexico's most poverty-stricken and violent regions, but major gaps still exist in other hard-hit regions (i.e., Guerrero, Hidalgo, and Veracruz). Church-linked human rights groups working in the indigenous Tarahumara highlands in Chihuahua have also made significant advances. Cross-border alliances with U.S. environmental NGOs such as the Texas Center for Policy Studies led to widespread critical discussion of a World Bank–funded forestry project, contributing to its suspension in 1991 when large-scale logging enterprises undermined community forestry initiatives and Indian rights over ejidal lands. Increased attention to the problems of police abuse and political violence, internationally as well as domestically, led to the creation of a governmental National Human Rights Commission, which is nominally committed to working with the NGO sector. International attention has been crucial for the growth and consolidation of the human rights movement.

NGO Convergence

NGOs are making important advances at the sectoral level and in some cases have formed important sectoral networks (i.e., housing, community health). Mexican NGOs still lag, however, in the formation of multisectoral networks that effectively articulate social movements, grassroots economic-development support work, and alternative public policy at the local and national levels (Lopezllera 1990). Three factors led to the formation of the first major national network: the 1985 earthquake, the political effervescence of 1988, and the government's new tax law initiative of 1989. In Mexico, NGOs are legally defined as "civil associations" or nonprofit organizations of individuals. In December of 1989, the Ministry of Finance sent a proposed law to the Congress called the "Miscellaneous Tax," which would treat NGOs and cooperatives as though they were large corporations, a threat both to philanthropic and to development projects. The government argued that these two types of organizations were used by profit-oriented companies to avoid taxes. From the NGOs' point of view, the government was attempting both to broaden its tax base and to "impose some political controls on autonomous sectors. But whatever the motive, the new tax threatened the existence and the work of those civil associations that wanted to serve society" (Reygadas 1991).

The convergence among the independent-minded NGOs was also speeded up by a June 1990 national meeting between welfare agencies and NGOs backed by the Mexican private sector and the Catholic Church. At this meeting, the participants discussed three main issues: (1) their status within the context of new tax laws, (2) the opportunity to participate in international debt swaps, and (3) the growing problem of extreme poverty. The Catholic Church's active role in earthquake relief, through its Community Support Fund, permitted it to consider whether to take advantage of international debt swaps for its welfare and development projects.

The June meeting served as a warning to the more independent minded NGOs that the government, the church, and the private sector were developing a new level of coordination that could displace and subordinate them. In response, some of the most representative of the left-oriented NGOs met to discuss their identity, the Salinas government, the new tax law, and the challenge of finding a more stable form of coordination. More than seventy-five NGOs founded the "Convergence of Civic Organizations for Democracy" in August 1990.[9]

The Second and Third National Encounters, which included 120 NGOs, followed quickly. The Convergence proposed an alternative tax law that would recognize its members' status as nonprofit agencies; the PRI-controlled Congress disregarded this proposal, however. At the third meeting, electoral democracy had become an important item for discussion, especially the twin problems of fraud and abstention. The Convergence then joined with the Mexican Human Rights Academy and the San Luis Potosí Human Rights Center to coordinate precedent-setting poll watching in the hotly contested August 1991 governor's race in San Luis Potosí. Their documentation of fraud played a key role in legitimating the opposition candidate's dramatic peaceful protest march on Mexico City, which convinced the president to reverse his decision to support the official results and led in turn to the fall of the PRI candidate. Because of logistical, social, and political constraints, however, the observers were unable to reach beyond the urban areas—a serious problem in a predominantly rural state. The Convergence also backed the Mexican Free Trade Action Network in an effort to democratize information about trinational trade talks as well as to include issues of labor, human rights, and the environment on the integration agenda.[10]

NGOs and Municipal Democratization

Until 1988, the PAN was the party that most successfully capitalized on growing discontent at the municipal level. However, after the surprisingly strong showing in 1988 of Cuauhtemoc Cárdenas' broad center-left nationalist presidential campaign, the pattern began to change. The first phase of this upsurge of electoral opposition created a sensation of real possibilities for change at the local level, especially for autonomous regional social organizations that successfully rode the presidential wave.[11]

After the massive antifraud protests in July and August of 1988, the coalition of semiofficial nationalist parties, former members of the official party (the Democratic Current), Catholics, the social left, and the independent left-wing Mexican Socialist party that had come together to support Cárdenas' candidacy began to come apart. Eventually, the semiofficial parties returned to the progovernment fold, abandoning the PRI's Democratic Current and the political party-oriented and grassroots left, which together formed the Party of the Democratic Revolution (PRD). The party-building effort began at the national level and soon faced the challenge of municipal and state elections without a political presence.

By late 1991, of the 191 municipalities in opposition hands, 97 were under PRD administration (down from a high of 116) and 47 were with the PAN. Most of the other non-PRI municipalities were in the hands of semiofficial parties that had briefly joined the Cardenista opposition in 1988. Most PRD victories were in villages and towns in a handful of states. The PAN remained a powerful force in key cities of the north, including several state capitals (e.g., Tijuana, Ciudad Juárez, Chihuahua, Durango, San Luis Potosí, Saltillo, and Mérida, farther south). Cárdenas had run especially well in urban areas, and even the official tally ceded him the crucial Mexico City metropolitan area. The PRD's efforts to capitalize on this early success had limited results, however, and led to important municipal gains only in the core states of Michoacán and Guerrero. These victories were often partial, since the government only recognized some of them. Repression was fierce; tanks were called out to dislodge protesters from town halls they claimed were theirs.

In 1990 and 1991, however, the PRD did not win partial electoral victories. Fraud and abstentionism were key factors behind this failure to consolidate the gains of 1988 at the local level. Almost as important, however, was the PRD's difficulty in incorporating those who had mobilized behind Cárdenas's presidential race.

The 1988 election represented a gigantic step toward finding political expression for a growing social discontent, but the transition from sectoral organizations to a representative political party at the local level proved remarkably difficult. In 1988, many viewed the wave of support for Cárdenas as one of the effects of the years of grassroots organizing. Taking advantage of a major split within the political class, many social movements joined together and entered the political arena. There is some truth to this view, but it is only partial. With the benefit of hindsight, it is more than likely that most Cárdenas voters were individual citizens who did not identify with or participate in social movements or political organizations, although they may have been formal members of official corporatist groups (Zermeño 1990). It is therefore quite consistent that large numbers of people supported Cárdenas, who symbolized nationalism, social reform, and honest government, yet felt no attraction to traditional forms of political party organization under new labels. Most of those who ended up in the PRD's top leadership came either from the PRI itself or from the Mexican Socialist Party, and their political style often reproduced traditional top-down patterns.

By the time the PRD's municipal advances had peaked, the NGOs were still trying to catch up with the events of 1988, and their role in municipal democratization efforts remained quite limited. The vast majority of international funding agencies were unwilling to finance electoral or alternative governance activity in Mexico, since it could be interpreted as foreign intervention in domestic politics. Even when political parties were not directly involved and the issue support for grassroots development efforts that might get involved in local electoral politics, foreign funders were extremely wary. Their wariness is understandable given the increasingly fine line between grassroots development and electoral politics. The result, however, has been very little NGO support for newly democratized municipal administrations, in a context in which the conventional public-sector resources for local services are often frozen because of political hostility (Paas 1991).

One of the problems is that new ways of thinking about the NGO role in local-level public administration are only beginning to emerge and to be debated. For example, opposition municipalities had their first meeting as late as September 1990 at the First National Municipalist Convention in Mexico City. Although the effort to bring together PRD municipal activists from all over the country was an important step, the dominant organizing concept turned out to be quite narrow. Instead of broadening the notion of municipal politics, the proposed Municipalist movement was based on opposition mayors alone—a structure that would exclude multiparty representation, not to mention possible new forms of citizen participation and representation in local government yet to be created.

Democratic municipal administration has a limited track record, and NGOs are learning how to offer constructive support. Examples include the Guerrero and Oaxaca cases of community-based sustainable resource management previously cited. The Assembly of Mixe Authorities in the Oaxaca highlands built a variety of teams to support grassroots development projects, bilingual legal services, and the defense of traditional culture. Several NGOs in the state of Morelos have opened a training center for staff members of democratic townships to prevent them from being absorbed by the official bureaucracy. The Equipo Pueblo, a key grassroots-support organization in the 1980s, helped to draw lessons from the Durango Popular Defense Committee's experience in electoral politics. In general, however, NGOs are still learning how to bring together social movements, community-based economic development, and democratic local government. Several have come together in the new Inter-Institutional Network, which is beginning to generate proposals and projects for increasing local autonomy and community participation in municipal planning and management through its Municipal Support Network. Founded by eleven NGOs in 1989, the Inter-Institutional Network emerged from progressive religious networks primarily working in housing, cooperatives, and popular education.[12]

The Political Underdevelopment of Mexican NGOs

Mexican NGOs have far to go before achieving the institutional life, the political impact, or the social presence of their counterparts in Chile, Brazil, or Peru. With a few notable exceptions, the presence of NGOs in Mexican politics and social-change efforts is remarkably limited.

The omnipresent role of the state is one key factor explaining the relative political underdevelopment of Mexican NGOs. Prior to its dramatic cuts in social spending in the 1980s, the Mexican state had a significant presence in the provision of basic services. While NGOs are the key actors behind community-based survival strategies in several South American countries, in Mexico, government agencies continue to play a leading role. Examples are the distribution of low-cost milk or the organization of rural food stores and community kitchens (*comedores populares*). Access to these social safety net programs is often conditioned on political loyalty to the ruling party, further limiting the space for independent community-development efforts by NGOs.

Another reason for the relative weakness of Mexican NGOs is their extremely limited access to external funding, at least before the 1985 earthquake. Many European and North American NGOs considered Mexico to be a democratic country well on its way toward industrial development, in short, a regional power with oil resources. Official development aid has also been relatively small, excluding macroeconomic debt and stabilization agreements. The U.S. Agency for International Development has had a very low profile in Mexico, since in aggregate terms the agency considers Mexico a "middle income" country (although it recently increased its support for environmental projects through U.S. NGOs). Until the mid-1980s, the Inter-American Foundation concentrated its grassroots-development activities outside the mainstream of social movements, supporting the business-oriented Mexican Rural Development Foundation and church-linked projects oriented toward popular education. Also, until recently, the European foundations' orientation toward political parties made it difficult for them to find appropriate counterparts in Mexico. For example, the Friedrich Ebert Foundation, linked to the German Social Democratic Party, supported the ruling political party and its trade-union branch, while the Christian Democratic Konrad Adenaur Foundation supported the Mexican Rural Development Foundation. The European foundations arrived late, however, and their resources had much less of a qualitative impact on Mexico's grassroots social change than they did in places that, proportionately, received more money earlier, such as Central America or Chile.[13]

Internal factors also account for some of the weakness of Mexican NGOs. A significant number of the pioneer NGOs dedicated their energies to welfare activities or to popular-education projects that were disconnected from the main lines of social-movement building in the 1970s. In sharp contrast to the Brazilian experience, for example, little communication or coordination took place for many years between the principal NGOs and most cutting-edge popular movements. This difference might have been due to the contrasting roles of the progressive church hierarchy in each country's popular movements—fundamental in the case of Brazil and marginal in most of Mexico. While most of Brazil's bishops sheltered movements for social change and democratization in the 1970s and 1980s, much of the Mexican Catholic Church hierarchy has been hostile or indifferent to social movements (with the notable exceptions of the states of Morelos, Oaxaca, and Chiapas).

In Mexico, while church-based actors focused on small groups, the mainstream popular movements were sustained by their own resources and by whatever they were able to extract from the government through mass mobilization. The differences between church-based NGOs and popular movements were not the result of the NGOs' lack of funding and political outreach, alone; they were also the result of the posture taken by many of these social organizations, which were strongly nationalistic and quite skeptical of NGOs' foreign funding, especially from governments.

Mexican NGOs have also been limited by their distance from national intellectual life. In contrast to many other Latin American countries, where NGOs constituted a key space for prominent intellectuals, many of Mexico's most creative thinkers worked either in universities or for the government. Only recently have intellectuals begun to flock to the NGOs, in part to compensate for the collapse in their standard of living as a result of budget cuts in higher education.

Many of the limiting patterns and circumstances just described have been changing rapidly since the late 1980s. The "divorce" between grassroots movements and NGOs has begun to reverse itself. Many grassroots-support organizations have become more politically flexible, shifting from consciousness raising among the unorganized poor to providing important technical assistance to self-managed development projects embedded in social movements that are autonomous from NGOs as well as from the state. NGOs have become more institutionally consolidated and have professionalized their work, becoming an important alternative for growing sectors of activists and technicians who offer concrete support services to grassroots development initiatives. Some social movements have created their own NGOs, such as the Popular Defense Committee of Durango's ecological program. The organizational and technical support offered by a growing number of NGOs to social movements is increasingly significant, and a comprehensive analysis remains to be done. In the context of grassroots development projects, the relationship, while not free of conflict, is fruitful and mutually enriching. Out of an atmosphere of competition and cannibalism, Mexican NGOs have created a climate of greater tolerance and understanding of differences.

Future Directions

Although Mexico's grassroots movements have a rich and diverse history, they have yet to democratize local government to a significant degree, and they have yet to create a broad-based, representative national political alternative. They have, however, become important counterweights to centralized state power in some regions and in certain policy areas.

One of the most important trends has been the shift from an emphasis on socioeconomic demands (*revindicaciones*) to political and electoral rights, both at the local and national levels. The results so far have been mixed, with the centralized state retaining a great deal of the political initiative. Until 1991, the most important steps toward pluralistic, representative local government have been taken at the municipal level, although one governorship was ceded to an opposition party in 1989. By 1992, the PAN won two more—one appointed and another elected.

There are many reasons behind the government's remarkable success, so far, at recovering the political initiative after its 1988 setback at the polls. Inflation control and economic growth are certainly appreciated after years of crisis and insecurity. The government also developed a sophisticated response to the shift of the grassroots movement toward the electoral arena that developed during the mid- to late 1980s. With PRONASOL, the president's National Solidarity Program, social welfare and infrastructure projects have been skillfully targeted to politically contested areas. PRONASOL is a catchall presidential strategy with many different programs, ranging from the simple relabeling of traditional federal revenue-sharing with states and municipalities to innovative rural development efforts inspired by past NGO successes.

PRONASOL projects are accompanied by a powerful official discourse on community participation and coresponsibility between the state and the citizens. These projects require the formation of Local Solidarity Committees, which in turn choose from a set menu of possible community improvement projects—electrification, road paving, repairs to school, and so on. To what degree attendance at public meetings will turn into genuine community participation remains an open question.

PRONASOL's political goal is to promote a direct link between the president and the local community, often bypassing local authorities and traditional political bosses.[14] While PRONASOL appears to decentralize, in practice it centralizes power within the presidency, provoking serious subterranean conflicts between Salinistas at the federal level and more traditional state authorities.

In spite of drawing many key staff members and practical lessons from NGOs, PRONASOL has had a mixed record with the more consolidated autonomous NGOs and social organizations, bargaining with some while bypassing others, in the name of delivering services directly to the base. Interestingly, PRONASOL blocked World Bank efforts to fund Mexican NGOs directly.

Within the wide range of PRONASOL activities, its revenue-sharing grants for building roads, bridges, and water systems are the most conventional and, therefore, the most open to potential political manipulation, although money is spent in opposition municipalities as well. These infrastructural projects appear to represent the bulk of PRONASOL spending. The rural development projects include some of PRONASOL's only production-oriented supports. The amounts are very small and symbolic, but they are an important substitute for the abrupt withdrawal of other state agencies that provided credit for peasant crops such as basic grains and coffee.

PRONASOL's most innovative projects are probably those carried out by the National Indigenous Institute, whose budget increased eighteen-fold during the first three years of the Salinas government in an attempt to make up for years of neglect of Mexico's most oppressed citizens. The institute's two largest lines of development were direct credit ("on-your-honor") for low-income indigenous coffee-producer organizations and the creation of NGO-style revolving credit funds, ostensibly managed by regional councils of indigenous organizations. As with any innovative government development program, the record has been mixed. For example, after two years in operation, five of Oaxaca's original twenty regional credit funds succumbed to local political elites and other conflicts, another ten still operated as branches of the regional INI office, while another five truly "took off" and became relatively autonomous, self-managed development agencies.

Social and political groups that press charges of electoral fraud and thereby contest the government's legitimacy tend to be excluded from the few remaining spigots of official social spending. In addition, because most Mexicans continue in a state of economic crisis, community-based organizations are obliged by their members to deal with immediate material needs. Thus, they are forced to strike a balance between their social and political priorities. The choice has been made more difficult by the daunting limitations faced by the PRD, which appeared in 1988 to have the potential to represent large sectors of hitherto disenfranchised citizens. However, the party has been dominated by political forces that are unaccustomed to balanced relationships with autonomous social movements and, therefore, have been unable to incorporate and represent them. A second factor is that, despite its partial successes on the municipal front, the PRD had difficulty making the transition from contestation to proposition. The central government and PRONASOL, in particular, have been closely attuned to these weaknesses, encouraging the social movements to find alternative, less confrontational forms of political representation outside the PRD.[15]

Local government has become a key arena for the expression of this tension between protest and proposition, confrontation and collaboration—even Juchitán, long a standard-bearer for leftist municipal power, entered into PRONASOL agreements with the government. (Although this scandalized some PRD leaders, local authorities from the Coalition of Workers, Peasants, and Students of the Isthmus decided that it was their prerogative to spend public money on public works.) After three years, PRONASOL officials proudly reported that they worked with all but two of Mexico's opposition municipalities. By implication, if opposition municipal movements managed to overcome the various biases and obstacles embedded in the electoral process, they had shown themselves strong enough to be worthy of access to some federal funding.

By the end of 1991, however, contestation of municipal power returned to the agenda. September and October 1991 witnessed mass civic movements that toppled fraudulently elected governors in the states of Guanajuato and San Luis Potosí. These were partial victories, however, since the results were negotiated elite compromises rather than the result of voter choice. Such civic mobilizations were followed by an even more remarkable movement that turned more micropolitical conflicts into national political issues. The fraudulent municipal elections in the Gulf Coast state of Tabasco denied the PRD two town halls. Local and state PRD leaders led a protest march to distant Mexico City, learning from the San Luis Potosí experience how to challenge state power peacefully, without provoking repression. Winning widespread popular support along the way, and with sympathy from church officials, the march was warmly received in Mexico City's main plaza. Negotiations produced PRD-led Municipal Councils, and the hard-line governor was removed from office a month later. The Tabasco protests put small towns on the democratic map in a new way and may point toward an upturn in the PRD's fortunes.

In conclusion, some local governments have become more democratic and/or pluralistic, either formally or in practice, but even the most positive achievements have been limited to blocking the imposition of traditional clientelist development policies, rather than pioneering innovative forms of participation in public administration. Few local governments have carried out creative social and economic policies on a significant scale. A growing number of experimental initiatives have emerged from small towns and villages, leading to a broadening and deepening of local democratization, especially in the areas of rural development and environmental policy. Even though Mexico is now an overwhelmingly urban nation and elections tend to be more closely monitored and cleaner in urban areas, it is ironic that there may be more opportunities for innovation in those exceptional rural areas that have become democratized.

Where there has been progress toward local-level democratization, NGOs have played an important support role. However, the transition from social demands and political opposition to a political alternative based on new proposals for locally based development policies has been difficult. In this context, NGOs in Mexico have been part of the problem as well as part of the solution. Many of them long rejected formal public administration, while others have entered the political arena as contenders. So far, neither type of NGO has focused seriously on developing alternative public policies.

In contrast to the South American experience, where NGOs often served as a bridge between political and social change, most NGOs in Mexico have been followers rather than leaders. The remarkably successful preemptive role of the state, combined with longstanding underfinancing from abroad, are key factors. The continuing obstacles confronting the democratization of the electoral system challenge all efforts to open up creative approaches to public administration. Both grassroots movements and NGOs face the classic challenge of Mexican politics: What kinds of new styles and institutions make it possible to change the system to a greater extent than one is changed *by* it?

Notes

A longer version of this article was published in *Alternatives* 17:2 (Spring 1992).

1. In the 1920s, when the political system was in flux, two kinds of governors were key. One type was the highly autonomous politico-military warlord, who ruled a personalistic political machine and occasionally rebelled against the national state. Another key variant was the more "modern" political machine-builder, who created an organized following based on interest groups, innovative policy reforms, and semicompetitive politics. These so-called "laboratories of revolution" served as important forerunners of what was to become the "inclusionary corporatist" reforms of the 1930s.

2. See Carlos Castillo Peraza, "La batalla por Mérida," *Nexos,* no. 158 (February 1991). Panista civic organizations formed the National Citizen's Front in 1991, led by a group called Integral Human Development and Civic Action. See *La Jornada,* 9 May 1991. See also Soledad Loaeza's historical *Clases Medias y Política en Mexico,* and María Luisa Tarrés, Middle-Class Associations and Electoral Opposition, in Joe Foweraker and Ann Craig, eds., *Popular Movements and Political Change in Mexico.*

3. Important urban popular movements emerged in Chihuahua, Monterrey, Zacatecas, Durango, Torreón, Acapulco, and Greater Mexico City, as well as in Oaxaca, Nayarit, Sinaloa, and Baja.

4. The most notable case at the time was the 1976 gubernatorial election in Nayarit. Most observers agree that the Popular Socialist Party candidate won, but its national leaders were willing to trade their victory for a senatorship.

5. The Ministry of Housing, the newly created Popular Housing Renovation agency, the political parties, and the key community organizations and their support groups.

6. The Chernobyl disaster provoked the emergence of a very broad movement against the Laguna Verde nuclear plant in Veracruz, an endeavor involving both civic groups and technical support and research. It is worth noting that an unusual alliance of indigenous peasants and ecologists blocked the construction of a planned nuclear installation at Lake Pátzcuaro in 1980—perhaps the first such victory in Latin America.

7. Because the systematic documentation of human rights violations in Mexico is relatively recent, it is difficult to draw conclusions about whether abuses have increased or decreased over the last decade or two. The independent print media have grown freer and bolder in recent years, which has led to better coverage, especially in the Mexico City daily, *La Jornada,* and the newsweekly, *Proceso.*

8. See, for example, the "Fray Francisco de Vitoria" Center's regular journal, *Justicia y Paz.* As an aside, the activities of the Mexican League for the Defense of Human Rights should also be noted. Their work is limited to the defense of "their" prisoners—those involved with a small ultraradical group known as the National Democratic Popular Front (FNDP). The FNDP is considered by some informed observers to be the civilian wing of a small clandestine military organization.

9. The network's members worked in nineteen states, and its leaders estimated that they identified with and provided services or support to as many as one in ten low-income Mexicans (Reygadas, op. cit., p. 20). They began publishing a bulletin, *Convergenica,* in May, 1991.

10. Since the launching of the "free trade versus fair trade" debate over the North American Free Trade Agreement, the Mexican Network has worked closely

with the Action Canada Network and the Washington-based Mobilization on Development, Trade, Labor, and the Environment. These lobbying networks are increasing dialogue between NGOs in Mexico, the United States, and Canada that goes beyond the free trade agreement.

11. Salinas' claim to victory was based on the so-called "green vote," a very high turnout, and PRI support in remote rural areas where access to information, freedom of assembly, and opposition political party presence was very limited (Barberán et al. 1989).

12. See its new international bulletin *Mexico Insight.* (Number "0" appeared in 1991.)

13. For example, according to World Bank estimates, international NGOs channel at most U.S.$10 million annually to Mexico's poorest states (Oaxaca and Chiapas), while Guatemala and Honduras receive over $40 to 80 million each.

14. As the president once told a long-time friend, a historic radical leader of the urban popular movement: "You were my teacher: everywhere I go I leave a nucleus of support."

15. The emergence of a new national network of local, regional, and state-level political parties may lead in new and unpredictable directions. Seventeen such groups met at the Second National Gathering of Local Parties and Organizations, issuing a strongly profederalist policy statement that appeared in *La Jornada,* 12 December 1991.

◆◆

11

Local Power and Development Alternatives: An Urban Popular Movement in Northern Mexico

Julio Moguel

Forces for Change

Grassroots social movements have flourished throughout Mexican history. In this century alone, Mexico has experienced innumerable cycles of social conflict—in addition to those that took place during the great revolutionary struggles of 1910 to 1917, which laid the foundation for modern Mexico. The latter decades of this century have witnessed a convergence of such movements, many of which share some or all of the following characteristics:

- They sprang up quickly in the wake of the social and political crisis of the late 1960s, with its tragic denouement at Tlaltelolco, the Mexico City square where hundreds of student demonstrators were killed.
- They emerged during the first major breakup of the official unions (i.e., those controlled by the Institutional Revolutionary party) when emerging forces found official or quasi-official channels unresponsive to their demands for urban plots, agrarian land, better housing, wages, and so on.
- As they grew from sectoral and regional groups into national-level organizations, they managed to evade for some time the centralized forms of political organization represented by the parties and traditional corporatist entities.
- Throughout their process of formation and development, they maintained informal and low-profile networks or channels of communi-

cation among the various groups and sectors they represented. Such networks were nourished by students, organic intellectuals,[1] and activists, many from the 1968 student movement.

- They took on similar national organizational forms, such as mass coordinating bodies (*coordinadoras*) organized by sector: peasants, teachers, and periurban dwellers.[2]

Typical of Mexican social movements is the "Francisco Villa" Committee for Popular Defense of Durango (CDP), one of the most active social and political groups and one that played an important role in the development of the coordinadoras. This group, along with the urban homesteaders or squatters movements of Chihuahua and Monterrey, was a founding member of the Mexican Urban Popular Movement and a decisive promoter of its development into the leading force among the urban popular movements of northern Mexico. The CDP and its allies represent the fullest expression of self-determination by urban homesteaders who, in this case, improved the quality of their lives after appropriating their settlement land. "Francisco Villa" shows, also, how society at large can be transformed when such groups, on their own initiative, decide to enter the political arena as a way to win control of municipal governments or gain parliamentary representation at the state and federal levels.

These groups, among the very first promoters of the National Coordinating Body of the Urban Popular Movement (CONAMUP) during its rise from 1979–1980 to 1985, continued to grow and evolve various organizational structures even after CONAMUP itself entered a period of limited growth. One of the most successful was the CDP, whose framework of growth rested upon two fundamental axes, (1) sustained evolution of its organizational methods and its concept of community development, and (2) sustained expansion of its areas of influence and endeavor. The background that follows provides some perspective on the development of this popular movement.

The Context

Durango, capital of the state of Durango, is a city of almost 400,000 residents located within the vast area of northern Mexico. The region has a fairly well-defined identity and one that sets it somewhat apart from such areas as the central, southern, and southeastern regions, where the Nahuatl, Otomi, Mayan, and Zapotecan cultures flourished. The North is not heavily populated, although it has a few large cities such as Monterrey, Ciudad Juárez, and Tijuana, and some smaller urban centers—Saltillo, Monclova, Laredo, Reynosa, Matamoros, Durango, Chihuahua, Torreón, and Ciudad

Victoria. Some of these cities (especially Monterrey) are home to old industries geared to the national market, and the modern cross-border assembly plants and automotive industries (directly tied to the U.S. economy) are flourishing. The rural areas of the North achieve the highest agricultural productivity in all of Mexico, with vast highly mechanized irrigated areas.

Popular Movements in the North

From the North emerged the most important social, political, and military factions of the revolution of 1910. This region was the site of the first major popular battles against the regime of Porfirio Díaz; it was also where the governing bloc of the late nineteenth century suffered its first major ruptures (Madero, Carranza, and the so-called "Sonora boys," all leaders of prerevolutionary Mexico), which opened the way for the popular uprisings that combined with the Constitutionalist and Villista movements to topple the Díaz dictatorship.

In more recent times, significant popular struggles occurred there in 1957 and 1958, with simultaneous land invasions in the northern states of Sonora, Chihuahua, and Sinaloa directed by the General Union of Mexican Workers and Peasants. At about the same time, the dominant Institutional Revolutionary Party (PRI) suffered its first major electoral setback in any state or territory when the National Action Party (PAN) won the elections in Baja California (although the results were overturned and the popular mobilization was harshly repressed).[3] From 1960 to 1964, other major popular struggles (primarily agrarian) developed that shared a common feature: all were based in social sectors that had broken with government-controlled organizations such as the National Peasant Confederation (CNC). These regional movements joined the organizational project of the National Liberation Movement, whose member groups became a fundamental social force. In 1963, a large number of these same agrarian forces formed the Independent Peasant Federation, the first important rural group organized outside of and in opposition to the traditional corporatist organizations (in particular, the CNC).

Other events were unfolding in the North, as well. In Chihuahua, for example, a guerrilla group emerged in 1963 to battle the region's tremendous social inequalities and, in particular, to struggle against the rule of the region's old political bosses (*caciques*). The band was virtually annihilated, however, when it attacked a military barracks in September of 1965. In 1967, the PAN took advantage of a major split within Sonora's dominant classes and sectors to deal the PRI a spectacular setback at the polls, winning seven municipalities in the state, including its capital. The first significant opposition victory to be recognized by the government, it foreshadowed a framework of contradictions that would unfold in the 1970s and 1980s on a much broader regional scale.[4]

By the early 1970s, the North was beginning to undergo significant economic changes in addition to its shifting political winds. For one thing, Mexico and the United States were moving toward greater economic integration. Large and midsized cities of the region experienced a renewed cycle of growth, due to the new trends of industrial development and to the rural-urban migration brought about by the economic crisis in the countryside.

In the late 1960s, a series of factors sparked new civic and social movements in the northern states. The social movement that developed in Durango in 1966 and 1970 (in separate cycles of mobilization) took on particular importance, as it was a multisectoral *and* multiclass struggle against mining exploitation by the industrial magnates of Monterrey, who removed iron from the Cerro del Mercado at an extremely low price and under conditions that prevented the people of Durango from establishing their own industry.

The national student movement of 1968—with its tragic outcome—spurred new concerns in the popular sectors of the North, radicalized many of their ideological positions, and triggered other splits in the traditional structures of corporatist power. From this context new popular actors emerged: in Chihuahua, the confluence of independent union struggles, peasant struggles for land and production reforms, and student and squatter struggles led to the founding in the early 1970s of the Committee for Popular Defense of Chihuahua. In the Northeast, a wave of urban land invasions by rural-urban migrants led to the formation of the Popular Front for Land and Freedom of Monterrey. These two were the first important urban-homesteader groups in the country.

In 1975 and 1976, a series of concurrent land invasions by Sonoran and Sinaloan peasants sparked one of the most bitter social and political conflicts in Mexico's modern history, leading to the fall of one governor and to a profound division between broad sectors of the landowning and industrial bourgeoisie of the North and the governing political bureaucracy. This division, combined with a major increase in overall social discontent, profoundly affected the federal elections of 1982, in which the PRI received only 68.4 percent of the vote. This was its lowest percentage in Mexico's entire electoral history.

In Durango, the percentage of PRI votes also declined, albeit to a lesser degree, dropping from 83.4 percent in the 1979 elections to 74.9 percent in the elections of 1982. Both locally and nationally, the PAN picked up most of the votes that shifted away from the PRI, increasing its national share from 10.8 percent in 1979 to 17.7 percent in 1982; in Durango, the PAN vote increased from 8.4 percent to 18.3 percent over those same years. These electoral trends also affected local elections in July of 1983, giving the PAN victories in seven of the most important municipalities in Chihuahua and winning the state capital.

The events of the first half of the 1980s reflected the shortcomings of the Mexican political system and led to its eventual modification. The seeds were sown by the 1968 student movement, which sparked a transitional process that unfolded along two lines. First, during the administration of Luís Echeverría Alvarez, the Mexican state undertook a major effort to regain lost consensus, adopting for this purpose a policy of "democratic opening" that greatly loosened the traditional bonds between the dominant centers and the subordinate classes or sectors. Second, the independent social movements multiplied and extended to all the sectors, initiating a new phase in the history of modern Mexico in which the PRI began to lose a major part of its political clientele and to be dangerously undermined by the emerging social forces.

Mexico's political crisis entered a new stage with the failure of Echeverría's neopopulism, kindled by a split among the dominant groups due to the government's expropriation of extensive, privately held agricultural areas in the Northwest. Following a political honeymoon during one presidential administration, a divorce occurred once again between the government and major sectors of private enterprise when the government nationalized the banking system in 1982, a measure taken to halt Mexico's dizzying economic spiral after the abrupt end of the oil boom. The PRI began to lose credibility and faced growing resistance, not only from independent popular groups developing in the 1970s but also from business groups that now began to vote for the PAN, the traditional right-wing party.

Within this overall context, the social and political forces linked together in the Committee for Popular Defense made advances in Durango—indirectly from 1973 to 1976, shielded by the democratic opening of Echeverría, and later by taking advantage of splits within the governing party and within the PAN after it had gained strength in the northern states. The CDP's mode of action—to advance upon the no-man's-land when conflict among more powerful groups made this possible—became a distinctive aspect of urban popular movements in Durango and Monterrey, following the lines advocated by China's Mao Zedong.

Origins of the CDP

The first incarnations of what years later would become Durango's Committee for Popular Defense, the Cerro del Mercado movements of 1966 and 1970 and the national student movement of 1968, were roughly concurrent with the formation of such organizations as the Committee for Popular Defense of Chihuahua[5] and the Popular Front for Land and Freedom of Monterrey.

Despite its lack of industry, the state of Durango experienced one of Mexico's largest waves of rural-to-urban migration during the 1970s, due to the economic crisis and to the decreasing pace of capitalization in rural areas. Its main cities (Durango, Gómez Palacio, and Lerdo) grew primarily around services, presenting limited employment options for a growing population. In addition, the end of the golden age of Mexico's economy began to affect established but underserved urban dwellers, who protested the lack of public services and/or their rising costs.

The first organizing group of the urban popular movement in Durango began to operate in 1972, propelled by activists from Mexico City who had participated in the student movement of 1968 and considered themselves Maoist (along the lines of the French interpretation of Maoism led by Charles Bettelheim[6]) and *consejista* (i.e., favoring assembly-style direct democracy). In their view, only a radical change in the country could bring about a popular government, but such a change could only take place through a very long process in which "the broad popular masses" would go "from the countryside to the city" or "from the periphery to the center" to surround the central powers of the state. This scheme, shared by urban groups from Monterrey and the city of Torreón, presupposed that the movement would advance through a peaceful process of expanding what they called "liberated zones." These zones comprised the poor neighborhoods of urban homesteaders (*colonias populares*).

The group directed its first efforts at helping some tenants in the city center protest high water rates. Soon, however, the activists allied themselves with groups calling for urban lots and housing, and together they organized mass land invasions. After some major setbacks, the first territorial "base" was "conquered" and became the División del Norte neighborhood.

Following in the wake of Durango's first colonia popular, the work of these grassroots activists unfolded along two basic lines. First, was the development of democracy within the colonia through block-by-block assemblies that were organized as decisionmaking bodies. Next, came the promotion of new settlements to meet mounting demands for urban lots and housing and to broaden the movement's political strength and realm of activity. Three years after the founding of División del Norte, a new cycle of invasions began whose first successes were the formation of the Emiliano Zapata and Lucio Cabañas colonias.

After seven years of social and political advances, the confluence of this and similar movements made it possible to formally establish the Committee for Popular Defense of Durango, or the CDP. From 1980 to 1985, the CDP grew and consolidated itself, making the most of the relative flexibility of the new governor, Salvador Gámiz Fernández. The two lines of work taken on by the enlarged group respected the original pattern: first, cooperative and collective work to develop the districts and promote internal democracy based on regular meetings by block, colonia, base, and intercolonia (or interbase) coordinating groups; second, territorial and sectoral advances and growth through invasions or purchases of land. In addition to the cooperative work, the ideological struggle during this phase took on additional dimensions: for example, new rules of community life led to diminished drinking during popular festivals; committees participated directly in the primary school programs; newly formed groups studied recreation and politics; auditoriums were built or established; and popular communication programs were developed. In 1983, the "José Revueltas" Cultural Center was formed in an effort to formalize and give a central role to other activities of this nature.

During this period, the CDP developed and consolidated its organizational structures. In 1982, the first general political commission was formed, followed by grassroots commissions. To its principal membership of rural-urban migrants, the CDP gradually added groups from other social sectors. Small merchants and some unions (the musicians' union, for example) joined the CDP. Organizing work began in the other two major cities of Durango (Gómez Palacio and Lerdo) and in various municipalities, with peasant groups.

The CDP Enters a New Phase

When the CDP reached this stage of development, it had no fewer than forty bases, of which over twenty-five were consolidated. About one-fifth of the city's population lived in these communities. In addition, the CDP organized support for a major sector of small merchants and became their main defender and promoter. Enjoying a certain degree of sympathy from the students and university workers of Durango and the support of the musicians' union, the CDP undertook a major statewide effort, establishing its own forces in the other two major cities while also extending its network into the rural areas.

This impressive process of extending its work locally and nationally (through CONAMUP and its contacts with the other mass coordinadoras) was the distinctive aspect of the CDP's growth until 1985. That particular year was fraught with difficulty due to a new cycle of repression by the state government, which now saw the organization as a threat—one growing and strengthening at a geometric pace. Among other attacks suffered in 1985 was an incident provoked in one of the colonias. A CDP activist was assassinated, and six others were wounded. The secretary general of the musicians' union was later assassinated, as well.

Faced with these conditions, the CDP shifted to a new phase of development and, with its new slogan "break down the fence," advanced to other levels of political activity. The CDP dropped its former reluctance to participate in elections, until then considered PRI-bourgeois areas of politics. The CDP participated in the 1986 elections to protect itself in the face of the government policy of repression, to open channels of communication with other sectors of civil society in Durango, and to reframe the struggle for reforms and for the rights of colonias to participate in managing certain areas of the public administration, above all in the municipalities. Other factors influenced the CDP shift, as well: PAN's struggle with the PRI in the North could be taken advantage of to provide a window of opportunity for swift gains and significant benefits. The PAN had already managed to take the most important municipality in the state, and all indications were that in the following elections there would be an even broader electoral shake-up.

The results were surprising, considering the traditionally weak position of the left in northern elections and the abstentionist tradition of the CDP. In the 1986 elections, with some 8,000 votes cast, the CDP won a seat in the state legislature and two city council seats in Durango, one in Súchil, and another in Coneto de Comonfort. This marked the beginning of a new phase for the CDP, whose first experience in the legislature and in municipal management took on particular importance; its capacity for bringing forth proposals, maintaining the initiative, and introducing new methods made a genuine impact. Certain meetings of the state legislature were filled with CDP activists, gathering to show support for their representative or to pressure the PRI and PAN speakers. Similar delegations crowded the meetings of the Durango city council.

With these changes, the CDP itself underwent major internal transformations; traditionally organized on the basis of direct and assembly-based democracy, the organization for the first time introduced the secret and universal ballot for the election of all leadership positions. Technical support structures were created in various areas. A legal office was established to consolidate and formalize the efforts of lawyers who until then had provided only limited support. The CDP began to move from the old concept of liberated zones to that of autonomous mass organizations, which were more flexible. In so doing, it left behind its former emphasis on strict controls over the CDP territory and also its overideologized political leadership. As the grassroots of the organization became increasingly complex, its leadership became more sophisticated as well.

The Elections of 1988 and 1989

In early 1987, the CDP began to discuss its participation in the 1988 federal elections. In so doing, it gave up the registry it had "borrowed" from the Revolutionary Workers Party (PRT) and prepared to enter into an electoral alliance with the Mexican Socialist Party (PMS), a much older organization and one better consolidated nationally.

The CDP generated extraordinary activism and mobilization in its campaign. As part of its strategy to grow and gain increasing impact on elections, the CDP mobilized its forces simultaneously in Durango, Gómez Palacio, and Lerdo around various demands. In February and May of 1988, the CDP greeted its presidential candidate, Heberto Castillo, with a turnout of over 10,000 CDP members and followers, considered by the national press to be the second largest in the PMS presidential campaign. The election campaign employed a vast grassroots operation, with heavy emphasis on political graffiti (*pintas*) and home visits.

In June, Heberto Castillo renounced his candidacy in favor of Cuahtémoc Cárdenas, son of former president Lázaro Cárdenas (1934–1940); Cuahtémoc Cárdenas himself had been governor of Michoacán from 1980 to 1986. Months earlier, Cárdenas had decided to leave the PRI, along with his colleagues of the Critical Line (*Corriente Crítica*). The CDP lost no time in accepting Cárdenas as its candidate and became the main force in Durango behind the National Democratic Front, a political alliance of several parties and organizations that backed the Cárdenas presidential election campaign.

In the elections of 1988, having attracted many of the political forces unallied with either the PRI or PAN, the CDP won a seat in the national Congress. It then began a new campaign on several fronts, capitalizing on the social and political strength it had accumulated and on the political shelter provided by its electoral victories. The CDP participated successfully in the public forums called by the state legislature to carry out electoral reform, and some of its proposals for changing Durango's election laws were included in the constitutional amendment passed by the Chamber of Deputies in November.

In November 1988, the CDP labored alongside the pro-Cárdenas forces, positioning itself to be a major force in the Party of the Democratic Revolution (PRD) headed by Cárdenas. During subsequent weeks, however, the situation began to change. First, a new electoral cycle was beginning for the Durango elections, in which municipal authorities and state legislative representatives were to be elected, and a serious conflict began to evolve regarding the division of the candidacies. Second, since September 1988, the CDP had been exploring the possibility of obtaining a registry of its own as a state political party.[7] In practical terms, it sought a greater margin of autonomy within the Cardenista alliance and thereby created the possibility of an eventual split in the previous electoral coalitions.

The situation became more complicated when the CDP announced, in early February 1989, that it would sign an agreement of *concertación* with the federal government—within the so-called National Solidarity Program (PRONASOL)—to carry out a series of social works and productive projects.

Outraging the local militants of the former PMS and the national militants of the PRD was the fact that the agreement would be signed in the presence of President Carlos Salinas de Gortari during a visit to Durango. The straw that finally broke the camel's back, however, was the CDP's decision to openly fight for and win its registry conditioned on the outcome of the 1989 local elections; this finalized the CDP's break with the PRD.

Now known as the Party of the Committee for Popular Defense, the CDP activists plunged into the campaign for the local elections held in July 1989, once again with many and varied mobilizations and experimental approaches to electoral participation. They repeated their meticulous grassroots organizing of 1988, and their candidate for mayor of Durango, Horténsia Nevárez,[8] contributed significantly to the perception of CDP's broadening base, as she came from the well-to-do class of Durango and was the wife of an industrialist in Monterrey. In addition, despite its split with the PRD, the CDP maintained a close electoral alliance with many organizations previously linked to the National Democratic Front.

The CDP's ability to mobilize around the elections was consolidated in the cities of Gómez Palacio and Lerdo and extended with good results to several rural municipalities, where the CDP enjoyed the support of the Unión de Pueblos "Emiliano Zapata."[9] The election results were impressive: two state deputies and twelve city council members in different municipalities. Most impressive, however, were its mayoral victories in Nombre de Dios and Súchil, awarded to the PRI but recaptured in a hard-fought battle against fraud. (Popular and civic pressure generated by the assassination of a CDP activist forced the electoral authorities and government to cede.)

Numerically, the CDP comfortably surpassed the legal minimum required to win its registry as a state political party. CDP became the third-ranking electoral force in the state of Durango, with 7.6 percent of the vote, yielding only to the PRI, which won 63.3 percent of the vote, and to the PAN, which took 21.6 percent.

CDP Support for Related Groups

During this period, the CDP was able to develop some organizational structures, such as the legal office previously mentioned,[10] but even more important was its support for the Ecological Defense and Preservation Committee (CDyPE), a civic association of technical personnel, peasants, and other concerned citizens who mounted a campaign against pollution of the Tunal River. This waterway, the principal river in the region, receives untreated wastewater from the city of Durango and waste from a cellulose plant.

Formed during 1988 and 1989, the CDyPE began its activities with an assessment of river pollution and its effects on production and health in the affected areas. The association set up a consultative process, involving the rural sectors, to promote as quickly as possible a series of midrange actions to reverse some of the worst effects of this pollution. Simultaneously, the group began a similar dialogue with institutions and businessmen to find a long-term solution and to draft a plan (the Emergency Ecological Program) that would address critical short-term problems.

The ecological program addressed the most urgent problems, especially those associated with production and with local public health. In the case of agriculture, clean water sources were needed for livestock, as well as for fish farming and crop irrigation. As for health, there was talk of building a specialized clinic in the affected area. Other demands and proposals were added, such as bringing in drinking water, repairing and building schools and sports fields, instituting first aid training, establishing medical dispensaries, and so on.

Within this framework there evolved the idea of production and ecological reserve units centered on a natural resource (a spring or reclaimed reservoir, for example) that could provide enough pure water to support productive livestock and crop agriculture at least temporarily. By September 1990, the Ecological Defense and Preservation Committee and the people of the area had reclaimed seventeen springs and developed a production and ecological reserve unit for each. Once the Emergency Ecology Program was consolidated, the reserve units set out to promote the Regional Plan for Productive Development and Ecological Recovery, whose main aim was to find intermediate or final solutions for productive development and ecosystem recovery in areas of environmental degradation. Efforts would depend on the local inhabitants' proposals and initiative. Overall, the plan encompassed some sixty initial activities in both city and countryside. Soon an intermediate financial plan was drawn up that included the possibility of government and business participation.

In early 1990, the CDyPE began a series of urban studies and actions to identify solutions to pollution caused by solid waste and the lack of basic services in some colonias. These activities were in addition to CDP mobilizations that, since 1988, had protested pollution from the municipal dump and to efforts to form ecological committees in each colonia.

A Truce with the Federales

The CDP of Durango was the first organization of its type to sign a concertación agreement with the Salinas de Gortari administration. Signed 13 February 1989, when the CDP was still linked to the Cardenista bloc and the war with the governor of Durango was at its peak, the agreement represented just over 3 billion pesos (approximately U.S.$1 million). Financed through this agreement were six tortilla machines, fifteen rustic kitchens, three sewing shops, one carpentry shop, fourteen primary schoolrooms, a walkway, electrification in six colonias, housing improvements and drinking water systems in seven colonias, and equipped day-care centers. A study was also funded to determine priorities for urban facilities in Durango, Gómez Palacio, and Lerdo.[11]

These initiatives addressed some of the most deeply felt needs of the CDP colonias, and their solution no doubt stemmed from the experience the CDP gained during its years of struggle, experience that taught its leaders how to maneuver and negotiate. Considering the CDP's years of struggle with the state government and several federal offices, the public signing of such an agreement in the presence of Salinas de Gortari was an unquestionable political victory for the opposition social forces.

A few days after signing, certain segments of the left openly criticized the CDP for what the leftists considered to be a betrayal of the opposition movements. Before long, however, the model began to be adopted by others, and similar agreements were signed by organizations of the National Union of Peasant Organizations, the Democratic Peasant Front of Chihuahua, and other branches of the urban popular movement. Also joining in the trend were forces of the Independent Federation of Agricultural Workers and Peasants, the National "Plan de Ayala" Network, and even organizations which, like the Coalition of Workers, Peasants, and Students of the Isthmus of Oaxaca (COCEI), were a militant part of the PRD. Not all of them signed in the presence of Salinas de Gortari, nor did the government take such pains in all cases to showcase the agreements. But even this can be recognized as an asset rather than a liability, if one considers how effectively the agreement strengthened the CDP organizational structures within the context of the acute conflicts of Durango. No less important was the consolidation of the CDP as the leading force of a large part of the urban popular movement in the North.

Conclusion

As we have seen, the CDP developed largely along two main paths. It saw itself, first, as a movement that "destroys" (insofar as it struggles against unjust ways of life, organization, and political domination) at the same time that it "builds" a new form of social interaction. In its first documents, for example, the activists who participated in the colonias speak of the "destruction-construction" dialectic. The second path is one of expansion: first, in the colonias populares; then, among the established colonias; still later, among other popular groups (especially small merchants and peasants); and finally, into general civil society in Durango, based on the CDP's leadership in a multiclass environmental alliance and on its electoral participation. Throughout this process (during which different aspects dovetailed at various phases), the CDP continued to grow and to develop key political links with other popular sectors in the state and country—in the latter case, through its participation in CONAMUP and in an informal network that spanned the other mass coordinadoras.

While following the first of its paths, the CDP maintained its community-based work and organizational structures for many years; these led to largely ongoing collective actions to build popular housing, install drainage and water systems, build streets, develop small shops for production, establish medical dispensaries, and build schools (as well as halls for parties and meetings). This self-organizational ability was based originally on the strength and stability of a charismatic leadership drawn primarily from post-1968 students; however, the CDP replaced this leadership with an organizational structure grounded in popular block-by-block organization, neighborhood assemblies, and occasional interneighborhood or interbase coordination that, later on, would form the general structure of the Committee for Popular Defense. The ideology or cultural mortar holding together this community-based movement encompassed two elements: the first was the systematic struggle against individualism and against the political and ideological domination of the PRI and corporatist organizations of the state, and the second was the idea that the masses or popular sectors are the ones who truly make history. CDP tools were (1) the people that it worked with; (2) the urban homesteading urge that fueled the takeover of a given territorial area; (3) the particular economic and political conditions of Durango; and (4) the fact that the underlying contradiction addressed lies not in production but in consumption.

The People

Although people renting lots and housing were the starting point for the CDP's organizational work, the target group soon expanded to include the squatters of Durango, who had come from the countryside and had no place to live. Most were extremely poor people who, when they were employed or pursuing an economic activity, worked in the informal sector. Uprooted and in desperate poverty, they quickly became a force willing to mobilize and organize, especially if it could lead directly to benefits.

The Territory

During its long formative stage, and even as a developed organization, the CDP expanded and consolidated itself through "conquests," either direct land invasion or purchase of a given compact territory. At present, the CDP comprises over sixty bases (large, medium, and small), of which most are fairly compact colonias populares. We are speaking of some 150,000 people, just over 100,000 of whom live in the city of Durango. The rest include inhabitants of the colonias populares of Gómez Palacio and Lerdo, small merchants from all three cities, and groups of peasants and other citizens organized in six or seven municipalities statewide. During its long history, the CDP has moved from its original conception of these colonias as "liberated zones" to one defining them as areas where autonomous mass organizations are being built or already exist. The fact that the CDP has a territorial life allows it to offer alternative options in areas dominated or influenced by PRI/PAN.

The Particular Conditions

In Durango, more than anywhere else in the country, the CDP developed in response to both economic and political conditions. For one thing, Durango has enjoyed relatively little economic development due to its lack of a self-sustaining industrial base. It has remained a state characterized by agriculture, forestry, and services, with fairly weak economic sectors that are largely subject to capitalist groups from Monterrey (in industry and commerce) and Chihuahua (in forestry and commerce). Another factor relates to the dominant political sectors of Durango, which have had differences of opinion with centers of federal power. These strains have played a decisive role in the CDP's growth, allowing it to take advantage of rifts within the local dominant groups, between local and national power groups, and between local power groups and the central government.

The Nature of the Principal Contradiction

Through its grassroots mobilization and negotiation, the CDP has systematically curbed state influence in areas of urban landownership, housing, and consumption. Even when its battles and energies are funneled into applied politics, the CDP almost never takes on the industrial sector or private enterprise, hence its contradictory stance of not tackling industrialists or economic elites but seeking political allies outside to check political enemies locally. The CDP has nearly always drawn support from one of the opposite poles of the contradiction: either against local elites with "cover" from the federal elites, or vice versa.

The CDP has solved a series of problems affecting the poor of Durango (just as CONAMUP and other popular organizations have done in other states). Under "normal" conditions—that is, without a supporting social and political vehicle such as the CDP—this population would have suffered greatly in a society that systematically expels them from the areas where they produce and live collectively, that treats them as a marginal population, and that humiliates them and dominates them socially and culturally. In contrast, the CDP has enabled them to build a collective identity, has generated important services for improving their living conditions, and has helped to prevent, or eradicate to a considerable degree, prostitution and the social degradation generated by extreme poverty.

For the small merchant sector, the CDP has been the main organization defending and promoting employment and higher incomes. As well, it has helped them develop a collective identity, one that encompasses a feeling of solidarity with the squatters and urban homesteaders and a strong sense of themselves as worthy participants in the larger society.

Issues of Survival

The CDP now faces all the pitfalls and problems that accompany most transitional processes. For example, its regional ambitions lead the CDP into political realms where it can advance only if it is capable of solving diverse and complex problems. In addition, given its dual role as a decisive player in Durango's development and also as the leading force of the urban popular movement in the North, the CDP now finds itself the focus of regional and federal political powers that include the presidency itself, which increasingly views the urban popular sectors as a new base of support for the Mexican state.

During the federal primary of 1991, the CDP and other related groups were unable to garner enough registered members to claim national status for their Worker's Party, thereby losing an opportunity to win parliamentary seats. At the same time, however, the Salinas government was at work trying to convert the urban popular sectors into one of its principal bases of support. By responding to social demands with PRONASOL economic resources, the government sought to cement a "new state-citizen relationship." Solidarity committees were established to link PRONASOL directly with base groups via autonomous community assemblies that were coordinated with local and regional plans. Eventually, two national organizational networks were in place: one rural, the other urban, and both directly connected to the state structure by the PRONASOL hinge.

In pursuing this strategy, the Salinas government challenged the organizational influence of the independent social left over the urban popular sector. Moreover, it employed many methods associated with the left, such as democratic assemblies and coordinadoras. Avoiding corporatist co-optation, PRONASOL created parallel structures separate from traditional PRI sectors and often in clear contradiction to local and regional power groups organized around the Agrarian Community Leagues, base committees from state organizations (such as the National Peasant Confederation), or other official groups.

The importance of this governmental policy is reflected in the formation of nearly five thousand solidarity committees in urban communities as well as in the ambitious urban land regulation undertaken by the government. It remains to be seen whether this path will create a solid and wide-spread social movement supportive of the state, and just how it will fit within the government's complex system of contradictions. Whatever the outcome, there is no doubt that this policy will affect the Mexican Urban Popular Movement—with consequences impossible to predict.

The CDP's decision to participate in the 1991 federal elections through a political party of its own (the Workers' Party), in an alliance with other forces, opened a new path for social movements of this type. Many criticized the process, considering it an unnecessary and perhaps harmful leap into *political* politics as opposed to the CDP's traditional *social* politics, which for years implied refusal to participate in elections. Nevertheless, it is hard to see this new direction as anything but an inevitable result of the CDP's own logic, its need to grow and develop, and its legitimate interest in broadening its social and political impact beyond the narrow confines of its sectoral and territorial bases.

Perhaps there was another way to proceed: the CDP might have established short-term electoral alliances with national political parties that already had their registries, thereby remaining an autonomous regional force affecting primarily the policies of the municipal governments and the state government of Durango. CDP activists, however, considered this an unattractive option for a variety of reasons: by 1988, the CDP had exhausted its extensive social development thrust (there were limits to the growth possible via land invasions and purchases); the colonias had by then secured and normalized land tenure and had obtained basic public services; and repression had been checked through street demonstrations, publicity, and negotiations. In addition, the CDP was encountering various problems in its alliances with certain national political parties; thus, when the CDP and forces friendly to it suddenly found the doors open to the possibility of obtaining federal-level registry, they crossed the threshold. Where this decision will lead them is difficult to predict.

Another critical aspect in the CDP's development rests with the social and productive enterprises it has been able to build, based on its concertación agreements with PRONASOL. Technical and administrative experience will be in short supply during the early stages; yet, these enterprises need to be competitive given the conditions imposed by the market, the intermediaries, and the monopolies. An additional difficulty will be the link between the economy and politics, as perennially scarce funds for mobilizing and developing the social organization tend to generate tensions over the use of savings and accumulation. Thus, the challenges of growth multiply.

The CDP will be tested philosophically, as well, as it tries to balance the party/movement equation. Where does the *movement* end and the party begin? It is difficult to answer this question and even more difficult to devise practical tactics and an overall strategy for both social and political action. The CDP is at a crossroads; the coin is in the air. The CDP is a social organization that has always ventured down dangerous and unknown paths and has generally emerged victorious. Soon, however, it will be put to possibly definitive tests. Then we will see what emerges during the third stage of its development.

Notes

1. "Organic intellectual," a term coined by Italian Marxist Antonio Gramsci, refers to professional or academically trained elites identified with the masses and their struggles.

2. The golden age of the coordinadoras spanned a five-year period, beginning around 1979 and declining during the early years of the Miguel de la Madrid administration. During that period they scaled up from sectoral and regional groups to national-level associations. In 1982–1983, for example, coordinadoras were the key force in the National Front for the Defense of Wages Against Austerity and High Prices, organized to confront the government's austerity policy and the cutbacks of workers' wages and standard of living. Later, they were the key elements of another national popular organization called the National Worker, Peasant, and Popular Assembly. From 1979 to 1984, working independently and together, coordinadoras carried out the broadest and most consistent political mobilizations and actions since the beginning of the political crisis unleashed in 1968.

3. PRI roots go back to 1928, when the National Revolutionary party (PNR) was founded by the country's governors to unite most of Mexico's political organizations into a single government-controlled body. In 1938, during the presidential term of Lázaro Cárdenas, it was renamed the Mexican Revolutionary Party (PRM) and took on its definitive structure as an "organization of sectors." In 1946, it was given the name of the Institutional Revolutionary Party (PRI).

4. The National Action party (PAN) was formed in 1939 as a response by some business sectors (especially from the North) to the popular and leftist politics of Lázaro Cárdenas. Since that time it has been the second largest national party, although it gained little electoral significance until the 1970s.

5. In addition to the Popular Front for Land and Freedom of Monterrey and the CDP of Durango, the CDP of Chihuahua stands out in the North as a major organization of squatters, or urban homesteaders. The CDP of Chihuahua pioneered the urban popular movement nationwide. Arising in the late 1960s, it developed in a manner very different from the Popular Front for Land and Freedom and the CDP of Durango. First, it arose not as an urban popular movement, but as a broad front of social organizations in which, during its initial phase, students, peasants, and some industrial workers were the most active. Only after a filtering process did it become an organization primarily of urban homesteaders. Second, its ideological and programmatic starting point had nothing to do with Maoism or *consejismo* (i.e., assembly-style direct democracy), so that its strategies of growth and development, as well as the way it defines and practices internal democracy and mobilizes and negotiates with the state, differ significantly from those of its parallel organizations in Monterrey and Durango. In the early 1970s, other urban popular organizations (or seeds of such organizations) arose in the country, especially in Mexico City, but some of them were defeated very quickly (such as the Campamento 2 de Octobre) or failed to play a significant role until the late 1970s and early 1980s.

6. See "Doce tesis sobre el nuevo liderazgo campesino en México: Notas

sobre la UNORCA," a paper presented by Luis Hernández at the April 1991 Congress of the Latin American Studies Association held in Washington, D.C.

7. According to Paul L. Haber, "the most convincing explanation as to why they decided to form their own party is that it turned out to be impossible to reach agreement to share power within the alliance. The specific problem that separated them was the selection of candidates. Although the July 1989 elections were for mayoralties and state legislators, knowing who would receive the legislative seats awarded on the basis of proportional vote counts was the thorniest point. The CDP had been displeased for some time about the fact that in its opinion the PRD (and, before that, the PMS) wielded undeserved influence in the alliance, simply because they were the ones with registry as a party. . . ." From Cárdenas, Salinas, y los movimientos populares de Durango, in Sergio Zermeño and J. Aurelio Cuevas (coordinators), *Antología sobre movimientos sociales en México en el decenio de los 80,* published in 1991 by the Centro de Investigaciones Interdisciplinarias de Humanidades, UNAM, Mexico City.

8. In her nomination acceptance speech, Horténsia Nevárez said: "I am a person who by fate has not gone without having my basic needs met. This in no way means that I am not familiar with the CDP. I respect, I understand, and I sympathize with your organization. Five years ago, I was coordinator of the "José Revueltas" Cultural Center, and there I discovered an honest, democratic CDP, with the authentic aim of solving the problem of the poor. . . . I am a social worker, I have worked in rural communities, in educational institutions. I was in charge of liaison with the colonias populares for the city government of Durango in 1983. . . ."

9. Although the Unión de Pueblos "Emiliano Zapata" participated in the struggle against pollution of the Tunal River, this was not its main cause. The group draws its members from certain peasant communities and rural groups near the city of Durango and concerns itself with agrarian and production issues. The CDP has been a strong supporter and, although the Unión de Pueblos is an independent organization, considers it a sister organization.

10. The José Guadalupe Victoria Law Office brought together lawyers closely linked to the CDP, who initiated a project to provide legal advice and support to members of the CDP colonias and bases. As a civil association, the office was declared formally separate from the CDP; this made it easier to extend its activities to groups outside the CDP.

11. The same day that the CDP colonias signed their concertación agreement, Salinas de Gortari signed a similar document with the National Confederation of Popular Organizations (CNOP), a group of PRI-affiliated colonias, for a total of 22.2 billion pesos. From the standpoint of total amounts, the differences between the CDP and CNOP projects were enormous. Nonetheless, most of the amount given the PRI-connected group was in the form of credit. Thus, in relative terms, there was practically no discrimination against the CDP colonias. In addition, it was evident that the CDP emphasized social works and productive activities, based on its organizational capability, and that the CNOP had inflated its budget and plans for the concertación agreement by targeting mainly public works.

12

NGOs, State, and Society in Peru: Anchors of the Utopian Vision

Baltazar Caravedo M.

Utopian Visions in
Peruvian Development

Just as dreaming is essential to conscious life, so too are utopian visions that maintain the unity of a people over time. Such visions are based on myths generating perceptions of reality or, at least, achievability. Strengthened by its underlying myth, a utopian vision may eventually become universally embraced, as in Peru, where first the middle class and then the rest of society have responded to successive utopian visions of development.

The period spanning roughly 1900 to 1930, for example, witnessed a centralist trend in Peru, due largely to the emerging middle sectors of Lima and the provinces, who believed that a growing and strengthening state would lead to development, reduce social and ethic disparities, and unify the country. In the mid- to late 1930s, this vision yielded to that of the "anti-imperialist state," which rejected foreign capital and investment as backward pacts favoring landlords and oligarchs and led its proponents to further strengthen the state, nationalize the country, and promote a top-down approach to development.

From 1930 to 1950, the state's economic role increased dramatically; the Central Reserve Bank, the development banking system (Banco Industrial, Banco Agrario, Banco Minero), the Corporación del Santa (iron and steelworks), and the Rubber Corporation were all created during this twenty-year period. In addition, the foundation of Peru's contemporary highway system was established. As a result, the state bureaucracy grew significantly during these years.

229

Political Organizations and Popular Groups

In the mid-1950s, new parties and political movements arose and, although beset with difficulties, played an important role in Peru for several decades. These groups—Popular Action and Christian Democracy, among them— called for reform of the state, pointing out its need to guarantee social justice, define the economic development model, and guarantee the right of citizen participation. Slowly, political parties gained legitimacy: presidential elections were held in 1931, 1936, 1939, 1945, 1950, 1956, 1962, and 1963; in 1963 and 1966, municipal elections took place. Not all election results were respected, however, nor were all contests free and fair. The 1936 elections, for example, were never concluded, and it is said that the 1939 election was fixed. The elections of 1950, held after almost two years of dictatorship, were manipulated by the executives. Twelve years later, in 1962, the electoral results were never implemented.

During this century, Peru's elections and democratic governments have often yielded to restricted democracies in which political parties have had virtually no legal existence (first Prado administration, 1939–1945, and Odría in 1950–1956) or to military dictatorships such as Benavides (1936–1939), the military junta led by Odría (1948–1950), and the junta headed by Pérez Godoy and Lindley (1962–1963). With the inauguration of Manuel Prado's second administration (1956–1962), the American Popular Revolutionary Alliance (APRA) was able to resume its public organizing after the interregnum of 1945–1948, and new parties were formed such as the aforementioned Popular Action and Christian Democracy.

In general, while the population enjoyed more opportunities to participate actively in political organizations, there was no apparent need to integrate the grassroots constituencies of those parties, as the usefulness of doing so was not perceived. Indeed, given Peru's tendency to vacillate between democracy and dictatorship, activists were often considered to be at a disadvantage, since during periods of dictatorship or political persecution they had the most to lose. During these repressive periods, no culture of party politics could survive.

In contrast to political organizations, popular or interest group organizations (*gremios*) were seen as more narrowly focused service or benefit providers concerned mainly with a relatively small membership base. As such, they escaped the persecution that political activists faced during periods of dictatorship. Depending on their negotiating capacity, organized interest groups often could win immediate results such as pay increases or greater social benefits. Moreover, they could engage in covert political organizing without running the risks that political parties faced. That is precisely what they did, at first directing their social and economic demands not at the state but at companies and property owners.

During the 1960s, APRA was resurrected and radicalized by Marxist insurgent organizations that shunned party activities, in part because they were prohibited and in part because political party activism was not the goal of these organizations. Over the years, APRA softened its anti-imperialist position and, from 1948 to 1956, primarily focused on winning the right to operate legally. This modification left a vacuum of sorts, which insurgents sought to fill. Inspired by the Cuban Revolution, Peruvian guerrilla groups organized in 1962, 1963, and 1965–1966 drew many followers from among the university students. The clandestine parties of the Marxist left developed a certain degree of influence in trade unions, giving direction to their struggles and helping to define their grievances. These groups, working to build a socialist or popular democratic state characterized by the undisputed leadership of a single party (which would represent the working class and constitute its leading force), eventually displaced APRA as the most influential force among workers and peasants.

In the late 1960s, Alvarado Velasco and the Peruvian armed forces took control of the government, citing the legal political parties' inability to reform the state; the growing threat from socialists, communists, and Marxists, who were winning more followers and engaging in certain military actions; and the country's declining socioeconomic dynamics. Political parties were forced either to go underground or to operate clandestinely, and these restrictions turned them once again toward organizing social and economic interest groups.

Decline of the Anti-Imperialist State

Many reforms took place under military rule, both agrarian and economic. During this period, for example, the expansion of the state and its direct action in the economy led to a popular image of the state as employer, or boss; society related to the state as a union relates to a company or workers to their employers. By the end of the 1970s, however, four realities had begun to emerge. First, certain reforms were unsuccessful. Agrarian reforms neither boosted agricultural production nor improved farmer and peasant incomes; indeed, overall agricultural production actually declined during this period. Economic reforms, for their part, failed to stimulate reinvestment or promote capital investment in production. When foreign enterprises were nationalized, their productivity also declined. In general, the reforms of this period led to an economic stagnation from which Peru has yet to recover.

Second (a more positive effect), political parties regained their legal status. Successive elections featuring more open debate on various aspects of national life led to questioning of the original Marxist theses. Gradually, the Marxist parties and organizations began to lose their influence over grassroots social and economic interest groups and unions.

Third, the cities played an ever more prominent role politically, yet were unable to boost production or create additional sources of formal-sector employment; a dramatic expansion in the informal sector ensued that diminished the social significance of the working class.

Fourth, provincial and departmental "defense fronts" sprang up to unite various provincial sectors in a struggle to achieve their long-neglected demands. These defense fronts positioned themselves similarly to the interest groups in their relationship with the state and employers. Encouraged by the decentralist currents that were gaining strength, first the defense fronts and then the municipal governments elected after 1980 (following return to civil rule) organized mobilizations. These and ensuing regional and local labor and civic strikes were undertaken as a way to force the central state to meet citizen demands.

As it became increasingly clear that the state could not meet the demands of the poorest and would, instead, forge alliances with large- and medium-scale business interests, radical expressions of discontent arose. To these were added the voice of one Peruvian NGO (later to play a significant role with the mass media) that initiated a systematic critique of the state's inability to support and legalize the thousands of informal-sector entrepreneurs in the main cities of Peru, especially Lima (de Soto 1986). Indeed, the Institute for Liberty and Democracy (ILD) carried its criticism of the central state to the point of labeling it the major enemy of national development.

It should be noted that political and ideological leaders of the decentralization movement do not all hold the view that the market should regulate resource allocation in the country. Indeed, some see the decentralizing state as a transition to the popular democratic state and believe that planning should predominate over the marketplace. (Decentralization would allow popular participation in such planning.) However, the ILD proposal for deregulation and debureaucratization of the state and ILD's criticism of the state as "mercantilist" by virtue of its pact with oligopolistic business interests implicitly supported the market as the principal regulating force. Despite their very different orientations and formulations, both perspectives reflected a strong critique of how the state had developed in Peru.

Decline of the Utopian Vision

During the 1980s, the image of a national utopia began to unravel. Although never collapsing completely, this vision appears to be slowly fading, provoking a vacuum of authority and sometimes giving rise to the feeling that political action is meaningless. For example, in the 1980s the close association between leftist parties and grassroots social and economic groupings began to come apart. Turning to politics, the parties began to work in parliament and in many municipal governments, spending less time organizing interest groups and unions. Whereas at one time the Marxist parties (now legally registered) dedicated themselves to organizing the working class for revolution and the dictatorship of the proletariat, they now struggle for political reforms without the grassroots contacts they cultivated in the past. Thus, the dictatorship of the proletariat appears either to have been abandoned as a goal or to no longer hold special appeal.

For many dissident militants of the legal left, ideological and political debate has replaced political action as a significant strategy. Yet the terrain upon which the political confrontations unfold is not exclusively ideological. Although the debate is replete with rational arguments, violence also sets the context for the Peruvian drama. The rise of terror as a political weapon has diminished the standing of the state and has revealed its weaknesses, incompetence, and deterioration. In proclaiming the need for a stronger and more authoritarian state, however, the terrorists have in effect helped reorient the (legal) leftist and Marxist political forces that have defended state expansion to promote development and national unity, forcing these groups not only to defend democratic methods but also to partially embrace promarket arguments. Furthermore, despite widespread and longstanding state corruption, low salaries, and adverse conditions, some government employees continue to provide services. Such employees engender an underlying base of support that prevents a complete collapse and total overthrow of the state.

Despite the unfolding democratic process of the 1980s, which was marked by several elections, the existing democracy was questioned not only by the insurgents but also by certain intellectuals and a number of political organizations. It was said, among other things, that Peruvian democracy cannot be based exclusively on general elections every five years and municipal elections every three;[1] that Peruvian democracy is weak because no adequate and efficient mechanisms of control exist to channel and resolve society's conflicts and contradictions; and that it fails to encourage or facilitate popular participation in drafting legislation.[2]

Perhaps the lack of viable alternatives to the traditional approach keeps political parties locked into their political bureaucratism, where they remain very distant from the needs and respect of civil society. This would explain, at least in part, why the 1990 elections brought to the presidency a man without a party who was unknown to most Peruvians.

Seeking a New Utopia

The Peruvian context raises certain questions regarding development. For example, if the state is no longer recognized as a development principal, what will provide the main stimulus? Will the dynamic agents of development now be individuals? Private enterprise? NGOs? Grassroots organizations?

Confronting the state's growing ineptitude—sometimes, its absence—

the popular and middle sectors have advanced four main organizational responses. First is the individual initiative seen in microenterprises, whereby the problems of underemployment, low income, and lack of dynamism in production and commerce are resolved to the benefit of and at the risk of each individual or family. Drawing upon the marketplace (preferably one that is free and spontaneous), individual microentrepreneurs become a force capable of promoting development. Second are the community organizations that emerge mainly to provide food through community kitchens and milk committees. In contrast to microenterprises, such initiatives are defensive in nature, attempts to maintain a standard of living by paying less for food and freeing mothers from certain tasks so they can work or attend to other matters in their own homes. Third are peasant and urban groups that organize to defend themselves against terrorist attacks or unwarranted actions by the police and armed forces. This response has taken the form of peasant patrols (*rondas campesinas*) and, more recently, urban patrols (*rondas urbanas*), which confront attacks from outside the locality and defend the community's economy and tranquility. Fourth are the NGOs that have sprung up to support individuals and groups mounting the three responses just described.

A new conception of development appears to be afoot in Peru, one that draws popular and middle sectors into the struggle to overcome the present crisis and ensure future development. Such a view removes development from the exclusive realm of the state or medium and large entrepreneurs and places it in the hands of the popular sectors—whether organizations or individuals and whether defensive or entrepreneurial initiatives.

NGO Development in Peru

Not until the second half of the 1970s did nongovernmental organizations become a major phenomenon in Peru, as prior to that time there were only a few such groups. Most prominent were the Institute of Peruvian Studies (IEP), which focuses on social science research; the Center for the Study and Promotion of Development (DESCO), which promotes grassroots development while also involving itself in research and dissemination; and the Center for Studies and Publications (CEP), which does pastoral work and provides research and reflection on society from a Liberation Theology approach. IEP and DESCO had secular origins, while CEP was affiliated with a religious order.

During the first half of the 1970s, at the height of the military government, the state grew considerably. New ministries emerged, the National Planning Institute revitalized itself, the National System to Support Social Mobilization (SINAMOS) was established, and state financial institutions were set up. Agrarian and economic reforms, as well as other enterprises, required qualified personnel to make them work; many of those people came from the universities.

At this stage of the seventies, the few NGOs that arose were very much bound to the concerns of the social sciences. During that period, Peruvian social scientists examined the Chilean political experience (the significance of Allende and the Popular Unity government), the Bolivian experience (the Torres government and People's Assembly), and the Peruvian experience (the military's high-profile, anti-imperialist developmentalist approach). More generally, social scientists addressed themselves to the advancement of Latin American development beyond dependency and to the organization of workers into a new democratic form. These concerns were mainly theoretical because the phenomena to be addressed were either multidimensional or continental in scope, as opposed to national. For a time, interest in researching the global processes prevailed. As a result, NGOs founded during the first stage of the military government were primarily research organizations such as, for example, the Las Casas Center in Cuzco established by the Dominican Order. After 1975, however, with the fall of Velasco and the transition from military to democratic civilian government, new NGOs arose that took their direction from the church and from professional groups (mainly leftist) associated with political parties.

When the central state, which had taken bold development initiatives, began to have problems, SINAMOS disappeared and other state agencies suffered cutbacks. Expectations vested in the state soon became frustrated. In addition, the universities entered a protracted period of crisis, one shared by the rest of the country. University salaries began to deteriorate, undercutting the incentive to find employment in academia. As both state and university grew weaker, so did the link between them.

The democratic opening that began in mid-1977, with the announcement of a Constituent Assembly, made possible the return of the traditional political parties and enabled the parties of the legal left to try their luck in the electoral arena. Although political life did not become as dynamic as would have been desirable, many professionals were drawn to politics, giving up their jobs to join in the struggle for power. In many cases, NGOs supported the political work of organizations that did not wish to fully enter legal political life.

In the late 1970s, the Peruvian economy experienced its first major crisis since 1967–1968, touched off by massive worker layoffs in 1977 that ended in a national strike on 19 July 1977. Economic and agrarian reforms were dismantled, and the idea that the "social property" sector should be favored above private property was discarded. External indebtedness began to pose a serious problem during this period, as debt servicing amounted to nearly 60 percent of export earnings—an unbearable burden. When the provincial and departmental defense fronts raised a series of regional demands, the state's inability to address these and the country's other development needs was associated with the crushing impact of the debt service.

In the marginal settlements (*pueblos jóvenes*) in Lima and other cities, inhabitants organized to demand that water and drainage systems be installed and that other services be provided. Newly emergent NGOs supported microentrepreneurs, interest groups and trade union organizations, neighborhood organizations, grassroots organizations struggling for social services, and groups fighting to preserve the gains won during the reformist stage of the military government. The NGOs also supported the political organizations, although not always openly.

With the 1980s, Peru entered a new phase of political life. After the drafting of Peru's constitution, elections were held in May 1980, bringing the country a democratically elected civilian government after twelve years of military rule. In November of that same year, municipal elections were held nationwide, and the traditional political parties returned to official political life on a strong footing. Also in that year, against prevailing sentiment, an armed struggle was launched that came to be known as Shining Path (Sendero Luminoso). A movement carried out by a political organization calling itself the Communist Party of Peru, Shining Path's ideological origins are Maoism adapted to Peru. Although viewed with skepticism initially, this terrorist force gradually won followers in certain parts of the highlands, using methods unknown in Peruvian insurrectional struggles during the 1960s. Shining Path also carried out actions in urban areas, including Lima, to attract attention and show that the new period of democratic life would not be easy.

Democracy did, in fact, fail to improve the lot of the population; it created no new jobs nor did it jump-start development. Galloping inflation led to figures never before seen in Peru's economic history, while wages swiftly deteriorated; soon, nutritional levels began to be a matter of concern. Yet the political organizations, although in power, curiously and paradoxically could do less and less to resolve the situation of the country's poorest sectors.

In the urban areas, especially Lima, neighborhood mothers organized to prepare food together as a way to cushion themselves against high prices. From their activities emerged the idea of community kitchens. At the same time, the mayor of Lima, Alfonso Barrantes, proposed that children of the pueblos jóvenes be given milk every day, which led to the organization of glass-of-milk committees.

Responding to grassroots needs and activities such as these, NGOs began to grow away from political organizations and to develop profiles of their own. However, like everything else in Peru, this was not a swift process. Slowly the NGOs took on a life of their own, developing objectives that grew out of their work rather than out of the political needs of the organizations for which they were created. The array of NGO services expanded, as did the range of beneficiaries. As the NGOs and parties loosened their ties, NGOs began on their own to provide support to the municipalities. Some became involved in designing development plans and providing advisory services for specific projects and activities. From 1984 to 1986, for example, NGOs helped design Lima's urban development plan.

Toward the end of the second administration of Fernando Belaúnde Terry (1983–1984), the country was in agony. The economic crisis had worsened, partly due to natural disasters (floods and droughts) in both northern and southern Peru. Inflation continued to climb, and it was estimated that by the end of 1985 it would reach nearly 250 percent annually. This, coupled with declining wages, produced the worst nutritional conditions ever. In addition, the debt burden became so crushing that by late 1984 and early 1985, Peru stopped paying some of the multilateral lending agencies.

Shining Path was making its presence increasingly felt during this period, not only through bombings and other forms of destruction but also through selective assassinations. The military began a counteroffensive that failed to spell out appropriate objectives and methods. Thus began the so-called dirty war, spurring human-rights organizations to protest as the army and terrorists systematically violated the rights of Peruvians. Such was the climate in which the presidential elections of 1985 were held.

The election of Alan García aroused great expectations, as he pledged to spend no more than 10 percent of export earnings for debt service. Accordingly, tension mounted between the Peruvian government and the International Monetary Fund. During the first year and a half of García's administration, inflation dropped by 60 percent annually; later, however, it climbed to figures higher even than under Belaúnde, reaching 3,000 percent a year by the end of his term. At first García embraced a policy of rapprochement with big business; later he lashed out against the private banking system in an effort to implement statist policies, which generated greater legal and ideological opposition and became a political movement. In his struggle against Shining Path, he took advantage of an uprising of Path prisoners to eliminate dozens of members, thus sharpening the internal confrontation without having an effective strategy.

During the second half of his term, García accelerated the decentralization process by creating eleven regions that could elect their own regional governments. This regionalization ushered in a new political dynamic in Peru; now, in addition to the municipal governments, there were regional seats of power.

Throughout this period, NGOs distanced themselves from political parties; newer NGOs, for example, often had either more conditional ties to the parties or none at all. Many NGOs began to believe, as well, that they should become less dependent on international donations and looked at ways to attain eventual sustainability. Human-rights activities picked up dramatically during these years as a result of terrorism and the dirty war. During the late 1980s, Peruvian NGOs began to increase their support to small-scale and microentrepreneurial productive activities, mainly in the urban areas, and continued their support of community kitchens and glass-of-milk committees. They also began to work with municipalities and, at the outset of the 1990s, expanded their activities to include support to the new regional governments. Interest in environmental issues also grew among Peruvian NGOs.

NGOs and Municipal Governments

Although municipal governments date back to the nineteenth century, until 1980 there were but a few occasions when they were chosen democratically. Now, however, mayors are chosen by direct election, and municipal council members are elected according to distributional guidelines; the winning slate is given 50 percent plus one of the seats (an absolute majority), while the other slates are given representation proportional to the number of votes they received. Mayors generally appoint key municipal officials.

Generally financed by transfer payments from the central government, municipal governments spend relatively little—usually less than 5 percent of the central government's expenditures (Delgado 1991). The 1979 constitution granted municipal governments more autonomy and strengthened their economic positions somewhat. Since 1980, for example, municipalities have increased their own revenues and become less dependent on the central government. Even so, they are not in good financial health.

Prior to 1980, municipal governments either relied on staffs or contracted the services of private consultants to carry out the most important municipal responsibilities. However, as the quality of internal professional support declined and the need for austerity grew, NGOs emerged as a promising alternative. As noted, NGOs played a key role in drawing up the Urban Development Plan for the municipality of Lima, a plan still in effect. The Institute for Peruvian Studies performed a demographic analysis of Lima, and the Development Studies Group investigated the structure of production.

During the 1980s, many political representatives and municipal officials were drawn from NGOs: Deputy Mayor Henry Pease was a member of the DESCO board of directors, and other members of the council were either NGO directors or staff. Appointees to various high-level posts also came from NGOs. Despite these prominent contributions to political life, however, Peruvian NGOs generally remain separate and apart from the political parties. Instead, they are turning their professional and technical expertise to the promotion and support of grassroots activities. In addition, they have proven to be open to new ideas. If, as is increasingly thought, development comes from below and has little to do with the state and if the NGOs express the demands of the organized population, NGOs now hold a privileged place in the structure of the new utopian vision.

NGO Forum on Environment

Over the past decades, Peru has endured institutional crises at every level; Lima itself is the core not only of institutional and political upheaval, but also of a dangerous level of environmental degradation.

Since 1989, alarm has been growing over urban environmental degradation in Lima and its environs. Two forums, created and orchestrated by NGOs, became the setting wherein municipal, regional, and federal officials could meet and discuss topics of shared interest with NGOs. The first such meeting, held in 1988, led to a position paper calling for joint government and private-sector efforts to reverse the growing environmental threat. A second forum, held in late 1991, produced a comprehensive environmental document, excerpts of which begin below.

These forums produced a diagnosis of environmental deterioration affecting natural resources of land, sea, and air, alerting municipal and regional officials to the alarming dimensions of the crisis. Among the short- and long-term recommendations by NGOs were (1) clearer divisions of labor and responsibility among government actors; (2) more stringent application of existing legislation through regulatory mechanisms; and (3) elaboration of additional legislation that could begin to reverse the environmental deterioration in the metropolitan region.

If the NGOs are themselves incapable of resolving the crisis, they have at least shown themselves willing to enter into a dialogue and to submit concrete proposals and examples of local-level environmental protection to beleaguered but still relatively powerful municipal authorities. The Lima forums provide a good example of NGO "proposal" rather than "protest," an offer to collaborate with rather than impede governmental decisionmaking. The following are excerpts from the second environmental meeting held in 1991.

Lima Charter II
Environmental Resources and Metropolitan Management

Ecological Hazards

Lima's deepening crisis is aggravated by its deteriorating environment, which the city government has thus far failed to address. One of the world's larger cities, Lima is growing at such a rapid pace that its intensifying socioeconomic and environmental problems have begun to affect the rest of Peru. Soil and water loss are prime examples: if population growth and distribution maintain their current pattern in the Chillón and

Lurín River Basins, the arable lands there will be lost over the next 25 years. Lands along the Rímac River will not endure even to the year 2000. And, assuming that agricultural land continues to diminish at current rates and Lima fails to curb its growth, groundwater will be dramatically reduced. If the city must then turn to surface water, large investments will be needed to draw water from the Lurín and Chillón rivers, expand the volume taken from the Mantaro, and even, perhaps, turn to the Chancay and Mala rivers.

Treatment cost will be very high, due to excessive surface water pollution. For example, the Rímac River, Lima's main water source, serves as a waste dump for no fewer than 402 mining, industrial, and sewage sources. In its final stretches, this river is an open-air garbage collector and sewer.

Lima suffers from air pollution, as well. Its climate is a contributing factor, as are its factories and refineries, all producing largely untreated emissions. Motorized vehicles and outside food vendors further contaminate the atmosphere, already stressed by the widespread practice of burning garbage and garden refuse.

Beaches escape few, if any, of Lima's polluting agents. The nearby seas are degraded by the direct and indirect discharge of approximately 700 million cubic meters of wastewater per year. Moreover, it is estimated that 900 tons of human excreta, from a variety of sources, are discharged daily at Lima's beaches. Microorganisms from the untreated waste deposited there cause several serious enteric diseases (such as cholera, typhoid and paratyphoid fevers, and several diarrheal phenomena) as well as viral diseases (polio, hepatitis A and B, and various enteroviruses). In addition, the sea floor is the repository of vast amounts of sewage sludge deposited each year, which settles to the bottom. Only part of this sludge is biodegradable; the rest consists of toxic metals that will inevitably affect the marine ecosystem, harming or eliminating most of the fish and shellfish in that zone—with the predictable effects upon consumers and the fishing industry. Considered separately or en masse, these indicators reveal the alarming reality of Lima's environmental emergency.

A Crisis in Government

Lima's environmental problems are aggravated by a critical lack of coherence in the metropolitan government, which suffers from a three-way overlap of functions and competencies involving itself, the central government, and public enterprises in charge of city services. This overlap creates serious problems in urban development planning and in the administration and decision making relating to public services.

Proposals for Action

To protect present and future generations, the problems experienced by Lima and the rest of Peru must be addressed quickly and expeditiously. The following measures must be undertaken:

- Declare a state of emergency and environmental danger in Lima to evoke the necessary sense of urgency regarding policy for its three

watersheds, its drinking water and sewage systems, its solid waste collection and disposal, and its electrical system.
- Ensure institutional implementation of the Ecological Belt of Metropolitan Lima to undertake the sectoral coordination needed to save our environmental resources.
- Create institutional and legal mechanisms to permit the various metropolitan agencies to coherently address environmental problems until the Lima Region is established.
- Implement an oversight program for environmental legislation aimed at achieving its effective implementation.

These emergency actions should be accompanied by proposals that ensure continuity of the policies over both medium and long term. Given that the problems of Greater Lima originate not only from within the area and as a result of its dynamics, but also from a national development pattern, we propose the following guidelines:

- Promote a type of education that values environmental resources and spreads awareness of the need to protect them.
- Bring about changes in the urban paradigm of development, reducing goals and expectations to achievable and sustainable levels.
- Promote decentralization of Peru's production as a means of curbing Lima's population growth and narrowing the gap between Lima and the rest of Peru.
- Increase public investment for sanitary infrastructure, and increase private investment in activities that help with environmental sanitation (recycling of wastewater for irrigation, collecting solid waste, etc.).

Within the framework of these proposals, there is a need for action on each of the environmental problems indicated above, taking into account the following considerations:

[Here, the charter moves into specific recommendations relating to soil, water, atmosphere, and marine ecology.]

The crisis that has gripped Peru for over a decade has contributed heavily to the degradation of its environmental resources and thus impinged upon its potential for development. National resurgence will require careful management of the environment in all spheres of Peruvian life. Thus, we call upon national and local authorities, grassroots organizations, political parties, NGOs, professional schools, labor organizations, churches, and all Peruvians to join together in this effort. (Lima Forum on Environmental Resources, Crisis, and Alternatives, June 1991.)

NGOs and Democratization

Bridging the Gap

Alternatives, an NGO quite similar in origin and program to São Paulo's Pólis,[3] links poor populations and municipal authorities in the northern section of Lima. This NGO plays a catalytic role in helping mayors of nine towns in Lima's Northern Cone cooperative with NGOs, thus facilitating the evolution of regional cooperation.

Estimated at approximately 1,520,000 inhabitants, the Northern Cone is a strategic territory for the development of Metropolitan Lima because of its accommodation of population growth. Furthermore, it includes Lima's largest agricultural areas which, along with developing small and medium industrial enterprises, constitute important economic resources. Much of its population lives in acute poverty. The activities of Alternatives affect about 10,000 of these residents directly and about 50,000 indirectly. Alternatives coordinates its work with the nine local governments of the Northern Cone through the Interdistrict Coordinator of Mayors.

The regionalization programs introduced during the García regime have been ineffective, particularly so in urban settings. An Organic Law of Municipalities sets forth definitions for municipal management but lacks precision when it comes to determining competencies. As now defined, relationships between provincial and district municipalities give rise to confusion, duplication of efforts, and conflicts. Although theoretically established by law, the autonomy of districts making up the metropolitan region stems from the will of the particular provincial government in power.

As well, the lack of institutionalized mechanisms and spaces for the participation of civil society makes it difficult to legitimate municipal governments. In some municipalities, social organizations have achieved a certain degree of success, which is evidence of the potential for popular participation. Nonetheless, these experiences suffer from a lack of continuity, since the groups created lacked an institutional structure to guarantee their ongoing reality. Thus, they often remain dependent on the political will of the mayor.

Alternatives is currently seeking to aid and encourage local governments of the Northern Cone in their decentralization and democratization efforts. Specifically, this NGO directs its efforts at promoting greater community participation in defining objectives and goals; helps to foster closer coordination among local governments, grassroots social organizations, NGOs, private entities, and international support agencies; and serves as a partner in projects addressing production, employment, food and nutrition, health, citizen rights, and democratization of the public agencies in the Northern Cone.

Through its participation in working groups (*mesas de trabajo*), Alternatives coordinates closely with other NGOs on activities in the Northern Cone. These groups bring together NGOs, mayors, and council members of Northern Cone districts to facilitate coordination of work plans. One group, for example, has worked with several successive municipal governments and, based on that experience, has formed the

Coordinating Commission for Northern Cone Planning. This commission works with municipal authorities, leaders of civic organizations, and NGOs in such areas as urban development, environment, health, food and nutrition, and job promotion. It focuses, as well, on government and has drafted a bill containing a plan for organizing the government of Metropolitan Lima. In March 1991, the first interdistrict meeting of the Northern Cone was held, attended by over 300 delegates that included representatives of grassroots organizations and district municipal governments. NGOs of the Cone have also begun to publish a bimonthly newspaper, *La Propuesta,* and Alternatives is publishing *Alerta-Emergencia,* which provides up-to-date information on the key aspects of the crisis and emergency programs.

In 1991, Alternatives formed a regionalization group to give this process direction and to assist municipal authorities with training, advisory services, policy and programs, assessment and planning, and—most important for democracy and efficiency—advisory services and training for the popular organizations and leaders. The regionalization group carries out its activities in coordination with other NGOs and technical resources of the Northern Cone.

Research projects and programs include publications on urban space, the government, and regionalization of the Cone; a study of draft legislation; a study of sanitation and the environment in the Northern Cone; a diagnostic study of the Cone; and an evaluation of Peru's regionalization process. In addition, Alternatives is building a data bank for the use of researchers and professionals as well as local authorities and organizations.

As a member of the NGO Working Group on Food and Agriculture, Alternatives participated in the Executive Committee of the Social Emergency Program and has undertaken a project to evaluate and improve popular nutrition. Finally, it has made a study of agricultural areas of the Cone to lay the foundation for a project that will protect these areas and their groundwater.

NGO Roles and Goals

According to the National Association of Centers (ANC), there were just over five hundred NGOs in Peru in 1990; DESCO counted seven hundred, and the National Planning Institute estimates that there are approximately six hundred NGOs. Most (67 percent) are located in Lima.[4]

The period of most rapid NGO expansion was from 1976 to 1985; during those years approximately 70 percent of the NGOs now operating were established. ANC figures indicate that 3 percent of the NGOs were established prior to 1970, 2 percent from 1971 to 1975, 26 percent from 1976 to 1980, 43 percent from 1981 to 1985, and 25 percent from 1986 to 1990. Clearly, NGOs are now cropping up at a somewhat slower pace.

During the period of greatest expansion, there occurred a relative decentralization of NGOs, and Lima's share fell somewhat (although it remained predominant). Their number and swift rise may be deceptive if one associates volume with efficiency, as Peruvian NGOs vary in size and capability. The largest have maintained their preeminence for several years: DESCO, for example, has sometimes had as many as 100 employees; the Las Casas Center and IEP are also large and relatively powerful. Some NGOs have grown considerably and now cover several areas of the country, with regional offices, branches, or subsidiaries. For example, organizations such as the Center for Research, Documentation, Education, Advice, and Service; the Center for Research, Education, and Development; and Habitat Perú all have offices outside of Lima, as does DESCO. Las Casas Center, originally established in Cuzco, now has offices in Lima.

Most prevalent, however, are the small-scale entities with ten to fifteen staff members; these NGOs expand and contract according to the financing they are able to garner. Indeed, some NGOs shut down for a time and then reestablish themselves. According to the findings of a World Bank mission to Lima, of the 500 to 600 NGOs registered, only 250 are operational (de Wit 1991). Developing simultaneously with the NGOs during the 1980s were cooperative efforts that in some cases culminated in the establishment of NGO networks (or *coordinadoras*) around certain issues. As of 1990, there were approximately fifteen such networks.

The relationship of NGOs to the state was a matter of some concern during the 1980s. In the 1970s, probably due to the dictatorial nature of the regime, pressure from political parties, and the nature of NGO programs and beneficiaries, there was little NGO-state cooperation. In the 1980s, however, greater interest developed around such contacts—despite the potential for philosophical clashes. For one thing, a share of international cooperation for NGOs comes through the state. In addition, coordination with the state is sometimes essential, as was the case with health actions to stem the cholera epidemic.

Compared with some other Latin American countries, Peru has many NGOs; together, they mobilize large amounts of human and financial resources. The question is, can NGOs make substantive contributions to popular groups and lay the groundwork for development within the new Peruvian context? Can NGOs play a development role in view of a strengthening neoliberal economic ideology and a climate of terror reigning in the areas where the poorest Peruvians live? Or should these organizations limit themselves to providing welfare assistance and defending human rights?

Impact of NGO Development Projects

Today, international development agencies increasingly view NGOs as organizations that can respond to the challenges of the present moment. Indeed,

NGOs have already played a significant role in Peru and worldwide. But what is their effective impact?

First of all, it is not easy to promote development in a country experiencing a lengthy recession and growing political, military, and social violence. Development cannot be promoted in all regions equally or with the same security, as military confrontations vary from region to region and from zone to zone. Levels of social organizations also vary by region and by zone. Thus, giving a group $100,000 to carry out a project will be more problematic in certain parts of the country than in others. In fact, the present context is such that expectations of yield on development funds will probably diminish. All of these factors create development limitations that cannot be overcome until peace comes to Peru.

In the development world, vestiges of clientelist and welfare-oriented tendencies remain to undercut current development endeavors. However, a self-critical, long-range perspective of NGO activities is gaining ground, and such a perspective helps to erode the clientelist and welfare-oriented approach of many NGOs and transform the expectations of beneficiaries long accustomed to manipulation and clientelist politics. A fundamental step in bolstering project efficiency is to create workable mechanisms for project selection and follow-up. In some cases project activities work only to a certain point (which undercuts the objective of the original proposal); in others, they are almost completely reformulated once they have been approved. The responsibility lies both with the NGO in charge of preparing the proposal and with the entity providing the funds (lending agency, foundation, or international NGO). As the flow of development funding to Peru is considerable, project impact should be a key concern.[5]

Final Reflections

Peru's prolonged economic crisis undercuts standards of living throughout the country and signals the need for reassessment and reformulation of development models. The country is witnessing the transition from a statist to a neoliberal myth, and the slow progress from one utopian vision to the other is perhaps the most dangerous challenge the country has to face. For, running against the current, a radical and violent movement seeks to expand and strengthen the state and is directly opposed to all of society as it is organized today.

The political parties' lack of legitimacy in Peru has led NGOs and other autonomous organizations to become repositories of a new utopian thought regarding development. It has also given them a more prominent role in combating the forces trying to destroy contemporary Peruvian society. In this sense, the NGOs—together with grassroots organizations from the 1980s—have become key players in upholding Peru's current democracy.

However, in a context marked by rising tides of both neoliberalism and violence, the NGO capacity to genuinely replace the state in promoting development is limited. Many development projects, for example, are carried out by NGOs that still retain clientelist and welfare vestiges and cannot meet project objectives and goals. Furthermore, the absence of the state has given regional and local governments a leading role for which they are ill-prepared. If the state in its central, regional, or municipal manifestations is not in a position to undertake a utopian vision of development, the NGOs alone are even less so. However, as collaborators, each may provide what the other lacks, in the process forging workable partnerships for genuine, sustainable development. Such partnerships hold a degree of promise for Peru's future.

Notes

1. This is an argument raised primarily by the most radical political groups calling for direct democracy, such as Popular Democratic Unity (UDP), headed by former Lima mayor Alfonso Barrantes and the Unified Mariátegui Party (PUM).

2. This argument is set forth mainly by the ILD.

3. See chapter 6, "Making Cities Livable," for a description of this Brazilian PVO, which focuses heavily on public transportation and solid waste collection.

4. The statistical information of this chapter is based on the document *El Perú en Cifras,* published by Cuanto, S.A. in 1991.

5. Donor agencies for Peruvian NGOs have mainly been European NGOs throughout the period under consideration. In 1990, North American NGOs (both U.S. and Canadian) contributed U.S.$17,971,000, or 39 percent of the total contributed by international NGOs in Peru. (This figure is based on information in *Programa Nacional Cooperación Técnica 1990,* published by DGCTI-INP in Lima, Peru.)

13

Topocrats, Technocrats, and NGOs

CHARLES A. REILLY

The road ahead will be bumpy for Latin America's democratizing states. Fragile economies and skewed distribution mechanisms have reinforced austerity, foreclosed populist options, and discouraged redistribution of wealth. The region has been outperformed by Asian "tigers," upstaged by Eastern Europe's emergence, eclipsed by extreme African poverty. But bad news for overambitious central governments may lead them to unexpected and efficacious allies through the gradual emergence of civil society, a complex and frequently unfamiliar terrain. As state-centered development strategies wane, interest is shifting to markets, free-trade agreements, and regional trading blocs. Within these changing state and market frameworks, can more vibrant civil societies lead to a fuller realization of citizenship? What kind of democracy will result?

Guillermo O'Donnell worries that an impoverished and indifferent "delegative democracy" is emerging in the region, and the Cavarozzi and Palermo study of neighborhood associations in Buenos Aires seems to support this somber interpretation. But the remaining case studies paint a more optimistic picture of engaged, rather than delegated, democracy. Whether optimistic or pessimistic, delegative, representative, or plebiscitary, all the cases deepen my conviction that the major issues of governance and citizenship will be resolved in the coming years at the municipal level. If the secondary citizenship nascent in civil society is to take on full meaning, it will have to occur next at the municipal level. Governance and civility, as well as democracy, are at stake in the cities and towns of Latin America.

NGO Diversity

Each national and local government context is different, as are the forms of collective action or NGO activity emanating from civil society. Luis Paulo

Teixeira, a community housing activist and leader in São Paulo, put it this way:

> Look, urban reform sews together the demands of specific movements: day care, landless, homeless, "bus-less," and those who don't participate at all in the life of the city. It is also the formulation of a dream, of the ideal of seeing everyone living well, with dignity, and being respected as a citizen—doing away with the city of exclusion, of apartheid, in favor of a city of sharing and equality (du Silva 1991: 7).

Such movements, dreams, and ideals bubble up from civil society, creating a form of secondary citizenship that percolates through myriad actors: NGOs and grassroots support organizations involved in service delivery; nascent social movements formulating demands; organized social movements and membership support organizations articulating demands and delivering services; and producers' organizations blending self-help with occasional protest.[1]

NGOs have complex sets of national and international relationships. They relate downward to their own networks of grassroots or base organizations. They relate laterally to other NGOs and build federations or consortia among equals. They may lead or anchor amorphous social movements. Increasingly, they provide services in association with state and municipal governments. They relate upward to national governments, though usually outside of the directly sponsored, corporatist framework that lingers in many countries.

Do Municipalities Govern?

Unlike some countries of the world, Latin American nations have no tradition of local-level clout. Each of the six countries discussed in this book shares Latin American centralist traditions in which corporatist structures rest on clientelist underpinnings. If state governments have historically enjoyed some autonomy in these countries, municipal governments have enjoyed little more than rhetorical nods to municipal autonomy unaccompanied by fiscal capacity. Although federalist principles enrich the oratory of national leaders and catchall constitutions usually contain some federal features, corporatist structures predominate, and the administrative, fiscal, and legislative capacity of local units is extremely curtailed. Yet municipal government is fundamental to democratization. As Manuel Castells put it,

> the municipality is the decentralized level of the state, the most penetrated by civil society, the most accessible to the governed, and the most directly connected to the daily life of the masses. Central state-municipal relations are the clearest indicator of the general relations between the State and civil society (1981: 300).

Austerity politics, sometimes enjoined on national governments by external actors (particularly the International Monetary Fund and the World Bank), contribute to de facto decentralization trends and to the breaking down of traditional, corporatist-clientelist patterns of interaction. The populist handouts of the past are quite impossible today; the Benefactor State is broke, and fiscal crises are endemic. Persistent Maoist challenges like Shining Path in Peru, sporadic social explosions (such as the food riots in Rosario, Argentina or Caracas, Venezuela), or random violence in cities of the hemisphere lend urgency to the situation. If "perception of threat" propelled middle- and upper-class sectors to support bureaucratic authoritarianism in the 1960s, today, new threats stimulate a different, more collaborative response. Faced with such problems, it is hardly surprising that financially strapped local politicians are searching for new partners. With their (foreign) resources and know-how, NGOs are especially attractive.

Experiments linking citizens' advisory councils and neighborhood associations with popular municipal administrations are a promising trend in many cities, whose previous mayors and prefects casually disregarded their councils and advisory colleagues. Administrative deconcentration has been driven more by overcrowded central cities, traffic jams, and pollution than by federalist ideals. Political decentralization is complicated by the legacy of national parties and representational mechanisms. Moreover, civilian control of the military is not yet firmly established. Thus, governance *and* civility remain in question.

Technocrats, Topocrats, and Negotiating NGOs

Democracy and development are inextricably linked. If a first generation of Latin American development agents was enamored of technocracy, a new, technically skilled generation seems to give more weight to place or locale—"topocracy." Territoriality has been reinforced by demographic trends—especially by the dramatic growth of urban populations. Intergovernmental relations and the peculiar attributes of each *layer* of government have grown more important as centralized, corporatist organizations recede in Latin America. Is this a universal trend?

Referring to intergovernmental relations in the United States during the 1970s, Samuel Beer (cited in McKay 1980) distinguished between "technocrats"—the professional bureaucrats of the modern state and "topocrats"—the intergovernmental lobby to which he attributes increasing territorial specialization (such as the National League of Cities, U.S. Conference of Mayors, National Governors' Conference, the International City Management Association, etc.). I would extend the term *topocrat* well beyond Beer's intergovernmental usage to include NGOs and political actors grounded in particular geographic areas. Technocrats with their expertise and topocrats linked to locality and intergovernmental bridge building were sources of social entrepreneurial initiative in the United States during the 1970s.

In Latin America, the central state has dominated development thinking and practice for four decades. Indeed, the state (meaning central government) was assumed by capitalists, socialists, world bankers, and military elites to be the arbiter and implementer of development. Armed with an array of (mostly) economic tools with which to tinker, these technocrats—the professional bureaucrats of the modern state—went to work.

Today in Latin America, topocratic vision and action (providing services to specified local populations, forging linkages between localities and reformers within the state apparatus, and strengthening regional networks) flow primarily from NGOs and social movements in civil society. A new, technically skilled generation gives more weight to locale or "topos"; these topocrats are loyal to territory, to decentralization, and to diversity. This regard for turf and territoriality has been reinforced by demographic trends—especially the challenges to democracy and development triggered by the dramatic growth of urban populations. While observers of the United States in the 1990s focus on the expanding suburbs as the territorial core of politics, in Latin America the contested arena is the city.

In many Latin American countries, the transition to democracy was accompanied by a variety of social movements—amorphous and sometimes ephemeral groupings of people focused on ethnic, gender, ecological, religious, and economic issues—often led by NGOs or tracing their intellectual and administrative impetus to NGO participation. NGOs often served as bridges between social movements and state and local governments, especially as the NGOs grow technically more competent.

To states strapped both for resources and for effective popular support, the NGO universe presents dilemmas as well as advantages. For example, NGOs are increasingly weaving international networks built on functional, sectoral, or ideological affinities quite beyond the traditional linkages of labor, business, and party structures. Environmental networks are a prime example. Their particular brand of foreign relations allows many NGOs to capture resources and channel them to projects within their nation. These activities, however, bring many NGOs into competion with their own governments for such resources. As well, this flow of international resources through the NGO sector—especially during times of austerity—introduces weighty issues of sovereignty and resource control. In 1980, more than U.S.$4.7 billion was transferred to Latin America, Africa, and South Asia from industrial nations through private channels (Brian Smith 1990: 7). In 1987, $5.5 billion was transferred through nongovernmental channels, $1 billion more than the amount contributed by the World Bank's International Development Association (World Bank 1991: 136).

National governments respond to the NGO phenomenon in various ways. In Brazil, for example, an office has been set up within the Ministry of Foreign Affairs to monitor international NGO resource transfers. New Chilean government agencies (FOSIS and ACI) were set up immediately after Aylwin assumed power in 1990 to serve as liaisons to the NGOs. Chilean NGOs had designated their representative to the new government *before* it was elected—and the newly installed democratic government quickly acknowledged the support. High officials of Mexico's Ministry of Agriculture recently requested funding from a U.S. donor agency for conference the ministry wished to have with Mexican NGOs. PRONASOL, an agency of the Mexican government, already seeks to link such organizations directly to the Mexican presidency. Each of these responses affects the emerging linkages between subnational governments and the NGO sector. Whether in economics or politics, informality blurs the boundaries between public and private spheres.

How Do NGOs Buttress Democracy?

In answering such a question, one might begin with the following analogy: voluntary associations and NGOs in democracies function like capillaries do in the body. The last stop for arterial blood outflow, capillaries are also the starting point for the return of venous blood to the heart and the means by which oxygen, nutrients, and wastes are exchanged between blood and tissues. Extending the metaphor to the body politic, voluntary associations and NGOs promote the exchange of information, financial resources, demands, and supports: the stuff of power. Capillaries/associations are one point at which the policymaker and policytaker converge, and thus the effects of policy may be known and adapted. (Implementation often changes objectives.) Policy monitoring and modification through these capillaries merit greater attention from managers and also from political scientists, who, when not engaged in intramural debates, usually pursue policymaking (design) more often than policy taking (outcomes).

In 1986, O'Donnell and Schmitter wrote on the grassroots social movement phenomenon (in which NGOs are significant actors) and acknowledged their potential for deepening the roots of democracy.

> Of particular interest . . . has been the literal explosion of grassroots movements, most of which have been organized around narrowly circumscribed territorial domains (barrios or parroquias). . . . They are numerous and their internal processes are quite often highly participatory and egalitarian. This has important implications for the emergent political culture of the transition. There are suddenly a multitude of popular forums—however ephemeral some of them may prove to be—in which the exercise and learning of citizenship can flourish in deliberations about issues of everyday concern. . . . Comprehensive social pacts or national-level policy reforms will not resolve such issues, and therefore, the emergent political process acquires elements of decentralization which may deepen its democratic roots (53).

Is there solid empirical evidence for celebrating democratic practice in NGOs and social movements? Observing a range of organizations in six Latin American countries, Albert Hirschman traced the sources of their "social energy," emphasizing what they learned from overambitious, revolutionary adventures of the 1960s.

> [T]he growth of collective action for economic advancement at the grass-roots . . . may simply be a reflection of an increasing and increasingly difficult-to-deny recognition of basic rights to be extended to all citizens. . . . Grassroots movements become more numerous, active, and vocal at a time when there is a great deal of talk about a new set of human rights to subsistence, education, health care, a safe environment, and participation in decision-making, in addition to such older human rights as freedom of religion, expression, movement, and so on (1985: 101).

If an awareness of rights impels them, what is the level of internal democracy in the NGOs themselves? Not surprisingly, it varies. A recently completed study of thirty grassroots support and membership organizations in Chile, Peru, and Costa Rica by Thomas Carroll assessed three attributes: service delivery efficiency, participation and accountability, and impact within the country. Of these thirty organizations, eighteen rated lower for the democratic criteria of participation/accountability than for service delivery; however, he concluded that, in both grassroots and membership support organizations, formal accountability mechanisms such as ownership and representation were not nearly as important as open consultative processes and a code of ethics that avoids paternalism and dependency. On the issue of leadership, he concludes: "In practice, dependence on a charismatic leader is less damaging for participation than for loss of flexibility and dynamism in later stages of organizational development" (1992: V-18).

What then is the best mix of leadership and dependency? What about rotation in office? How do NGOs resolve the succession problem? Does Roberto Michels's "iron law of oligarchy"[2] prevail, or do membership organizations somehow avoid the pitfalls of bureaucratization and maintain accountability? What goes on in the gray zones, where there are many gradations between absolute ideals and relative exercise of democracy? Do voluntary associations and social movements speak to such issues as representational versus direct democracy? Several ongoing studies of membership organizations in rural settings are exploring these questions further.[3]

Science of Management

An unexpected endorsement of efficiency through decentralized democratic practices emerges from studies of the contemporary business firm. Let us hear from the science of management for ideas derived from business approaches to decentralization, customer satisfaction, and effective service delivery. According to Thomas Peters, "the times demand that flexibility and love of change replace our long-standing penchant for mass production and mass markets, based as it is upon a relatively predictable environment now vanished" (1988: xii).

Peters offers a set of standards for business organizations in "a world turned upside down," guidelines equally pertinent for public and private-sector agencies engaged in service delivery:

- Create total customer responsiveness.
- Pursue fast-paced innovation.
- Achieve flexibility by empowering people.
- Learn to love change.

Peters offers "a new view of leadership at all levels." Prescriptions selected from his long list would radically change service delivery, whether by the public or private sector and whether north or south of the Rio Grande. Here are a few:

- Specialize, create niches, differentiate.
- Become obsessed with listening.
- Reconceive the middle manager's role.
- Eliminate bureaucratic rules and humiliating conditions.
- Pursue "horizontal" management by undermining and displacing "vertical" bureaucracy.
- Measure what is important.
- Decentralize information, authority, and strategic planning.
- Demand total integrity.

Such daunting management prescriptions are far from internalized within the business community and certainly not yet incorporated into public management. They reflect a change in corporate strategies from massive scale to microprecision, from centralized control to decentralization, from repetitive mass production to innovative research and development, from mass to local markets, and from rigidity to "flexible specialization."

We have discussed democratizing NGOs and decentralizing management strategies. What are the mechanisms that can bring democratizers and decentralizers together? Let me borrow some concepts useful for examining intergovernmental relations and for recognizing the de facto linkages between public and private spheres at the local level.

Negotiations, Pacts, and Bureaucratic Rings

It has been convincingly argued that patrimonial legacies and the path of transition toward democracy are crucial for the shape and substance of subsequent democratic practice at the national level. The authors have chronicled a wide variety of negotiations, agreements, concertation, contracts, and cost sharing between public-private actors in Latin American cities. Pacts among elites have been instrumental in many Latin American transitions, as have "bureaucratic rings," a concept first elaborated by Fernando Henrique Cardoso (1975) to explain technocratic-military alliances in authoritarian Brazil.

Cardoso identified bureaucratic rings during his analysis of the change from parliamentary and party-dominated politics to a technocratic-military configuration during the 1960–1970 period in authoritarian Brazil. Cardoso argued that political decisionmaking occurred in "bureaucratic rings," semiformal but influential circles of government ministers, technocrats, financiers, and heads of parastatal entities. Unlike earlier forms of politics rooted in state and municipal alliances, bureaucratic rings operated primarily at the federal level within the state apparatus. As the authoritarian regime penetrated the periphery and its technocratic ethos trickled down through federal agencies, these rings became operative at state and local levels as well (Reilly 1981).

Today, bargaining and compromise have entered the lexicon of technocrats and topocrats at all layers of democratizing societies—not merely the national level. Integral to other Latin American democratic transitions has been the concept of pacts. The Colombian and Venezuelan cases led Terry Karl (1986) to analyze "foundational pacts," or "pacts to make pacts," as basic to the democratic transitions in these two countries. Such pacts, or negotiated compromises, guarantee threatened elites (both military and civilian) that certain prerogatives will be assured, for example, amnesty for the military, property rights for the landed, rules for arbitrating between labor and capital, and so on. Assurance that their fundamental interests will be respected enlists compromise and collaboration from otherwise reluctant elites at the outset of the transition. O'Donnell and Schmitter point out the downside of this practice.

> Ironically, such modern pacts move the polity toward democracy by undemocratic means. They are typically negotiated among a small number of participants representing established (and often highly oligarchical) groups or institutions; they tend to reduce competitiveness as well as conflict; they seek to limit accountability to wider publics; they attempt to control the agenda of policy concerns; and they deliberately distort the principle of citizen equality. Nonetheless, they can alter power relations, set loose new political processes, and lead to different (if often unintended) outcomes (1986: 37–38).

Operating below the national level, pacts—like bureaucratic rings— reflect elite arrangements. However they are instrumental to introducing democracy. A feature of NGO-municipal relationships in most of the case studies discussed here is the rather novel and pragmatic approach to negotiation, bargaining, compromise, and pactmaking now in evidence among NGOs, social movements, and local government elites. Sometimes products of stalemate, these negotiations also reflect a willingness of both governors and governed to work out partial solutions to immediate problems. Totalistic responses are neither demanded nor expected. Tolerance is on the rise. Impetus and energy flow in both directions, instead of solely from government and private-sector elites. Initiative, vitality, and diversity abound in voluntary associations, movements, and grassroots organizations, whose interests are being heard—sometimes for the first time. Conflict is a normal part of this two-way process; conflict management, however, has become more socialized.

I would argue that interaction with NGOs (assuming a certain degree of internal democratic practice) does positively influence the democratic content of local governments. In other words, the relationships between NGOs and local governments can be a cause as well as an effect of enhanced democratic practice. A product of democracy, such negotiations can also produce it.

Latin American Cities: From Conflict to Collaboration

> Ever since the seventeenth century, political philosophers have been hunting for the secret of alchemical transformation from the brutish chaos of conflict to the serene life of cooperation.
> —Adam Przeworski, *Democracy and the Market*

Our look at contemporary Latin American cities reveals both conflict and cooperation—few alchemists but many problemsolvers.

The interactions between NGOs and local governments cited in these chapters range from adversarial and conflictive to competitive or surrogate to collaborative and even consensual. There were examples of NGOs serving as surrogates when local government services have proven particularly ineffective (the expansion of NGO health care in Chile, garbage collection in Brazil, or self-help housing in Argentina exemplify this pattern).

The adversarial position of NGOs throughout authoritarian periods typifies the opposite extreme. Where the adversarial position has been superseded, NGOs often provide research and development and serve as experimental sites. They test social innovations that might be transferred to the public sector (pilot projects testing curriculum reform for Colombian primary schools, for example) or sustained joint ventures such as creating and maintaining community schools in Northeast Brazil. Successful NGOs may expand or multiply and consolidate networks, as Chilean NGOs have done in health care or the community schools have done in Brazil. Some NGO efforts, however, may never spill over into the public sector, instead subsisting as enclaves for a privileged clientele until external funding dries up. However, these are hot houses rather than laboratories.

A new spirit of pragmatism is at work in Latin America today, giving rise to patterns of interaction that may feature explicit pacts or implicit bargains. Negotiations ebb and flow, with tradeoffs and varying degrees of collaboration within different arenas. From discussions of national transitions to democracy let me borrow some concepts useful for examining intergovernmental relations and for recognizing the de facto linkages between public and private spheres at the local level. Based on the chapters included here and impressions derived from my field visits to the sites, I'll sketch where these case studies fit on the continuum.

The chapters in this book chronicle cases that illustrate the changing relationships between local government and civil society in a number of Latin American cities. The transition from confrontation to policy collaboration, from protest to proposal, is very clear in Mexican social movements and producer organizations. The popular defense committees of Durango, Mexico, evolved over two decades from confrontation to collaborative ventures in land titling, self-help housing, consumer affairs, and environmental protection. Frequently, these efforts achieved collaborative status until, most recently, the formation of a political party seeking elective office set the movement into channeled competition once again. Julio Moguel has captured this history in his chapter and in various publications over the past several years.

In the Fernandes and Piquet survey, Brazilian NGO leaders expressed some ambivalence but also generally agreed upon the need for increased governmental regulation of the NGO sector. They were adamant, however, that NGOs should maintain an autonomous stance outside the state. Collaboration, not absorption or co-optation, was the watchword. Brazilian health movements follow this pattern, moving from adversarial stances to more collaborative ventures with sympathetic municipal and state administrations. Working in another sector is Pólis, an NGO created by "action researchers" specifically to provide training and information-management services for municipal governments and to disseminate workable ideas for social problem solving. The identification and promotion of efficient approaches to solid waste sorting and recycling is one example of cooperation between an NGO (in this case, Pólis) and local government on a major urban environmental problem. Pólis also advocates transportation financing schemes that charge producers as well as consumers and employers as well as workers, thus accommodating the fiscal requirements of city governments by ending direct subsidies.

Loveman's chapter traces the evolution of Chile's large and heterogeneous NGO sector, which played a significant role in the transition to democracy; for example, NGOs furnished many leaders for cabinet and sub-cabinet positions in the concertación government. He also suggests new roles for NGOs in consolidating democracy. The study of primary health care in Chile by Judith Salinas and Giorgio Solimano covers a period when

320 of the 335 local municipal officials (prefects) appointed by the Pinochet dictatorship continued in power well after a democratically elected national government had settled into office (municipal elections were held 28 June 1992). The case studies of six NGOs, three of them contracted by the Ministry of Health for primary health-care services, illustrate the comparative advantage of having NGOs work with specific target populations. Cooperation, rather than conflict, has characterized the Chilean public/private health-care programs to date, with formal contracts and agreements as their vehicle. In a different chapter, Caravedo cites Peruvian cases that also rely on formal cooperative agreements for service delivery, including soup kitchens and school lunch programs.

Incremental progression from welfare to development has characterized programs of Argentine NGOs responding to poor people's needs. Rosario, Argentina, the site of Martínez Nogueira's case study, illustrates the transfer of know-how and experience in promoting community organization and housing. NGOs involved in these efforts have become surrogates by default, since neither its financial nor its human resources permit the municipal government to deal with low-income housing. "We can't do it ourselves," Rosario's mayor remarked as he welcomed NGOs to train municipal government workers in self-help housing techniques. This city had been the scene of major riots a few years before—clearly an incentive for public- and private-sector actors to get along.

Historically, most Latin American NGOs forged their institutional identity through resistance to authoritarian regimes. In Chile and Brazil, for example, NGOs provided space for "secondary citizenship" and jobs for dissidents, giving vicarious democracy a chance to take root. As the transition to democracy unfolds, these NGO schools for democracy continue to redefine their roles. In Chile and Peru, for example, many NGO leaders are tapped for positions in government ministries.

Are democratic tendencies deepened through NGOs and social movements? Mounting evidence suggests that they are. While it is true that both often depend on charismatic leaders and rotation in office may be slow, it is also true that NGO and movement personnel usually demonstrate more inclusive attitudes, habits of internal democracy, accessibility, and direct links and responsiveness to the popular sectors. Moreover, in many Latin American countries an important generational shift in NGO leadership is taking place as younger social entrepreneurs, unmarked by years of authoritarian strictures, launch NGOs like Pólis that are characterized by specialization and technical proficiency.

Can NGOs transfer their attitudes, values, habits, and behavior, to the local state? On this point, some cautionary remarks may be in order. Authoritarian tendencies are deeply rooted in these societies, as O'Donnell (1984) and da Matta (1987) have argued with regard to both Argentina and Brazil (and few Mexican or Chilean analysts would disagree). NGOs are not the sole relevant actors, and political representation (with the exception of opposition under authoritarian regimes) is a recent phenomenon. The parties traditionally monopolizing political organization (but seldom *representation*) in these countries clearly do not exhaust the potential of civil society.

In some settings, older parties have lost their social bases or become tarnished by identification with military regimes. Elsewhere, a proliferation of new parties signals pluralism and inefficacy at the same time. The weak performance of parties and diminished clout of unions increases the importance of the "informal sector of the polity" and escalates representational roles of the NGO community. In countries like Chile, where huge numbers of people once participated intensely and extensively through political parties, or in Mexico, where they did not, one important issue will be to see how continuous and how autonomous a role NGOs will play. The withering away of NGOs and social movements is a possibility, but one even less likely than the disappearance of the state.

Toward a Democracy Without Adjectives

Mexican historian Enrique Krauze reflected generalized distaste for qualifying democracy with words like "tutelary," "popular," "formal," and so on, by titling his 1986 book *Democracy Without Adjectives* (Mexico: Editorial Planeta). We have suggested here that Latin American NGOs and social movements buttress the preliminary stages of such a democracy. Unfortunately, democratic governance is problematic. Democracy, like development, is reversible. Now, after electoral interludes have taken place, is a good time to assess the evolution of democratic performance in Latin America.

Political analysts and the international community have celebrated elections and welcomed civilians to office. Such events are not insignificant achievements, but electoral fervor and farewells to uniformed executives ensure neither the genesis nor the deepening of democracy. Will the interplay between NGOs and local governments serve democratic practice more effectively in the future than centralized governments, parties, and institutions have in the past?

Before exploring the thorny issue of democratic performance, let us clarify some concepts. In the broadest terms, we are examining an always reversible and uncertain process of designing and implementing norms for taking power, as well as practices for assuring accountability. The political expression of interests and values may find many channels: parties and associations, functional and territorial units, individual and collective vehicles. Robert Dahl (1971) defined the Western model of democracy or "polyarchy," as one that includes separation of powers, regular and competitive elections, freedom for all groups, tolerance, pluralism, full participation, and human rights in economic, social, civic, and political spheres.

Scholars, inspired by de Tocqueville and reinforced by the Western European experience, presumed that there was some correlation between economic development and democracy: the ideal pattern of evolution moved from liberalization through democratization, progressing toward enjoyment of the benefits of political, economic, and social democracy for increasing numbers of the population.

De Tocqueville insisted upon links between associational activity and increasing equality of conditions. Independent groups and autonomous group activities were fundamental to his reading of democracy as it operates in North America. Each of the countries we have examined has made progress in this direction, although in many others (several in Central America spring to mind), not even the threshold of substantive liberalization has been achieved. Although a facade of democratic elections has been superimposed, elected civilians remain subject to vetos and overriding opposition by military officers, while the majority of people exist in abject poverty, their most fundamental human rights merely illusions. The Charter of the Organization of American States and the United Nations Universal Declaration of Human Rights recognize representative democracy as a basic principle of governance and as a basic human right. Most Latin American constitutions agree. Declaring rights, however, is rarely enough, as O'Donnell and Schmitter observe: "The constitution and civil code may proclaim these rights but their violation may be buried in administrative regulations, suffocated by informal norms, or masked by secret agreements" (1986: 42).

Liberalization/Democratization

> Would it not then be simpler for the government to dissolve the people and elect another?
>
> —*Bertolt Brecht*

The people are not so easily dissolved, once convinced they are citizens. Political liberalization marks a departure from autocracy, "an opening that results in the broadening of the social base of the regime without changing its structure" (Przeworski 1991: 66) or "the process of making effective certain rights that protect both individuals and social groups from arbitrary or illegal acts committed by the state or third parties" (O'Donnell and Schmitter 1986: 7).

Democratization refers to "the progressive extension of the citizenship principle to encompass a wider range of eligible participants and a wider scope of domains in which collective choice among equals (or their representatives) can make binding decisions on all" (O'Donnell and Schmitter

1986: 8). Political scientists have produced better chronicles of and performance criteria for the transition *to* democracy than for its consolidation. Democracies are different (vive la difference!) and consolidated democracies are permanently in need of revitalization. Extending the citizenship principle, rather than the shallow electoral arena, is where democracy becomes germane in the Americas today.

Latin Americans (and East Europeans) can learn a great deal from other models of democracy, especially from constitutions and institutions crafted to ease the tension between majority rule and minority interests and values. Some democracies qualify majority rule and protect minority rights through constitutional provisions (bills of rights); others guarantee autonomy of local or regional governments (federalism); coalition governments may incorporate all parties (consociationalism); or some democracies may negotiate social pacts between major groups like business and labor (neocorporatism). Blends of these democratic forms have already appeared in new constitutions and recent practice within the region.

There are, then, many forms of democracy. Here is an inclusive, contemporary definition, inspired by de Tocqueville, influenced by Dahl, and updated by reflection on European and North and Latin American variants: "Modern democracy is a system of governance in which rulers are held accountable for their actions in the public realm by citizens, acting indirectly through the competition and cooperation of their elected representatives" (Schmitter and Karl 1991: 76).

The most common and effective way of protecting minorities and introducing majorities to democracy lies in organization, in the everyday operation of nongovernmental organizations, interest associations, and social movements. Uncertainty and trust are two underrecognized characteristics. Adam Przeworski emphasized democracy's uncertainty "because it is a system of decentralized strategic action in which knowledge is inescapably local" (1991: 49). Bellah wrote, "Democracy requires a degree of trust that we often take for granted. . . . Democracy itself is not so much a specific institution as a metaphoric way of thinking about an aspect of many institutions" (1991: 12). The multiplicity and diversity of institutions and organizations is key. In effect, the tale begins with citizens.

The Qualities of Citizenship

Enthusiasts of democratization, myself included, are prone to exaggerate the virtues of citizens and the value of citizenship. One political philosopher recommended more "chastened, or subdued approaches to citizenship" (Flathman 1989). A subdued approach is particularly useful for examining democratization as evidenced in interaction between local governments and NGOs, baptized "supercitizens" by Rubem Cesar Fernandes. Ideal types of citizenship overshadow its partial realizations like the noonday sun overwhelms subtle pastels—gradations of color reappear only as the sun goes down. Assessing democratic performance, then, requires working around the clock. In this normative arena of citizenship, we have to become accustomed to more and to less, and also to more-or-less. The exercise of citizenship seldom approximates the ideal.

In an assessment of neocorporatism, Philippe Schmitter argued that democratic performance standards are grounded in the citizenship principle and implemented through various blends of decision rules and institutions, and that they flourish through a combination of qualitative relationships that includes, among others, participation, access, responsiveness, and accountability. With its package of mutual rights and obligations, the citizenship principle is at the core of the exercise.

> [It] involves both the right to be treated by fellow human beings as equal with respect to the making of collective choices and the obligation of those implementing such choices to be equally accountable and accessible to all members of the polity. Inversely, this principle imposes obligations on the ruled, that is, to respect the legitimacy of choices made among equals, and rights of rulers, that is to act with authority (and to apply coercion when necessary) to promote the effectiveness of such choice, and to protect the polity from threats to its persistence (1983: 8).

The shapes of the institutions and rules enveloping the citizenship principle are open, flexible, and culturally specific. They are rooted in particularistic history, although often influenced by models drawn from other settings. The French and U.S. constitutions have been diffused widely. For example, in formulating their new constitution, Brazilians shopped for elements from continental Europe to California. They were attracted by German representational and district schemes as well as by the initiative, referendum, and recall mechanisms of the California State Constitution. Catchall constitutions such as Brazil's, and the politicization attending their formulation, evoke momentary enthusiasm but sail deep and slow in the water, weighted down by many contradictory elements and interests. Colombians are now exploring various models as they write a new constitution.

Institutions set the rules of the game—the formal and informal channels for decisionmaking, the frameworks that make citizenship operative and confirm it as preferable. The range of such institutions and organizations vary from society to society and, within any specific society, change over time. There is no tabula rasa, no clean start, no chance to abstract from history. Each emerging democracy must cope with legacies involving compromise with alternative ways of allocating values and exercising authority. Whether Latin clientelism (*cacicazgo, coronelismo*) or its second cousin, the machine politics of U.S. cities, the legacies live on. By themselves, institutions cannot guarantee the exercise of citizenship, as they require some degree of trust and consensus from the people involved. Such institutions endure only "when they evoke self-interested spontaneous compliance from all major political forces" (Przeworski 1991: x). Qualitative factors like participation, access, responsiveness, accountability, and competition give life to the institutional fabric. Here are some definitions for these elusive and relative qualities, the core of a matrix for identifying types of democracies and assessing their effectiveness.

Participation.   Taking part in a public activity or enterprise. In political terms, participation is taking place when individual citizens play active and equal roles in collective decisionmaking (Schmitter 1983). To the discussion of political participation, Marshall Wolfe and Matthias Stietel add an important element, that of bringing in people who have usually been excluded from the political process (1994).

Access.   Open to the influence of all citizens, as when public authorities consider the preferences and demands of all citizens—organized and unorganized—evenhandedly when making public choices.

Accountability.   Holding officials answerable through regular processes. It is significant that there is no single word for this concept in Spanish and Portuguese, obliging us to resort to such unwieldy substitutes as *transparencia* (transparency), and *rendir cuentas* (to account for). At the core of accountability is a system that allows citizens some degree of regular consultation with elected officials and the possibility of redress.

Responsiveness.   Reacting readily or easily to suggestion or appeal. The "collective property of a democratic ruling class which guarantees that citizens' needs will be met and hence, exercise of public power will be legitimate" (Schmitter 1983: 9).

Competitiveness.   Striving for power by two or more rivals, following procedural rules for alternation or succession.
    Local-level politics can be both a starting point and a lifelong school for citizen-ruler interaction. This is not an idealized, rose-colored notion of citizenship but the everyday negotiating, pact making, compromise, and disenchantment that is the stuff of politics. The matrix of qualitative traits listed here finds expression in NGOs and social movements, providing both short-run exposure to democratic practice and long-run experience in the deepening of democratization and civic culture.

Consensual and Consociational Democracy

The qualitative relationships just described give content to institutional forms and create a permanent tension between the ideal and the real. There are many types of democracy that have the capacity to contain these qualitative relationships. Lipjhart's comparative work on consociational democracy (1977) provides an indispensable backdrop. Mansbridge's distinction between "adversarial and consensual democracy" is particularly relevant at the local level and should be part of an inclusive normative framework.

> Democracy, as practiced in the United States and Western Europe, is a hybrid idea that incorporates conflicting assumptions. In one vision of democracy, the system creates fair procedures for resolving conflicts of interest; in another, it encourages deliberation about how best to promote the common good. Practicing politicians in the United States and Western Europe tend to understand democracy in only one of these two ways. For them, democracy is an adversary system that assumes conflicting interests and sets up fair procedural rules under which each side attempts to "win". . . . [On the other hand] in deliberative democracy, citizens talk with one another about public problems. . . . While it does not rule out the possibility that the participants' interests fundamentally conflict, it aims at the creation of a common good. It works through persuasion, not power. . . . Each nation must work out the deliberative innovations, and the mix of adversary and deliberative institutions, that fits its own patterns of cleavage, its own history, and its own culture (1990: 2).

Unfortunately, it seems that many elites in Latin American societies endorse the adversarial version, while the masses subscribe to deliberation. The challenge to Latin Americans today will be to bring adversarial and deliberative visions of democracy together, especially at the local level. The deliberative or consensual normative framework can encompass cultural diversity, Iberian heritages, Amerindian or Afro-Brazilian legacies, numbers and intensities, the de facto pluralism of Latin American societies, and the diffusion of Western concepts incorporated into the already codified or still evolving constitutions of the region. It can absorb the intensity of minority group issues and yet accommodate the majority.

Just as if majority rule must be circumscribed to ensure minority rights at the national level, minority, or elite, control of decisionmaking and resource allocation as is the case with local-level politics in Latin America, must be controlled as well. There is a conspicuous absence of real majority rights in Latin American countries. National and local concerns are not always congruent. The democratic process is more complex than simplistic top-down or bottom-up models allow. But the qualitative traits of democracy—some level of trust despite conflict, openness to negotiating, and institutional embodiments of these qualities—must operate at all levels, or both citizenship and civil society lack meaning.

Within such a context and meaning, subnational governmental units become most relevant to democratization, development, and the fulfillment of human needs. The "local state," social movements, and NGOs fit comfortably into the scheme. By examining public (and private) policy at the local level, implications for citizenship become more specific.

Purposive Policy for More Civil Societies

Society is civil when it is formed by men (and women) locked together in
argument....We hold certain truths; therefore we can argue about them.
—John Courtney Murray, *We Hold These Truths*

This normative view of deliberative democracy (and development) has policy implications, given the rapidly changing relationships between popular
organizations and local governments. Throughout this volume, we have
been discovering, documenting, and analyzing joint government and private efforts that, despite austerity, effectively meet the basic human needs
of some citizens as a contribution to a more civil society. Expanding the
productive potential of each society is, of course, fundamental, but it is not
the focus here. Rather, we are seeking to expand citizenship through more
effective and more responsive social policies that confirm the benefits and
obligations of citizens through the units of government closest to them.
Territoriality is key and self-help a motif, precisely because resources are
so scarce.

Policy is here construed quite simply as a guide to action and, as such,
can be the property of both government *and* citizenry, public *and* private
spheres. The aim of social policy is to improve the living conditions of specific human populations within the limits of available capacity. Distributive
and, especially, redistributive social policy is usually a disputed process;
giving to some and taking away from others is seldom pacific. Yet, there
are some indications from these chapters that conflict decreases and pragmatism increases when resources are generally scarce. One unintended
consequence of austerity is the demise of state paternalism/populism, or, as
Caravedo put it, the "benefactor state."

The policies of interest to many are those aimed at improving the living conditions of poor people and those creating a more favorable environment for such improvement. Poverty means more than lack of adequate
income; it also means little access to information, to networks of social
support, and to participation in the decisions that shape people's lives.
Social policy begins by assessing two things: the significant living conditions of a specific population and those environmental conditions that most
directly influence their situation. The preferred outcomes from among a
range of possibilities must be identified, as well as the activities that will
achieve the outcome at the least cost (not just monetary, but social cost).
Finally, a linkage between action and outcome must be established, one
that allows improvement in both the pursuit of purpose and the purposes
pursued (Meehan and Reilly 1982).

Policy monitoring and policy modification should receive at least as
much emphasis as policymaking and outcomes. This "ideal typical"
description of social policy from a grassroots development perspective
leads to an important caveat. In grassroots democracy and development,

much of the action lies not in the sphere of public policy but beyond, in the arena of programs and projects. Here, people wage their struggle for survival.

Efficacious and responsive policy needs to be grounded in local settings; ultimately, all policy, like all politics, is local. Enlightened and democratic policymaking relies on the people involved to organize, design, carry out, and assess their own initiatives. It creates space and tolerates their demands, their interests, and their efforts to acquire more equitable shares in society's resources.

The production, demand, distribution, and self-provisioning of goods and services are integral parts of the policy environment and policy repertory, even while falling outside the conventionally understood sphere of "authoritative allocation of values." If science is construed as creating tools for anticipating, controlling, or affecting events in the environment, and policy is seen as a guide to action, then policy and science can converge. To improve the living conditions of poor people, social policy and purposive inquiry can and should be complementary.

Beyond Ideologies of Privatization

Privatization is a universal buzz word, rapidly losing meaning. In Latin America, it is associated primarily with turning over government enterprise to private investors and, to a lesser degree, with parallel changes in the provision of services. But no matter how great the preferences for privatization and how strident the advocates for the "withering away of the state," there are some limitations to this movement. As economist William Glade put it:

> The attempted disengagement of government from much of its direct intervention in the economy does not ordinarily imply a "retreat of the state" in any aggregate sense, as statists have alleged and antistatists have hoped. Much remains to be done to get the fiscal house in order. Yet so vast are the unmet needs for public investment in social overhead projects and infrastructure, and for government spending on elemental welfare, that it is hard to imagine a future in which public-sector activity would actually contract. It is a question, rather, of realigning priorities and diverting funds now absorbed in underwriting inefficiency to uses that benefit the needier segments of society and build the human and organizational capital on which broad economic advancement in the late twentieth century and beyond necessarily rests (1991: 17).

Junk bonds and savings-and-loan debacles in the United States confirm that privatization is no panacea, unassisted markets do not always "get the prices right," and government regulation cannot be cavalierly dismissed during privatization. Protectionist policies in many Latin American countries have shielded local entrepreneurs from market competition and granted them hefty subsidies for a long time. (The first "privatized" state enterprises in Argentina, airline and telecommunications, are being sold to Spanish *state* enterprises.) If both public and private efforts underwrite inefficiency, how can they be combined or realigned, and in what measure and with what division of labor, to improve the lot of society? For starters, let's broaden the definition of privatization to include a significant role for NGOs and social movements of the not-for-profit sector. Let us begin with the local state.

Parcelizing Sovereignty and Expanding Citizenship Through Local Policy

Can municipalities in Latin America begin to function as polities rather than as instruments of a central state? Can states and provinces become more than middle managers? Fiscal capacity is an obvious first step, but the ability to design and enforce effective taxation strategies has thus far eluded central as well as local states. Some progress has been made, however, in setting up revenue-sharing arrangements across governmental units, in generating revenues from local property-holders, and, most recently, in collecting user fees for certain services. Municipal governments are often as poor in human capital as they are in physical resources, but they have one great advantage; they are well positioned to evolve and guide purposeful action.

The dual challenge to policymakers at all levels is deceptively simple. Can they fashion purposive and corrigible public policy? Can they improve their performance based on results achieved? Three steps will help public authorities meet this challenge:

1. Clearly state the policy and its purpose in human terms.
2. Set up a monitoring system that can produce an inventory of the living conditions of specific populations, and record the effects of actions.
3. Gather the information thus produced and use it to guide successive activities (Meehan 1990a; Meehan and Reilly 1982).

If policy is understood as a guide to action and rule making for particular cases, it must be made, monitored, and modified where its implications can be foreseen; that is, usually closer to the bottom than to the top of the pyramid. Local authorities thus have an enormous advantage. Indeed, proximity to and knowledge of its citizens is the major advantage local governments enjoy in making policies purposive. Local governments, as well as associations within civil society, are improving their abilities to fashion such a policy apparatus and learning to be more attentive to the locally defined hierarchy of need.

I would argue that collaboration between local governments and NGOs has contributed substantially to expanding citizenship for the excluded. Through the production of goods and the delivery of services, NGO and social movement roles have increased dramatically in recent years. They contribute significantly to the human and organizational capital on which economic advancement rests. Their comparative advantage lies in having relatively well-identified client populations and relatively manageable numbers, a luxury seldom available to government programs, which (ostensibly) employ standardized programs and policies to service entire populations—despite the obvious heterogeneity of those populations. NGOs serve as laboratories and extensionists, while making governance feasible. The secondary citizenship of membership in NGOs and social movements converts readily into primary citizenship, with rights and obligations initially concretized through local-level governments.

Citizen equality, direct participation, voluntary associability, accountable representation, unrestricted political choice, honest apportionment, public disclosure, and competition and alternation between incumbents and challengers are relevant to every level of government. Introducing parliamentary sovereignty and ensuring a policy climate tolerant of voluntary associations begin, but do not end, at the center. Sovereignty can be distributed, with power and privilege dispersed across units rather than concentrated at the top or bottom.

Antagonisms between NGOs and state inherited from the authoritarian past linger but have begun to ebb. Development cooperation agencies are at a crossroads, exploring through which institutions, and for how long, reduced amounts of aid will be channeled. Drawing from the case studies, let us focus on the elements of a more enabling and inclusive policy environment. The first step will be to open the Pandora's box of policy ownership.

Policy Owners: State, Civil Society, or Markets?

The boundaries between public and private policy have always been blurred. If policy is understood quite simply as a guide to action, the realm of social policy need have no single master—neither state, nor market, nor civil society. Whichever the former master, today's resource constraints, demographic trends, and social volatility require that new combinations be found and joint ventures tested. (Perhaps more attention to markets in the social policy mix will not only create jobs, but begin to legitimate diversity.) In Latin America, state-woven safety nets rarely work for the majority. Thus, radical retooling, joint ventures, and self-provisioning are the order of the day. We are at the threshold of a different breed of social policy, operational at both middle and base levels of the social pyramid. This policy has emerged from bargains and pacts, from negotiations over interests and values—all carried out in the public view. It is incremental and pragmatic, diversified and decentralized. It bears residual effects of the transition to democracy and shapes democracy's consolidation. It is state-influenced, but not state-monopolized. Its boundaries are fluid. Like life, it is full of contradictions.

Redefining the roles of state, society, and market in policymaking is not limited to Latin America. Lester Salamon writes that "powerful forces are leading the [U.S.] voluntary sector away from its recent role as a partner [to the state] in public service toward greater integration into the private, market economy" (1989: 12). Resource scarcity, a shift from producer to consumer subsidies, changing demographics, and recent emphasis on cultural rather than economic explanations of poverty have hastened the trend, according to Salamon. In welfare states of the North, the government will become less of a philanthropist, and market forces will increasingly shape public policy.

Yet Latin America is not the United States. The cases included here suggest either a different stage in the same sequence or, more likely, movement in a different direction. Privatization has not yet effectively grappled with poverty. Privatized health care and fee-for-service schemes in Brazil and Chile have simply abandoned the poor, whose subsistence budgets do not allow for paying fees. Microentrepreneurs in the heralded informal economy generally earn too little to cover costs for basic services, let alone provide for accumulation and growth.

Given the scale of poverty, the scarcity of resources, the potential for social explosions, the historic role of the central state, and the limits to migration, organizations of civil society and a democratizing state are finding more in common and forming incipient partnerships. After years of estrangement, they have begun joint ventures unheard of only a few years ago; rapprochement usually begins with conflict, followed by division of labor and hesitant cooperation. If state benevolence has faded, state and civil society representatives together have begun to invite their counterparts from the market to invent private philanthropy (or redirect it in self-sustaining directions). Self-interested national and international business investors now nudge states toward friendlier regulatory environments for private philanthropy, just as together they have accommodated adjustment measures to recover international credit standing. "Anti-politics" has influenced national elections, but not so much as to push people uncritically into the exclusive embrace of the market. For most of the poor, the informal economy remains a survival tactic rather than an engine of growth. It is more likely, then, that the triangle of state, civil society, and market will endure, with "negotiated interaction" between all three.

If policy must engage market forces and the organized interests of civil society at the national level, what of subnational politics and the redefinition of local power? Decentralization and changing intergovernmental relations have dramatically affected social policy in Latin America. Increasingly, resources managed by local governments, traditionally based on transfers, will have to be generated locally. Local politics, usually associated with clientelism, may yield to more participatory arrangements, especially to the degree that NGOs and social movements learn to use newly minted leverage and to articulate their interests more effectively. Merging frontiers between public and private sectors may contribute to strengthening participatory local governments and lead to more inclusive, diversified social policy.

The Poetry of Local Politics

Local-level "bodies politic" are learning to interact constructively with voluntary associations, NGOs, and social movements. At this local level, the qualitative aspects of democracy are crucial and perhaps least practiced. Echoing de Tocqueville and American philosopher John Dewey, a new, more open and active localism, instead of closed and insular parochial communities, is essential to democracy.

> Whatever the future may have in store, one thing is certain. Unless local communal life can be restored, the public cannot resolve its most urgent problem, to find and identify itself. But if it is reestablished, it will manifest a fullness, a variety, and freedom of possession and enjoyment of meanings and goods unknown in the contiguous associations of the past. For it will be alive and flexible as well as stable, responsive to the complex and world-wide scene in which it is enmeshed. While local, it will not be isolated. Its larger relationships will provide an inexhaustible and flowing fund of meanings upon which to draw, with assurance that its drafts will be honored. Publication is partial and the public which results is partially informed and formed until the meanings it purveys pass from mouth to mouth. That and only that gives reality to public opinion. We lie, as Emerson said, in the lap of an immense intelligence. But that intelligence is dormant, and its communications are broken, inarticulate and faint until it possesses the local community as its medium (Bellah 1991: 263).

Dewey's commentary expresses a fuller sense of vital local democracy, which he held out as a yet-to-be-attained ideal for the United States in 1927. His maxims are worrisome to those who fear that American democracy is today ebbing away before homogenizing mass media or divisive demographics, face-to-face communities replaced by network sound bites and market manipulators. They surface the question of whether the mechanisms of democracy being shipped overseas are too narrowly conceived, too uncommunitarian, and tied to electioneering more than to democracy. As a Salvadoran friend reminded me, "You Americans forget that elections are but one note in the symphony of democracy."

Throughout this book, we have read of NGOs and social movements in Latin America that display Dewey's sort of creativity, openness, and linkages to the outside world. Perhaps the know-how for recovering this ideal can be repatriated. Admittedly, the legacies of clientelism are profound, but they are not omnipotent. New mechanisms for qualitative participation are spreading across levels of central, state/regional, and local government (although further research is required to chronicle their emergence and assess their effectiveness). Where is the poetry of Latin American democracy, and what are its specific mechanisms? How well do they work, and how good do they sound? Political participation begins to include a range of mechanisms and activities well beyond the familiar electoral arena, such as plebiscites, referenda, initiatives, petitions and recalls, concertation, constituent relations, new parties, pressure groups, neighborhood councils, hearings and ombudsmen, ethnic organizations, citizen protests through mass movements, and so on. Not alchemy, but hard work and purposive talk transforms secondary citizenship into primary.

Accountability includes the changing role of the media and access to it (whether network television or neighborhood loudspeakers); liability through courts or special tribunals; and polling and similar tools of the trade. Access implies expanded areas of inclusion—to information, to networks, to skills, to legal advice, and to productive assets. Responsiveness means clarifying what citizens must do or endure to get attention and force action—natural disasters and emergencies, boycotts and marches, and, increasingly, coalition building and alternate political parties. Fax machines and microcomputers, not TV, have democratized communications, and now two-way information flows between organizations of the poor.

It is our contention that NGOs and social movements of civil society can effectively mediate social demands and supports, especially at the local level. Given the cleavages within Latin American societies, whether based on status, class, ethnicity, language, or gender, NGOs provide institutional channels and settings for acquiring attitudes and learning behavior that can be institutionalized into nonviolent competition for office and influence. While social movements sometimes evaporate once immediate goals are met (or frustrated), NGOs frequently have great staying power. The combination of social movements and NGOs make extensive and intensive participation more feasible than ever before.

The formal structures of federal, state, and local layers of government appear tidy when compared with the multiple layers and shapes of associations in civil society. But closer examination reveals informal linkages, bureaucratic rings, topocrats, and intergovernmental lobbies percolating through the public sphere. These mechanisms of the informal polity help keep government permeable to civil society. NGOs, grassroots groups, and social movements are indeed heterogeneous, sometimes ephemeral, often opportunistic. Some are unrelated to the poor and are unlikely instruments for effective social policy. But collectively, they constitute the basis and

foundation of civil society and, as such, have become key vehicles for purposive social policy. Beyond celebration of their emergence, it is time to
record how well they perform. This volume illustrates some pioneers and
underlines their potential.

Whose Democracy?

Authoritarian regimes and countries in transit toward democracy are not the
only ones assessing public and private responsibilities for social policy. In
the "welfare states" of the North—whether Europe, the United States, or
Canada—disillusionment with the state's role in the social sector brings
attacks from right and left and pleas for markets over politics. Enthusiastic
requests from Eastern Europe for guidance on how to change both markets
and politics have launched vendors of American democracy into the world
marketplace. Is the U.S. model relevant? Adequate? Exportable?

Modesty, rather than megalomania, seems called for now. Exporting
hybrid varieties of adversarial democracy without incorporating native,
deliberative strains is a recipe for failure. While there are many virtues in
American society, beginning with the Articles of Confederation and the
federalist insights of the founders of the republic, it is doubtful that the
United States offers an exemplary model of intergovernmental relations or
urban poverty problem solving for Latin America. I firmly believe that
Latins will do well to invent their own version, dipping into their own legacies, borrowing from de Tocqueville and the best in critical American
thought (rather than thoughtless transfer of techniques), studying European
models (Spain and Germany have relevant constitutions), and sampling
portions of other models that best fit Latin contexts, histories, and cultures.

I agree with those political scientists who argue that the type of democracy consolidated depends in part on contagion, on available models, and
on the mode of transition; more importantly, however, it depends on the
quality of relationships being worked out at the grassroots. NGOs and social
movements bring a new representational quality to Latin America. Together with local governments, they have become an important setting for dealing with expanding democratic practice and for seeking joint resolution of
human needs.

In the opening chapter, we listed a number of programmatic and policy
recommendations for maximizing NGO contributions to both development
and democracy. Whether allocated through politics, through markets, or
through the associations of civil society, policies (or programs or strategies) must somehow reach clients, consumers, citizens, and constituents.
Democracy is everywhere the offspring of compromise. It is never all that
it could be. But the blending of democracy and development noted by de
Tocqueville is even now taking place in Latin America, unfolding in a

unique manner resembling neither U.S. models nor Latin legacies. More-over, it is being carried out at the grassroots by Latin Americans. New de Tocquevilles are needed to chart their inventions.

Notes

1. For a typology and analysis of the performance characteristics of effective grassroots support organizations (GSOs), see Thomas Carroll's *Intermediary NGOs: The Supporting Link in Grassroots Development* (1992).

2. Michels's "iron law" posits that inclusive, participatory organizations inevitably become rigid and excluding, dominated by a narrow elite (1959).

3. Jonathan Fox and Luis Hernández (1989) identified "intermediate instances of participation" at crucial turning points in a major Mexican campesino organization's evolution. See also Candido Grzbowski, Lynn Stephens, Gonzalo Falabela, et al., in Fox and Hernández 1992.

Selected Bibliography

CHARLES A. REILLY, ELISAVINDA ECHEVERRI-GENT, AND LAURA MULLAHY

An Introduction

Democratization

Several convergent streams of literature will be deepened by the flow of ideas, actions, and policies analyzed in these chapters and in the bibliography. The first stream examines patterns and pitfalls of transitions to and consolidation of democracy, drawing from South American and some Southern European cases. Focused principally on the structures of the central state, these studies track the shift from corporatist and bureaucratic authoritarian patterns to more inclusive, but tentative, democratic tendencies toward delegative if not representative democracy. Schmitter, Whitehead, Lowenthal, Linz, Lipset, and Diamond have contributed to this literature in the North, and while many Latin American scholars have produced works on democratization, outstanding comparative work has been done by O'Donnell, Weffort, Cardoso, and Moises, and by members of the Latin American Council of Social Sciences (CLACSO) network (Calderón, Borja, et al.). Work on the changing role of political parties and representation is now well under way (for example, Scully and Mainwaring, forthcoming).

Corporatism seems to have passed out of fashion for the moment, but, influenced by Southern Europe, one can usefully posit a transitional path toward democracy that moves from state through societal corporatism as civil society emerges. The legacies of clientelism and corporatism linger on; complementary informal and formal mechanisms for containing and channeling social energy, demands, and supports pervade macro, micro, and mezzo levels, sometimes yielding to more technocratic and more participatory forms. Fernando Henrique Cardoso, in his analysis of authoritarian Brazil during the 1970s, argued that a great deal of policymaking occurred through "bureaucratic rings" or circles composed of technocratic elites—including highly placed government officials, the military, and rep-

273

resentatives of peak associations—functioning outside of Congress or other representative institutions. (In international finance circles, "bureaucratic rings" describes the decisionmaking processes that buttressed the "Washington consensus" on structural adjustment policies of the 1980s.) At the local level as well, topocrats and technocrats (territorial and sectoral elites) dominate the agenda, their interests consistently at the forefront.

The literature on the rapid decay of Communism and the painful efforts to replace it with markets, if not democracy, in Eastern Europe and Russia is not considered here. But the events themselves are a reminder, not only that the geopolitical context of East-West relations has dramatically changed with implications for the South, but also that the pace of transition has been accelerated to a degree previously undreamed of by incrementalists of the North. Centralized governments equipped with command and control economies proved ineffective in many ways. Fragile social fabrics; festering ethnic, territorial, and religious cleavages; inexperience with markets—all pose weighty questions for those who are concerned with the fragility of civil society and the vulnerability of nascent democracy. They may find some encouragement from Latin American efforts chronicled in this volume. Adam Przeworski's *Democracy and the Market* (1991) is one of the first comparisons of political and economic reforms in Latin America and Eastern Europe.

Civil Society: NGOs and Social Movements

A second stream of publications examines the emergence of civil society and its role in development, especially through nongovernmental development organizations and social movements. Alan Wolfe's *Whose Keeper* (1989) and Charles Maier's *Changing Boundaries of the Political* (1987) reintroduced "civil society" to North American debate. Uphoff and Esman pioneered work on local rural development organizations worldwide. Through its journal, *Grassroots Development,* and through a cluster of monographs, the Inter-American Foundation has contributed to this body of literature, supporting recent work by Thomas Carroll, Jonathan Fox, Albert Hirschman, Sally Yudelman, Marion Ritchey-Vance, Judith Tendler, Sheldon Annis, Peter Hakim, and Patrick Breslin, among others. A major effort has gone into identifying sources of social energy, mapping the NGO universe, presenting a typology, assessing NGO performance, and then exploring how internal democracy within NGOs and social movements contributes to external democracy in the broader society.

In 1987, the journal *World Development* issued a seminal edition on NGOs in development, and David Korten's advocacy of NGOs and people's movements has stimulated much useful thought and debate. Bilateral and multilateral development agencies have taken up the NGO theme, their rhetoric sometimes outstripping commitments, depending on resource availability, structural constraints, efficacy of "policy dialogue," and their readiness to engage amorphous civil society. Brian Smith called attention to the political agenda lurking behind private aid flows of the 1980s, noting the substantial volume (U.S.$4 billion in transfers) through "private development aid" in 1980, which, according to the World Bank, reached $5.4 billion by 1987. Fernandes and Piquet report in this volume that over one hundred Brazilian NGOs received $28 million from international private donors during 1991, not much in light of an external debt of $120 billion, but very significant, he argues, on the social side of the ledger. Throughout Latin America, debt and deficit loom larger than trade and aid, and civil society is expected to cancel debts it did not incur. Responsibilities as well as rights crowd the agendas of the NGOs and social movements of civil society.

Municipal Administration and Urbanization

The third literature stream is nascent, still finding its way. It includes recent research in Latin America through CLACSO, which has begun to systematically examine municipal governments in a comparative framework and to assess their (potential) role in both development and democratization. Supported by the Institute for International Cooperation of Spain and drawing on experiences of popular participation in Spanish cities, this body of research has begun to chart the potential and limitations of municipal government in hitherto centralized states. A prime example is the volume edited by Francisco Calderón, Jordi Borja, et al. (1989) entitled *Descentralización y Democracia: Gobiernos Locales en América Latina.* Already published volumes emanating from IAF research include Marcela Jiménez, *Municipios y Organizaciones Privadas* (1990) in Chile and Martínez Nogueira's publications on Argentina (1989). Manuel Castells (1983) ventured a theoretical framework for local democracy drawn from Spanish and Latin American cases in *The City and the Grassroots: A Cross-Cultural Theory of Urban Social Movements.*

A complementary body of research on public administration during the 1960s and 1970s evolved through the steadfast technical contributions of agencies like the Brazilian Institute for Municipal Administration that stimulate and sustain the municipalist agenda. Many early efforts to strengthen municipal administration were prematurely bureaucratized or colonized by central government actors. Perhaps these efforts at municipal government and administration were ahead of their time and can be usefully resuscitated for the 1990s. Research from urban planners, including the Megacity project and the International Institute for Environment and Development, has contributed sound information to policymakers concerned with subnational governments.

The present volume blends NGO development literature with this nascent municipal government research, emphasizing collaboration and conflict between public and private actors in a variety of Latin American settings. It documents emerging NGO transitions from adversarial to collaborative and sometimes surrogate activities and explores the rights and obligations flowing from the limited scope of citizenship enjoyed by the poorest residents of these countries. The bibliography includes works cited by authors of individual chapters, citations of relevant literature by country, and comparative works on relations between government and civil society, especially at the subnational level.

Latin American Democratization, Local Government, and Nongovernmental Organizations

Author Unknown

————. 1992. Centros históricos y política urbana. *Medio ambiente y urbanización* 9, no. 38 (marzo).

————. 1992. Iniciativas locales para el medio ambiente. *Democracia local: Revista del capítulo latinoamericano de IULA y CELCADEL* 34 (enero-marzo).

————. 1991. *Democracia 2000: Los grandes desafíos en América Latina.* Bogotá: Tercer Mundo Editores.

————. 1991. Gobierno local en áreas metropolitanas de América Latina. *Medio ambiente y urbanización* 9, no. 35 (junio).

————. 1990. Community-Based Organizations: How They Develop, What They Seek and What They Achieve. *Environment and Urbanization* 2, no. 1 (April).

————. 1990. ONGs, habitat y desarrollo en América Latina. *Medio ambiente y urbanización* 32 (septiembre).

————. 1989. Gobiernos locales en América Latina. *Medio ambiente y urbanización* 7, no. 28 (septiembre).

————. 1985. *Estado, participação política e democracia.* Ciencias sociais hoje, vol. 3 Brasilia: Editorial Coordenação.

————. 1984. Movimiento urbano popular. *Nueva Antropología* 6, no. 24 (junio).

————. 1982. *Comunicación y democracia en América Latina.* Lima: Desco/CLACSO.

————. 1979. Organizing Policy. Community Organizing Strategy. Special Issue of *Social Policy* 10 (September-October).

Altimir, Oscar. 1981. The Extent of Poverty in Latin America. World Bank Staff working paper no. 552. Washington, D.C: World Bank.

Amin, Samir. 1991. El problema de la democracia en el tercer mundo contemporáneo. *Nueva Sociedad* 112 (marzo-abril): 24–39.

Annis, Sheldon, and Peter Hakim, eds. 1988. *Direct to the Poor: Grassroots Development in Latin America.* Boulder, Colo.: Lynne Rienner.

Anthony, Harry A. 1979. The Challenge of Squatter Settlements: With Special Reference to the Cities of Latin America. *Human Settlement Issues* 3.

Aron, Raymond. 1990. *Democracy and Totalitarianism: A Theory of Political Systems.* Ann Arbor: University of Michigan Press.

Ashford, D. E. 1976. *Democracy, Decentralization and Decisions in Subnational Politics.* Sage Professional Papers in Comparative Politics, vol. 5. Beverly Hills: Sage.

Bahl, Roy. 1982. *Urban Government Financial Structure and Management in Developing Countries.* Washington, D.C.: USAID.

Bahl, Roy et al. 1981. *Strengthening Local Level Fiscal Performance.* Syracuse: Maxwell School.

Barber, Benjamin R. 1992. Jihad vs. McWorld. *The Atlantic Monthly* (March): 53–63.

Bellah, Robert N. et al. 1991. *The Good Society.* New York: Alfred A. Knopf.

Beltrão, Helio. 1984. *Descentralização e liberdade.* Rio de Janeiro: Editora Record.

Bielsa, Rafael. 1935. *El problema de la descentralización administrativa.* Buenos Aires: J. Lajouane & Cía.

Blitzer, Silvia et al. 1988. *Outside the Large Cities: Annotated Bibliography and Guide to the Literature on Small and Intermediate Urban Centres in the Third World.* London: International Institute for Environment and Development.

———. 1983. *Las ciudades intermedias y pequeñas en América Latina: Una bibliografía comentada.* Buenos Aires: Ediciones CEUR.

Boisier, Sergio. 1987. *Ensayos sobre descentralización y desarrollo regional.* Santiago: CEPAL-ILPES.

Borja, Jordi. 1989. *Estado, descentralización y democracia.* Bogotá: Foro Nacional por Colombia.

Borja, Jordi et al. 1987. *Descentralización del estado, movimiento social y gestión local.* Santiago: FLACSO.

Bowden, Peter. 1979. The Administration of Rural Development. *Journal of Administration Overseas* 18, no. 3: 193–201.

Brasileiro, Ana Maria. 1973. *O municipio como sistema político.* Rio de Janeiro: Fundação Getulio Vargas, Instituto de Documentação.

Breslin, Patrick. 1990. *Development and Dignity.* Arlington: Inter-American Foundation.

Brett, E. A. 1988. Adjustment and the State: The Problem of Administrative Reform. *IDS Bulletin* 19, no. 4: 4–11.

Bruhns, F. C., F. Cassola, and J. Wiatr, eds. 1974. *Local Politics, Development and Participation.* Pittsburgh: Center for International Studies, University of Pittsburgh.

Buci-Glucksmann, C. 1982. Hegemony and Consent. In *Approaches to Gramsci,* ed. A. Showstack Sassoon, 116–126. London: Writers and Readers Publishing Cooperative Society.

Calderón, Fernando G., and Mario R. dos Santos. 1991. *Hacia un nuevo orden estatal en América Latina. Veinte tesis sociopolíticas y un corelario.* Santiago: CLACSO/Fondo de Cultura Económica.

Calderón, Fernando G., and Mario R. dos Santos, coords. 1989. *Centralización/descentralización del Estado y actores territoriales.* Vol. 5, no. 6. Buenos Aires: CLACSO, Biblioteca de Ciencias Sociales.

———. 1987. *Los conflictos por la constitución de un nuevo orden.* Buenos Aires: CLACSO.

Calderón, Fernando G. et al., eds. 1989. *Descentralización y democracia: Gobiernos locales en América Latina.* Santiago: CLACSO/SUR/CEUMT.

Campbell, Tim. 1989. Urban Development in the Third World: Environmental Dilemmas and the Urban Poor. In *Environment and the Poor: Development Strategies for a Common Agenda,* ed. H. Jeffrey Leonard et al., 165–187. Washington, D.C.: Overseas Development Council.

Caporaso, James A. 1989. *The Elusive State: International and Comparative Perspectives.* London: Sage.

Caputo, David A., and Richard L. Cole. 1974. *Urban Politics and Decentralization.* Lexington, Mass.: Lexington Books.

Cardoso, Fernando Henrique. 1975. *Autoritarismo e democratização*. Rio de Janeiro: Paz e Terra.

Carlessi, Carolina, ed. 1989. *Gestión popular en salud: Organizaciones no guber-namentales de desarrollo políticas sociales. Algunas experiencias peruanas*. Lima: Alternativa/CESIP/FOVIDA.

Carnoy, Martin. 1978. *The State and Political Theory*. Princeton: Princeton University Press.

Carothers, Thomas. 1991. *In the Name of Democracy*. Berkeley: University of California Press.

Carrión, Diego et al. 1986. *Ciudades en conflicto: Poder local, participación popular y planificación en las ciudades intermedias de América Latina*. Quito: Editorial El Conejo.

Carrión, F., and P. Velarde. 1991. *Municipio y democracia: Gobiernos locales en ciudades intermedias de América Latina*. Santiago: Ediciones Sur.

Carroll, Thomas. 1992. *Intermediary NGOs: The Supporting Link in Grassroots Development*. West Hartford, Conn.: Kumarian.

Castells, Manuel. 1983. *The City and the Grassroots: A Cross-Cultural Theory of Urban Social Movements*. Berkeley: University of California Press.

———. 1981. *Crisis urbana y cambio social*. México: Siglo Veintiuno Editores.

———. 1977. *Ciudad, democracia y socialismo*. México: Siglo Veintiuno Editores.

Cavarozzi, Marcelo, and Manuel A. Garretón. *Muerte y resurrección: Los partidos políticos en el autoritarismo y las transiciones del Cono Sur*. Santiago: FLAS-CO.

Cheema, G. Shabbir, and Dennis A. Rondinelli. 1986. *Urban Services in Developing Countries: Public and Private Roles in Urban Development*. New York: St. Martin's.

———. 1983. *Decentralization and Development: Policy Implementation in Developing Countries*. Beverly Hills: Sage.

———. 1978. *Urbanization and Rural Development: A Spatial Polity of Equitable Growth*. New York: Praeger.

Chubb, John E., and Paul E. Peterson, eds. 1989. *Can the Government Govern?* Washington, D.C.: Brookings Institution.

Clark, John. 1991. *Democratizing Development: The Role of Voluntary Organizations*. West Hartford, Conn.: Kumarian.

Clark, Terry. 1974. Community Authority in the National System: Federalism, Localism, and Decentralization. In *Comparative Community Politics*, ed. Terry Clark, 21–51. Beverly Hills: Sage.

Cochrane, Glynn. 1983. Policies for Strengthening Local Government in Developing Countries. Working paper, no. 582. Washington, D.C.: World Bank.

Cohen, John M., and Norman T. Uphoff. 1980. Participation's Place in Rural Development: Seeking Clarity Through Specificity. *World Development* 8: 213–235.

———. 1976. *Rural Development Participation: Concepts for Measuring Participation for Project Design, Implementation and Evaluation*. Ithaca, N.Y.: Cornell University Press.

Cohen, Joshua, and Joel Rogers. 1984. *On Democracy: Toward a Transformation of American Society*. New York: Penguin Books.

Collier, David, ed. 1979. *The New Authoritarianism* in Latin America. Princeton: Princeton University Press.

Conyers, D. 1986. Future Directions in Development Studies: The Case of Decentralization. *World Development* 14, no. 5: 593–603.

————. 1983. Decentralization: The Latest Fashion in Development Administration? *Public Administration and Development* 3, no. 2 (April–June): 97–109.

Cornelius, Wayne A., and Robert V. Kemper. 1978. Metropolitan Latin America: The Challenge and the Response. In *Latin American Urban Research.* Vol. 6. London: Sage.

Corporación de Salud y Políticas Sociales (CORSAPS). 1991. *Participación en salud: Lecciones y desafíos.* Santiago: CORSAPS.

Cotler, Julio et al. 1987. *Para afirmar la democracia.* Lima: Instituto de Estudios Peruanos.

Dahl, Robert. 1990. Social Reality and 'Free Markets.' *Dissent* (spring): 224–228.

————. 1971. *Polyarchy: Participation and Opposition.* New Haven: Yale University Press.

————. 1956. *A Preface to Democratic Theory.* Chicago: University of Chicago Press.

de la Court, Thijs. 1990. *Beyond Brundtland: Green Development in the 1990s.* New York: New Horizons.

Delgado Navarro, Juan. 1985. Desarrollo integral del municipio. *Estudios municipales* 1 (enero-febrero): 91–96.

de Mattos, Carlos A. 1989. La descentralización, ¿una nueva panacea para enfrentar el subdesarrollo regional? *Revista Paraguaya de sociología* 74 (enero-abril): 95–116.

————. 1989. Falsas expectativas ante la descentralización. *Nueva sociedad* 104 (noviembre-diciembre): 118–126.

de Mello, Diego L. 1983. Modernización de los gobiernos locales en América Latina. *Revista interamericana de planificación* 17 (junio): 185–202.

de Soto, Hernando. 1989. *The Other Path: The Invisible Revolution in the Third World.* New York: Harper and Row.

de Soto, Hernando. 1986. *El otro sendero: La revolución informal.* Lima: El Barranco.

de Tocqueville, Alexis. 1954. *Democracy in America.* Vol. 2. New York: Vintage Books.

Diamond, Larry. 1990. Three Paradoxes of Democracy. *Journal of Democracy* 1, no. 3 (Summer): 25–58.

————. 1989. Beyond Authoritarianism and Totalitarianism: Strategies for Democratization. *The Washington Quarterly* (winter): 141–163.

Diamond, Larry, Juan Linz, and Seymour M. Lipset. 1989. *Democracy in Developing Countries: Latin America.* Boulder, Colo.: Lynne Rienner.

Domínguez Company, Francisco. 1981. *Estudios sobre las instituciones locales hispanoamericanas.* Caracas: Academia Nacional de la Historia.

Drabek, Anne Gordon. 1987. Development Alternatives: The Challenge for NGOs. *World Development* 15 (autumn).

Draibe, S.M. 1990. As políticas de combate a pobreza na América Latina. *São Paulo em Perspectiva* 4, no. 2 (April–June): 18–24.

Drake, Paul W., and Eduardo Silva, eds. 1986. *Elections and Democratization in Latin America, 1980–1985.* San Diego: University of California.

Durning, Alan B. 1989. People Power and Development. *Foreign Policy* 76 (fall): 66–82.

Eckstein, Susan. 1989. *Power and Popular Protest: Latin American Social Movements.* Berkeley: University of California Press.

Economic Commission for Latin America and the Caribbean. 1990. *Changing*

Production Patterns with Social Equity. Santiago: Economic Commission for Latin America and the Caribbean (ECLAC).

Edel, Matthew, and Ronald G. Hellman, eds. 1989. *Cities in Crisis: The Urban Challenge in the Americas.* New York: Bildner Center for Western Hemisphere Studies.

Egaña, Rodrigo, ed. 1989. *Una puerta que se abre: Los organismos no gubernamentales en la cooperación al desarrollo.* Santiago: Taller de Cooperación al Desarrollo.

Eisenstadt, S. N., and René Lemerchand, eds. 1981. *Political Clientelism, Patronage and Development.* Beverly Hills: Sage.

Eisenstadt, S. N. and L. Roniger. 1984. *Patrons, Clients and Friends: Interpersonal Relations and the Structure of Trust in Society.* Cambridge: Cambridge University Press.

Elazar, Daniel J. 1981. The Rebirth of Federalism: The Future Role of the States as Polities in the Federal System. *Commonsense* 4, no. 1: 1–8.

Elkin, Stephen L. 1975. Cooperative Urban Politics and Interorganisational Behaviour. In *Essays on the Study of Urban Politics,* ed. Ken Young, 158–184. London: Macmillan.

Esman, Milton F., and Norman T. Uphoff. 1984. *Local Organizations: Intermediaries in Rural Development.* Ithaca: Cornell University Press.

Evans, Peter B. et al., eds. 1985. *Bringing the State Back In.* Cambridge: Cambridge University Press.

Fals Borda, Orlando. 1986. El nuevo despertar de los movimientos sociales. *Revista foro* 1, no. 1: 76–83.

Ferreira de Oliveira, Sergio. 1986. Administração participativa: Bases para a definição. *Revista de administração municipal* 33, no. 181 (outubro-dezembro): 42–59.

Ferreira dos Santos, Carlos Nelson. 1981. *Movimentos urbanos no Rio de Janeiro.* Rio de Janeiro: Zahar Editores.

Ferrin, Cynthia L. 1989. *The Small Farmer Sector in Uruguay: A Partnership in Development Cooperation.* Arlington: Inter-American Foundation.

Fesler, F. W. 1965. Approaches to the Understanding of Decentralization. *Journal of Politics* 27, no. 3: 536–566.

Fisher, Tania. 1987. A gestão do municipio e as propostas de descentralização e participação popular. *Revista de administração municipal* 34, no. 183 (abriljunho): 18–35.

Flanigan, W., and E. Fogelman. 1971. Patterns of Democratic Development: An Historical Comparative Analysis. In *Macro-Quantitative Analysis: Conflict, Development and Democratization,* ed. John V. Gillespie and Betty A. Nesvold, 475–497. Beverly Hills: Sage.

Flathman, Richard E. 1989. *Toward a Liberalism.* Ithaca: Cornell University Press.

Foucault, Michel. 1984. Space, Knowledge and Power. In *The Foucault Reader,* ed. P. Rabinow, 239–256. New York: Pantheon Books.

Fox, Jonathan. 1992. Leadership Accountability in Regional Peasant Organizations. *Development and Change* 23, no. 2 (April): 1–36.

Fox, Jonathan, and Luis Hernández. 1989. Offsetting the Iron Law of Oligarchy: The Ebb and Flow of Leadership Accountability in a Regional Peasant Organization. *Grassroots Development Journal* 13, no. 2: 8–15.

Foxley, Alejandro. 1979. Políticas de estabilización y sus efectos sobre el empleo y la distribución del ingreso: Una perspectiva latinoamericana. *Crítica y Utopía Latinoamericana de Ciencias Sociales* 4: 9–94.

Foxley, Alejandro et al., eds. 1986. *Development, Democracy, and the Art of*

Trespassing. Essays in Honor of Albert O. Hirschman. Notre Dame: University of Notre Dame Press.

Friedmann, John. 1992. *Empowerment: The Politics of Alternative Development.* Cambridge: Blackwell.

———. 1988. *Life Space and Economic Space: Essays in Third World Planning.* New Brunswick and Oxford: Transaction Books.

———. 1964. *The Social Context of National Planning Decisions: A Comparative Approach.* Bloomington: CAG Occasional Paper.

Friedmann, John, and Clyde Weaver. 1979. *Territory and Function: The Evolution of Regional Planning.* London: Ernold Arnold.

Fundación Jorge Estéban Roulet. 1989. *Municipalismo y democracia.* Buenos Aires: Fundación Jorge Estéban Roulet, Centro de Participación Política.

Furtado, Celso. 1979. Modernización versus desarrollo. *Crítica y utopía latinoamericana de ciencias sociales* 4 (otoño): 95–140.

Gant, G. F. 1979. *Development Administration: Concepts, Goals and Methods.* Madison: University of Wisconsin Press.

Garcia Delgado, D. et al. 1989. *Descentralización y democracia: Gobiernos locales en América Latina.* Buenos Aires: FLACSO.

Germani, Gino et al. 1985. *Los límites de la democracia.* Buenos Aires: Consejo Latinoamericano de Ciencias Sociales.

Glade, William. 1991. *Privatization of Public Enterprises in Latin America.* San Francisco: ICS.

Goehlert, Robert. 1983. *Policy Studies on Local Affairs.* Monticello: Vance Bibliographies.

González Casanova, Pablo. 1980. La crisis de Estado y la lucha por la democracia en América Latina. *Socialismo y Participación* 10 (May): 117–124.

Goulet, Denis. 1989. *Incentives for Development: The Key to Equity.* New York: New Horizons.

———. 1989. Participation in Development: New Avenues. *World Development* 17, no. 2 (February): 165–178.

Graham, Lawrence S. 1990. *The State and Policy Outcomes in Latin America.* New York: Praeger.

———. 1982. Intergovernmental Relations in Comparative Perspective: Results from Five Countries. Paper presented at the Annual Meeting of the American Society for Public Administration, Honolulu, April 1982.

———. 1980. Centralization Versus Decentralization: Dilemmas in the Administration of Public Service. *International Review of the Administrative Sciences* 46, no. 3: 219–232.

Grindle, Merilee S., and John W. Thomas. 1991. *Public Choices and Policy Change: The Political Economy of Reform in Developing Countries.* Baltimore: Johns Hopkins University Press.

Grupo de Assessoría e Participação do Governador, GAP. 1981. *Democracia participativa: Uma certa ideia.* São Paulo: Governo do Estado de São Paulo.

Gutierrez Mayorga, Alejandro. 1988. *Municipalidades y revolución.* Managua: Centro de Investigación y Asesoría Socioeconomica.

Hamilton, Alexander et al. 1866. *The Federalist: A Commentary on the Constitution of the United States,* no. 29. Philadelphia: J.B. Lippincott.

Hanna, William John. 1985. Contemporary Urbanization Research in Latin America. *Comparative Urban Research* 6:1–2.

Hardoy, Jorge. 1990. Building and Managing Cities in a State of Permanent Crisis. Working paper, no. 187. Washington: Woodrow Wilson Center.

————. 1989. *Las ciudades intermedias y pequeñas en el desarrollo latinoameri-cano*. Buenos Aires: Ediciones GEL.

Hardoy, Jorge E., and David Satterthwaite. 1986. *Small and Intermediate Urban Centres: Their Role in Regional and National Development in the Third World*. London: Hodder and Stoughton.

Hardoy, Jorge E. et al. 1990. *The Poor Die Young: Housing and Health in Third World Cities*. London: Earthscan.

Hartlyn, Jonathan, and Samuel A. Morley, eds. 1986. *Latin American Political Economy: Financial Crisis and Political Change*. Boulder, Colo.: Westview.

Hawley, Willis et al. 1976. *Theoretical Perspectives on Urban Politics*. Englewood Cliffs: Prentice-Hall.

Hicks, Ursula. 1960. *Development from Below*. Oxford: Clarendon.

Hirschman, Albert O. 1985. *Getting Ahead Collectively: Grassroots Experiences in Latin America*. New York: Pergamon.

Hoyo d'Addona, Roberto. 1985. La hacienda pública municipal. *Estudios munici-pales* 1 (enero-febrero): 13–22.

Instituto Político Nacional de Administradores Públicos (IPONAP) and Instituto de Estudios Políticos, Económicos y Sociales (IEPES). 1982. *El desafío munici-pal*. México: Instituto Nacional de Capacitación Política.

Inter-American Foundation. 1990. *A Guide to NGO Directories*. Arlington: Inter-American Foundation.

————. 1977. *They Know How*. . . . Arlington: Inter-American Foundation.

International City Management Association. 1992. *Cities International: Municipal Development Programs Worldwide* 3, no. 1 (Spring).

Isuami, E. A. 1990. *Crisis, estado y opciones de política social*. UNICAMP: Seminario Internacional Sobre la Economía, el Estado y la Salud (julio). foto-copia.

Jelin, Elizabeth. 1987. *Ciudadanía e identidad: Las mujeres en los movimientos sociales latinoamericanos*. Geneva: UNRISD.

Jimenez Castro, Wilberg. 1965. *Los dilemas de la descentralización funcional: Un análisis de la autonomía institucional pública*. San Jose: Escuela Superior de Administración Pública para America Central (ESAPAC).

Johnson Rebaza del Pino, Jaime. 1985. *Estructura y gestión del Estado descentral-izado*. Lima: Centro Peruano de Estudios para el Desarrollo Regional.

Kann, Mark E., ed. 1983. *The Future of American Democracy: Views from the Left*. Philadelphia: Temple University Press.

Karl, Terry L. 1986. Petroleum and Political Pacts. In *Transitions from Authoritarian Rule* vol. 2, ed. Guillermo O'Donnell et al. Baltimore: Johns Hopkins University Press.

Katzenstein, Peter J., ed. 1978. *Between Power and Plenty: Foreign Economic Policies of Advanced Industrial States*. Madison: University of Wisconsin Press.

Kaufman, Robert R. 1988. *The Politics of Debt in Argentina, Brazil and Mexico: Economic Stabilization in the 1980s*. Berkeley: Institute of International Studies.

Keil, T. J., and C.A. Eckstrom. 1974. Municipal Differentiation and Public Policy: Fiscal Support Levels in Varying Environments. *Social Force* 52, no. 3 (March): 384–395.

Kesselman, Mark. 1972. Research Perspectives in Comparative Local Politics: Pitfalls and Prospects. *Comparative Urban Research* 1, no. 1: 10–30.

Kesselman, Mark, and Donald Rosenthal. 1974. *Local Power and Comparative Politics*. Beverly Hills: Sage.

Korten, David C., and Rudi Klauss, eds. 1984. *People-Centered Development: Contributions Toward Theory and Planning Frameworks.* West Hartford, Conn.: Kumarian.

Landim, Leilah. 1988. Non-Governmental Organizations in Latin America. *World Development* 15 (supplement): 29–38.

Laurelli, Elsa, and Alejandro Rofman, eds. 1989. *Decentralización del Estado: Requerimientos y políticas en la crisis.* Buenos Aires: Ediciones CEUR/Fundación Friedrich Ebert.

Lefeber, Louis, and Lisa North, eds. 1980. *Democracy and Development.* Toronto: CELARC, York University.

Lembruch, Gerhard, and Phillipe C. Schmitter, eds. 1982. *Patterns of Corporatist Policy-Making.* Sage Modern Politics Series, vol. 7. London: Sage.

Leonard, David, and Dale R. Marshall, eds. 1982. *Institutions for Rural Development for the Poor: Decentralization and Organizational Linkages.* Berkeley: Institute for International Studies, University of California.

Leonard, David et al. 1981. *Decentralization and Linkages in Rural Development: The Partnership of Central and Local Organization.* Berkeley: University of California.

Leonard, H. Jeffrey et al. 1989. *Environment and the Poor: Development Strategies for a Common Agenda.* Washington: Overseas Development Council.

Lewis, John P. et al. 1988. *Strengthening the Poor: What Have We Learned?* Washington, D.C.: Overseas Development Council.

Lindblom, Charles E. 1980. *The Policy-Making Process.* Englewood Cliffs: Prentice-Hall.

———. 1977. *Politics and Markets: The World's Political-Economic Systems.* New York: Basic Books.

Linz, Juan J., and Alfred Stepan, eds. 1978. *The Breakdown of Democratic Regimes: Crisis, Breakdown and Reequilibration.* Baltimore: Johns Hopkins University Press.

Lipjhart, Arend. 1989. Democratic Political Systems: Types, Cases, Causes and Consequences. *Journal of Theoretical Politics* 1, no. 1 (January): 33–48.

———. 1977. *Democracy in Plural Societies: A Comparative Exploration.* New Haven, Conn.: Yale University Press.

Little, P.D. 1979. *Local Level Projects: A Diachronic Study of AID's Public Finance Projects.* Washington, D.C.: USAID.

Lobo, Thereza, and Fernando Rezende. 1985. Competencias tributarias em regimes federativos. *Revista de administração municipal* 32, no. 175 (abril/junho): 24–35.

Lordello de Mello, Diogo. 1984. Associações de municipios: Experiencia na América Latina. *Revista de administração municipal* 31m bi, 172 (julho/setembro): 56–63.

———. 1983. Modernización de los gobiernos locales en América Latina. *Revista interamericana de planificación* 17, no. 66: 223–257.

Loveman, Brian, and Thomas M. Davies, Jr. 1989. *The Politics of Antipolitics.* Lincoln: University of Nebraska Press.

Lowenthal, Abraham F., ed. 1991. *Exporting Democracy: The United States and Latin America.* Baltimore: Johns Hopkins University Press.

Lowi, Theodore J. 1966. American Business Public Policy: Case Studies and Political Theory. *World Politics* 16 (July): 677–715.

Maier, Charles S. 1987. *Changing Boundaries of the Political.* Cambridge: Cambridge University Press.

Mansbridge, Jane. 1990. *Hard Decisions.* Report from the Institute for Philosophy and Public Policy. (winter): 2–4.

———. 1983. *Beyond Adversary Democracy.* Chicago: University of Chicago Press.

Mansbridge, Jane, ed. 1990. *Beyond Self-Interest.* Chicago: University of Chicago Press.

Martes, A.C.B. 1989. *A política e os movimentos sociais.* São Paulo: CEBRAP. Mimeographed.

Martínez Nogueira, Roberto. 1988. *Las relaciones entre las organizaciones no gubernamentales de desarrollo y el Estado.* (Septiembre.) Mimeographed.

Martínez Nogueira, Roberto et al. 1990. *La trama solidaria: Pobreza y micro-proyectos de desarrollo social.* Buenos Aires: GADIS.

Mawhood, Phillip. 1974. Decentralization for Development: A Lost Cause? In *Local Politics, Development and Participation,* ed. F. C. Bruhns, F. Cassola, and J. Wiatr, 231–236. Pittsburgh: Center for International Studies, University of Pittsburgh.

McKay, David H. 1980. The Rise of the Topocratic State: U.S. Intergovernmental Relations in the 1970's. In *Financing Urban Government in the Welfare State,* ed. Douglas Ashford, 50–70. London: Croom Helm.

Medellín, Pedro, ed. 1989. *La reforma del Estado en América Latina.* Bogotá: Fundación Friedrich Ebert de Colombia.

Meehan, Eugene J. 1990a. *Ethics for Policymaking: A Methodological Analysis.* New York: Greenwood.

———. 1990b. *The University and the Community.* St. Louis: University of Missouri. Mimeographed.

Meehan, Eugene, and Charles Reilly. 1982. Local Development in Rural Latin America. In *Progress Extension and Community Development.* Vol. 1. London: John Wiley & Sons.

Mesa Lago, Carmelo. 1992. *Health Care for the Poor in Latin America and the Caribbean.* PAHO Scientific Publication, no. 539. Washington, D.C.: Pan American Health Organization.

Meyer, Jack A., ed. 1982. *Meeting Human Needs: Toward a New Public Philosophy.* Washington, D.C.: American Enterprise Institute.

Michels, R. 1959. *Political Parties.* New York: Dover Publications.

Montgomery, John. 1988. *Grassroots Participation in Third World Development.* Baltimore: Johns Hopkins University Press.

———. 1987. Probing Managerial Behavior. *World Development* 15:7.

Morris, Arthur, and Stella Lowder. 1992. *Decentralization in Latin America: An Evaluation.* New York: Praeger.

Morse, Richard M., and Jorge E. Hardoy, eds. 1992. *Rethinking the Latin American City.* Washington, D.C.: Woodrow Wilson Center.

Muñoz, Heraldo, ed. 1985. *Crisis y desarrollo alternativo en Latinoamérica.* Santiago: Centro de Estudios de la Realidad Contemporanea.

———. 1982. *From Dependency to Development: Strategies to Overcome Underdevelopment and Inequality.* Boulder, Colo.: Westview.

Murray, John Courtney. 1960. *We Hold These Truths.* New York: Sheed and Ward.

Nef, Jorge. 1988. The Trend Toward Democratization and Redemocratization in Latin America: Shadow and Substance. *Latin American Research Review* 23, no. 3: 131–153.

Nelson, Joan M. 1979. *Access to Power: Politics and The Urban Poor in Developing Nations.* Princeton: Princeton University Press.

Novak, Michael, ed. 1980. *Democracy and Mediating Structures: A Theological Inquiry.* Washington: American Enterprise Institute.
Nunes, Edison. 1991. *Municipio y democracia. Gobiernos locales en ciudades intermedias de América Latina* 17. Santiago: Ediciones SUR.
O'Donnell, Guillermo. 1992. Delegative Democracy? Working paper, no. 172. Notre Dame: Helen Kellogg Institute for International Studies.
O'Donnell, Guillermo, and Philippe Schmitter. 1986. *Tentative Conclusions about Uncertain Transitions,* vol. 4 of *Transitions from Authoritarian Rule.* Baltimore: Johns Hopkins University Press.
O'Donnell, Guillermo, Philippe Schmitter, and Lawrence Whitehead, eds. 1988. *Transitions from Authoritarian Rule: Comparative Perspectives,* 4 vols. Baltimore: Johns Hopkins University Press.
Osorio, Jorge, and Luis Weinstein. 1988. *La fuerza del arco iris: Movimientos sociales, derechos humanos y nuevos paradigmas culturales.* Santiago: Consejo de Educación de Adultos de América Latina.
Paas, Dieter et al., eds. 1991. *Municipio y democracia: Participación de las organizaciones de la sociedad civil en la política municipal.* México: Fundación Friedrich Naumann.
Padua, Jorge N., and Alain Vanneph. 1986. *Poder local, poder regional.* México: Colegio de México-CEMCA.
Paul, Samuel. 1982. *Managing Development Progress: The Lessons of Success.* Boulder, Colo.: Westview.
Payne, Douglas W. 1992. Latin American Democracy: In Search of the Rule of Law. *Freedom Review* 23, no. 1 (January-February): 48–50.
Perelli, Carina, and Juan Rial. 1991. *Partidos políticos y democracia en el Cono Sur.* Montevideo: PEITHO Sociedad de Análisis Político.
Peters, Thomas. 1988. *Thriving on Chaos.* New York: Harper and Row.
Picard, Louis A., and Raphael Zariski, eds. 1987. *Subnational Politics in the 1980s: Organization, Reorganization and Economic Development.* New York: Praeger.
Piore, Michael J., and Charles F. Sable. 1984. *The Second Industrial Divide: Possibility for Prosperity.* New York: Basic Books.
Portes, Alejandro et al., eds. 1989. *The Informal Economy: Studies in Advanced and Less Developed Countries.* Baltimore: Johns Hopkins University Press.
Przeworski, Adam. 1991. *Democracy and the Market: Political and Economic Reforms in Eastern Europe and Latin America.* Cambridge: Cambridge University Press.
Rabinovitz, Francine F. 1969. Urban Development and Political Development in Latin America. In *Comparative Urban Research: The Administration of Politics of Cities,* ed. Robert T. Daland, 98–99. Beverly Hills: Sage.
Raimondi, Equequiel et al. 1991. Democracia, ajuste e integración. *Nueva sociedad* 113 (mayo-junio): 156–163.
Ralston, Leonard, James Anderson, and Elizabeth Colson. 1982. *Voluntary Efforts in Decentralizing Management.* Berkeley: Institute of International Studies, University of California.
Rechkiman, Benjamin, and Gerardo Gil Valdivia. 1981. *El federalismo y la coordinación fiscal.* México: UNAM, Instituto de Investigaciones Juridicas.
Reilly, Charles. 1993. Ideas, Action and Policy. In *Inquiry at the Grassroots,* eds. William Glade, and Charles Reilly.
———. 1989. *The Democratization of Development: Partnership at the Grassroots.* Arlington: Inter-American Foundation Annual Report, pp. 16–20.
———. 1984. Intergovernmental Relations in Austere Times: Mexico and Brazil.

Paper delivered at the annual meeting of the American Political Science Association, August 30–September 2, Washington, D.C.

Ritchey-Vance, Marion. 1991. *The Art of Association: NGOs and Civil Society in Colombia.* Arlington: Inter-American Foundation.

Ritter, Archibald, and David Pollock, eds. 1983. *Latin American Prospects for the 1980s: Equity, Democratization, and Development.* New York: Praeger.

Roberts, Bryan. 1978. *Cities of Peasants: The Political Economy of Urbanization in the Third World.* Beverly Hills: Sage.

Rondinelli, Dennis. 1990. Financing the Decentralization of Urban Services in Developing Countries: Administrative Requirements for Fiscal Improvements. *Studies in Comparative International Development* 25, no. 2 (summer): 43–59.

———. 1985. Equity, Growth, and Development. *American Planning Association* 5, no. 4 (autumn): 434–448.

———. 1981. Government Decentralization in Comparative Perspective: Theory and Practice in Developing Countries. *International Review of Administrative Sciences* 2: 133–145.

Rondinelli, Dennis et al. 1989. Analysing Decentralization Policies in Developing Countries: A Political Economy Framework. *Development and Change* 20, no. 1 (January): 57–87.

Rondinelli, Dennis, John R. Nelis, and G. Shabbir Cheema. 1983. Decentralization in Developing Countries: A Review of Recent Experience. World Bank Staff Working paper, no. 581. Washington, D.C.: World Bank.

Roque, Miguél Angel. 1935. *La descentralización administrativa.* Buenos Aires: Talleres Gráficos "Accinelli."

Rosenthal, D.B. 1980. Bargaining Power in Inter-Governmental Relations. *Publius* 10: 5–44.

Rouquie, Alain et al. 1985. *Como renascem as democracias.* São Paulo: Editora Brasiliense.

Rowat, G., ed. 1980. *International Handbook on Local Government Reorganization.* New York: Greenwood Press.

Rudolph, Lloyd I., and Susanne Hoeber Rudolph. 1979. Authority and Power in Bureaucratic and Patrimonial Administration: A Revisionist Interpretation of Weber on Bureaucracy. *World Politics* 31, no. 2 (January): 195–227.

Sady, Emil J. 1962. Improvement of Local Government and Administration for Development Purposes. *Journal of Local Administration Overseas* 1: 135–148.

Salamon, Lester M. 1989. The Voluntary Sector and the Future of the Welfare State. *Nonprofit and Voluntary Sector Quarterly* 18, no. 1 (spring): 11–24.

Sanguinetti, Julio Maria. 1991. *El temor y la impaciencia: Ensayo sobre la transición democrática en América Latina.* Buenos Aires: Fondo de Cultura Económica.

Schmitter, Philippe. 1983. Democratic Theory and Neo-Corporatist Practice. Working paper, no. 74. Florence: European University Institute.

Schmitter, Philippe, and Terry L. Karl. 1991. What Democracy Is . . . and Is Not. *Journal of Democracy.* 2, no. 3 (Summer): 75–88.

Schmitter, Philippe, and Gerhard Lehmbruch, eds. 1979. Trends Toward Corporatist Intermediation. *Contemporary Political Sociology.* Vol. 1. London: Sage.

Schulz, Ann. 1979. *Local Politics and Nation-States.* Santa Barbara: Clio.

Shefter, Martin. 1987. *Political Crisis, Fiscal Crisis: The Collapse and Revival of New York City.* New York: Basic Books.

Smith, Brad. 1987. *Building a Learning Network: Annual Report.* Arlington: Inter-American Foundation, pp. 31–32.

Smith, Brian. 1990. *More Than Altruism*. Princeton: Princeton University Press.

Stokes, Bruce. 1978. *Local Responses to Global Problems: A Key to Meeting Basic Human Needs*. Worldwatch paper, no. 17. Washington: Worldwatch Institute.

Tarrow, Sidney. 1989. *Struggle, Politics and Reform: Collective Action, Social Movements, and Cycles of Protest*. Occasional paper, no. 21. Ithaca: Cornell University, Center for International Studies.

———. 1977. *Between Center and Periphery: Grassroots Politicians in Italy and France*. New Haven: Yale University Press.

Tendler, Judith. 1982. *Turning Private Voluntary Organizations into Development Agencies: Questions for Evaluation*. Discussion paper, no. 12. Washington: USAID.

Titmuss, Richard. 1974. *Social Policy: An Introduction*. New York: Pantheon Books.

Torrealba Narvaez, Luis. 1982. La reforma administrativa municipal de Venezuela. *Boletín de la academia de ciencias políticas y sociales* 39 (septiembre): 89–118.

UNICEF. 1989. *Participación de los sectores pobres en programas de desarrollo local*. Santiago: UNICEF.

Uphoff, Norman. 1986. *Local Institutional Development: An Analytical Sourcebook with Cases*. West Hartford, Conn.: Kumarian.

Uphoff, Norman, John M. Cohen, and Arthur Goldsmith. 1979. *Feasibility and Application of Rural Development Participation: A State of the Art Paper*. Ithaca, N.Y.: Center for International Studies, Cornell University.

Urrutia, Miguél. 1983. *Gremios, política económica y democracia*. Bogotá: Fondo Cultural Cafetero.

Urrutia, Miguél, ed. 1991. *Long-Term Trends in Latin American Economic Development*. Washington, D.C.: Inter-American Development Bank.

Valla, V. V., and S. A. V. Siquiera. 1989. O centro municipal de saúde e a participação popular. In *Demandas populares, políticas públicas e saúde*, ed. N. R. Costa et al. 91–115. Rio de Janiero: Editorial Vozes/Abrasco.

Walsh, Sandra. 1978. *Bibliography on Local Government*. Monticello: Council of Planning Librarians.

Wasserstrom, Robert. 1985. *Grassroots Development in Latin America and the Caribbean: Oral Histories of Social Change*. New York: Praeger.

Weffort, Francisco C. 1992. *New Democracies, Which Democracies?* Occasional paper no. 198. Washington, D.C.: Woodrow Wilson International Center for Scholars.

———. 1991. America Astray. Working paper, no. 162, July. Notre Dame: Kellogg Institute.

———. 1984. *Por qué democracia?* São Paulo: Editora Brasiliense.

Weffort, Francisco, et al. 1984. *A democracia como proposta*. Rio de Janeiro: IBASE.

Welin, H. H. 1970. Elasticity of Control: An Analysis of Decentralization. *Journal of Comparative Administration* 2 (August): 125–209.

Wickwar, W. Hardy. 1970. *The Political Theory of Local Government*. Columbia: University of South Carolina Press.

Williams, Arthur R. 1981. *Measuring Local Government Performance: Assessing Management, Decentralization, and Participation*. Ithaca, N.Y.: Rural Development Committee, Cornell University.

Willmott, Peter, ed. 1987. Local Government, Decentralization and Community.

discussion paper, no.18. Presented at a March conference held at the Political Studies Institute London.

Wolfe, Alan. 1991. Three Paths to Development: Market, State, and Civil Society. Paper presented at the International Meeting of NGOs and the United Nations System Agencies, August 6–9, Rio de Janeiro.

Wolfe, Alan. 1989. *Whose Keeper? Social Science and Moral Obligation.* Berkeley: University of California Press.

Wolfe, Marshall, and Matthias Stietel. 1994. *A Voice for the Excluded.* London: Zed Books.

Wolfe, Marshall. n.d. *Popular Participation.* Geneva: United Nations Research in Social Development.

Wolfinger, Raymond E. 1971. Nondecisions and the Study of Local Politics. *American Political Science Review* 65, no. 4 (December): 1063–1080.

World Bank and Oxford University. 1992. *World Development Report.* Washington, D.C.: World Bank.

World Bank. 1991. *Urban Policy and Economic Development: An Agenda for the 1990s.* Washington, D.C.: World Bank.

World Bank and Johns Hopkins University. 1991. *World Development Report.* Baltimore: Johns Hopkins University Press.

———. 1991. *World Tables.* Baltimore: Johns Hopkins University Press.

Yudelman, Sally. 1987. *Hopeful Openings.* West Hartford, Conn.: Kumarian.

Yuhnke, Robert. 1991. Air Pollution and Urban Transportation. In *Economic Development and Environmental Protection in Latin America,* ed. Joseph S. Tulchin, and Andrew I. Rudman. Boulder, Colo.: Lynne Rienner.

Zenha, Francisco Salgado. 1988. *As reformas necessarias.* Lisbon: Reproscan.

Argentina

Bonaparte, H. M. 1990. Los que llegaron del interior. *Rosario, historias de aquí a la vuelta,* p. 6. Rosario: Universidad Nacional del Litoral.

Buthet, Carlos. 1988. *El encuentro de entidades no gubernamentales para el desarrollo y algunas experiencias de articulación con el Estado.* Cuadernillo (occasional paper) no. 3. Cordoba: Servicio Habitacional y de Acción Social, SEHAS.

Castagna, A., J. L. Pellegrini, and M. L. Woelflin. 1990. Desarrollo de la actividad industrial. *Rosario, historias de aquí a la vuelta,* p. 5. Rosario: Universidad Nacional del Litoral.

Cavarozzi, Marcelo. 1986. Peronism and Radicalism: Argentina's Transitions in Perspective. In *Elections and Democratization in Latin America,* ed. Paul Drake, and Eduardo Silva. San Diego: Center for Iberian and Latin American Studies, University of California at San Diego.

CEPAD. 1990. *La situación laboral en el Gran Rosario.* Rosario: CEPAD.

Cragnolino, Silvia. 1990. Rosario: Del poblado a la ciudad. *Rosario, historias de aquí a la vuelta,* p. 3. Rosario: Universidad Nacional del Litoral.

CRICSO. n.d. *Crisis socio-económica y su impacto en un proyecto de desarrollo social,* Rosario: CRICSO.

Davis, J. Emmeus. 1991. *Contested Ground: Collective Action and the Urban Neighborhood.* Ithaca, N.Y.: Cornell University Press.

del Franco, A. 1989. Consideraciones organizacionales acerca del Programa

Alimentario Nacional (PAN). In *¿Cómo enfrentar la pobreza? Estrategias y experiencias organizacionales innovadoras,* ed. B. Kliksberg. Buenos Aires: GEL.

Feijoo, María del Carmen, and Elizabeth Jelin. 1987. Women from Low Income Sectors: Economic and Democratization of Politics in Argentina. In *The Invisible Adjustment: Poor Women and the Economic Crisis.* New York: UNICEF.

García Delgado, R., and J. Silva. 1985. El movimiento vecinal y la democracia: Participación y control en el Gran Buenos Aires. In *Los nuevos movimientos sociales,* vol. 2, ed. Elizabeth Jelin. Buenos Aires: CEAL.

Herzer, H., and P. Pirez. 1988. El municipio entre la descentralización y la crisis. In *Gobierno de la ciudad y crisis en Argentina,* ed. H. Herzer and P. Pirez. Buenos Aires: GEL.

Martínez Nogueira, Roberto. 1989. Procesos sociales y aprendizaje: la emergencia social en Argentina. Serie documentos de trabajo, no. 9. Buenos Aires: Grupo de Análisis y Desarrollo Institucional y Social, GADIS.

———. 1988. Tensiones y complementariedades entre el Estado y las organiza-ciones no gubernamentales en los programas de promoción y apoyo a microempresas. Serie documentos de trabajo, no. 5. Buenos Aires: Grupo de Análisis y Desarrollo Institucional y Social, GADIS.

Milofsky, Carl. 1988. Networks, Markets, Culture and Contracts: Understanding Community Organizations. In *Community Organizations: Studies in Resource Mobilization and Exchange,* ed. Milofsky, C. New York: Oxford University Press.

Nuñez Miñana, H., and A. Porto. 1982. *Subsidios hacia y/o desde los partidos del Gran Buenos Aires a través de la finanzas públicas.* Vol. 7. Buenos Aires: CFI.

O'Donnell, Guillermo. 1988. State and Alliances in Argentina, 1966–1973. In *Bureaucratic Authoritarianism,* ed. Guillermo O'Donnell. Berkeley: University of California Press.

———. 1984. Y a mí, ¿qué me importa? Sociabilidad y autoritarismo en Brasil y Argentina. Working paper, no. 9. Notre Dame: Kellogg Institute.

Pelliza, M. Celina. 1989. Un nuevo 'mirar' para las ONG. *Boletín de desarrollo social* 7 (agosto): 11–13.

Pirez, Pedro. 1990. Ciudades intermedias en la Argentina. Gestión local y política local. *Revista foro* 11:28.

———. 1989. El municipio y la organización del estado en la Argentina. *Medio Ambiente y Urbanización* 7:28 (septiembre).

Ramos, Peralta, and Carlos H. Waisman, eds. 1987. *From Military Rule to Liberal Democracy in Argentina.* Boulder, Colo.: Westview.

Rock, David. 1975. *Politics in Argentina, 1890–1930: The Rise and Fall of Radicalism.* Cambridge: Cambridge University Press.

Smith, Peter. 1978. The Breakdown of Democracy in Argentina, 1916–1930. In *The Breakdown of Democratic Regimes: Latin America,* ed. Juan Linz, and Alfred Stepan. Baltimore: Johns Hopkins University Press.

———. 1974. *Argentina and the Failure of Democracy.* Madison: University of Wisconsin Press.

Smith, W. C. 1991. Hyperinflation, Macroeconomic Instability, and Neoliberal Restructuring in Democratic Argentina. Mimeographed.

Thompson, Andres A. 1989. La emergencia social y las organizaciones no guberna-mentales. Preguntas y dilemas. *Boletín de desarrollo social* 7 (agosto): 14–18.

———. 1988. *El desarrollo social y la cooperación internacional: El papel de las organizaciones no gubernamentales (ONG) en la Argentina.* Buenos Aires: CEDES-PREAL.

Toutoundjian, Beatriz. 1988. *Ciudades de Rosario y Santa Fe: Aspectos de la situación social reciente a la luz de los cambios operados en sus respectivos mercados de trabajo.* Buenos Aires: CFI.

Brazil

Author Unknown

———. 1990. Administrações populares. *Proposta: Experiencias em educação popular* 45 (agosto): 45–60.

———. 1980. Associação Brasileira de Municipios. In *Dez anos de municipalismo no Brasil: Atividades da Associação Brasileira de Municipios: Relatorios anuais, 1969–1979.* Rio de Janeiro: Associação.

Azevedo, S., and A. A. P. Prates. 1990. Movimentos sociais, ação coletiva e planejamento participativo. Belo Horizonte. Mimeographed.

Bandecchi, Pedro Brasil. 1974. *O municipio no Brasil e sua função política.* São Paulo: n.p.

Brant, Vinicius Caldeira. 1989. *São Paulo: Trabalhar e viver.* São Paulo: Editora Brasiliense, Comissão Justiça e Paz de São Paulo.

Brasileiro, Ana María. 1973. *O municipio como sistema político.* Rio de Janeiro: Fundação Getulio Vargas, Instituto de Documentação.

Caccia Bava, Silvio. 1991. *Taxa transporte: Uma alternativa de financiamento para os transportes públicos municipais.* São Paulo: Pólis.

Cann, Kenneth T. 1964. *The Structure of Local Government Finance in Brazil with Comments on its Relationship to Community Development.* Madison: Land Tenure Center, University of Wisconsin.

Cardoso, Fernando Henrique. 1980. Regime Político e Mudanza Social. *Revista de cultura e política* 2: 7–20.

———. 1972. *O modelo político brasileiro.* São Paulo: Difusão Europeia do Livro.

Cohn, Amélia. 1988. De política da desigualdade à proposta de equidade. Saõ Paulo: Universidade de São Paulo. Mimeo.

Covre, Maria de Lourdes. 1986. *A cidadanía que não temos.* São Paulo: Editora Brasilense.

da Matta, Roberto. 1987. Carnival Culture as a Problem. Working paper, no. 79. Notre Dame: Kellogg Institute.

da Silva, Ana Amélia. 1991. Ambiente urbano e qualidade de vida. *Pólis* 3 (special edition): 1.

———. 1991. Reforma urbana é o direito a cidade. Pólis 1: 1.

de Freitas, Eugenio. 1985. Promovendo o desenvolvimento local e enfrentando o desemprego: Uma experiencia de Jaragua. *Revista de administração municipal* 32, no. 177 (outubro/dezembro): 56–61.

de Mattos, Carlos A. 1989. Falsas expectativas ante la decentralización. *Nueva sociedad* 104 (noviembre-diciembre): 118–126.

Dillinger, William. 1982. *Regional Aspects of State and Local Finance in Brazil.* Washington, D.C.: International Development Bank.

Donnangelo, M. C. F. and L. Pereira. 1976. *Saúde e sociedade.* São Paulo: Livraria Duas Cidades.

dos Reis Velloso, João Paulo et al. 1991. A ecologia e o novo padrão de desenvolvimento no Brasil. From National Forum 4: How to Avoid Another Lost Decade, November 25–28. São Paulo: Livraria Nobel.

dos Santos, Wanderley Guilherme. 1990. *Público e privado no sistema brasileiro.* Rio de Janeiro. Mimeographed.

―――. 1979. *Cidadanía e justicia: A política social na ordem brasileira.* Rio de Janeiro: Editora Campus.

Draibe, S.M. 1990. As políticas de combate à pobreza na América Latina. *São Paulo em perspectiva* 4, no. 2 (abril/junho): 18–24.

Fernandes, Rubem Cesar, and Leandro Piquet Carneiro. 1991. *NGOs in the Nineties: A Survey of Their Brazilian Leaders.* Arlington: Inter-American Foundation.

Fernandes, Rubem Cesar, and Leilah Landim. 1986. Um perfil das ONGs no Brasil. *Comunicações do ISER* 2 (novembro): 44–56.

Frieden, Jeffrey. 1987. The Brazilian Borrowing Experience: From Miracle to Debacle and Back. *Latin American Research Review* 22, no. 1: 95–131.

Instituto Brasileiro de Administração Municipal. 1982. *Instituto Brasileiro de Administração Municipal: 30 Años.* Rio de Janeiro: IBAM.

International City Management Association. 1992. *Cities International: Municipal Development Programmes Worldwide* 3, no. 1.

Jacobi, Pedro. 1989. *Movimentos sociais e políticas públicas: Demandas por saneamiento básico e saúde, São Paulo 1974–1984.* São Paulo: Editora Cortez.

Landim, Leilah. 1988. *Sem fins lucrativos: As organizações não-governamentais no Brasil.* Rio de Janeiro: ISER.

Mahar, Dennis J. 1983. Financing State and Local Government in Brazil. World Bank Staff Working paper, no. 612. Washington: World Bank.

Mello, C.G. 1977. Saúde e assistência médica no Brasil. In *Coleção saúde em debate.* São Paulo: Cebes/Hucitec.

Moises, Jose Alvaro. 1980. Crise política e democrática, a transição dificil. *Revista de cultura e política* 2 (agosto-outubro): 9–36.

Muçouçah, Paulo Sergio. 1990. A coleta seletiva do lixo. In *Inovação Urbana,* no. 1. São Paulo: Pólis.

NEPP/UNICAMP. 1989. *Brasil 1987: Relatório sobre a situação social do país.* Campinas: UNICAMP.

Nunes, Edison. 1990. Carencias e modos de vida. *São Paulo em perspectiva: Fundação SEADA* 4, no. 2 (abril-junho): 2–8.

―――. 1989. Carencias urbanas, reivindicações sociais e valores democráticos. *Revista de cultura e política* 17 (junho): 67–92.

O'Donnell, Guillermo. 1989. Privatización de lo público en Brasil: Microescenas. *Nueva sociedad* 104 (noviembre-diciembre): 118–126.

Paulson, Belden H. 1984. *Local Political Patterns in Northeast Brazil.* Madison: Land Tenure Center, University of Wisconsin.

Pedreira, Mauricio, and Carol Goodstein. 1992. Blueprint for an Eco-Safe City. *Américas* 44, no. 4: 6–15.

Pólis. 1989. *Movimiento Popular.* São Paulo: Pólis.

Prefeitura do Município de São Paulo. 1991. *Plano diretor de São Paulo: Ao alcance de todos.* São Paulo: Prefeitura do Município de São Paulo.

Reilly, Charles. 1981. Development, Public Policy and Local Politics in Authoritarian Brazil. Ph.D. diss., University of Chicago. Ann Arbor, Michigan: University Microfilms.

Schwartzman, Simon. 1982. *Bases do autoritarismo brasileiro.* Rio de Janeiro: Editora Campus.

Sherwood, Frank P. 1972. *Institutionalizing the Grassroots in Brazil: A Study in Comparative Local Government.* San Francisco: Chandler.
Simões Junior, José Geraldo. 1991. *Cortiços em São Paulo: O problema e suas alternativas,* vol. 2. São Paulo: Pólis.
Singer, Paul and Vinicius Caldeira Brant. 1980. *São Paulo: O povo em movimento.* São Paulo: Editora Brasileira de Ciencias.
Tavares Bastos, Aureliano Cândido. 1937. *A provincia: Estado sobre a descentralização no Brasil.* São Paulo: Companhía Editora Nacional.
Wils, Frits. 1991. NGOs and Development in Brazil, An Overview and Analysis. The Hague. Mimeographed.

Chile

Author Unknown

———. 1990. *Transición y municipio: Democratización del gobierno local y participación.* Santiago: Proyecto Educación para la Democracia.
———. Various years. *Memoria de Actividades.* Santiago: Academia de Humanismo Cristiano.

Abalos, José A. 1987. Las instituciones de apoyo en Chile, una síntesis. *Cooperación internacional al desarrollo* 1: 17–32.
Abalos, José A., and Rodrigo Egaña B. 1989. La cooperación internacional al desarrollo frente a los cambios políticos en Chile. In *Una puerta que se abre: Los organismos no gubernamentales en la cooperación al desarrollo,* ed. Rodrigo Egaña, 327–356. Santiago: Taller de Cooperación al Desarrollo.
Affonso, Almino et al. 1970. *Movimiento campesino chileno* 1: 165–170. Santiago: ICIRA.
Agurto, Irene, and Carlos Piña. 1988. *Las organizaciones no gubernamentales de promoción y desarrollo urbano en Chile. Una propuesta de investigación.* Discussion Paper, no. 110. Santiago: FLASCO.
Ahumada, J. 1985. El gobierno y la administración local: Tradición y cambio en los ochenta. Santiago: ILPES (junio). Pamphlet.
Arellano, José P. et al. 1982. *Modelo económico chileno: Trayectoria de una crítica.* Santiago: CIEPLAN.
Arteaga, Ana María, and Eliana Largo V. 1989. Los ONG en el area de la mujer y la cooperación al desarrollo. In *Una puerta que se abre: Los organismos no gubernamentales en la cooperación al desarrollo,* ed. Rodrigo Egaña, 327–356. Santiago: Taller de Cooperación al Desarrollo.
Barria, Lilíana, and Margarita de la Cuadra. 1989. INPROA y su trabajo con la mujer campesina. Santiago: INPROA. Pamphlet.
Bertoni, Nora, Sergio Pezoa, and Judith Salinas. 1991. *Las ONG de salud en Chile: Una contribución a la estrategia de atención primaria.* Santiago: PROSAPS/CORSAPS.
Bitar, Sergio. 1986. *Chile, Experiment in Democracy.* Philadelphia: ISHI.
Borel Chieyssal, Edmundo. 1976. *Algunos aspectos administrativos del gobierno regional y perspectivas de desarrollo del nuevo municipio chileno.* Santiago: Departamento de Administración, Facultad de Ciencias Económicas y Administrativas, Universidad de Chile.
Brown, L. David. 1979. Organizaciones voluntarias privadas y coaliciones para el

desarrollo. In *ONG, estado y cooperación internacional, una introducción al tema,* Francisco Vío Grossi, 185–209. Santiago: Secretaria General del Consejo de Educación de Adultos de América Latina.

Cancino D., Bernardita. 1990. *Los cambios en las ONG a partir del nuevo escenario político.* Santiago: Taller de Cooperación al Desarrollo, Cooperación Internacional al Desarrollo.

Cleaves, Peter S. 1969. *Developmental Processes in Chilean Local Government.* Berkeley: Institute of International Studies, University of California.

Culagovski, M. 1985. *Afiliación y participación social a nivel local: Algunos resultados de la encuesta de participación comunal.* Discussion Paper, no. 70 CED (enero).

Delpiano, A., and D. Sánchez, eds. 1984. *Educación popular en Chile: 100 experiencias.* Santiago: CIDE-FLACSO.

de Vylder, Stefan. 1974. *Allende's Chile: The Political Economy of the Rise and Fall of the Unidad Popular.* Cambridge: Cambridge University Press.

Díaz C., Eugenio. 1989. Cooperación al desarrollo y sindicalismo urbano: 1973–1988. In *Una puerta que se abre: Los organismos no gubernamentales en la cooperación al desarrollo,* ed. Rodrigo Egaña, 327–356. Santiago: Taller de Cooperación al Desarrollo.

Díaz C., Eugenio, and Sergio Gómez. 1990. *Nuevos dilemas para las ONG chilenas.* Santiago: Taller de Cooperación al Desarrollo, Cooperación Internacional al Desarrollo.

Downs, Charles et al., eds. 1989. *Social Policy from the Grassroots: Nongovernmental Organizations in Chile.* Boulder, Colo.: Westview.

Egaña, Rodrigo. 1990. Relaciones entre ONGD y donantes en el período de transición democrática en Chile. Santiago: Taller de Cooperación al Desarrollo, Cooperación Internacional al Desarrollo. Pamphlet.

Ffrench-Davis, Ricardo. 1973. *Políticas Económicas de Chile, 1952–1970.* Santiago: CIEPLAN, Ediciones Nueva Universidad.

Gomez, Sergio. 1989. Nuevas formas de desarrollo rural en Chile. In *Una puerta que se abre: Los organismos no gubernamentales en la cooperación al desarrollo,* ed. Rodrigo Egaña, 327–356. Santiago: Taller de Cooperación al Desarrollo.

Hardy, C. 1989. *Organizarse para vivir: Pobreza urbana y organización popular.* Santiago: Programa de Economía del Trabajo.

Huerta, Mario, and Luis Pastene. 1988. *La iglesia chilena y los cambios sociopolíticos.* Santiago: Pehuén.

Jansana, Loreto. 1989. *El pan nuestro.* Santiago: PET, Editorial Tiempo Nuevo.

Jiménez, Marcela et al. 1989. *Desarrollo local: Municipio y organismos no gubernamentales.* Santiago: Escuela de Trabajo Social, Pontificia Universidad Católica de Chile.

Jiménez, Marcela, ed. 1990. *Municipios y organizaciones privadas: Lecciones y proyecciones de algunas experiencias.* Santiago: Ediciones Mar del Plata.

Landsberger, Henry, and Fernando Canitrot. 1967. *Iglesia, intelectuales y campesinos.* Santiago: ISORA, Editorial del Pacífico.

Lipjhart, Arend. 1977. *Democracy in Plural Societies.* New Haven: Yale University Press.

Lladser, María T. 1989. La investigación en ciencias sociales en Chile: Su desarrollo en los centros privados, 1973–1988. In *Una puerta que se abre: Los organ-*

ismos no gubernamentales en la cooperación al desarrollo, ed. Rodrigo Egaña, 213–270. Santiago: Taller de Cooperación al Desarrollo.

———. 1986. *Centros privados de investigación en ciencias sociales en Chile.* Santiago: AHC/FLASCO.

Loveman, Brian. 1991. NGOs and the Transition to Democracy in Chile. *Grassroots Development* 15, no. 2: 8–19.

———. 1988. *Chile, The Legacy of Hispanic Capitalism.* 2d ed. Oxford: Oxford University Press.

Marshall, T., M. Saez, and Judith Salinas. 1991. *Participación en salud: Lecciones y desafíos.* Santiago: CORSAPS.

Ministry of Health, Primary Care Department. 1990. Health Policy and Nongovernmental Organizations Seminar. October 9–10. Mimeo.

Pardo V., Lucia, ed. 1990. *Instituciones de fomento y de apoyo a talleres productivos y pequeñas empresas o negocios.* Santiago: AID/FINAM, Departamento de Economía, Facultad de Ciencias Económicas y Administrativas, Universidad de Chile.

Pinto, Anibal. 1964. *Chile, una economía difícil.* México: Fondo de Cultura Económico.

Pozo, Hernán. 1981. La situación actual del municipio chileno y el problema de la municipalización. *Contribuciones* 7: (julio).

Raczynski, Dagmar, and Claudia Serrano. 1988. Planificación para el desarrollo local? La experiencia de algunos municipios de Santiago. *Colección Estudios CIEPLAN* 24 (junio): 37–62.

———. 1987. Administración y gestión local: La experiencia de algunos municipios en Santiago. *Colección Estudios CIEPLAN* 22 (diciembre): 129–151.

Razeto, Luis. 1983. Las organizaciones económicas populares. Santiago: Programa de Economía del Trabajo (PET). Mimeographed.

Salinas, Judith, ed. 1989. *Equipo de salud: Salud y promoción social.* Catastro de Instituciones de Santiago. Santiago: INFOCAP.

Sánchez, Daniella. 1987. Instituciones y acción poblacional: Seguimiento de su acción en el período 1973–1981. In *Espacio y poder, los pobladores,* ed. Jorge Chatêau et al. Santiago: FLACSO.

Smith, Brian. 1982. *The Church and Politics in Chile: Challenges to Modern Catholicism.* Princeton: Princeton University Press.

Spoerer, Sergio. 1987. La diplomacia informal: América Latina, Europa y los no gubernamentales. *Revista nueva sociedad* (julio-agosto): 45–51.

SUR (Equipo Urbano). 1986. Movimiento de pobladores y poder local en Chile. *Revista foro* 1, no. 1 (septiembre): 4–15.

Thiesenhusen, William. 1966. *Chile's Experiments in Agrarian Reform.* Madison: University of Wisconsin Press.

Tulchin, Joseph S., and Augusto Varas, eds. 1991. *From Dictatorship to Democracy: Rebuilding Political Consensus in Chile.* Boulder, Colo.: Lynne Rienner.

Valenzuela, Arturo. 1978. *The Breakdown of Democratic Regimes: Chile.* Baltimore: Johns Hopkins University Press.

———. 1978. *Political Brokers in Chile: Local Government in a Centralized Polity.* Durham, N.C.: Duke University Press.

Walton, Gary M. 1985. *The National Economic Policies of Chile.* Greenwich: Jai.

Zahler, Roberto et al. 1978. *Chile, treinta y cinco años de discontinuidad económica: 1940–1975.* Santiago: Instituto Chileno de Estudios Humanísticos.

Colombia

Author Unknown

————. 1991. Cooling It. *The Economist* (March 30): 42–43.
————. 1987. Ciencia Política. *Revista trimestral para América Latina y España* 9, no. 4 Trimestre.

Alvarez A., Orion. 1988. Participação dos cidadães no governo municipal—o caso colombiano. *Revista de administração municipal* 35, no. 187 (abril-junho): 52–61.
Antorveza, Adolfo Triana. 1988. *La Organización del Estado Colombiano.* Bogotá: Cuadernos del Jaguar.
Bailey, John J. 1976. Pluralist and Corporatist Dimensions of Interest Representation in Colombia. In *Authoritarianism and Corporatism in Latin America,* ed. James M. Malloy. Pittsburgh: University of Pittsburgh Press.
Bustamante, Edgar, ed. 1988. *El gran libro de Colombia. Circúlo de lectores.* Vol. 1. Bogotá: Editorial Printer Colombiana.
Casasbuenas, Constantino. 1989. Las ONGs y los movimientos sociales en Colombia. *Revista foro* 8 (febrero): 32–41.
————. 1988. Descentralización y adminstración municipal. *Economía Colombiana* Special edition (octubre).
Castro, Jaime. 1986. *Elección popular de alcaldes.* Bogotá: Editorial Oveja Negra.
Fundación Foro Nacional por Colombia. 1991. *El impacto de la reforma municipal en Colombia. Estudio de 8 municipios.* Bogotá: Fundación Foro Nacional por Colombia; Informe Final de Investigación.
Londoño, Rocío. 1991. Problemas laborales y teestructuración del sindicalismo. In *Al filo del caos. Crisis política en la Colombia de los años 80,* ed. Francisco Leal and Leon Zamoso. Bogotá: Tercer Mundo Editores, Instituto de Estudios Políticos y Relaciones Internacionales.
López-Alves, Fernando. 1990. Explaining Confederation: Colombian Unions in the 1980s. *Latin American Research Review* 25, no. 2.
Ocampo, José Antonio. 1992. Reforma del Estado y desarrollo económico y social en Colombia. *Análisis político* 17 (septiembre a diciembre).
Office of the Presidency. 1991. *La revolución pacífica: Plan de desarrollo económico y social 1990–1994.* Bogota: Office of the Presidency, National Planning Department.
Perfetti, Juan José. 1992. Los beneficiarios del gasto público social al final del decenio de los ochenta. *Análisis político* 15 (enero a abril).
Revéiz, Edgar, and María José Pérez. 1986. Colombia: Moderate Economic Growth, Political Stability, and Social Welfare. In *Latin American Political Economy: Financial Crisis and Political Change,* ed. Jonathan Hartlyn and Samuel Morley. Boulder, Colo.: Westview.
Santana Rodríguez, Pedro. 1989. *Los movimientos sociales en Colombia.* Bogotá: Ediciones Foro Nacional por Colombia.
————. 1989. Movimientos sociales, gobiernos locales y democracia. *Revista foro* 8 (febrero): 20–31.
————. 1983. *Desarrollo regional y paros cívicos en Colombia.* Bogotá: Centro de Investigación y Educación Popular.
Sarmiento Anzola, Libardo. 1992. La revolución pacífica: Una mirada premoderna

sobre los derechos sociales en Colombia. *Economía Colombiana* 238 (febrero-marzo).

Tavera, Helena Paez de. 1989. *Protagonismo de mujer: Organización y liderazgo feminino en Bogotá.* Bogotá: PróDemocracia-Fundación Friederich Naumann.

Urrutia, Miguel. 1982. *Winners and Losers in Colombia's Economic Growth of the 1970s.* Cambridge: Cambridge University Press.

Wilde, Alexander W. 1978. Conversations Among Gentlemen: Oligarchical Democracy in Colombia. In *The Breakdown of Democratic Regimes: Latin America,* ed. Juan J. Linz and Alfred Stepan. Baltimore: Johns Hopkins University Press.

Mexico

Author Unknown

———. 1991. PRD: El partido que nació el 6 de julio o el que se fundó el 5 de mayo de 1989. *El cotidiano* 7 (julio-agosto):42.

———. 1991. Pros, contras y asegunes de la 'apropriación del proceso productivo.' *El cotidiano* 39 (enero-febrero).

———. 1988. Las mujeres tenemos la palabra. Paper presented at the 3d Encuentro Nacional de Mujeres de la CONAMUP. México: Equipo Pueblo.

Acosta, Marieclaire. 1992. Prólogo. In *America's Watch. Los derechos humanos en México.* Mexico: Planeta.

Aguilar Camín, Hector. 1988. *Después del milagro.* México: Cal y Arena.

Alatorre, Gerardo, and Jasmine Aguilar. 1990. Las ONGs en el ámbito rural: Su identidad y su papel como instancias de apoyo a grupos campesinos en aspectos productivos y ecológicos. Paper presented at forum on rural social movements, UNAM, October.

Aldrete Haas, José Antonio. 1990. The Decline of the Mexican State? The Case of State Housing Intervention (1917–1988). Ph.D. diss., Massachusetts Institute of Technology.

Alonso, Jorge, ed. 1986. *Los movimientos sociales en el valle de México.* 2 vols. Mexico City: CIESAS.

Americas Watch. 1991. *Unceasing Abuses: Human Rights in Mexico One Year After the Introduction of Reform.* New York: Americas Watch.

Amnesty International. 1991. *Mexico: Torture with Impunity.* New York: Amnesty International.

Barberán et al. 1989. *Radiografía del fraude.* Mexico: Editores Nuestro Tiempo.

Bartra, Armando. 1992. La ardua construcción del ciudadano. In *Autonomía y nuevos sujetos sociales en el desarrollo rural,* ed. Julio Moguel, Carlota Botey, and Luis Hernández. Mexico: Siglo Veintiuno Editores.

Bennett, Vivienne. 1992. The Evolution of Urban Popular Movements in Mexico Between 1968 and 1988. In *From Protest to Proposal: The Making of Social Movements in Contemporary Latin America,* ed. Arturo Escobar, and Sonia Alvarez. Boulder, Colo.: Westview.

Bezaury, Josefina Aranda, ed. 1988. *Las mujeres en el campo.* Oaxaca: UABJO.

Bizberg, Ilan. 1988. Poder local y acción sindical en situaciones de enclave: Las elecciones en Monclova en 1978–1982. In *Poder local, poder regional,* ed. Jorge Pauda, and Alain Vanneph. México: Colegio de México/CEMCA.

Boehm de Lameiras, Brigitte. 1987. *El municipio en México.* Michoacán: Colegio de Michoacán.

Bohrquez, Gerardo. 1989. Tendencias actuales del movimiento urbano popular en México. *El cotidiano* 31, no. (septiembre-octubre): 31.

Bray, David. 1991. The Struggle for the Forest: Conservation and Development in the Sierra Juárez, Oaxaca. *Grassroots Development* 15, no. 3: 12–23.

Carabias, Julia, Carlos Toledo, and Javier Caballero. 1990. Aprovechamiento y manejo de los recursos naturales renovablesen la región de la Montaña de Guerrero. In *Recursos naturales, técnica y cultura. Estudios y experiencias para un desarrollo alternativo,* ed. Enrique Leff, Julia Carabias, and Ana Irene Batis. Mexico: UNAM/SEDUE/UNEP.

Carr, Barry, and Ricardo Anzaldúa, eds. 1986. *The Mexican Left, the Popular Movements and the Politics of Austerity.* La Jolla: Center for U.S.–Mexican Studies.

Chapela, Gonzalo. 1991. De bosques y campesinos: Problemática forestal y desarrollo organizativo en torno a diez encuentros de comunidades forestales. *Cuadernos desarrollo de base* 2: 135–166.

Chevalier, Francois. 1989. La libertad municipal, antigua y permanente revindicación mexicana. *Revista mexicana de sociología* 51 (abril-junio):2.

Colegio de México/UNICEF. 1988. Organizaciones no gubernamentales que trabajan en beneficio de la mujer. Documentos de trabajo, no. 2. México: Colegio de México/UNICEF.

Cook, Maria. 1990. Organizing Opposition in the Teachers' Movement in Oaxaca. In *Popular Movements and Political Change in Mexico,* ed. Joseph Foweraker and Ann Craig. Boulder, Colo.: Lynne Rienner.

Cordera, Rolando. 1989. Estado, crisis y privatización: Una perspectiva mexicana. *Nueva sociedad* 104 (noviembre-diciembre): 118–126.

Cornelius, Wayne, Judith Gentleman, and Peter Smith. 1989. *Mexico's Alternative Political Futures.* Monograph Series, no. 30. San Diego: Center for U.S.–Mexican Studies.

Coulomb, René. 1991. Democratización de la gestión urbana. *Ciudades* 9.

Cruz, Marcos et al. 1986. *Llegó la hora de ser gobierno. Durango: Testimonios de la lucha del Comité de Defensa Popular, General Francisco Villa.* México: Equipo Pueblo.

de la Rosa, Martín, and Charles Reilly, eds. 1985. *Religión y política en México.* México: Siglo Veintiuno.

Díaz Gomez, Floriberto. 1988. Principios comunitarios y derechos indios. *México indígena* 25 (septiembre).

Diskin, Martin, Steven Sanderson, and William Theisenhuesen. 1987. *Business in Development: A Workable Partnership. Issues in Grassroots Development.* Arlington: Inter-American Foundation.

Dresser, Denise. 1991. Policy and Politics in the Face of Economic Restructuring: The Case of the National Solidarity Program in Mexico. *Current Issues Brief,* occasional paper. Mexico: Center for U.S.–Mexican Studies.

Elías Gutierrez, Sergio. 1987. El municipio y los gobiernos de los Estados. In *El municipio en México,* ed. Brigitte Boehm de Lameiras, 297. Zamora: Colegio de Michoacán.

Enzástiga Santiago, Mario. 1986. La unión de colonias populares de cara al movimiento urbano popular, recapitulación histórica. In *Los movimientos sociales en el valle de México,* vol. 1, ed. Jorge Alonso. Mexico City: Ediciones de la Casa Chata/CIESAS.

Esteva, Gustavo. 1987. *Towards Creating a People's Space.* Alternatives, no. 12.

Fernández, Eduardo. 1991. Municipio y partidos políticos. *El Financiero* (25 November).

Foweraker, Joe and Ann L. Craig, eds. 1990. *Popular Movements and Political Change in Mexico.* Boulder, Colo.: Lynne Rienner.

Fox, Jonathan. 1992a. Democratic Rural Development: Leadership Accountability in Regional Peasant Organizations. *Development and Change* 23 (April):2.

———. 1992b. *The Politics of Food in Mexico: State Power and Social Mobilization.* Ithaca: Cornell University Press.

———. 1989. Toward Democracy in Mexico? *Hemisphere* 1, no. 2 (winter): 40–43.

Fox, Jonathan, and Gustavo Gordillo. 1989. Between State and Market: The Campesinos' Quest for Autonomy. In *Mexico's Alternative Political Futures,* Monograph Series, no. 30, ed. Wayne Cornelius, Judith Gentleman, and Peter Smith, 131–172. La Jolla: UCSD, Center for U.S.–Mexican Studies.

Gayabet, Luisa et al. *Mujeres y sociedad.* Guadalajara: Colegio de Jalisco/ CIESAS.

Gerez, Patricia. 1991. Movimientos sociales ambientalistas en México. *Cuadernos desarrollo de base* 2: 255–276.

Guillén López, Tonatiuh. 1990. La ideología política de un municipio de oposición. El PAN en Ciudad Juárez (1983–1985). Frontera Norte 2 (enero-junio):3.

Haber, Paul. 1992. Collective Dissent in Mexico: The Political Outcome of Contemporary Urban Popular Movements. Ph.D. diss., Columbia University.

Harvey, Neil. 1990. The New Agrarian Movement in Mexico 1979–1990. Research Paper, no. 23. London: University of London Institute of Latin American Studies.

Hernández, Luis. 1990a. Las coordinadoras de masas. *El cotidiano* 7 (julio-agosto):36.

———. 1990b. Respuestas campesinas en la época del neoliberalismo. *El cotidiano* 7 (enero-febrero):30.

———. 1990c. La unión de ejidos "Lázaro Cárdenas." *Cuadernos desarrollo de base* 1: 9–114.

———. 1989. Convención nacional de instituciones de servicio y asistencia social. *Pueblo* 12 (enero):140.

Hernández, Luis, and Gabriela Ejea, eds. 1991. Cafetaleros: La construcción de la autonomía. *Cuadernos desarrollo de base* 3.

Hernández, Ricardo. 1987. *La coordinadora nacional del movimiento urbano popular: Su historia, 1980–1986.* México: Equipo Pueblo.

Instituto Nacional Indigenista. 1990. *Programa nacional de desarrollo de los pueblos indígenas 1991–1994.* Mexico: INI.

Juárez, Irma. 1990. Taller nacional de crédito alternativo al campo. *Sociológica* 5 (mayo-agosto):13.

Leff, Enrique, Julia Carabias, and Ana Irene Batis. 1990. *Recursos naturales, técnica y cultura. Estudios y experiencias para un desarrollo alternativo.* México: UNAM/SEDUE/UNEP.

Loaeza, Soledad. 1988. *Clases medias y política en México.* México: Colegio de México.

Lopezllera Méndez, Luis. 1990. Las organizaciones civiles por la autogestion de los pueblos. *IFDA Dossier,* no. 77 (mayo-junio).

———. 1988. *Sociedad civil y pueblos emergentes.* México: Promoción del Desarrollo Popular.

López Monjardin, Adriana. 1988. Los procesos electorales como alternativa para la disidencia rural. In *Las sociedades rurales hoy,* ed. Jorge Zepeda Patterson. Zamora: Colegio de Michoacan.

————. 1986. *La lucha por los ayuntamientos: Una utopía viable.* México: Siglo Veintiuno/UNAM.

Maier, Elizabeth. 1990. La coordinadora de mujeres 'Benita Galeana' (Las Benitas): Una experiencia en el desarrollo de la lucha género/clase en México. Mimeo.

Martínez Assad, Carlos. 1985. Nava: De la rebelión de los coheteros al juicio político. In *Municipios en conflicto,* ed. Martínez Assad, 55–74. México: GV/IIS/UNAM.

Martínez Assad, Carlos, and Alicia Ziccardi, 1989. Política y gestión municipal en México. In *Descentralización y democracia—Gobiernos locales en América Latina,* ed. Jordi Borja et al., 286–336. Santiago: CLACSO-SUR-CEUMT.

Massolo, Alejandra. 1983. Las mujeres en los movimientos sociales urbanos de la ciudad de México. *Revista Iztapalapa* 9 (junio).

Meza, Gilberto, and Antonio Padilla. 1991. *Los nuevos electores, actores sociales e insurgencia municipal en el México de los '80s.* México: El Nacional.

Middlebrook, Kevin. 1986. Political Liberalization in an Authoritarian Regime: The Case of Mexico. In *Transitions from Authoritarian Rule: Latin America,* ed. Guillermo O'Donnell, Philippe Schmitter, and Laurence Whitehead. Baltimore: Johns Hopkins University Press.

Moguel, Julio. 1991. La necesaria reforma del 115 constitucional. *Unomásuno* 25 (noviembre).

————. 1990. National Solidarity Program Fails to Help the Very Poor. *Voices of Mexico* 15 (October–December).

————. 1989. La COCEI y su triunfo sin retorno. *Pueblo* 12 (agosto): 146.

————. 1987. *Los caminos de la izquierda.* México: Juan Pablos.

Moguel, Julio, ed. 1990. *La historia de la cuestión agraria mexicana.* Vol. 9. Mexico City: Siglo Veintiuno/CEHAM.

Montano, Agustín. 1985. *Manual de administración municipal.* Mexico City: Editorial Trillas.

Myhre, David. 1991. Campesinos as Bankers: Democratizing Finance in Rural Mexico. Paper presented at XVI Congress of the Latin American Studies Association, April, in Washington, D.C.

Nuñez, Oscar. 1990. *Innovaciones democrático-culturales del movimiento urbano-popular.* México: UAM-Azcapotzalco.

Padua, Jorge, and Alain Vanneph, eds. 1986. *Poder local, poder regional.* México: Colegio de México, Centro de Estudios Sociológicos.

Poniatowska, Elena. 1980. *Fuerte es el silencio.* México: Era.

Ramírez Saiz, Juan M. 1988. Autogestión y movimiento urbano popular. In *Movimientos sociales y autogestión.* México: Fundación Friedrich Naumann.

Reygadas, Rafael. 1991. Convergencia para la democracia. *Este país* (septiembre): 20.

Rubin, Jeffrey. 1990. Popular Mobilization and the Myth of State Corporatism. In *Popular Movements and Political Change in Mexico,* ed. Joe Foweraker, and Ann L. Craig, 247–267. Boulder, Colo.: Lynne Rienner.

————. 1987. State Policies, Leftist Oppositions, and Municipal Elections: The Case of the COCEI in Juchitán. In *Electoral Patterns and Processes in Mexico,* Monograph Series, no. 22, ed. Arturo Alvarado. La Jolla: UCSD, Center for U.S.–Mexican Studies.

Salazar, Hilda. 1991. Organizaciones no gubernamentales de vivienda. Unpublished monograph. México: Servicios de Apoyo Local.

Schteingart, Marta, and Alejandra Massolo, eds. 1987. Participación social y el sismo. *Cuadernos de trabajo*. Vol. 1. México: Colegio de México/UNICEF.

Schteingart, Marta, and Luciano d'Andrea, eds. 1991. *Servicios urbanos gestión y medio ambiente*. Mexico: Colegio de Mexico/CERSE.

Senties, Yolanda. 1987. *Organización de la participación ciudadana municipal*. México: Centro Nacional de Estudios Municipales, Secretaría de Gobernación.

Staudt, Kathleen. 1987. Programming Women's Empowerment: A Case from Northern Mexico. In *Women on the US–Mexico Border: Responses to Change*, ed. Vicki Ruiz, and Susan Tiano, 155–173. Boston: Allen & Unwin.

Stephen, Lynn. 1992. Women in Mexico's Popular Movements. *Latin American Perspectives* (winter).

———. 1991. The Gendered Dynamics of Rural Democratization: Brazil, Chile and Mexico. Paper presented at International Congress of Americanists, New Orleans.

———. 1990. Popular Feminism in Mexico. *Z Magazine* 2:2.

Szekeley, Miguel, and Sergio Madrid. 1990. La apropriación comunitaria de recursos naturales, Un caso de la Sierra de Juárez, Oaxaca. In *Recursos naturales, técnica y cultura. Estudios y experiencias para un desarrollo alternativo*, ed. Enrique Leff, Julia Carabias, and Ana Irene Batis. Mexico: UNAM/SEDUE/UNEP.

Taibó, Paco Ignacio. 1990. A New Politics with Deep Roots. *The Nation* (10 December).

Taibó, Paco Ignacio, and Rogelio Vizcaino. 1990. *Las dos muertes de Juan Escudero*. México: Cuadernos de Joaquín Mortiz.

Tarrés, María Luisa. 1990. Middle-Class Associations and Electoral Opposition. In *Popular Movements and Political Change in Mexico*, ed. Joe Foweraker, and Ann Craig, 137–149. Boulder, Colo.: Lynne Rienner.

Torres, Blanca. 1986. *Descentralización y democracia en México*. México: Colegio de México.

Vargas Llosa, Mario. 1991. Mexico: The Perfect Dictatorship. *New Perspectives Quarterly* 8 (winter):1.

Velasco Rocha, Ana Bertha, and Blanca Cortes Montano. 1988. Una experiencia feminista: El centro de apoyo a la mujer de Colima. In *Mujeres y sociedad*, ed. Luisa Gabayet et al. Guadalajara: Colegio de Jalisco/CIESAS.

Villa Aguilera, Manuel. 1988. *¿A quién le interesa la democracia en México? Crisis del intervencionismo estatal y alternativas del pacto social*. México: Coordinación de Humanidades.

Zabin, Carol. 1989. Grassroots Development in Indigenous Communities: A Case Study from the Sierra Juarez in Oaxaca, Mexico, Ph.D. diss., University of California.

Zermeño, Sergio. 1990. Crisis, Neoliberalism and Disorder. In *Popular Movements and Political Change in Mexico*, ed. Joe Foweraker, and Ann L. Craig. Boulder, Colo.: Lynne Rienner.

Peru

Author Unknown

———. 1991. *Lima Forum on Environmental Resources, Crisis, and Alternatives*. June. Lima: SASE.

———. 1989. *Regionalización y gobiernos locales*. Lima: Tarea, Ipadel.

Armani, Domingos. 1988. Una ONGD en busca de su identidad. Paper presented at the course-workshop, Gestión y políticas institucionales para ONGD de América Latina, Rio de Janeiro, 10–28 August 1987. Lima: IRED-DESCO.

Arnillas, Federico. 1986. El movimiento popular urbano. In *Movimientos sociales y educación popular en el Perú* 9: 29–44. Lima: Nuevos Cuadernos CELAIS.

Ballón, Eduardo. 1986. Estado, sociedad y sistema político peruano: Una aproximación inicial and movimientos sociales y sistema político. El lento camino de la democratización: Síntesis nacional. In *Movimientos sociales y democracia: La fundación de un nuevo orden,* ed. Eduardo Ballón. Lima: DESCO.

Caravedo, Baltazar. 1988. *Descentralismo y democracia.* Lima: Gredes.

Caravedo, Baltazar, and A. Pillado, eds. 1993. *ONGDs, desarrollo y cooperación internacional en el Perú de hoy.* Lima: SASE.

Carroll, T., D. Humphreys, and M. Scurrah. 1990. Organizaciones de apoyo a grupos de base en el Perú: Una radiografia. *Socialismo y participación* 50 (junio). Lima: CEDEP.

CELADEC. 1983. *Villa El Salvador: De arenal a distrito municipal.* Lima: Servicio Documental Especial CELADEC.

Collier, David. 1976. *Squatters and Oligarchs: Authoritarian Rule and Policy Change in Peru.* Baltimore: Johns Hopkins University Press.

Cotler, Julio, ed. 1987. *Para afirmar la democracia.* Lima: Instituto de Estudios Peruanos (IEP).

———. 1978. A Structural-Historical Approach to the Breakdown of Democratic Institutions: Peru. In *The Breakdown of Democratic Regimes: Latin America,* ed. Juan J. Linz, and Alfred Stepan. Baltimore: Johns Hopkins University Press.

Dammert, José. 1992. *Construyendo juntos el futuro.* Lima: DESCO.

Degregori, Carlos Iván et al. 1986. *Conquistadores de un nuevo mundo. De invasores a ciudadanos en San Martín de Porres.* Lima: Instituto de Estudios Peruanos.

Delgado, Angel. 1991. Economía municipal. In *Construyendo un gobierno metropolitano: Políticas municipales 1984–1986,* ed. Henry Pease. Lima: IPADEL.

de Wit, Tom. 1991. World Bank report of visit to Peru, May 1991.

Díaz-Albertini, Javier. 1988. *La promoción urbana: Balance y desafíos.* Serie Materiales, no. 1. Buenos Aires: CEDYS.

———. 1987. La formulación de estrategias de vida y los centros de promoción en el Perú. In *Estrategias de vida en el sector urbano-popular,* ed. R. Haak, and J. Díaz-Albertini. Lima: DESCO.

Díaz Palacios, Julio. 1990. *Municipio: Democracia y desarrollo.* Lima: Moquegua Publicaciones Labor.

Mariátegui, José Carlos. 1971. *Seven Interpretative Essays on Peruvian Reality.* Austin: University of Texas Press.

Mejía Navarrete, Julio Victor. 1990. *Estado y municipio en el Perú.* Lima: Consejo Nacional de Ciencia y Tecnología.

Padrón, Mario. 1988. Los centros de promoción y la cooperación internacional al desarrollo en América Latina. El caso peruano. In *Las organizaciones no gubernamentales de desarrollo en el Perú,* ed. Mario Padrón, 23–87. Lima: DESCO.

———. 1982. *Cooperación al desarrollo y movimiento popular: Las asociaciones privadas de desarrollo.* Lima: DESCO.

Pease, Henry. 1988. Experiencias de democracia local y ONGD. In *Las organizaciones no gubernamentales de desarrollo en el Perú,* ed. Mario Padrón, 23–87. Lima: PREAL-DESCO.

Salazar, Carlos, ed. 1990. *Gestión y políticas institucionales en ONGDs.* Lima: DESCO-IRED.

Smith, Michael. 1992. *Entre dos fuegos, ONGs desarrollo y violencia política.* Lima: IEP.

Soberón, Luis. 1986. *Las ciencias sociales y el desarrollo rural en el Perú.* Lima: FOMCIENCIAS.

Vergahen, Koenraad. 1990. *La promoción de la autoayuda. Un desafío a la comunidad de ONGs.* Lima: DESCO-CEBEMO.

INDEX

Academy of Christian Humanism (Chile), 121, 124, 129, 130*tab,* 131, 143*n4*

Acapulco Workers' Party (Mexico), 182

Accountability, 258, 260, 262; governmental, 115, 181, 187; in nongovernmental organizations, 2

ACI. *See* Agency for International Cooperation (Chile)

ACT. *See* Catholic Rural Action (Chile)

Agency for International Cooperation (Chile), 18, 137, 140, 141, 251

Agrarian Community Leagues (Mexico), 225

Agriculture: community, 103; cooperativism in, 122; production, 29, 49, 231; urban, 123

AHC. *See* Academy of Christian Humanism (Chile)

Alfonsín, Raúl, 35

Allende, Salvador, 119, 143*n9*

Alternatives (Peru), 241, 242, 243

American Popular Revolutionary Alliance (Peru), 230, 231

Analysis, Decentralization, and Management (Mexico), 193, 198

APRA. *See* American Popular Revolutionary Alliance (Peru)

Argentina, 4; civil society in, 29–44; clientelism in, 36–37, 40; economic crises, 34; La Esperanza project, 53–54tab, 58–61; La Paloma project, 53–54*tab,* 61–63; neighborhood associations in, 29–44; nongovernmental organizations in, 13, 14–15, 45–68; Peronist influences, 31–32, 51; political parties in, 3, 35, 48, 51, 67–68; protest in, 1, 14; social policy configuration in, 12*tab;* transition to democracy in, 29–44; Unión y Parque Casas project, 53–54*tab,*

55–58; urbanization in, 27, 32, 33, 49–50

Assembly of Mixe Authorities (Mexico), 183, 203

Assembly of Zapotec Authorities (Mexico), 183

Association of Relatives of Political Prisoners (Chile), 128

Associations, 116; academic, 172; business, 180; civil, 200; community, vii, 167, 171, 176; development, 33, 40, 46, 47; dissidence in, 43–44; housing, 124; leadership in, 41–44; neighborhood, 7, 14, 24, 29–44, 46–47, 50–52, 53*tab,* 167, 170, 236, 247; professional, 172; of squatters, 40; voluntary, 50, 251

Austerity, vii, 2, 14

Authoritarianism, vii, 3, 12, 13, 16, 34, 35, 43, 47, 72, 128, 145, 174, 181, 230, 254, 255, 257

Aylwin, Patricio, 137, 140, 143*n3,* 143*n9,* 144*n11,* 251

Betancur, Belisario, 168

Brazil, 4; civil society in, 72; Curitiba project, 104–105; democratization in, 17; Favela Monte Azul project, 106–107; "Garbage That Isn't Garbage" project, 105, 108; health care in, 8–9, 85–97; Luiz Freire Center, 10–11; modernization in, 72; nongovernmental organizations in, 10–11, 13, 15–17, 71–84, 85–97; political parties in, 3, 73, 74*tab;* protest in, 1, 14; public health in, 85–97; "Purchase of Garbage" project, 105; social movements in, 7; social policy configuration in, 12*tab;* transportation in, 109–115; urbanization in, 27, 85, 109, 110;

ABOUT THE CONTRIBUTORS

Silvio Caccia Bava has served, since 1987, as president of Pólis—the Institute of Research, Training, and Advisory Services in Social Policy—in São Paulo, Brazil. Coordinator of social research programs at CEDEC from 1986 to 1989, he has conducted research for the National Council for Research and Development, the UN Research Institute for Social Development, and the Urban Research Center at New York University. His work on urban issues has been published extensively. In June 1992, Caccia Bava coordinated the "Urban Problematic" session for the International NGO Forum at the United Nations Conference on Environment and Development (UNCED) in Rio de Janeiro. Recently named director of the National Public Transportation Association, Caccia Bava developed the transportation fee concept discussed in this volume.

Baltazar Caravedo M., economist and sociologist, currently serves as director of Analysis and Evaluation for Development (SASE), a research institution that analyzes and evaluates development projects. He also directs a monthly publication, *Informe regional,* which tracks regionalization and decentralization in Peru. Director of the Inter-American Foundation's local support system in Peru, Caravedo is presently concluding an evaluation of Peruvian environmental NGOs.

Leandro Piquet Carneiro is a researcher at the Institute for Religious Studies (ISER) in Rio de Janeiro. His research interests include party and electoral systems and quantitative methods for social research.

Marcelo Cavarozzi, an Argentine political scientist, has directed the Center of State and Society Studies (CEDES) in Buenos Aires since 1975. His publications include *Autoritarismo y democracia* (1983) and Political Cycles in Argentina since 1955, a chapter in *Transitions from Authoritarian Rule,* vol. 2. Cavarozzi is currently establishing a program on democratic governance and economic restructuring at the National Autonomous University of Mexico (UNAM).

Amélia Cohn, a sociologist, is a researcher at the Center for Studies of Contemporary Culture (CEDEC), where she currently serves as vice president. She also teaches at the University of São Paulo and has written several articles and books. Cohn is currently studying popular movements and the right to health in São Paulo and analyzing local health administration in four municipalities of São Paulo.

Rubem Cesar Fernandes is an anthropologist who teaches at the National Museum at the Federal University of Rio de Janeiro and coordinates the research division of the Institute for Religious Studies (ISER) in Rio de Janeiro. His recent studies include *Protestants, Evangelicals, and Pentecostals in Greater Rio* and *Religion and Social Movements in Brazil and Eastern Europe: A Comparative Approach.*

Jonathan Fox teaches Latin American politics at the Massachusetts Institute of Technology. He has lived and worked in Mexico for three of the last ten years, studying the interaction between social movements and the state. He has done field research as well in Brazil, the Philippines, Chile, Nicaragua, and Costa Rica. Fox has most recently published *The Politics of Food in Mexico: State Power and Social Mobilization.* He also edited *The Challenges of Rural Democratization: Perspectives from Latin America and the Philippines.* Recent articles by Fox have appeared in *Development and Change, LASA Forum, Report on the Americas, Grassroots Development, Cuadernos desarrollo de base,* and *Investigación económica.*

Luis Hernández, an anthropologist, focuses his work on social and rural movements and agrarian development. Currently, Hernández divides his time between the Center of Studies for Change in the Mexican Countryside (CECCAM) and the National Network of Coffee-Producing Organizations (CNOC), both IAF-funded projects. A contributor to various Mexican journals and magazines, Hernández has also published *Autonomía y nuevos sujetos sociales de desarrollo rural del siglo XXI.*

Brian Loveman, a professor of political science at San Diego State University, has written extensively on Chilean history and politics, the military in Latin America, and labor and agricultural reform. Loveman's most recent book, *The Constitution of Tyranny,* is an investigation into the origins of regimes of exception and military rule in Latin America.

Roberto Martínez Nogueira, is professor of economics and sociology at the University of Buenos Aires. His extensive research includes work at the Torcuato Di Tella Institute, the Center for Research on State and Society, and the Economic Commission for Latin America. Martínez Nogueira was a founding member of the Group for Institutional Social Development and Analysis (GADIS) and served as its director. He recently formed the Foundation for the Strengthening of Social Management and Organization (FORGES), a public-policy study center in Buenos Aires.

Julio Moguel is an economics professor and researcher in the Department of Economics at the National Autonomous University of Mexico (UNAM). In 1987, he earned an award for his coverage of popular urban movements in the newspaper *Unomásuno.* He has written numerous articles and books on social movements and the Mexican agricultural sector. A member of the Guadalupe Victoria law firm in Durango, he also edits *La jornada's* biweekly supplement, *La Jornada del Campo.* His NGO involvement since 1986 includes Equipo Pueblo, a Mexico City–based NGO that focuses on economic development and participatory democracy, and another NGO, Debase, of which he is director.

Laura Mullahy collaborated with Charles Reilly on the publication of *New Paths to Democratic Development in Latin America* while employed by the Inter-American Foundation during 1992. She is currently editing a monthly publication on local-level environmental initiatives for the Center of Environmental Research and Planning in Santiago.

Vicente Palermo is on the faculty of the Complutense University in Madrid.

Charles A. Reilly directs research and thematic studies for the Inter-American Foundation. Most recently, he and William Glade coedited *Inquiry at the Grassroots,* a sampling of grassroots development research carried out by doctoral fellows of the Foundation. Reilly directed the Mary Knoll Center for Integral Development in Guatemala and has taught in Brazil and Mexico as well as at the University of California in San Diego.

Judith Salinas is a social worker and a professor of public health at the University of Chile's Institute of Nutrition and Food Technology. A founding member of Chile's Health and Social Policy Corporation (CORSAPS), she has worked in the Ministry of Health, since 1990, as head of the Social Participation Unit in the Department of Primary Health Care.

Pedro Santana Rodríguez teaches sociology and philosophy at Rosario University in Bogotá, Colombia. He has directed research on civics and decentralization, the topic of his chapter, since the early 1980s. His most recent research project, The Impact of Reform in Eight Colombian Municipalities, was sponsored by the Ford Foundation and will be published in Colombia. For the past four years, Dr. Santana has overseen a comparative study on government in large Latin American cities, published as *Bogotá 450 Años: Retos y Realidades* and *Vivir en Bogotá.*

Giorgio Solimano, a founding member and former president of CORSAPS in Chile, held high-level positions in Chile's Ministry of Health during the Allende and Aylwin administrations. He is a professor of public health at the University of Chile Medical School and at Columbia University in New York City.